THE
Presidents
OF THE
Church

Edited by Leonard J. Arrington

THE Presidents OF THE Church

BIOGRAPHICAL ESSAYS BY

JAMES B. ALLEN
LEONARD J. ARRINGTON
WILLIAM G. HARTLEY
DEAN C. JESSEE
SCOTT KENNEY
EDWARD L. KIMBALL
JOSEPH FIELDING McCONKIE
MERLO J. PUSEY
PAUL THOMAS SMITH
HEIDI S. SWINTON
RONALD W. WALKER

Deseret Book
Salt Lake City, Utah

First printing March 1986
Second printing October 1986

Library of Congress Cataloging-in-Publication Data
Main entry under title:

    The Presidents of the Church.

    Includes bibliographies and index.
    Contents: Joseph Smith / Leonard J. Arrington—
Brigham Young / Leonard J. Arrington—John Taylor /
Paul T. Smith—[etc.]
    1. Church of Jesus Christ of Latter-day Saints—
Presidents—Biography.   2. Mormon Church—Presidents—
Biography.   I. Arrington, Leonard J.
BX8693.P74   1986   289.3'32'0922 [B]   85-31117
ISBN 0-87579-026-7

CONTENTS

PREFACE

In 1941, Preston Nibley, a writer for the *Church News*, *Improvement Era*, and other Latter-day Saint publications, wrote the biographies of the first seven presidents of The Church of Jesus Christ of Latter-day Saints under the title *The Presidents of the Church*. Published by Deseret Book Company, the book went through a second printing the next year, and, indeed, through a succession of printings in the years that followed. As the existing president died and a new one was sustained, the author added new chapters. In 1957, *The Presidents of the Church* became even more authoritative when Preston Nibley was sustained as Assistant Church Historian. By the time of his death in 1963, the book had gone through nine printings.

After Elder Nibley's death, additional printings were made under the supervision of the LDS Church Historian's Office. With the creation of the Church Historical Department in 1972, the book was revised and enlarged under the direction of the Church Historian, and a thirteenth edition was issued in 1974. That printing included biographies of Presidents Joseph Fielding Smith, Harold B. Lee, and Spencer W. Kimball, each of whom had been sustained since the death of Elder Nibley.

With the acceleration in research that has occurred in recent years, it is clear that there is need for a completely new volume on the presidents of the Church. Far more information is now available on each of the presidents than was available to Elder Nibley. Deseret Book Company has therefore encouraged me to supervise the preparation of this new volume with completely new biographies of each of the presidents. With their approval, I have chosen Latter-day Saint historians who have immersed themselves in the papers of the presidents they have written about. In the three instances in which, for personal or other reasons, the biographers have found it necessary to withdraw, I have filled in by preparing the biographies myself.

It should be emphasized that this book is intended for general Latter-day Saint readers, young and old, who wish an introduction to each of the presidents of their church. For the pleasure of the reader, we have avoided footnotes and have, instead, presented a brief bibliographical note at the end of each chapter that indicates the sources used in preparing the essay. We have tried to be factual, honest, insightful – and interesting. The writers have enormous respect and admiration for the men they have written about, and we have not attempted to submerge that feeling. I am sure that the reading of these lives will be as faith-promoting for those who read it as it has been for those of us who have written it.

LEONARD J. ARRINGTON

THE
Presidents
OF THE
Church

JOSEPH SMITH
Leonard J. Arrington

The Prophet of the Restoration has been portrayed as a philosopher, community builder, poet, military commander, revelator, and visionary. But the rapid growth of the church he was instrumental in founding, and of which he was the president for its first fourteen years, suggests a warm and attractive personality that appealed to all ages and classes of people. Joseph Smith, divinely appointed to restore the gospel in this dispensation, was a vigorous and resourceful, but also a jovial and exciting, leader. Examination of the wealth of material that relates to his life impresses one that his personal qualities, as well as his teachings and revelations, played a prominent role in the Restoration. To use a word often heard today, Joseph Smith possessed charisma.

JOSEPH SMITH WAS THE FOURTH CHILD among nine in the family of Joseph Smith, Sr., and Lucy Mack Smith, who lived in Vermont and western New York State. On both sides he was descended from "old Americans." The Smiths had come to America in 1638 and settled in Topsfield, Massachusetts. They later moved to New Hampshire, then to Vermont. The Macks had gone to Connecticut in 1682, and later moved to

---

In writing this chapter, I have benefited particularly from the research and writing of Richard L. Bushman.

New Hampshire and then to Vermont, where Lucy Mack met and married Joseph Smith, Sr. Their son Joseph Smith, Jr., was born in Sharon, Windsor County, Vermont, on December 23, 1805.

The family into which young Joseph was born was hard-working and frugal – typical of many on the New England frontier. At Joseph's birth, his father was thirty-four and his mother twenty-nine. They had three children: Alvin, seven; Hyrum, five; and Sophronia, two. Joseph's younger brothers and sisters included Samuel H. (born in 1808), Ephraim (1810, died as a baby), William (1811), Catherine (1812), Don Carlos (1816), and Lucy (1824). Although Joseph, Sr., and Lucy began marriage under favorable circumstances in Tunbridge, Vermont, he lost his farm in 1803 through a venture with a dishonest partner. Without property, their life for the next few years was a story of frequent moves. The Smiths lived in several villages in central Vermont and New Hampshire before migrating to western New York in 1816.

Because of the family's circumstances, the Smith children had to work hard on their own and neighboring farms. Such education as they received came primarily from their father, who had been a schoolteacher, and their mother, who grew up in a family with cultural attainments. Much of Joseph's early life was spent within the circle of his family and a small number of acquaintances and neighbors in the villages where they lived.

It was a religious home, even though family members were not contented to be active in a particular denomination. Joseph's mother had been brought up under adverse conditions; two sisters and several of her friends had died, and she found her chief consolation in religion. She read the Bible and engaged frequently in prayer, and her mind was often turned to thoughts of eternity and the final judgment. His father, also from a "worthy, respectable, amiable, and intelligent family," as Lucy's brother Stephen described him, was reserved or freethinking on the subject of institutional religion.

The Smith family were forced to undergo many reverses. They lost their land, were cheated out of an inheritance, and suffered from serious health problems. Joseph, Sr., taught school, cleared land, and worked on farms and roads, and he and his boys earned the respect of neighbors by their industry, frugality, and neighborly helpfulness. Their reputation as workers was such that they were invited to labor in nearby villages. Even Lucy brought in income by painting oil table-cloths. The various family work assignments necessitated frequent moves. During the time Joseph, Jr., was growing up — that is, until he was fourteen — the family moved seven times.

When Joseph was seven, a typhoid epidemic swept through the upper Connecticut Valley where they lived, and all of the children fell ill. Joseph seemed to recover from the illness, but infection set in his bone, requiring an operation to cut out the diseased portion. There was no anesthesia at the time, but young Joseph was determined to "tough it through," as he said. According to his mother, he refused wine or brandy and told the doctors that they didn't need to bind him with cords. "I will have my father sit on the bed and hold me in his arms," he said. Fortunately, the family had secured the services of one of the most renowned surgeons in New England, and the operation was a success. Nevertheless, Joseph was incapacitated for three years while his leg healed. During those three years, ages seven to ten, he was either in bed or on crutches. As an adult, he walked with a slight limp. His childhood experience may well have accelerated his love and sympathy for children; there are many stories of his holding and comforting children as an adult.

Joseph was ten or eleven when the family moved from Norwich, Vermont, to Palmyra, in western New York State, a distance of three hundred miles. Joseph, Sr., had gone on ahead to prepare the way, leaving Lucy, a resolute and determined woman, to travel with their eight children. Late-winter snow was still on the ground, and the journey required three to four weeks.

PALMYRA WAS A BOOMING TOWN with perhaps 3,000 inhabitants, including two tailors, a blacksmith, several saddlers, a cooper, two lawyers, and a physician. There was a bookstore, a tannery, a harness shop, a distillery, two drugstores, and four taverns. The county seat was Canandaigua, fifteen miles south of Palmyra. To obtain cash with which to buy land, Lucy once more painted oil tablecloths, various members of the family sold refreshments from a small shop and peddled them by cart when crowds gathered for celebrations and revivals, and the older boys worked for farmers needing extra hands for harvesting, digging wells, and landscaping. Occasionally one or more worked on the construction of canals, an important activity in the region. After two years of this labor, the Smiths were able to buy a farm two miles south of Palmyra in what would later become the township of Manchester. There they built, in the words of Lucy, "a snug log house, neatly furnished," which provided sleeping spaces for ten people in its four rooms: six boys from two to nineteen, two girls six and fifteen, and the parents.

The family now devoted most of their effort to clearing the land and preparing it for the planting of crops. According to Lucy, the men's labor was prodigious — they cleared thirty acres the first year. This enabled them to sell potash and pearl ash from the burnt trees, considerable cordwood, and some maple sugar. They apparently grew corn for the family and animals on the first land they cleared. They also sold brooms, baskets, cakes, sugar, and molasses, and very likely they fished, trapped, and hunted. Joseph, Jr., says that he worked as an errand boy for the local general store and for nearby farmers. They were making good progress; as Lucy wrote, "We began to rejoice in our prosperity; our hearts glowed with gratitude to God for the manifestations of His favor that surrounded us."

The family was not caught up with material concerns to the exclusion of spiritual anxieties. Joseph, Sr., continued to have dreams and visions that were important enough for him to relate them to Lucy and the family. Each of the dreams dwelt with the search for healing, for salvation, for beauty. It is also apparent that Joseph, Sr., Lucy, and the older children were affected by the frequent revivals and by the enticements of the local Presbyterian, Methodist, Baptist, and Quaker churches.

Joseph, Jr., began to be concerned about religion when he was twelve. "My mind became seriously imprest with regard to the all important concerns for the wellfare of my immortal soul," he later wrote, "which led me to searching the scriptures." When Lucy, two of her sons, and her older daughter decided to join the Presbyterian Church, Joseph, Sr., and the other sons held back. Joseph, Jr., as he later wrote, was "somewhat partial to the Methodist sect," and he almost united with them. But, as he told Alexander Neibaur, he "could feel nothing." He felt uncomfortable with the "stir and division amongst the people." Instead of continuing with "the great love" that new members manifested at the time of their conversion, Joseph wrote in his history, they began to manifest "bad feelings" toward those of other faiths or those of no faith at all. There was "great confusion" as "priest contended against priest" and "convert against convert." Religious life was "a strife of words and a contest about opinions."

The scriptures, Joseph thought, "contained the word of God," and he had a strong desire to find where salvation was to be found and how one might be redeemed. Which church was right? What was the way to salvation? He mourned for his own prospects and for the prospects of the world.

In addition to his extended labor on behalf of the family, Joseph sought to improve himself. He went to meetings of a young people's debating society, joined a "probationary class" of the Methodist Church, and, of course, continued to read the scriptures. Concerned with the welfare of his immortal soul, he was impressed with the verse in James: "If any of you lack wisdom, let him ask of God, that giveth to all men liberally, . . . and it shall be given him." (James 1:5.) This verse, wrote Joseph, "seemed to enter with great force into every feeling of my heart. I reflected on it again and again, knowing that if any person needed wisdom from God, I did."

The youth prayed for help in the spring of 1820, when he was fourteen years old. He went to a clearing in the nearby woods, where he had previously left his ax in a stump. A "pillar of light" came down and rested on him, he said, and he was "filled with the spirit of God." "The Lord opened the heavens upon me," he wrote, "and I saw the Lord and he spake unto me saying, 'Joseph, my son, thy sins are forgiven thee, go thy way, walk in my statutes, and keep my commandments.' " It was a message of forgiveness and redemption that satisfied his yearning.

But there was more. The world, he was told, had turned aside from the gospel; "their hearts are far from me." The Lord promised to deal with their ungodliness and to "bring to pass that which hath been spoken by the mouth of the prophets and apostles." Joseph, grateful for this assurance of the Lord's concern, declared that he "was filled with love . . . the Lord was with me."

Joseph's vision gave him peace of mind about his spiritual standing, but it did not interrupt his temporal labors. He and his brothers and father continued to clear and fence additional acres, to plant trees and crops, and, when opportunities arose, to work on nearby farms. Regular schooling was still out of the question. A neighbor recalled that the Smiths held school at night and studied the Bible. Joseph later reported that he "was merely instructed in reading, writing, and the ground rules of arithmetic."

His spiritual experience, however, caused him, as he recalled in his history, to have a "cheery temperament," and, strangely enough, this was a cause of anxiety. Contemporary religion set strict limits upon individual behavior and activity. Those having a "conviction of sin," as Joseph had, could not listen to a violin without feeling guilty, could not dance, could not laugh or tell jokes, could not make light of things, had to display solemnity, sobriety, and sorrowfulness. "I was guilty of levity," Joseph wrote, "and sometimes associated with jovial company." According to the tradition under which he had grown up, this behavior was "not consistent with that character which ought to be maintained by one who was called of God, as I had been. . . . I felt condemned for my weakness and imperfections," he wrote.

On September 21, 1823, when Joseph was seventeen, he waited until the others in the family had gone to sleep and then began an intense supplication to God. While he was praying, he felt the room growing lighter and lighter. Suddenly a person appeared in the light, standing above the floor. Joseph recalled: "He had on a loose robe of most exquisite whiteness. It was a whiteness beyond anything earthly I had ever seen; nor do I believe that any earthly thing could be made to appear so exceedingly white and brilliant. His hands were naked, and his arms also, a little above the wrist; so also, were his feet naked, as were his legs, a little above the ankles. His head and neck were also bare. I could discover that he had no other clothing on but this robe, as it was open, so that I could see into his bosom. Not only was his robe exceedingly white, but his whole person was glorious beyond description, and his countenance truly like lightning."

The being, who identified himself as Moroni, assured Joseph that he (Joseph) still enjoyed the acceptance of God, that God had a work for him, and his mission would be quite unlike any that he had dreamed of. He told the young man about a book "written upon gold plates, giving an account of the former inhabitants of this continent, and the source from whence they sprang. . . . The fulness of the everlasting Gospel was contained in it, as delivered by the Savior to the ancient inhabitants." Moroni also told Joseph about two stones in silver bows: "The possession and use of these stones were what constituted 'seers' in ancient or former times," Joseph wrote, adding that "God had prepared them for the purpose of translating the book." More was said, and Joseph understood that he was destined to play an important role in preparing for the return of Christ.

After delivering the message, the angel disappeared. But while the startled Joseph was trying to grasp the meaning of it all, the room began to brighten again. Moroni reappeared, and he repeated every word he had said before. Then he ascended a second time, only to appear a third time to repeat the same message.

Shortly after the third appearance came the dawn, and the family began to stir to do the morning chores. That morning, as he and his older brother and father worked at harvesting the wheat, Joseph stopped, as if in deep thought. Urged on by his brother, he resumed work, but soon stopped again. Noticing the young man's drained face, his father sent him back to the house, but while he was attempting to climb the fence, Joseph fainted and for a time lay unconscious. As he came to, he saw Moroni standing over him once more. The angel repeated the message a fourth time, this time directing Joseph to tell his father. Joseph returned to the field and related to his father what had transpired. Joseph, Sr., accepted his son's story and told him that he must be careful to follow the instructions of the angel.

The plates the angel had described lay in a hill about three miles south and east of the Smith farm. Having seen the hill in vision the night before, Joseph knew just where to look for them. He dug away the earth and uncovered a stone box within which were the plates, the Urim and Thummim, and a breastplate. Considering the indigent circumstances of the Smith family, Joseph could hardly avoid thinking of their worth — what they would bring on the market. That this thought should occur to the young man angered Moroni, who once more appeared, rebuked him for impure motives, and told him that, as Joseph reported, "the time for bringing them forth had not yet arrived." He was to go to the hill the next year for further instructions. According to Lucy, Joseph had to wait "until he had learned to keep the commandments of God — not only till he was willing, but able, to do it."

That evening Joseph told all of the family about the angel and the plates. They all believed and rejoiced that God was about to give them "a more perfect knowledge of the plan of salvation and the redemption of the human family." They went through a period of "sweetest union, happiness, and tranquility."

But the misfortunes and sorrows that had followed them in Vermont and New York came upon them again. Less than two months after Joseph went to the hill, his oldest brother, Alvin, became critically ill, and in a few days he was dead. On his deathbed he urged Joseph to "be a good boy and do everything that lies in your power to obtain the record."

IN THE SMITH HOUSEHOLD and on the farm, work went on. To raise money to help them complete a new frame house, young Joseph continued working for established farmers. He worked in Colesville, New York, for Joseph Knight, who had a gristmill and carding machine in addition to farms. Knight is reported to have said that Joseph was "the best hand he [Knight] ever hired." Joseph was also recommended to Josiah Stowell, who put him to work in his various enterprises, including using seerstones to look for buried treasure at Stowell's Pennsylvania farm. From the folklore of the region, it is apparent that the people had a fascination for spirits, treasure, and magic. Tales circulated of people finding lost mines and buried treasures by means of dreams, divining rods, and stones. This lore traces back many centuries and blended in with the orthodox Christian faith of the times. The people believed that supernatural powers aided and opposed humans as they sought to make their living. The invisible powers mentioned in the scriptures were real and, as Richard Bushman has written, "belief in angels and devils made it easy to believe in guardian spirits and magical powers." Joseph told both Josiah Stowell and Joseph Knight about the angel who had visited him and about the engraved book.

Despite their association with some of this activity, members of the Smith family continued to labor in their accustomed way; the angel had warned Joseph that, as Joseph later wrote, "Satan would try to tempt me" and that the greed of money diggers was a manifestation of Satan, not God. Joseph went through a period of orienting himself toward his heaven-sent task of obtaining and translating the Book of Mormon. He said that seeing with a stone, such as the seerstone in the hill, was "a gift from God," while "peeping" was "nonsense." Gradually members of Joseph's family and some of his friends began to see that Joseph's gifts were divine and were intended to discern God's will for His people. As he had been commanded, Joseph visited the hill each year on the anniversary date of Moroni's first appearance.

While Joseph was working for Stowell in Harmony, Pennsylvania, he became acquainted with Emma Hale, the tall, dark-haired daughter of a family with whom he boarded. Emma later visited the Stowells in Bainbridge, across the border in New York; the romance blossomed. Joseph and Emma were married January 18, 1827. Joseph was twenty-one, and Emma twenty-two. They made their home first in Manchester, where Joseph farmed with his father.

In September 1827, fully persuaded that Joseph realized that the plates were to be looked upon as history rather than as wealth, and that he would use his gifts and talents in the service of God rather than for personal or family enrichment, the angel commanded him to take the plates from their ancient hiding place in the hill—the place now called the Hill Cumorah. During the night of September 21-22, Joseph and Emma drove to the hill, where he took possession of the plates and concealed them for the time being in an old birch log. Later he retrieved the plates, placed them in a specially built cherry box, and buried the box under the hearthstones in the west room of his father's home.

Just north of the Smith farm was the farm of Martin Harris, a prosperous farmer, who had employed Joseph and who knew him to be a good worker, honest, and trustworthy. Upon hearing about the sacred plates, Martin agreed to help Joseph with the translating. However, there was so much interference in the township—neighbors' insistence on seeing the plates, surreptitious attempts to steal them, and demands that they be marketed and the revenue shared—that Joseph and Emma, assisted with a gift of fifty dollars from Martin, left to join Emma's family in Harmony. There they moved into a small two-room house owned by Isaac Hale, Emma's father. Joseph later purchased the house, in which they lived for the next two and one-half years.

Not long after Joseph and Emma moved to Harmony, he began translating the plates, which they had hidden in a barrel of beans for protection. The process of translation was not mechanical. There was more to it than possession of the plates and the translating instrument. Joseph's mind had to be properly prepared and attuned. With Emma's help, he began by copying some of the characters from the plates and translating them. He gave a sample of the characters to Martin Harris, who took them to two noted linguists in New York City to see if they could recognize and translate them. The most famous of the two, Professor Charles Anthon of Columbia University, apparently satisfied Martin that the characters resembled those from Egyptian sources and that Joseph's preliminary translation appeared to be correct. Although Anthon's later account is somewhat different, Martin believed that the un-schooled Joseph must be benefiting from divine inspiration. "God hath chosen the foolish things of the world to confound the wise," he advised Pomeroy Taylor, a Palymra printer and historian.

The translation began in earnest in the early spring of 1828, with Martin Harris acting as scribe. By the middle of June, 116 pages of foolscap had been completed. Then, in response to pleas from his wife — and perhaps to quiet his own fears as well — Martin asked Joseph if he could take the manuscript home to Palmyra. He agreed to show the manuscript only to his brother and his wife, his father and mother, and his wife's sister. While he was gone Emma gave birth to a son, who died the same day. Emma was so ill that Joseph tended her night and day for two full weeks. During her illness, Joseph began to be anxious about the manuscript and Martin Harris's failure to return. As soon as he could, Joseph left Emma with her mother and set out for Manchester. When he saw Martin, he knew something was wrong. The manuscript had disappeared, he learned; though Martin had searched for it many days, it was never recovered. The angel also repossessed the interpret-ers that had assisted Joseph.

There were bitter lamentations in the Smith household in Palmyra. "The heavens seemed clothed with blackness," Lucy wrote. Joseph paced the floor in deep grief. When he returned the next month to Harmony, Lucy wrote, he engaged in "mighty prayer before the Lord." Ultimately he was promised by revelation — the first revelation written by the youthful prophet — that the interpreters would be returned to him on September 22, the anniversary of his meetings with Moroni for the preceding four years. "The works and the designs, and the purposes of God cannot be frustrated, neither can they come to naught," the Lord declared. "My work shall go forth, for inasmuch as the knowledge of a Savior has come unto the world, through the testimony of the Jews, even so shall the knowledge of a Savior come unto my people—and to the Nephites, and the Jacobites, and the Josephites, and the Zoramites, through the testimony of their fathers." (Doctrine and Covenants 3:1, 16-17.)

Joseph received the interpreters again on September 22 and did some translating, with the help of Emma. But his primary occupation was to work the land that Isaac Hale sold to him. In late fall he and Emma visited Joseph Knight, and he gave Joseph some food, a pair of shoes, and three dollars. They also received visits from his parents and others who came to ask what role they might play in the work. In February 1829, Joseph received a revelation addressed to his father that began, "Now behold, a marvelous work is about to come forth among the children of men." All must serve God with "heart, might, mind and strength." (D&C 4:1-2.) All must prepare themselves to be worthy of the great work that lay ahead.

As she assisted Joseph, Emma had no trouble believing him. When he was translating, she said, the plates lay on the table wrapped in a linen cloth. "I once felt of the plates as they thus lay on the table," she said, "tracing their outline and shape. They seemed to be pliable like thick paper, and would rustle with a metallic sound when the edges were moved by the thumb, as one does sometimes thumb the edges of a book." She sometimes moved them around on the table as her work required it. "I am satisfied that no man could have dictated the writing of the manuscripts unless he was inspired," she concluded, "for, when acting as his scribe, [Joseph] would dictate to me hour after hour; and when returning after meals, or after interruptions, he would at once begin where he had left off, without either seeing the manuscript or having any portion of it read to him. . . . It would have been improbable that a learned man could do this; and, for one so ignorant and unlearned as he was, it was simply impossible."

14

In April 1829 Joseph and Emma were visited by his brother Samuel, who was accompanied by a schoolteacher in Palmyra, a man named Oliver Cowdery. A twenty-one-year-old native of Vermont, Oliver had boarded with the Smiths. While working as a store clerk, he had become acquainted with David Whitmer, who was the first to tell him of the golden plates. Now he had come to learn more about them. After talking with Joseph late into the evening after his arrival in Harmony, Oliver decided to stay and help him. They began working together on April 7. "These days were never to be forgotten," wrote Oliver. "To sit under the sound of a voice dictated by the inspiration of heaven, awakened the utmost gratitude of my bosom." Oliver, who had had experience previously with a divining rod, was told that his gift was from God, but that it must be exercised only for the purpose of teaching spiritual truths.

To ensure that they not be interrupted until the translation was completed, Joseph Knight supplied them with nine or ten bushels of grain, five or six bushels of potatoes, a pound of tea, a barrel of mackerel, and some lined paper.

In mid-May, while translating the portion of the record that dealt with the visit of Jesus to the ancient inhabitants on the North American continent, Joseph and Oliver, according to the latter's account in the *Messenger and Advocate*, worried that "none had authority from God to administer the ordinances of the gospel." They went down to the nearby Susquehanna River to pray about it. As they were praying, Oliver wrote, an angel descended in a cloud of light, declared that he was John the Baptist, and laid his hands on their heads to ordain them. "Upon you my fellow servants, in the name of the Messiah I confer the Priesthood of Aaron, which holds the keys of the ministering of angels, and of the gospel of repentance, and of baptism by immersion for the remission of sins." (D&C 13.) John told them they would later receive a higher priesthood as well as the power to lay on hands for the gift of the Holy Ghost. Under instructions from John, Joseph then took Oliver into the river and baptized him, and Oliver did the same for Joseph. Then they ordained one another. They experienced special gifts from heaven, including the gift of prophecy, and fully understood that they were to organize a church with Joseph as First Elder and Oliver as Second Elder. "[We] were filled with the Holy Ghost, and rejoiced in the God of our salvation," wrote Joseph in his history.

Having received the gift of the Holy Ghost, Joseph and Oliver were now more enlightened and could understand more fully the scriptures they were translating. When they related their experience to Joseph's brother Samuel, who was still staying with them, he prayed for understanding, was convinced, and Oliver baptized him as well. When their brother Hyrum came to visit later that month, he also was eager to become involved and was cautioned through revelation not to preach "until you shall have my word, my rock, my church, and my gospel, that you may know of a surety my doctrine." (D&C 11:16.) Hyrum was baptized a month later in Seneca Lake.

During the latter part of May, after two months of work, Oliver Cowdery wrote David Whitmer asking if they could work in his father's house in Fayette, New York, to complete the translation. The Whitmers, Pennsylvania Germans who had gone to New York in 1809, were friends of Oliver and later of the Smiths. Peter and Mary, the parents, had seven children, three of whom were married and lived close by. All of them were interested in the work of translation, and several of them joined with the Smiths in becoming witnesses for the existence of the plates. In June Oliver baptized Peter Whitmer, Jr., and Joseph baptized David Whitmer.

The day after they arrived at the Whitmer farm, Joseph and Oliver resumed translating. "It was laborious work," wrote David Whitmer, "for the weather was very warm, and the days were long, and they worked from morning till night." From time to time some of the writing was done by others—John Whitmer, Emma Smith, and Christian Whitmer—but most of it was done by Oliver. Once again, it was not an automatic process. One evidence was related by David Whitmer: "One morning when he [Joseph] was getting ready to continue the translation, something went wrong about the house and he was put out about it. Something that Emma, his wife, had done. Oliver and I went upstairs and Joseph came up soon after to continue the translation, but he could not do anything. He could not translate a single syllable. He went downstairs, out into the orchard, and made supplication to the Lord; was gone about an hour—came back to the house, and asked Emma's forgiveness and then came upstairs where we were and then the translation went on all right. He could do nothing save he was humble and faithful."

Joseph and his associates found many eager listeners in the Fayette region, giving them opportunities to teach and explain the principles of the gospel, and they baptized a few. It was during this period that Oliver, Martin Harris, and David Whitmer became witnesses to the plates and the interpreters, and that another group of eight members of the Whitmer and Smith families were shown the plates, given the opportunity of examining them, and willingly signed a statement that they knew "of a surety that the said Smith has got the plates of which we have spoken."

On June 11, 1829, Joseph deposited the title page of the Book of Mormon with the clerk of the district court for Northern New York and obtained a copyright. Shortly thereafter he reached an agreement with Egbert B. Grandin, a Palmyra bookseller, printer, and publisher, to have the book published. Martin Harris mortgaged his farm for $3,000 as security. Oliver was instructed to make an extra copy of the manuscript for security reasons, and the first twenty-four pages were delivered to Grandin in August. By the end of March 1830, the entire Book of Mormon was printed, bound, and ready for sale.

WHILE JOSEPH AND OLIVER were completing the translation, Joseph was instructed to organize the Church of Jesus Christ. The day given for this purpose was April 6, 1830. The preponderance of evidence suggests the organizational meeting was held at the home of Peter and Mary Whitmer, in the township of Fayette, Seneca County, New York. A sizable group of believers attended, including about fifteen from Manchester, where the Smith family lived; another twenty from Colesville, some one hundred miles distant, where the Joseph Knight family resided; and twenty or so from the farming vicinity around Fayette. And, of course, there were the six elders who were selected to be the nucleus and incorporators of the new church: Joseph, Hyrum, and Samuel Smith, Oliver Cowdery, and Peter and David Whitmer.

The organization was an all-day affair. Although the later memories of those who were present do not always agree, there was apparently a baptismal service in the morning, probably in Lake Seneca, about four miles from the Whitmer home. There was also singing, and many exciting conversations comparing notes on the Book of Mormon, on recent revelations to the Prophet Joseph Smith, and on plans for the spread of the gospel. No doubt lunch was served in which the visitors shared food they had brought with them. It was a joyful occasion, for at last the Lord's church was to be established in this dispensation.

Early in the afternoon the Prophet called everyone together in the twenty-foot-square Whitmer living room. The meeting was opened with solemn prayer; then Joseph asked if those present accepted him and Oliver Cowdery as their "teachers in the things of the Kingdom of God," and whether they should "proceed and be organized as a church." The vote, which was presumably with the uplifted hand, was unanimously affirmative. Following the pattern outlined in a revelation, the Prophet then laid hands on Oliver and ordained him an elder of the Church of Jesus Christ, and Oliver in turn ordained Joseph an elder. They then laid their hands on the individual members present who had been baptized and conferred on them the gift of the Holy Ghost.

This was followed by a solemn sacrament service, in which they broke bread, blessed it, and partook. Wine was blessed, and everyone was invited to touch it to their lips in memory of the Savior.

According to Joseph Knight, the Prophet then gave instructions on "how to build up the church" and exhorted the listeners to be faithful, "for this is the work of God." They sang, they prophesied, they manifested heavenly gifts, they rejoiced.

The Prophet Joseph received the revelation on the organization and functioning of the Church, now sections 20 and 21 of the Doctrine and Covenants. All were now members of the Church of Jesus Christ. Some men were ordained to offices in the priesthood.

There were further baptisms after the meeting. Among those baptized during the day, in addition to the six elders, were Joseph Smith, Sr., Lucy Mack Smith, Martin Harris, Sarah Witt Rockwell, Orrin Porter Rockwell, and probably others. The mother of the Prophet wrote: "When Mr. Smith [Joseph Smith, Sr.] came out of the water, Joseph stood upon the shore, and taking his father by the hand, he exclaimed, with tears of joy, 'Oh, my God! have I lived to see my own father baptized into the true Church of Jesus Christ!' "

All observers who later left reminiscences mention the strong emotional overtones of the meeting, and particularly the depth of the young Prophet's feelings. He could hardly contain his emotions—he prayed, he wept, he exulted, he praised God. "His joy," wrote Joseph Knight, "seemed to be full."

The Book of Mormon had been published, elders had been ordained, the Church had been organized, and the stage had been set for the spread of the gospel throughout the world. Joseph was now to demonstrate hitherto unsuspected qualities of leadership. Following the pattern in the Book of Mormon, he empowered elders to baptize, administer the sacrament, bestow the Holy Ghost, ordain other priesthood officers, take the lead in meetings, and bless children. Priests could do the same except for bestowing the Holy Ghost, blessing children, and ordaining elders. Teachers and deacons were assistants to the priests. At the head of the Church were Joseph Smith and Oliver Cowdery, First Elder and Second Elder respectively. Basically, every worthy adult male convert was ordained to the priesthood shortly after baptism, but it was clearly understood that the Book of Mormon rule applied: "All their priests and teachers should labor with their own hands for their support." (Mosiah 27:5.) Not long afterward Joseph and Oliver were designated apostles; and others were selected in 1835. A revelation announcing the restoration of the Melchizedek Priesthood, with offices for high priests, seventies, and elders, came in 1832.

Another evidence of leadership was Joseph's announcement of a revelation on the day the Church was organized in which he was told: "A record shall be kept among you; and in it thou shalt be called a seer, a translator, a prophet, an apostle of Jesus Christ, an elder of the church through the will of God the Father, and the grace of your Lord Jesus Christ." (D&C 21:1.) The revelation further admonished members of the church: "Give heed unto all his [Joseph's] words and commandments which he shall give unto you as he receiveth them, walking in all holiness before me." (D&C 21:4.)

The first baptized members of the church were Joseph's family and close friends, but with the distribution of the Book of Mormon, the sermons of early volunteer missionaries, and the letters of early converts to their families and friends, the number of converts quickly increased. Some were persons of considerable substance, such as Joseph Knight, Thomas Marsh, Solomon Chamberlain, Parley Pratt, and W. W. Phelps. Before long small congregations or branches of enthusiastic members had been formed in Manchester, Fayette, and Colesville, New York.

AT A SPECIAL CONFERENCE of the Saints on September 26, 1830, at Fayette, New York, the minutes record that Joseph was appointed "to receive and write revelations and commandments" for the Church. Equally important, the conference decided to launch a major missionary outreach to the Indians. Oliver Cowdery and Peter Whitmer, Jr., and later Parley P. Pratt and Ziba Peterson, were called to leave in October. As they headed toward "the borders by the Lamanites" (D&C 28:9), which at that time was on the western edge of Missouri, they stopped at Kirtland, in northeastern Ohio, to present the gospel message to a man named Sidney Rigdon, who had been associated with Parley Pratt in the Campbellite movement. Rigdon, who had been a Baptist minister and had broken with Alexander Campbell, was pastor of a group in Mentor, Ohio, to whom he was teaching what he believed to be pristine Christianity. When Elder Pratt and his fellow missionaries presented him with the Book of Mormon, he was immediately impressed, and he was baptized two weeks later. More than one hundred of his followers in Mentor, Painesville, and Kirtland, Ohio, similarly accepted baptism, and together they formed a branch in nearby Hiram, Ohio. Among them was Edward Partridge, a prominent shopkeeper, who would later figure prominently in the Church.

David Whitmer declared, "Rigdon was a thorough Bible scholar, a man of fine education, and a powerful orator," a man who contributed much to the infant church. When Joseph Smith received news of the new branch, he recalled a revelation he had received in September that instructed, "Ye are called to bring to pass the gathering of mine elect. . . . They shall be gathered in unto one place upon the face of this land." (D&C 29:7-8.) In December, after meeting Sidney Rigdon and Edward Partridge, the Prophet announced that the Saints were to "go to the Ohio." (D&C 37:1.) The entire church was to go there and wait for Oliver's return from Missouri with news of the location of a permanent gathering place, a New Jerusalem like that predicted by John the Revelator and the Book of Mormon prophet Ether. By early spring of 1831, Joseph and most of the one hundred fifty or more New York Saints were in the Kirtland area.

SCARCELY TWENTY-FIVE YEARS OF AGE, Joseph now began a new phase of his life. Having left behind the sacred places in New York—the Hill Cumorah; the place of the First Vision; the Smith farmhouse, where he had first seen the Angel Moroni; the Peter Whitmer farm, where he had finished the translation of the Book of Mormon and organized the Church—he was now the leader of a new community as well as of a new church.

Joseph's first thoughts were of his loved ones—arranging a place for Emma, who was pregnant with twins (a boy and a girl, who died shortly after birth in April), and finding a home for his parents and brothers and sisters. More than one hundred

PRESIDENTS OF THE CHURCH

disciples were in Kirtland to greet him when he arrived during the first week of February. He answered many questions on doctrine, many questions on church and civic affairs.

In the months before he was introduced to the Book of Mormon, Sidney Rigdon had broken from Alexander Campbell over a dispute as to the wisdom of attempting to duplicate the common sharing of the early Christians, as described in the Acts of the Apostles: "All that believed were together, and had all things common; and sold their possessions and goods, and parted them to all men, as every man had need." (Acts 2:44-45.) Campbell and his followers in Mentor and Kirtland had established a communal society called "The Family." When Joseph arrived in Kirtland, one of his first acts was to ask that "The Family" abandon the common-stock principle in favor of what he called "the more perfect law of the Lord." A week later, a revelation was received outlining what was referred to as the Law of Consecration and Stewardship. (D&C 42.) On the basic principle that the earth and everything on it belong to the Lord, members were asked to "consecrate" or deed their economic property to the Presiding Bishop of the Church, who had previously been designated as Edward Partridge. The bishop would then grant an "inheritance" or "stewardship" to each family out of the properties so received, the amount depending on the wants and needs of the family, as determined jointly by the bishop and the prospective steward. The stewardship might be a farm, building lot, store, workshop, or mill, or simply an appointment as a teacher or physician. Family heads were asked to consecrate annually their surplus production to the bishop's storehouse; this would be distributed to the aged and the needy and would also be used to provide funds for publications, lands, temples, schools, and similar projects. There was to be freedom of enterprise, freedom in the management of properties, and freedom to buy and sell, but at the same time the interests of the group were protected and the growth of the Church was facilitated. There would also be help for needy members coming from New York and other areas.

THE NEXT FEW YEARS, for Joseph Smith as well as for the Church, were marked by great growth, fuller understanding of the gospel message, and intensification of the religious experience, but also by persecution and forced removal from several gathering places. What was there about the Prophet that drew people to him? Granted that he was sustained during the remaining years of his life as Prophet, Seer, and Revelator and President of The Church of Jesus Christ of Latter-day Saints, it is also necessary to view him as a person. Why were people so fond of him? Why did they follow him so willingly and obediently? What evidences did they see that proved his prophetic calling?

In the early years in Kirtland, it is clear that Joseph, who was fully conscious of the responsibility of his prophetic calling, sought to make himself worthy of it — worthy to call upon the Father for counsel and blessings, and worthy to ask his followers to make the sacrifices necessary to accomplish the building of the latter-day kingdom of God. In his diary, for example, Joseph habitually introduced brief prayers at the beginning or end of a daily entry:

"Oh may God grant that I may be directed in all my thoughts."

"Lord bless my family and preserve them."

"O Lord deliver thy servant out of temptations and fill his heart with wisdom and understanding."

"A great congregation paid good attention [today]. Oh God seal our testimony to their hearts."

The diary also furnishes evidence of Joseph's sincere search for personal salvation. His sermons are so prophetic and theological that we do not think of him seeking salvation for himself. He reveals truth after truth, he exhorts and gives direction, but he also prays to be forgiven, to have help in overcoming his weaknesses. "This evening I feel better in my mind than I have for a few days back. Oh Lord deliver thy servant out of temptations." Another: "The Lord is with us, but I have much anxiety about my family." As with all of us, Joseph experienced occasional periods of uneasiness and guilt.

Nor was he complacent about his personal standing before the Lord. In a perfectly forthright manner he sought to improve his own standing with God. "I have visited a grove which is just back of the town almost every day," he wrote to Emma in 1832. "There I can be secluded from the eyes of any mortal and there give vent to all the feelings of my heart in meditation and prayer." Joseph had no doubt about his calling or the validity of his revelations; he was blessed and he was inspired. But, as Richard Bushman has written, he did not "glide effortlessly into his prophethood."

In addition to prayer and seeking to maintain a close relationship with God, Joseph renewed his close study of the Bible in Kirtland. It was obvious to him that there were mistakes in the Bible—mistakes in translation and in interpretation. "Many plain and precious things," as the Book of Mormon prophet Nephi had written, had been omitted or taken away. So Joseph made revisions in the text as he went through it. These alterations were not based on learning but on revelation. Under inspiration he even supplied new incidents and long prophecies. Just as he had been the instrument in providing the Book of Mormon for the Latter-day Saints as a guide to their religious faith, so he provided new information about the words of God to Moses, and more information about the life of Enoch. "To the joy of the little flock," wrote Joseph, "did the Lord reveal the doings of olden times from the prophecy of Enoch." The Prophet did not have an opportunity to publish the "Inspired Bible" during his lifetime, but it has since been made available to modern readers, and many passages from and references to it are included in the modern LDS edition of the King James Version of the Bible.

Another aspect of this theological preparation was Joseph Smith's attempt to develop an educated lay ministry. In Kirtland he established a school of the prophets, and later a school of the elders, to teach men (and occasionally women as well) the doctrines of the Kingdom, and to train them to be effective missionaries and officers. Since the restored gospel included all truth, not just religious and theological truth, a variety of topics was covered in these training sessions — English grammar, penmanship, history, geography, mathematics, and Hebrew, as well as theology and church government. An 1832 revelation (D&C 88) had commanded the establishment of the school and the importance of seeking wisdom "out of the best books." Members were to "teach one another" and to learn "by study and also by faith." In a subsequent revelation (D&C 90), the Saints were told to "become acquainted with all good books, and with languages, tongues, and people." So serious were the sessions of these schools that they began at sunrise, in the spirit of fasting and prayer, and continued until four in the afternoon, after which the participants broke their fast and partook of the sacrament together. Joseph Smith wrote that because of "the things revealed, and our progress in the knowledge of God," great joy and satisfaction enriched the lives of the members of the school.

Consistent with his prophetic calling and his attempt to prepare himself to fully understand the Bible and the secular learning of the times, Joseph openly exhibited his love for the Saints and his desire to be to them what a "man of God" ought to be. One early convert wrote: "In Kirtland, when wagon loads of grown people and children came in from the country to meeting, Joseph would make his way to as many of the wagons as he well could, and cordially shake the hand of each person. Every child and young babe in the company were especially noticed by him and tenderly taken by the hand, with his kind words and blessings. He loved innocence and purity and seemed to find it in the greatest perfection with the prattling child."

Evaline Burdick Johnson remembered that when she was a child in Kirtland, one day her mother had put her in on the floor to play while the mother cleaned house. The little girl, hearing a man's voice, looked up and saw a tall, smiling man come up the steps. He called to the mother and she told him to come in. "When he saw me," said Evaline, "he came and picked me up and sat me on his left arm and crossed the room to a large mirror. We both looked into the glass. He then turned and sat me down and asked where father was. When he went out of the room, mother called me to her and told me he was the Prophet of the Lord, and what a good man he was."

Another woman told of "the tender sympathy and brotherly kindness he ever showed toward me and my father-less child. When riding with him and his wife Emma in their carriage, I have known him to alight and gather prairie flowers for my little girl." Still another girl wrote that she was in a cottage meeting at which the Prophet was speaking. She had become tired and sleepy, and when she began to whimper, the Prophet stopped speaking, sat down on a bench behind him, and motioned to her to come to him. He put her on his lap and patted her, and she went off to sleep while he completed his sermon. Surely the Lord called Joseph to be prophet for his human qualities as well as for his revelatory capabilities.

As THE RESULT OF THE MISSION of Oliver Cowdery and his fellow missionaries to the Missouri River, Joseph appointed a central gathering place for the Saints in Jackson County, in western Missouri. By the fall of 1833, about twelve hundred Saints, most of the members of the Church who had gathered at Kirtland, had gone on to Missouri. However, Kirtland remained the residence of Joseph Smith and more than a thousand Saints until 1838. During this period Joseph and his associates had to acquire land and establish industries that would provide the means of a livelihood for incoming settlers. As the community grew, the old settlers in the region began to fear a Mormon take-over. Just as there had been religious persecution in New York, Ohioans likewise now tried to discourage the Saints and their leaders from settling in their state, this time on religious grounds, but also for political and economic reasons.

On occasion, these hostile efforts were violent and well-orchestrated. On March 24, 1832, an angry crowd of about fifty men attacked Joseph Smith and Sidney Rigdon. The mob first broke into the residence of Elder Rigdon, carried him from his home, and dragged him by his heels along the frozen ground. Then they covered his body with tar. One man had taken a feather pillow from the Rigdon home, and he and several others sprinkled the feathers over the church leader's tarred body. Next, they went to the home of Joseph and Emma Smith. Emma was ill and Joseph was staying up to look after little Joseph and Julia Murdock, twins whom Joseph and Emma had adopted after the death of their mother in childbirth. Little Joseph was ill with a fever. The mob broke into the house, forced Joseph out, carried him to a lonely meadow, and beat him. While being carried to the field, he was choked until he became unconscious. When he awoke, he saw the tarred and bloody body of Sidney Rigdon stretched out on the ground. They tore off his clothes, and one man, who was so affected by the mob spirit that he could not control himself, fell on Joseph like a "mad cat" and scratched his body with sharp nails, muttering, "That's the way the Holy Ghost falls on folks!" Others attempted to force into Joseph's mouth a vial of what he thought was poison, but he broke the vial with his teeth and it fell to the ground, leaving him with a chipped tooth. Then they covered him with a coat of tar and feathers.

Eventually the mob disappeared, leaving Joseph in the meadow. For some time he lay there, struggling to get up but too weak to walk. Finally, seeing two lights in the distance, he arose and made his way toward one of them. When he arrived home and Emma saw his body darkened with tar, she thought it was blood, and she fainted. That night some of his friends remained with him, removing the tar and washing his body.

The next day was Sunday, and the Latter-day Saints gathered to worship at the usual hour. The Prophet, now cleaned up, was prepared to take charge. Although his flesh was "all scarified and defaced," he preached to the congregation as usual and noted that some of the men who had participated in the mobbing the previous night were in attendance. During the afternoon he baptized three converts.

However, the sequel to this harrowing experience was bitter. Sidney Rigdon was delirious for several days, and some of his problems in later years might well have been generated by this experience. Because the mob had left the door open, little

27

Joseph Murdock was exposed to the stinging cold weather and died five days later. He was the first person to die as a consequence of persecution aimed at the Saints.

CONSCIOUS OF THE THREATS against his life, the Prophet left for a mission to Missouri, leaving Emma and Julia with friends in Kirtland. But the problems for the Saints in Missouri were even worse than they were in Kirtland. There, an angry mob, led by a militant minister, destroyed the Mormon store and printing establishment, tarred and feathered the bishop, and finally, in November 1833, drove the Saints from their homes with whippings and plunder. Many houses were burned, livestock was killed, and furniture and other domestic property were seized and carted away. The Saints complained to Governor Daniel Dunklin, who promised to restore their homes to them if they would provide him with a posse of assistance.

Joseph decided to take the governor's offer seriously and began recruiting a band of more than one hundred loyal Saints to go help their brethren in Missouri. The expedition would take axes, saws, chisels, spades, hoes, and other tools for the Missouri settlers, as well as food, bedding, clothing, teams, and wagons for themselves. The 2,000-mile round trip would require at least forty days each way.

Zion's Camp, as the expedition was called, left Kirtland on May 1, 1834. By the time they reached Missouri, they numbered 205 men, 11 women (wives of recruits, taken along as cooks and washerwomen), and 7 children. Since their twenty-five wagons were loaded with arms, supplies, and relief provisions for the embattled Saints in Missouri, they walked the distance.

The Prophet, with a new kind of leadership responsibility, took advantage of the opportunity to train the people. He appointed general officers and divided the band into companies of twelve (like the twelve tribes of Israel), with each electing a captain from its own ranks. Within each camp, two of the men were assigned to attend to cooking, two to see that fires were made, two to pitch the tent at night and strike it in the morning, two to "fetch and provide water," two to see to the horses and wagon, one to assist the captain to maintain liaison, and one, a captain, to supervise so that "all things are done in order."

Joseph exhibited remarkable patience. One of the young travelers, who was only sixteen at the time, kept a daily account of their progress. He wrote: "The Prophet . . . never uttered a murmur or complaint, while most of the men in the camp complained to him of sore toes, blistered feet, long drives, scanty supply of provisions, poor quality of bread, bad corn dodger, 'frouzy' butter, strong honey, maggoty bacon and cheese, etc. Even a dog could not bark at some men without their murmuring at Joseph. If they had to camp with bad water, it would nearly cause rebellion. *Yet we were the Camp of Zion*, and many of us were careless, thoughtless, heedless, foolish or devilish, and yet we did not know it. Joseph had to bear with us and tutor us like children." Joseph's patient and forgiving nature was on exhibit throughout the journey.

By the time the expedition reached Missouri, Governor Dunklin had changed his mind. Fearful of a civil war, he withdrew his support of the Saints, and they were never to regain their lands in Jackson County. The opposing army of Missourians was broken up when a timely storm arose, and members of the Zion's Camp were directed by revelation to disband and return to their homes in the East. When the members of the camp were called together once more in Kirtland in February 1835, they each received a special blessing. Twelve men, nearly all of whom were former members of the camp, were chosen to constitute the first Quorum of Twelve Apostles of the Church, and seventy others were chosen to constitute the First Quorum of Seventies.

Brigham Young, who was a member of the camp, afterward said, "This was the starting point of my knowing how to lead Israel." "I watched every word and summed it up," he said, "and I knew just as well how to lead this kingdom as I know the way to my own house." He concluded, "I would not exchange the knowledge I have received this season for the whole of Geauga County [Ohio]; for property and mines of wealth are not to be compared to the worth of knowledge."

NOT LONG AFTER THE SAINTS arrived in Kirtland, Joseph Smith announced that a sacred temple was to be built. For the new church, that was a remarkable accomplishment, for by the time the three-story structure was dedicated in 1836, there were fewer than five hundred Latter-day Saints in the Kirtland area, all struggling for survival. The $60,000 building was dedicated March 27, 1836, followed by a "pentecost" that lasted several days longer. There were solemn prayers, partaking of the Lord's Supper, fasting, the ordinance of washing of feet, speaking in tongues, and prophesyings. Some of those participating experienced the presence of heavenly beings for part of the proceedings. Joseph Smith and Oliver Cowdery reported that, in a sacred moment in the temple, they received instruction from, in turn, Moses, with the keys of the gathering and the return of the Ten Tribes; Elias, with the keys of the dispensation of Abraham; and Elijah, with the keys of redemption and sealing. Joseph later conveyed all of these keys to the Twelve Apostles, with the instruction for their use in building up the kingdom of God on earth.

Kirtland went through a period of building and growth. "Every countenance was lit up with a smile," wrote Warren Cowdery. Many persons believed that "the set time of the Lord to favor Zion had come." This expansion was in part a result of the Prophet's program of economic development. As Brigham Young said later, Joseph took heaven and earth and made them shake hands. But there were a few converts who thought the Prophet should follow a more limited policy; he had no business interfering in "temporalities." When a bank that he had promoted failed, a small group organized to depose him. "It was a crisis," declared Brigham Young, "when earth and hell seemed leagued to overthrow the Prophet and Church of God. The knees of many of the strongest men in the Church faltered." As Joseph had declared, temporal and spiritual things were inseparably connected, but because his temporal management did not always accord with what a few thought was wise or correct, they declared him to be a fallen prophet. Eventually he was forced to leave Kirtland, in the dead of night, in January 1838.

Even as he was fleeing from persecution in Ohio, however, there is one documented story that reveals Joseph Smith's capacity for quiet heroism. One evening he was driven by a young companion to a friend's house for supper. As they were finishing their meal, they heard a disturbance outside. A mob had gathered and were angrily yelling threats of murder, demanding that the host surrender Joseph and his friend to them. Instead, the host led Joseph and the friend through a back door and helped them get away in the darkness.

When the mob discovered that their quarry had escaped, riders were dispatched along the road they thought Joseph and his companion would take. Joseph's companion tells the rest of the story:

"Joseph and I did not take to the main road, but walked through the woods and swamps away from the road. We were helped by the bonfires [lit by their pursuers]. Pretty soon I began to falter in our flight. Sickness and fright had robbed me of strength. Joseph had to decide whether to leave me to be captured by the mob or to endanger himself by rendering aid. Choosing the latter course, he lifted me upon his own broad shoulders and bore me with occasional rests through the swamp and darkness. Several hours later we emerged upon the lonely road and soon reached safety. Joseph's herculean strength permitted him to accomplish this task and saved my life."

Joseph Smith was welcomed to the community of Saints in Missouri, as he wrote to friends, "with open arms and warm hearts." Long anxious to have their leader live with them, the Saints promised to provide for the Prophet's physical needs so that he would have "nothing to do but attend to the spiritual affairs of the church." At Far West, Missouri, he laid cornerstones for a proposed temple and supervised the planning of agricultural, commercial, and industrial enterprises.

Nevertheless, there was a repetition of the troubles in Ohio. The old settlers did not welcome the influx of Mormons, and certain Church members reacted against some of the Prophet's policies. Ministers and apostates organized mobs to oppose the Saints and attempt to drive them out, and finally, Governor Lilburn W. Boggs, fearful of civil war, ordered the Saints to leave the state or be exterminated. Homes of the Saints were burned, livestock was killed, and seventeen Church members were massacred at Haun's Mill. Some of the Saints organized a secret paramilitary band to take vengeance on their enemies, but Joseph Smith could see that this was a mistake, and he excommunicated their leader.

As units of the Missouri militia approached the Saints in October 1838, a "bloody massacre" seemed imminent, as Heber C. Kimball reported. Anxious to avoid bloodshed, Joseph Smith, Sidney Rigdon, Parley P. Pratt, Lyman Wight, and George Robinson went to negotiate with state officials under a flag of truce. Instead of treating them with respect, however, militia officials seized the group (and Hyrum Smith and Amasa Lyman the next day). An order was issued to have Joseph and the others shot, but Colonel Alexander Doniphan, a secondary Missouri officer, courageously refused to carry out the order. Instead of court-martial and execution, the prisoners were taken on November 2 to Jackson County (and subsequently elsewhere) for prison and trial.

JOSEPH AND HIS ASSOCIATES remained in jail in Liberty, Missouri, for almost six months—until the middle of April 1839, when they were allowed to escape. For much of that time their feet were bound together in chains. Most of the time they were in the dungeon of the jail, without light to read or write. Nevertheless, the closeness of his brethren and their unity and love in affliction must have helped maintain Joseph's spirits. "Brother Robinson is chained next to me," he wrote, "he that has a true heart and a firm mind. Brother Wight is next, Brother Rigdon next, Hyrum next, Parley next, Amasa next, and thus we are bound together in chains as well as the cords of everlasting love. We are in good spirits and rejoice that we are counted worthy to be persecuted for Christ's sake."

Perhaps because of this mutual sharing and the opportunity

presented for contemplation, the time in Liberty Jail was one of the most productive periods in the Prophet's life. The letters he wrote to Emma and his friends are full of tenderness and insight. He and his companions prayed, sang songs, and shared life experiences. He received revelations, some of the most beautiful and poetic in the Doctrine and Covenants. "The Lord has chosen his own crucible to try us," he wrote, "a trial of our faith equal to that of Abraham or any of the ancients." But such trials, he asserted, "only give us the knowledge necessary to understand the minds of the ancients."

As his letters demonstrate, Joseph yearned for the companionship of family and friends. He candidly told them of his love and desires, without embarrassment or subterfuge. He often asked Emma please to write, and friends please to visit—"If you would come and see me in this lonely retreat, it would afford me great relief of mind." The miseries of enforced seclusion made him lonely. He wrote to Emma of life "within the walls, grates, and screeking iron doors of this lonesome, dark, dirty prison." He longed not just for the comforts and peace of home, but to see and touch and talk to his children. "Oh God grant," he wrote, "that I may have the privilege of seeing once more my lovely family, in the enjoyment of the sweets of liberty and social life. To press them to my bosom and kiss their lovely cheeks would fill my heart with unspeakable gratitude." As for Emma's letters, "I received your letter which I read over and over again. It was a sweet morsel to me."

Joseph's prison letters reveal plainly his concern for his family. "I want you should not let those little fellows forget me," he wrote after five months of imprisonment. "Tell them father loves them with a perfect love, and he is doing all he can to get away from the mob to come to them." (By this time he and Emma had four children: Julia, eight, adopted; Joseph, six; Frederick, three; and Alexander, one.) "Do teach them [the children] all you can, that they may have good minds. Be tender and kind to them. Don't be fractious to them, but listen to their wants." One envisions him turning each over in his mind as he sat in jail. "Tell little Joseph he must be a good boy. Father loves him with a perfect love. He is the eldest and must not hurt those that are smaller than him, but comfort them. Tell little Frederick father loves him with all his heart. He is a lovely boy. Julia is a lovely little girl. Love her also. She is a promising child. Tell her father wants her to remember him and be a good girl." As for his wife: "Oh my affectionate Emma, I want you to remember that I am a true and faithful friend, to you and the children, forever. My heart is entwined around you forever and ever. Oh may God bless us all."

WHEN JOSEPH AND HIS COLLEAGUES escaped from jail, probably with the connivance of the jailer, his first task was to find lands on which the exiled Saints could be settled. Through a fortunate set of circumstances, he was able to acquire considerable land in Commerce, Illinois, and recommended that the Saints gather there. Within a year, most of the Saints expelled from Missouri had settled in Commerce and had begun to build a city, which Joseph renamed Nauvoo—Hebrew for "beautiful location."

Nauvoo was on the east bank of the Mississippi River, near the head of what were called the Des Moines Rapids, about two hundred miles north of Saint Louis. Joseph and his colleagues laid out a city plat in squares, began to erect many fine residences, and prepared for a stream of immigrants from Great Britain and from the eastern and southern United States. A university was chartered by the state legislature; a municipal militia, the Nauvoo Legion, was organized; schoolhouses were built; and artisans began working on the construction of a temple.

In Nauvoo Joseph announced new revelations for the government of the Church and for missionary efforts abroad; made new attempts to establish cooperative industries; continued to try to get political candidates to favor the Saints; and introduced a number of new practices. He was an innovative, imaginative, and aggressive leader. At the same time, he was an attentive husband and father, an ever-genial host, and a loyal friend. His great spiritual power brought joy and comfort to the Saints, but his human qualities were likewise special. He had the ability to establish a bond of brotherliness that drew in persons of all ages and of many diverse cultural groups. "He possessed," wrote one admirer, "the innate refinement that one finds in the born poet or in the most highly cultivated intellectual and poetical nature." In the words of another, he was "very sociable, easy, cheerful, obliging, kind and hospitable — in a word, a jolly fellow." Still another described him as "kind and considerate, taking a personal interest in all people, considering everyone his equal." All would have agreed that he was "a fine, noble looking man."

The Prophet had great respect for women, perhaps an outgrowth of his love and admiration for his mother, Lucy, and his wife, Emma. Just as Joseph Smith, Sr., had treated Lucy as a partner, so Joseph, Jr., treated Emma as a partner: she was a partner in his business affairs, a spokeswoman for the Church when he was away or in hiding, and a confidante in his most private concerns. In Joseph's diary are countless references to his doing things with Emma. Mercy Thompson recalled his tenderness with Emma: "I saw him by the bed-side of Emma, his wife, in sickness, exhibiting all the solicitude and sympathy possible for the tenderest of hearts and the most affectionate of natures to feel." His letters to Emma and Emma's letters to him suggest a warm and affectionate relationship.

Young people in Nauvoo continued to regard Joseph as their special friend. One person later recalled: "Passing the Prophet's house one morning on my way to school, I heard him call to me and ask what book I read in at school. I replied, 'the Book of Mormon.' He seemed pleased, and took me into the house where he gave me a copy of the Book of Mormon to read in at school. It was a gift greatly prized by me."

Margarette McIntire Burgess, walking to school with her brother one morning, had a similar experience: "It had been raining the previous day, causing the ground to be very muddy, especially along that street. My brother Wallace and I both got fast in the mud, and could not get out, and of course, child-like, we began to cry, for we thought we would have to stay there. But looking up, I beheld the loving friend of children, the Prophet Joseph, coming to us. He soon had us on higher and drier ground. Then he stooped down and cleaned the mud from our little, heavy-laden shoes, took his handkerchief from his pocket and wiped our tear-stained faces. He spoke kind and cheering words to us, and sent us on our way to school rejoicing."

Aroet Hale recalled. "Here [in Nauvoo] as a boy I became personally acquainted with the Prophet Joseph. He was fond of children and frequently used to come out of the mansion [Joseph's home] and play ball with us boys. Joseph would always conform to the rules. He would kitch [catch] till it came his turn to take the club [bat], then, being a very stout man, he would knock the ball so far that we used to holler to the boy that was going for the ball to take his dinner while he was at it. This used to make the Prophet laugh. Joseph was always good-natured and full of fun. I have seen him set down on the carpet in his office in the mansion and pull sticks with the Nauvoo police."

Edwin Holden, who first saw Joseph Smith in New York in 1831, wrote: "In 1838 Joseph and some of the young men were playing various out-door games, among which was a game of ball. By and by they began to get weary. He saw it, and calling them together he said, 'Let us build a log cabin.' So off they went, Joseph and the young men, to build a log cabin for a widow woman. Such was Joseph's way, always assisting in whatever he could."

Because he was both popular and a source of spirituality, he was always surrounded by people—people wanting advice, people seeking help, people who simply enjoyed his company. This must have been somewhat of a problem for Emma, because she never knew how many to cook for. But she must have been up to it: "When I want a little bread and milk," Joseph told William W. Phelps, "my wife loads the table with so many good things it destroys my appetite." He enjoyed wrestling, circulated socially without reserve, often uttered jokes for the amusement of his companions, and, as one early convert wrote, "moved upon the same plane with the humblest and poorest of his friends." As did other church officials, he also performed manual labor; there are many references in his journals to digging ditches, carrying the trunks of arriving passengers into the Mansion House, picking apples, plowing in his garden, hoeing potatoes, and drawing wood.

One afternoon Andrew Workman and others were sitting on a fence near the Prophet's home, listening as the Prophet spoke to them. A man came up and said that the home of a poor brother who lived some distance from town had burned down the night before. The men all began to get long faces and say how sorry they were. But, Andrew wrote, "Joseph put his hand in his pocket, took out five dollars, and said, 'I feel sorry for this brother to the amount of five dollars; how much do the rest of you feel sorry for him?' "

THE SAINTS LIVED AT PEACE with their Illinois neighbors at first, but later a mobocratic spirit arose similar to the one that had driven them from Ohio and Missouri. The Prophet was harassed by lawsuits, trumped-up arrests, and threats on his life. To make certain that the work would go on in his absence should anything happen to him, he turned over the keys of his authority to the Council of the Twelve in March 1844.

Even in the anxiety produced by the attempts on his life, however, Joseph's concern for the welfare of the Saints was paramount. In early June 1844, the Nauvoo Legion was called out to disperse a mob in an outlying area. When another mob approached the city, the Prophet asked the Junior Legion if they could provide some protection. Seventy-five members of the Legion were living in Macedonia, a few miles from Nauvoo. Though it had been raining and the roads were bad, all but eight of the young men went afoot, in places having to wade waist-deep in water. "We reached Nauvoo about daylight," wrote one of the men, John L. Smith, "and encamped in front of Foster's big brick house near the temple. Our camp equipage was placed on the side street." He continues:

While I was guarding the baggage, Joseph the Prophet rode up to the log, reached his hand to me and inquired after [relatives]. He held me by the hand and pulled me forward until I was obliged to step upon the log. When turning his horse sideways he drew me step by step to near the end of the log, when, seeing that each foot left marks of blood upon the bark, he asked me what was the matter with my feet. I replied that the prairie grass had cut my shoes to pieces and wounded my feet, but they would soon be alright. I noticed the hand he raised to his face was wet and looking up I saw his cheeks covered with tears. He placed his hand on my head and said, "God bless you, my dear boy," and asked if others of the company were in the same plight. I replied that a number of them were. Turning his face toward Mr. Lathrop [who ran the store], the Prophet said, "Let these men have some shoes." Lathrop said: "I have no shoes." Joseph's quick reply was, "Let them have boots, then." Joseph then turned to me and said, "Johnny, the troops will be disbanded and return home. I shall go to Carthage for trial, under the protection the governor will give." Then, leaning toward me, with one hand on my head, he said, "Have no fear, for you shall yet see Israel triumph in peace."

Soon afterward, Joseph and his brother Hyrum left Nauvoo, intending to escape westward. But after intensive prayer and discussion, they decided to return, "like lambs to the slaughter." Joseph wrote in his personal journal, "I told Stephen Markham that if I and Hyrum were ever taken again we should be massacred, or I was not a prophet of God." He said good-bye to his family and friends, and surrendered to Illinois authorities. "If my life is of no value to my friends it is of none to myself," he declared. On June 27, 1844, from a jail cell in Carthage, Illinois, he wrote to his wife, "Dear Emma, I am very much resigned to my lot, knowing I am justified, and have done the best that could be done. Give my love to the children and all my friends."

That morning, sensing a conspiracy of the Carthage militia to do away with Joseph, some friends tried to persuade Governor Thomas Ford to protect the prisoners. The governor replied, "You are unnecessarily alarmed. The people are not that cruel." He then disbanded the 1300-man militia and set out for Nauvoo to reassure the Saints. While he was away, many members of the militia daubed mud on their faces and set out for the jail. By afternoon all of the Prophet's friends who had been with him in the Carthage jail had been forced to leave except apostles John Taylor and Willard Richards. As the mob approached, they were fired upon with blanks by guards who were apparently part of the conspiracy. One group of attackers then stormed up the stairs. Within minutes, Joseph and Hyrum were shot to death and Elder Taylor was severely wounded. Someone shouted, "The Mormons are coming," and the attackers fled.

Samuel Smith, brother of Joseph and Hyrum, carried the bodies of the martyrs back to Nauvoo, where thousands of grieving Saints filed by to see them for the last time. The bodies were hidden and later buried privately. (They are now buried on a lot near the old Smith mansion in Nauvoo.) The anti-Mormon raids continued, with pitifully inadequate protection from the state militia, and the Saints left Nauvoo in the late winter and spring of 1846. The "City of Joseph," as it had been renamed after the death of the Prophet, now lay deserted.

TWO MONTHS BEFORE HIS DEATH, Joseph the Prophet wrote his own epitaph: "I love you all. I am your best friend, and if persons miss their mark, it is their own fault. . . . You never knew my heart; no man knows my history; I cannot tell it. I shall never undertake it. If I had not experienced what I have, I should not have believed it myself. I never did harm any man since I have been born into the world. My voice is always for peace, I cannot lie down until my work is finished, I never think any evil nor do anything to the harm of my fellow man. When I am called at the trump of the archangel and weighed in the balance, you will all know me then."

In the words of his associates, the Prophet had done more for the salvation of men in this world, save Jesus only, "than any other man who ever lived in it." (D&C 135:3.)

SOURCES

Biographies of Joseph Smith include Lucy Mack Smith, *Biographical Sketches of Joseph Smith the Prophet and his Progenitors for Many Generations* (Liverpool, England, 1853); Edward W. Tullidge, *Life of Joseph Smith the Prophet* (Plano, Illinois, 1880); George Q. Cannon, *The Life of Joseph Smith, The Prophet* (Salt Lake City, 1888); John Henry Evans, *Joseph Smith, An American Prophet* (New York: Macmillan, 1933); Preston Nibley, *Joseph Smith the Prophet* (Salt Lake City: Deseret News Press, 1944); Daryl Chase, *Joseph the Prophet* (Salt Lake City: Deseret Book, 1944); Leon R. Hartshorn, *Joseph Smith: Prophet of the Restoration* (Salt Lake City: Deseret Book, 1970); Donna Hill, *Joseph Smith, the First Mormon* (New York: Doubleday, 1977); and Francis M. Gibbons, *Joseph Smith: Martyr, Prophet of God* (Salt Lake City:

Deseret Book, 1977). The best treatment of his early life is in Richard L. Bushman, *Joseph Smith and the Beginning of Mormonism* (Urbana and Chicago: University of Illinois Press, 1984).

Other books and articles that have been especially useful include, in order of publication, the following:

B. H. Roberts, ed., *History of the Church of Jesus Christ of Latter-day Saints. Period I. History of Joseph Smith, The Prophet, By Himself,* 6 vols. (Salt Lake City: The Church of Jesus Christ of Latter-day Saints, 1902); Edwin F. Parry, ed., *Stories About Joseph Smith the Prophet* (Salt Lake City: Deseret Book, 1934); Leonard J. Arrington, "The Human Qualities of Joseph Smith, the Prophet," *Ensign* 1 (January 1971): 35-38; Jan Shipps, "The Prophet Puzzle: Suggestions Leading Toward a More Comprehensive Interpretation of Joseph Smith," *Journal of Mormon History* 1 (1974): 3-30; James B. Allen and Glen M. Leonard, *The Story of the Latter-day Saints* (Salt Lake City: Deseret Book, 1976); T. L. Brink, "Joseph Smith: The Verdict of Depth Psychology," *Journal of Mormon History* 3 (1976): 73-83; Richard L. Bushman, "The Character of Joseph Smith: Insights from His Holographs," *Ensign* 7 (April 1977): 10-13; Thomas G. Alexander, "The Place of Joseph Smith in the Development of American Religion: A Historiographical Inquiry," *Journal of Mormon History* 5 (1978): 3-17; Leonard J. Arrington and Davis Bitton, *The Mormon Experience: A History of the Latter-day Saints* (New York: Alfred A. Knopf, 1979); Andrew F. Ehat and Lyndon W. Cook, eds., *The Words of Joseph Smith* (Provo, Utah: Brigham Young University, 1980); Milton V. Backman, Jr., *The Heavens Resound: A History of the Latter-day Saints in Ohio, 1830-1838* (Salt Lake City: Deseret Book, 1983); Dean C. Jessee, *The Personal Writings of Joseph Smith* (Salt Lake City: Deseret Book, 1984); Linda King Newell and Valeen Tippetts Avery, *Mormon Enigma: Emma Hale Smith* (Garden City, New York: Doubleday, 1984).

In the interests of the reader, I have taken a few liberties with the quotations by correcting some of the spelling and adding punctuation, and in a place or two I have changed a tense or a pronoun to comport with the style of the narrative.

LEONARD J. ARRINGTON is Lemuel Redd Professor of Western History and director of the Joseph Fielding Smith Institute for Church History at Brigham Young University. A former Idahoan, he was awarded the Ph.D. at the University of North Carolina. He is author of *Great Basin Kingdom: An Economic History of the Latter-day Saints* (Cambridge, Massachusetts: Harvard University Press, 1958); *Brigham Young: American Moses* (New York: Alfred A. Knopf, 1985); and co-author with Davis Bitton of *The Mormon Experience: A History of the Latter-day Saints* (New York: Alfred A. Knopf, 1979); and *Saints without Halos: The Human Side of Mormon History* (Salt Lake City: Signature Books, 1982).

BRIGHAM YOUNG
Leonard J. Arrington

Next to the Prophet Joseph Smith, Brigham Young is probably the most widely known Latter-day Saint in our history.
Because he led a community of 16,000 to settle the Great
Basin, supervised the immigration of another 80,000, and
founded 350 different settlements, most historians, whether
or not members of The Church of Jesus Christ of Latter-day
Saints, regard him as one of the great colonizers in American
history. He was also the first governor of Utah, serving two
terms, the first Superintendent of Indian Affairs of Utah Territory, founder of many Western enterprises and industries,
head of one of the largest families in American history, and
president of the Church for thirty (or thirty-three, depending
on how one calculates it) years. His statue is that of the one
Latter-day Saint in the rotunda of the National Capitol in
Washington, D.C., and he has been the subject of many widely
selling biographies. Although he was obviously a person of
many important accomplishments, his own reaction to his
fame was the following comment: "I care nothing about my
character in this world. I do not care what men say about me.
I want my character to stand fair in the eyes of my Heavenly
Father."

I am grateful for the help of Rebecca Cornwall, Ronald K. Esplin, Ronald W.
Walker, and Dean C. Jessee in preparing this chapter.

BRIGHAM YOUNG did not start out life obviously destined to become a colonizer, governor, and prophet. Born in Whitingham, Vermont, on June 1, 1801, he was the ninth child in a Vermont farm family of eleven children, and was raised on hard work and good sense. His father, John Young, had been a soldier in the Revolutionary War army of George Washington, and had engaged in subsistence farming in Massachusetts before moving to Vermont just prior to Brigham's birth. Brigham's mother, Abigail (Nabby) Howe, also from Massachusetts, was ill with consumption (tuberculosis) during his childhood, and so he had to perform many duties inside the house as well as outside. Because of the Young family's poverty and their location on the frontier of settlement, Brigham had only eleven days of schooling. "We never had the opportunity of letters in our youth," he said, "but we had the privilege of picking up brush, chopping down trees, rolling logs, . . . and of getting our shins, feet, and toes bruised. . . . I learned to make bread, wash the dishes, milk the cows, and make butter. . . . I learned how to economize, for my father had to do it."

Brigham gained from his youth a practical approach to life and an ability to fend for himself. His mother died just as he turned fourteen, leaving his training to the sole direction of his father, whom he described as a stern moralist. "It used to be a word and a blow with him," said Brigham, "but the blow came first."

"When I was young," he later recalled, "I was kept within very strict bounds, and was not allowed to walk more than half-an-hour on Sunday for exercise." Brigham rebelled against all this and came to believe that life should be enjoyed. "The proper and necessary gambols of youth having been denied me, makes me want active exercise and amusement now," he said. "I had not a chance to dance, . . . and never heard the enchanting tones of the violin until I was eleven years of age; and then I thought I was on the highway to hell if I suffered myself to linger and listen to it. I shall not subject my little children to such a course of unnatural training, but they shall go to the dance, study music, read novels, and do anything else that will tend to expand their frames, add fire to their spirits, improve their minds, and make them feel free and untrammeled in body and mind."

Let everything come in its season, he said. There is a time to dance and a time to pray; a time to work and a time to sing. And we must always keep learning. "The Lord Almighty has designed us to know all that is in the earth, both the good and the evil, and to learn not only what is in Heaven, but what is in Hell," so we should not expect ever to get through learning. He went on: "Tight-laced religious people of the present generation have a horror at the sound of a fiddle. They do not realize that all good music belongs to heaven; there is no music in hell. We should delight in hearing harmonious tones made by the human voice, by musical instruments, and by both combined. Every sweet musical sound that can be made belongs to the Saints and is for the Saints. Every flower, shrub, and tree to beautify, and to gratify the taste and smell, and every sensation that gives to man joy and felicity are for the Saints, who receive them from the Most High."

Brigham's father later moved to Chenango County in central New York State, where Brigham apprenticed himself in the building trade, becoming a carpenter, joiner, painter, and glazier all in one. Here he was brought up "amid those flaming, fiery revivals so customary with the Methodists" — the church of his parents. The preachers urged him to pray and get saved. As to that, he had "but one prevailing feeling" in his mind: "Lord, preserve me until I am old enough to have sound judgement, and a discreet mind ripened upon a good solid foundation of common sense." In the meantime, he tried to live a pure life, although he was not afraid to expose iniquity when he saw it. He always admired morality and integrity: "I never saw a day in which I did not respect a good, moral, sensible man far more than I could respect a wicked man." He could not remember ever having stolen, lied, gambled, taken too much drink, or disobeyed his parents. Still, he was not disposed to attach himself to any church until, at the age of twenty-one, he became a Methodist like his father.

In Chenango County Brigham met and married, at age

twenty-three, Miriam Works, and took her sixty miles west to Port Byron, where he worked as a house and sign painter. In Port Byron he found that he could not make an honest living as a painter; to make money, he would have to adulterate the linseed oil, and this he would not do. So he got out of the business and moved to Oswego, on Lake Ontario, where he built a large tannery and joined a little group of citizens who, like him and his bride, were seeking religious truth. "How sweet our communion in old Oswego," wrote one of his associates there. "How encouraging our prayers, and enlivening the songs we used to sing."

With some of the others, Brigham took the scriptures simply and at face value. Common sense and morality were not enough for a religion when the Bible said there should be an organization, with officers and offices. As far as the spirit and application of their religion went, the churches were all right with him, but with regard to doctrine, he did not see any that altogether suited him. So he waited patiently, read the Bible, and all the time prayed earnestly that God would help him keep out of the "snares of folly," to use his words, until the Lord himself revealed his church.

Brigham's search for truth and prosperity took the Youngs to Mendon, two counties further west, where they joined the Congregational church and Brigham gained a reputation as a skilled craftsman. A year before Brigham's death one of his fellow church members there, George Hickox, wrote to him: "I shall always remember how kind you were to me when I had fever and ague." He then invited Brigham to a celebration banquet: "The Congregational Church People are to have a grand Centennial Supper the 22nd inst. My daughter is to have the centennial table and the most interesting [item] will be one of the chairs you made for me when you were in Mendon. We would be very happy to have you come and occupy it." Brigham, delighted that his chair had proved so sturdy, wrote back: "I have no doubt that many other pieces of furniture and other specimens of my handiwork can be found scattered about your section of country, for I have believed all my life that that which was worth doing was worth doing well, and have considered it as much a part of my religion to do honest, reliable work, such as would endure, . . . as to attend to the services of God's worship on the Sabbath."

This appreciation for quality stayed with Brigham; he always preferred a good watch to a cheap, temporary one. When he ordered a carriage, it was to have solid fittings and genuine leather. But his Puritan background also stayed with him; though he ordered carpet of "good sized, well twisted thread, made of long-stapled, coarsish, good wool," when it came to color, "I want red entirely rejected, and let the colors be selected of the yellow, brown, cinnamon, orange . . . &c. &c."

This reputation as an exacting workman and artisan accompanied Brigham wherever he did business, and rarely did he disappoint anyone. While living in Mendon in the late 1820s, he incurred two debts that went unpaid for years, one that the seller later could find no record of and would not let him repay, and one that he himself had forgotten. In 1866, having found a slip indicating he did indeed owe the debt, he instructed his son John to go through Monroe County on his way east and repay, to the heirs if the lender was no longer alive, those two debts totaling ten dollars.

EARLY IN 1830 Brigham Young first saw the Book of Mormon, a copy that Samuel Smith had just brought from Palmyra, New York, where it was fresh off the press. Samuel had sold it to Phineas Young, Brigham's brother; Phineas had given it to his father and then to his sister Fanny, and she gave it to Brigham — or something like that, for there are different accounts. Joseph Smith's mother, recording the history of that copy, says that "all received it without hesitancy, and rejoiced in the truth thereof." But Brigham remembers his conversion as not so sudden — more in keeping with his psychological makeup:

> When the Book of Mormon was first printed it came to my hands in two or three weeks afterwards. Did I believe, on the first intimation of it? The man that brought it to me, told me . . . "This is the Gospel of salvation; . . . you must be baptized for the remission of sins, or you will be damned." "Hold on," says I. The mantle of my traditions was

over me, to that degree, and my prepossessed feelings so interwoven with my nature, it was almost impossible for me to see at all; though I had beheld, all my life, that the traditions of the people was all the religion they had, I had got a mantle for myself. Says I, "Wait a little while; what is the doctrine of the book, and of the revelations the Lord has given? Let me apply my heart to them. . . ."

I examined the matter studiously for two years before I made up my mind to receive that book. I knew it was true, as well as I knew that I could see with my eyes, or feel by the touch of my fingers. . . . Had not this been the case, I never would have embraced it to this day. . . . I wished time sufficient to prove all things for myself.

So Brigham, while immediately attracted to the book, in his practical way sought to become acquainted with the people who professed to believe it, not to try and find fault with them, but, to use his words, "to see whether good common sense was manifest; and if they had that, I wanted them to present it in accordance with the scriptures."

Now we begin to see a change in Brigham Young, a dismantled Brigham. About the first thing the new convert to Mormonism did was to set out on a mission, in his own area and in the region of his birth. Brigham confessed, "When I first commenced preaching, I made up my mind to declare the things that I understood, fearless of friends and threats, and regardless of caresses. They were nothing to me, for if it was my duty to rise before a congregation of strangers and say that the Lord lives, that He has revealed Himself in this our day, that He has given to us a Prophet . . . and if that was all I could say, I must be satisfied as though I could get up and talk for hours. . . . Had it not been for this feeling, nothing could have induced me to have become a public speaker." On another occasion he said, "When I began to speak in public, I was about as destitute of language as a man could well be. . . . How I have had the headache, when I had ideas to lay before the people, and not words to express them; but I was so gritty that I always tried my best."

In 1832, the same year of his baptism, Brigham's wife died, leaving him with two small children. In mourning, Brigham left his children with Vilate Kimball, wife of Brigham's friend

Heber C. Kimball, and set off on a mission with his brother. First they traveled toward Kirtland, Ohio, preaching to the branches on the way. "We exhorted them and prayed with them and I spoke in tongues," Brigham said. Some of the congregation thought it was of God and some of the devil. Arriving in Kirtland, he said, "we rested a few minutes, took some refreshment, and started to see the Prophet [Joseph Smith]. . . . We went to his father's house and learned that he was in the woods chopping. We immediately repaired to the woods where we found the Prophet, and two or three of his brothers, chopping and stacking wood. Here my joy was full at the privilege of shaking the hand of the Prophet of God, and receiving the sure testimony, by the spirit of prophecy, that he was all that any man could believe him to be as a true Prophet."

Later this staid, stern, practical man Brigham Young, at the beginning of a friendship that would revise both the tenor and course of his life, met in prayer with the Prophet and the brethren and again spoke in tongues. "Some said to [Joseph] they expected he would condemn the gift Brother Brigham had, but he said 'No, it is of God.' " And after Brigham left the room, the Prophet reportedly said, "The time will come when Brother Brigham Young will preside over this Church."

Leaving Kirtland, Brigham and Joseph Young went to Canada. This mission seems to have been an intense period for Brigham, a period of decision. It was probably during this mission that, as he said, "I made up my mind . . . that I would be governed by certain principles and among them I decreed that women should not govern me neither should my passions of lust or anger, but I would be boss over myself, my passions and appetites." Many years later he wrote to his son Joseph as Joseph left on a mission: "We feel proud before the Lord when we think what you are doing in the great cause and Kingdom of our God. Be faithful, my son. You went out as a child; we trust you will return a flaming Elder of salvation. Keep yourself pure before the Lord. Your father before you has done it."

UPON HIS RETURN FROM CANADA, instead of resettling in Mendon, Brigham gathered his daughters with a small company of Saints from his vicinity and moved to Kirtland, later coming back to get his parents. In February 1834 he married Mary Ann Angell. He worked at carpentry and painting, accumulating $6,000 in property, before he was forced out of Ohio, but mostly he traveled and preached as requested by the Prophet. With a gift for constancy, he became one of Joseph Smith's most loyal co-workers. Brigham had a gift for clinging to what he believed was right without equivocation of any kind; there were no shades of right for him. If Joseph was a prophet, he was *right* even when he seemed to be wrong. If Joseph had his weaknesses, that was not Brigham's concern: "What man has ever lived upon this earth who had none?"

Every gift is a two-sided coin, and the other side to the staunch simplicity of Brigham's early years was that he did not recognize many of the forces that worked upon human personality. He could not comprehend hurt feelings, disillusionment, dissent, pride, or mercy toward those who gave in to such temptations. Thus, he himself was not emotionally prepared to reduce some of those temptations. Nevertheless, his gift was a great protection — of seeing to the crux of a matter and to the crux of a man or woman.

About 1836 there was a crisis in Kirtland, when "the knees of many of the strongest men in the church faltered." "Earth and hell seemed leagued to overthrow the Prophet and [thus the] church of God," wrote Brigham. At a meeting in the upper room of the temple, some of the brethren discussed deposing the Prophet and putting David Whitmer in his stead. Brigham recalled the incident in his history as follows:

> I rose up, and in a plain and forcible manner told them that Joseph was a Prophet, and I knew it, and that they might rail and slander him as much as they pleased. They could not destroy the appointment of the Prophet of God, they could only destroy their own authority, cut the thread that bound them to the Prophet and to God, and sink themselves to hell. Many were highly enraged at my decided opposition to their measures, and Jacob Bump (an old pugilist,) was so exasperated that he could not be still. Some of the brethren near him put their

50

hands on him, and requested him to be quiet; but he writhed and twisted his arms and body, saying, "How can I keep my hands off that man?" I told him if he thought it would give him any relief he might lay them on. This meeting was broken up without the apostates being able to unite on any decided measures of opposition. . . . During this siege of darkness I stood close by Joseph, and with all the wisdom and power God bestowed upon me, put forth my utmost energies to . . . unite the quorums of the church.

In those days Brigham Young was not the mild-mannered, controlled Brigham of later days. He was more explosive; he defended Joseph Smith with a ferocity as though it were his own ego he were protecting, or all the ideals hammered into him during his Puritan childhood.

In 1837 Brigham led a large company of Saints to a short-lived Zion in Missouri. Of his experiences there he said very little: "Mobocracy prevailed there to such an extent, that, with my co-religionists, I was compelled to leave the state on pain of extermination. The privations which our people endured, being driven out of the State in the depth of an inclement winter, stripped of their property or compelled to leave it behind them, no human tongue can tell or pen write."

From Missouri the Saints were driven to Illinois, where they founded Nauvoo in a swamp jutting out into the Mississippi River. Brigham did not spend a great deal of time in Nauvoo, at least while Joseph Smith lived, for he was either in England preaching the gospel or in the eastern United States declaring the Prophet's candidacy for U.S. president. Of the latter task he said: "You might ask what we think about Br. Joseph's getting the election this year. You know all about it. We shall do all we can and leave the event with God. The God of Heaven will do just as he pleases about it."

As to his mission to England in 1839 through the spring of 1841, it mellowed him. Remarriage and fatherhood and sickness had mellowed him, but that voyage across the Atlantic humbled him immensely. Told with very humble spelling in his diary, his troubles seem the more touching. To begin the journey, he wrote, they had "eight days contrary wind," and then "fare wind and a pleasant sail for four days." Near

Newfoundland, he wrote: "I was verry sick and destressed in my head and stomick. I felt as though I could not endure menny such voiges as I had indured for two years or sence I started on my mision. And ware it not for the power of God and his tendere mercy I should despare, but the Lord is my strength. . . . when the winds ware contry [contrary] the Twelve agread to humble themselves before the Lord and ask him to calm the sease and give us a fair wind. We did so and the wind emeditly changed and from that time to this it has blone in our favor." Here Brigham rejoiced when he was sometimes able to find, as he diarized, "a comfortable home." And here the Twelve, of whom he was the president, labored and suffered and grew closer together.

Wilford Woodruff, also in England, wrote about Brigham Young: "Elder B. Young labored with me in this vineyard [Herefordshire] about one month. I obtained much benefit as well as all the Saints from his instruction and council, for he is mighty in council and endowed with much wisdom." This more than any other mission seems to have made Brigham strong and eventually even happy. He would write cautiously to his cousin Willard Richards: "Be careful not to lay this letter with the New Testment wrightings. If you doe, som body will take it for a text after the Malineum [and] contend about it." Or, "Give my love to [the church in Liverpool, but] I due not say greet them with a holy kis."

BRIGHAM CAME HOME a calmer, gentler man. Reunited with his family in their primitive cabin, he wrote in his diary, "This evening I am with my love alone by the fireside for the first time in years." To Parley P. Pratt he wrote, "I can say I never felt better in my life then I have sence I came home last summer. I never injoyed my famely better, the society of my famely and frends are indeard to me. . . . I must come to a close. My wife is sick and groning and I must wate upon hir a little." When sent on another mission in 1844, he wrote home to Mary Ann, "This is a plesent evening on the Lake but I feele lonsom. O that I had you with me this somer I think I should be happy. Well I am now because I am in my cauling and duing my duty, but [the] older I grow the more I desire to stay at my own home insted of traveling."

That was two weeks before the assassination of the Prophet Joseph Smith. Brigham was troubled by "scores of Devels" on this mission, particularly at Kirtland, and on the day the Prophet was murdered, days before he heard anything about it, he was mournful and depressed without any apparent cause. Though he had read accounts of it in Boston papers, he had read so much nonsense about the Mormons in the eastern press that he had not believed it.

Not until July 16, 1844, when a letter arrived in Petersboro, New Hampshire, where he and Orson Pratt were attending a conference, did he realize the accounts to be true. Brigham's first thought was "whether Joseph had taken the keys of the Kingdom with him from the earth." He recalled, "Brother Orson Pratt sat on my left; we were leaning back in our chairs. Bringing my hand down on my knee I said, 'The keys of the Kingdom are right here with the Church.'" Within two days he was back in Boston to send a letter to "the Elders and Saints scattered abroad." Those with families in Nauvoo were to return there as soon as convenient; he was going there and would meet with them in council. Then, with his letter written, the senior president of the apostles fell upon his bed and sobbed. Even many weeks later, when other Saints vented their grief by talking, discussing how many barrels of tears were shed the day Joseph and Hyrum were brought from Nauvoo, Brigham wrote to his daughter Vilate: "I cannot bare to think enny thing about it."

The death of Joseph Smith was perhaps the greatest crisis the Church faced, for it was equally an internal crisis. As one member recalled, "The Latter-day Saints universally had such an abiding faith in the protecting care of the Lord over His Prophet, who had been so many times arrested upon frivolous charges trumped up by evil designing persons, actuated solely by the spirit of persecution; and from all of these our Heavenly Father had delivered him; until the Latter-day Saints, including myself, almost were led to believe that he had a charmed life, that mobs would not have power to destroy him. Consequently, after his martyrdom it can readily be imagined what the feelings of the people were in regard to his successor."

The line of succession had not been clearly determined, and the people did not know whom to believe. Brigham Young defended the authority of the Council of the Twelve. At a general meeting of the Saints, Sidney Rigdon made his claims to leadership, and that afternoon Brigham rose to refute him. He afterwards wrote in his diary, "My hart was swolen with compasion toards [the people]." Scores of journals testified that the "voice, manner, expression, and in fact, . . . personal appearance" of Brigham as he spoke to the people were those of the Prophet Joseph Smith. The people took it to be a divine manifestation that the mantle had fallen upon Brigham.

So Brigham had gotten himself another mantle, this time not of tradition but the mantle of the Prophet. There began to be wisps of evidences that this was a new experience for him. "This is my councel and orders," he wrote in January 1846. "Thus is the whisperings of the Spiret . . . to me. . . . I feele as though Nauvoo will be fild with all maner of abomnations and it is no place for the saints and the spiret whispers to me that the Bretherin had better get away as fast as they can." Some of the captains of the companies thought it would be better to wait to leave Nauvoo until the bitterest months were past, but "the feelings of the council," the clerk reported, were undivided: "if we are here 10 days—that our way will be hedged up. . . . We want to be 500 miles from here before they [enemies of the Saints] are aware of our move."

For the third time the Latter-day Saints abandoned a flourishing community they had created out of wilderness. They walked and rowed across the Mississippi in the middle of an icy February, camped at Sugar Creek, Iowa, in the mud, and then, as soon as they were ready, started out across Iowa toward the Missouri River. Here we learn how traumatic the death of Joseph had been to Brigham—to all the Saints. Brigham wrote to his brother, "Due not think . . . I hate to leve my house and home. No, far from that. I am so free from bondedge at this time that Nauvoo looks like a prison to me. It looks plesent ahead but dark to look back." Even out on the winter prairie, the Saints were happy to be away from Nauvoo. It was a place of gloom and danger.

THE 1846 EXODUS was one of the accomplishments that made President Young famous, but executive ability was not so much what made the Saints learn to love him. During the exodus they became acquainted with the new prophet. At Hickory Grove, the camp historian recorded, he "was out in the rain all day arranging the waggons, pitching tents, chopping wood and so on — until all were comfortable." At Garden Grove "at seven o'clock the Pres. shouldered his cross [axe] and walked to the creek, where he was engaged at chopping and raising the bridge till eleven."

Brigham could be irascible, too, for the drive toward Winter Quarters was a time of many vexations: Indian troubles, illness, ill-prepared Saints, mud, and more mud. Not being in danger as the Twelve were, many of the people could have remained longer in Nauvoo to advantage, but instead, the historian wrote, "they have crowded on us all the while and have completely tied our hands," and when they arrived at the tabernacle camps "they are not willing to do anything that will benefit any person but themselves." To a leader who had referred a matter to Brigham that should have been settled easily, he wrote: "What in the name of the Lord did you think when you referd old Mr. ____ to me to assis him . . . ? I will tell you what assistance I might render him. It is this, I have some men in the company that are thives and bogas makers [counterfeiters] and bogas men enny way you may put them. Unles they can due something to bring destres [distress] upon the saints they are in torment like a worm in the fire."

The camp was no longer how Brigham had described it in March as "the most perfect peace that ever a camp had, not a word of contencion through the hole camp." Malnutrition, exposure, and thoughtless behavior were taking their toll on Brigham's temper.

And though he could be politic in negotiations, Brigham

Young had no great forgiveness for his enemies. One person recounted, "Bro. Brigham arose and [made] some pointed and appropriate remarks. He called upon the Lord to bless this place for the good of the saints, and curse every Gentile who should attempt to settle here with sickness, rotenness, and death." As one of the Saints declared, in a Fourth of July toast:

> To all mobocrats, anarchs, and lovers of lies
> May their portion be with mosquitoes and flies
> And all who uphold them and live their ease
> May their portion be with bedbugs and fleas.

The story of the journey to the Great Basin has not really been told yet in our literature. It is an epic, but the way to tell it is to tell the stories of individuals, until the bits and pieces all fall together into an epic. On his first journey across the Plains, with the pioneer company of 1847, Brigham was accompanied by his young plural wife, Clara Decker. It was a rigorous, nerve-wracking voyage during which President Young became miserably ill with Colorado tick fever. Yet Clara came through the voyage with immense respect, even reverence for her prophet-husband, who had been patient, solicitous of her needs, and a gentleman to her and to the men in the company.

This reverential attitude toward Brigham Young from most of his wives and children has to be one of the most impressive accomplishments of the man. He was extremely solicitous of his family. He wrote to Mary Ann from a wagon train: "I doe think the Lord has blest me with one of the best famelyes that eney man ever had on the earth. I due hope the children will be good and mind there mother when I am gon. My son Joseph you must not goe away from home and Brigham also must stay at home. How due [you] sapose I would feele when I came home and find one of my children destoyed by the Indians. I pray this may not be the case. . . . I am glad you are not a going to come on this sumer for I want to be with my famely when they come this jorney. . . . I want the bretheren to keep my famely whilst I am gon and not supress them."

Part of his magic with his children was the respect the

mothers instilled in them for their father, but part was the respect and courtesy he had for the mothers and the children alike. Not long before he died, he spoke in public to the parents of the Church:

I will give a few words with regard to your future lives, that you may have children that are not contentious, not quarrelsome. Always be good-natured yourselves, is the first step. Never allow yourselves to become out of temper and get fretful. Why, mother says, "this is a very mischievous little boy or little girl." What do you see? That amount of vitality in those little children that they cannot be still. . . . They are so full of life . . . that their bones fairly ache with strength . . . and activity. . . . Do not be out of temper yourselves. Always sympathize with them and soothe them. Be mild and pleasant. . . . Now, mother, listen to this—never ask a child to give up that which it should not have. Step up kindly and put the article where it belongs.

Although an affectionate and indulgent father, Brigham was not devoid of firmness. During the family devotion one evening a noisy baby girl "was running about and squealing with laughter." Brigham stopped his prayer, caught the baby, took her to her mother, and returned to his chair, where he again knelt and quietly concluded the family prayer.

Brigham's wives had plenty of spirit, particularly one or two, such as Harriet Cook, who Brigham was certain would make a good sheriff: if she once determined to get her man, she would get him. When told about a husband who had blacked his wife's eye, he said, "I have women in my family that would have killed that Brother in a moment if he had treated them in the way he has [her]. But I govern my family by kindness. I tell them what is right and I get them to obey me without whipping them. If I cannot get my family to do as I wish them without quarreling with them I will not say a word about it." And though a good deal of credit for the truth of that statement goes to the wives, and if one discounts sarcasms, which he used in a pinch, it was true.

Brigham was a stickler for self-discipline and self-control. There was peace and order in his homes because he and his wives schooled their feelings and because they carefully ordered home affairs. There must have been a good deal of behind-the-scenes planning to ensure smoothness in the operation of the Beehive House and Lion House. The wives worked out the chores between themselves; each had her wash day and a family chore to do. Each had an account at the family store and later with ZCMI. The husband's contribution was an ingenious innovation here and there and a prompt attention to the family schedule.

Each adult and older child had a private lamp, and when anyone went out in the evening, that person's lamp would be lit and set with the others on a table in the parlor. When the person returned, he or she would douse his or her lamp, and when only one lamp remained lit, the owner of it was to bolt the door.

Prayer time was strictly attended. When many of the children were older and became lax in their attendance, their father set himself down and dictated a letter "for the perusal of my family": "There is no doubt but that my family . . . will acknowledge that my time is precious to me as theirs is to them. When the time appointed for our family devotion and prayer comes, I am expected to be there; and no public business, no matter how important, has been able to influence me to forego the fulfilment of this sacred duty which I owe to you, to myself, and to God.

"I do not wish to complain of you without a cause," he continued, but at prayer time lately he had noticed that one wife might be visiting, several children were scattered about town, "another has gone to see Mary, and another to see Emily, and I may add, etc., etc., etc." His counsel, which he expected them "to receive kindly and obey," was to be home by six-thirty each evening so as "to be ready to bow down before the Lord to make . . . acknowledgements to Him for His kindness and mercy and long-suffering towards us. . . . Your strict attendance to my wishes in this respect will give joy to the heart of your Husband and Father."

Brigham Young was a good psychologist; he always believed that the influences of childhood remained with a person all his life, making example a necessity. "I can say that I am not prepared to bring up a child in the way it should go," he once said, "and yet I probably come as near to it as any person that lives." He took great pride in his children and in his success as a parent, much more so than in his remarkable accomplishments as economic developer of the Great Basin Kingdom. To his public successes he seemed to maintain a sort of detachment, as though he hadn't really done them himself.

LATTER-DAY SAINTS SEE THE WISDOM of his viewing himself as an agent of God, and they also know that without the staunch, believing men and women around him, his success would have disintegrated. President Young had a great talent for selecting those workers who would be useful to the kingdom; he was a discerning judge of men and women. Even when he personally clashed with a person, he was able to see that person's fitness for serving the Lord.

One reason for occasional clashes was that President Young had an iron will. Most of the time he was right; but he could make mistakes, and he did not always take kindly to someone pointing them out. His ability to see beyond the exterior of a man was perhaps what attracted him to Edwin D. Woolley. E. D. was a blunt man, so much so that he often offended. Brigham looked beyond the words and saw an honest, kind, practical man, and he made him a bishop. Bishop Woolley turned out to be one of the best bishops in the history of the Church. But once he exercised a little too much independence of Brigham's counsel, and the president gave him a severe tongue lashing, adding, "Now I suppose you will go off and apostatize." "No, I won't," retorted the bishop. "If this were your church I might, but it's just as much mine as it is yours. In fact, it's the Lord's church."

Perhaps the source of other words between Bishop Woolley and Brigham Young lay in Brigham's distaste for pretension. He was a simple man. Something in his Puritan background made him appreciate directness and plainness, finding gold in unsuspected places, such as in Heber C. Kimball, of whom

Brigham said, "You cannot, the best of you, beat brother Kimball's language. You may call up the college-bred man, and he cannot beat it." Without doing wrong, for he was very attentive to the poor in and out of his ward, Bishop Woolley still loved a red carpet, and this irked Brigham Young, who commented once that if Bishop Woolley should fall off his horse while crossing the Jordan River on the way to his pasture, those searching for him should not expect him to be floating downstream; they would more likely find him swimming upstream, obstinately contending against the current. Brigham could not fail to admire Bishop Woolley's pertinacity and stick-to-it-iveness.

Brigham Young's modesty and humility were part of his strength: he was a simple, backwoods artisan who resisted the trappings of wealth and power. What endeared him to the Saints was that he could not resist an appeal from an open, honest man or woman. He was always creating jobs for new immigrants. He was as eager for the young women as for the young men to obtain an education; and when he learned, probably from a wife or one of his own daughters, that the daughter of a friend in an outlying settlement was sixteen and longed to go to school, he wrote her father offering free board and even tuition if necessary. In various years he was paying the tuition of from eleven to seventeen students not of his own family. When he heard that a missionary was coming home after several years, he would write the wife to expect her husband before such-and-such day. When a woman he had never met wrote from Tooele that she longed to attend conference but had no transportation, he arranged for the bishop in Tooele to bring the sister to the Beehive House, where she could stay during conference. It was the individual acts of concern that proved to the Saints that their prophet loved them and had not been corrupted by the immense power attributed to him by outsiders. It was impossible for outsiders to see Brigham Young's influence in the way the Latter-day Saints saw it.

The Saints loved Brigham because he was not self-righteous, not overly proud of himself. "There are weaknesses manifested in men [and women] that I am bound to forgive," he declared, for "I am right there myself. I am liable to mistakes, I am liable to prejudice, and I am just as set as any man that lives in my feelings. But I am where I can see the light, and I try to keep in the light." One should not underestimate his spiritual capacity. He prayed often, worked for months on the Nauvoo Temple so it could be completed enough to do ordinance work before the Saints left Illinois, visited the Salt Lake Endowment House frequently to participate in sacred ceremonies, had faith to be healed, and healed others by the strength of his own faith. His own contributions to Latter-day Saint doctrine were not negligible.

No man ever gave more stirring talks about living one's religion in the real world of struggle and conflict. In fact, his sermons were especially designed for the Saints of his day. He emphasized the necessity of "working out one's salvation" by making the earth green and productive and by building better homes and communities. He recognized the importance, the indispensability, of religious ordinances, worship, and Christian love, but he also stressed temporal salvation. Indeed, he saw a direct connection between religion, happiness, and the quality of one's daily labor. As he wrote to his son Willard in 1875: "Every human being will find that his happiness very greatly depends upon the work he does, and the doing of it well. Whoever wastes his life in idleness, either because he need not work in order to live, or because he will not live to work, will be a wretched creature, and at the close of a listless existence, will regret the loss of precious gifts and the neglect of great opportunities. Our daily toil, however humble it may be, is our daily duty, and by doing it well we make it a part of our daily worship."

In another letter, this time to his son Feramorz, Brigham wrote: "You will find that much of the happiness of this life consists in having something worthy to do and in doing it well. . . . It is our attention to our daily duties that makes us men, and if we devote our lives to the service of heaven, our faithfulness therein will eventually fit us with our Heavenly Father in eternity to dwell. Aspire to acquire knowledge that you may be able to do more good and also to progress in your sphere of life; but remember that you will win only by trust in the Lord, by present contentment, and by doing faithfully that which you have in hand. . . . No one advances who imagines himself too good or too big for present duties."

Brigham Young was particularly offended by Saints who were idle, who lacked the spirit of improvement, who wasted the "capital stock" — time — that God had given them. Husbands, for example, should make benches for their wives to set their water pails on, fix the garden fence, hoe the garden, set out trees, and make the yard look neater. He said: "I have seen men, year after year, without a chair in their houses. If I ask them why they do not go to work and make some chairs, they say, 'We don't know how.' Then why not go to work and learn how? Do as I did when I went to learn the carpenter and joiner's trade. The first job my boss gave me was to make a bedstead out of an old log that had been on the beach of the lake for years, waterlogged and watersoaked. Said he, 'There are the tools; you cut that log into right lengths for a bedstead, hew out the side rails, the end rails, and the posts, get a board for a head board, and go to work and make a bedstead.' I went to work and cut up the log, split it up to the best of my ability, and made a bedstead that, I suppose, they used for many years." In his travels he took opportunity to notice the homes and yards of his followers, and he went out of his way to compliment those who constantly labored to improve their home environment.

The importance of cooperation was another topic President Young underscored. The Saints must work together — cooperate in building the kingdom of God. This included organized cooperation in migration, in the settlement of villages, in the establishment of new industries, in the building of railroads and telegraph lines, and in the sharing of scarce provisions with those in need of help. Under his direction, they labored cooperatively to dig canals, build fences, and construct roads; to erect gristmills and tanneries; to pasture cattle and sheep, build schools, erect walls as a protection against Indians, and operate a general community store. For a period they even had their own mint and currency printing press. As Brigham intended, each community was essentially self-sufficient until well after his death.

Larger enterprises beyond the means of the villagers were planned and financed by the general church headquarters in Salt Lake City. These included cotton and woolen mills, iron foundries, a beet sugar factory, high-line canals, and, of course, railroads and telegraph lines. All such enterprises were financed by voluntary tithes, which meant that each man and his team labored for the Church one day in ten and contributed one-tenth of his crops, one-tenth of the increase in livestock, and one-tenth of the produce and other home productions. These donations went to a local tithing house, which used the contributions in kind to support laborers on public works. Some idea of President Young's task as Trustee-in-Trust of the Church can be had by imagining what it would be like if the receipts of the Church today consisted primarily of steel, used tires, soft drink bottles, cast-off clothing, mohair, magazines, and necklaces. He was always encouraging members to donate their best to the Lord. For example, the following chastisement in 1855: "Some are disposed to do right with their surplus property, and once in a while you will find a man who has a cow which he considers surplus, but generally she is of the class that would kick a person's hat off or eyes out, or the wolves have eaten off her teats. You will once in a while find a man who has a horse that he considers surplus, but at the same time he has the ringbone, is broken-winded, spavined in both legs, and has the pole evil at one end of the neck and a fistula at the other and both knees sprung."

Unquestionably, the Latter-day Saint capacity for dedicated cooperative labor and discipline, and the virtuosity of Brigham's economic leadership, made survival possible in a region widely regarded as uninhabitable.

ADMINISTRATION OF THIS VAST NETWORK of institutions and villages must have been a constant preoccupation. One of Brigham's close friends, George A. Smith, once commented: "To conduct his private affairs would seem work enough for any man." But, in addition, he personally superintended everything of a public nature too. As his secretary reported in 1866, "His general appearance is careworn. He attends to balls every week, and is an accomplished dancer. He dances, too, with glee and a zest that might not be surpassed by a boy of eighteen. He personally superintends the theatre, visiting every portion of the house almost every evening. He attends Bishop's meetings, visits the endowment house on almost every occasion, being as near as a man can be 'everywhere present.' "

As one studies Brigham Young's manner and policies, several things become clear. First, he had a high opinion of women and of their worth to the community of Saints. "If the women have not achieved as much as the men," he said, "it is because the women have no wives to help them." Under his leadership, Latter-day Saint women exercised an important influence in agriculture, medicine, economic and business development, literature, and politics. And in doing all of this, they were also serving as fine, warm, and loving wives, mothers, and daughters. President Young said: "We think the sisters ought to have the privilege to study various branches of knowledge that they may develop the powers with which they are endowed. Women are useful, not only to sweep houses, wash dishes, make beds, and raise babies, but they may also stand behind the counter, study law and physic [medicine], or become good bookkeepers, and all this to enlarge their sphere of usefulness for the benefit of society at large. In following these things they but answer the design of their creation."

Second, Brigham encouraged the kind treatment of the American Indians. "I wish to impress [all] with the necessity of treating the Indians with kindness, and to refrain from harboring the revengeful, vindictive feeling that many indulge in. I am convinced that as long as we harbor in us such feelings towards them, so long they will be our enemies, and the Lord will suffer them to afflict us." He continued: "Why should men have a disposition to kill a destitute, naked Indian, who may steal a shirt or a horse and think it no harm, when they never think of meting out a like retribution to a white man who steals, although he has been taught better from infancy? . . . We exhort you to feed and clothe them so far as it lies in your power. Never turn them away hungry from your door, teach them the arts of husbandry, bear with them in all patience and long suffering, and never consider their lives as equivalent for petty stealing."

Third, he encouraged the Saints to maintain a reverence for animal life and for nature. Even as the Saints were crossing the Plains, he laid down a rule that they must be kind to their animals. "The more kind we are to our animals," he said, "the more will peace increase and the savage nature of the animal kingdom will vanish away." Severe punishment was meted out to those who beat their oxen or their horses and mules. And after they reached the Great Basin, a Humane Day was held once a year at which there were talks on being kind to animals and on proper treatment of animals.

When the Saints first arrived in the Great Basin, Brigham declared: "You are commencing anew. The soil, the air, the water are all pure and healthy. Do not suffer them to become polluted. . . . Strive to preserve the elements from being contaminated. . . . Keep your valleys pure, keep your towns pure, keep your hearts pure, and labor as hard as you can without injuring yourselves. . . . Build cities, adorn your habitations, make gardens, orchards, and vineyards, and render the earth so pleasant that when you look upon your labors you may do so with pleasure, and that angels may delight to come and visit your beautiful locations. . . . Your work is to beautify the face of the earth, until it shall become like the Garden of Eden."

This was not just rhetoric. When the Saints celebrated the anniversary of their arrival in the Salt Lake Valley on the 24th of July of each year, they often went to one of the canyons east of Salt Lake City. The celebration of 1860, for example, held at Brighton at the top of Big Cottonwood Canyon, was magnificent enough to warrant coverage in the New York *Herald*. The reporter who described the affair tells how at dusk of the last day, after all the wagons had gone home and the dust had settled on the canyon road, he beheld a singular spectacle: "By 9 o'clock the last team had left the camp-ground," but one man remained behind "to see that all the fires were extinguished." That man, he discovered, was

Brigham Young himself. "The Prophet," wrote the reporter, "left the last, satisfied that all was right, and that his disciples had enjoyed themselves to their hearts' content."

Fourth, Brigham Young believed that people needed recreation, and he sought to facilitate this by encouraging drama, music, and dance in Nauvoo, during the crossing of the Plains, and in the Salt Lake Valley and the settlements to the north and south. For this purpose he built the Social Hall shortly after the Saints' arrival in the Salt Lake Valley, and later, in 1862, he built the Salt Lake Theater, which was for many years the finest theater between Chicago and San Francisco. "I built that theatre," he said, "to attract the young of our community and to provide amusement for the boys and girls rather than have them running all over creation for recreation. Long before that was built," he went on, "I said to the bishops, 'Get up your parties and pleasure grounds to amuse the people.'. . . Whenever we get into the Kingdom of Heaven, where God and Christ dwell, we shall find something more to do than to 'sit and sing ourselves away to everlasting bliss.' The mind of man is active, and we must have exercise and amusement for the mind as well as the body. . . . We say to the bishops and to everybody, exercise yourselves, provide innocent amusement for the youth, attract the minds of children, and get the upper hand of them and be on the lead."

This emphasizes his belief that the practice of religion was to be, to use his expression, a "happifying" experience. The gospel had transformed his own life, and it had the potential of providing joy for others. "Mormonism," he said, "has made me happy, . . . has filled me with good feelings, with joy and rejoicing." All of this was a product of the way in which the gospel of Christ had liberated him from the despondency that the religions of his day had induced. "I feel like shouting hallelujah, all the time," he said, "when I think that I ever knew the Prophet Joseph Smith."

For Brigham Young, Mormonism was not just an abstract set of beliefs, a promise of pie in the sky by and by, but a way of life that demanded practical daily solutions that stretched into all eternity. He saw the earth and man's experience upon it as part of a great divine plan of cosmic importance that would offer salvation to mankind and guarantee happiness and unity to those who accepted it, a plan in which the Latter-day Saints would play a key role. And as their spiritual leader, he would have a directing part in it, for he believed that God had blessed him with abilities and that it was his responsibility to benefit his fellowmen "to promote their happiness in this world and [prepare] them for the great hereafter. My whole life is devoted to this service," he once told a New York editor. The thing that made Mormonism unique, he said, was its ability to gather people of every tongue, creed, tradition, and degree of education and weld them together into a harmonious whole. "A creed that can take the heterogeneous masses of mankind and make of them a happy, contented, and united people has a power within it that the nations know little of. That power is the power of God. This labor, to unite the world in all that is good and praiseworthy, is the mission of the Latter-day Saints, and with the help of the Lord they intend to continue their labors until the knowledge of God shall cover the earth as the waters now cover the mighty deep."

Although it was important to settle as many communities as possible, immigrate as many converts as possible, and improve the level of living so that, by toil and thrift, each family could enjoy a competence, the primary goal of the community, Brigham Young believed, should be the improvement of the individual, and this is the reason for the emphasis on education and on the organization of improvement societies during his lifetime—an emphasis that continues to this day. "Brothers and sisters," he said, "the greatest and most important labor we have to perform is to cultivate ourselves." The Latter-day Saints "have been taken from the coal pits, from the ironworks, from the streets, from the kitchens and from the barns and factories and from hard service in the countries where they formerly lived." They belong to "the poorest of the poor," and it is the job of all to "cultivate their minds" so they can attain to a full development of their powers. The Great Basin, he said, is a great place to raise Latter-day Saints. "Here we can cultivate every science and art calculated to enlarge the mind, invigorate the body, cheer the heart, and ennoble the soul of man. . . . Here we can receive and extend that pure intelligence which is unmingled with the jargon of mystic Babylon." And, he said, the Saints can be completely confident of the future—of the providences of God—if they work hard, plan well, and trust in God. This is the way to achieve as God wants them to do, he said—as persons, as families, as communities.

Brigham's attention to every Saint's need and to every detail is indicated by the following letter, in his own handwriting, which was sent to Miss Rose Canfield, a teacher in Plain City, Utah. The newly discovered letter, which shows how much his penmanship and spelling had improved over the years, is dated January 7, 1867:

> I will take the liberty of writing you with my own hand, beleving it will be more gratifying and that you will not think me the worse for my mistakes.
>
> From my earliest recolection I knew God had a use for me if I should be weak as clay in His hands. I do not glory in my want of learning, but I will say that the Lord has more use for a practicle-minded boy or girl without book-lerned prejudice and traditions.
>
> We have lately taken the moto of education. I wish you to impress upon the minds of the children the vertue of practable education. Perhaps thay can be urged to this by lisning to some of the successful men [and women] of this territory. Do not neglect arithmatic, book-keeping, law, and medasine. Call on Br. Geddes if you need books. God bless you. Brigham Young.

President Young believed in introducing new inventions and taking advantage of improved technology. When the transcontinental telegraph was being extended from the Missouri River to the West Coast in 1861, he wanted to hurry it up and to give the Saints the experience they would need in erecting their own line, so he contracted to build the transcontinental line from the western edge of Nebraska to the eastern edge of California. When the line was finished, he established a special telegraph school in Salt Lake City and asked each local settlement to send one or two teenagers to attend the school. At the same time, priesthood quorums were assigned to get out poles, string the wire, and construct an office in each settlement. Within a year, five hundred miles of line were in operation in what was the only important telegraph system in the nation constructed and operated cooperatively by a church group. Brigham dedicated the line on December 1, 1866, by sending the first message, which was worded as follows: "To President Lorin Farr and Bishop Chauncey W. West and the Saints in the Northern Country who gave up freely when called upon. Greeting: In my heart I dedicate the line which is now completed and being completed to the Lord God of Israel whom we serve and for the building up of His Kingdom, praying that this and all other improvements may contribute to our benefit and the glory of our God, until we can waft ourselves by the power of the Almighty from world to world to our fullest satisfaction. BRIGHAM YOUNG."

Finally, there are many examples of his tender regard for his people. He shed tears when he saw people suffer, he intervened when he saw anyone being taken advantage of, and he often visited those who were in mourning. His letterbooks contain hundreds of letters designed to cheer up the downhearted and chastize the unscrupulous. His relationship with his followers is perhaps best told in a diary entry of Charles Walker, an early settler in St. George. A celebration was being held in St. George in which the Saints paid their respects to President Young on his seventy-fifth birthday, and later there was a special meeting for "old folks." After the meeting Brigham asked Brother Walker for a copy of the song Brother Walker had composed for the dedication of the temple there. The diary recounts a precious experience that he would never forget: "After meeting I went home and got the song and took it to him [President Young]. He treated me very kindly and asked me to sit beside him and take dinner with him. I spent the time very pleasantly and found him to be very polite, genial, and sociable, and I felt quite at home in chatting over the work on the temple, old times and other general topics. In bidding him goodbye, he took my hand in both of his and said, 'God bless you, Brother Charley, and God has blessed you, hasn't He?' It seemed that in an instant all the blessings I had ever received were before me. My emotion was too much to answer him, and I chokingly said, 'President Young, I have learned to trust in the Lord.' "

MANY OUTSIDE OBSERVERS, in writing favorably about Brigham Young, have failed to acknowledge the influence of Joseph Smith on Brigham. They tend to view Joseph as a visionary person, while Brigham is seen as a sincere, well-grounded, authentic authority. Perhaps they should consider Brigham Young-the-Realist's own viewpoint in the matter: To the end of his days, the influence of Joseph Smith was in everything he did. The Prophet's plans, teachings, and dreams were in the back of his mind at every phase of establishing the cooperative commonwealth in the Great Basin.

Brigham was very modest about his own accomplishments. When W. W. Phelps once referred to him as the man like unto Moses raised up by the Lord, Brigham asked him by what authority he had said a thing like that. "Joseph is gone and you are left to lead the people," Phelps answered. President Young responded, "That is no argument at all. I may die and others may be left; that does not prove that I or they would be the one referred to. If I thought I was the man, I would not tell of it. But I think I am the great man that none of the Prophets ever thought of or spoke of."

Whether or not the prophets spoke of either of them, Joseph Smith and Brigham Young complemented each other. Brigham was not as imaginative or creative as Joseph. Inspired by God, Joseph Smith was a well of creativity in almost everything he tackled. He advanced new views on almost every conceivable subject, and it is amazing how well most of them stand analysis. One can interpret many of Brigham's policies as simply attempts to implement what Joseph had suggested. Sometimes he may have been a little too faithful in implementing them, for Joseph's policies, intended for his day, were not always practical. But Brigham was resourceful, intelligent, firm, and capable enough to carry them out, and if he saw that one would not work, he was sensible enough to abandon it and try another.

Brigham Young had an acute sense of where Joseph Smith had led him, and how the gospel had changed the course of his life. It was not at all as one biographer said, that Mormonism would not have become great without Brigham Young, but Brigham Young might have become great without Mormonism. Brigham Young was the most dramatic example of what happened to all the pioneers: of the Lord taking the small of the earth and making them mighty. Brigham was a conscientious, ambitious carpenter, with modest aims and modest accomplishments, who would have made for himself a modest position in his home county. The restored gospel put his sights on something outside himself and expanded him as a husband, father, and man. His experiences and the spirit of the Lord made him over; when he met challenges that overwhelmed him, he would say, "I have the grit in me and I will do my duty anyhow." The challenges sharpened his powers, belief gave him confidence, and these things he could have found only in Mormonism. When he attained power, the mantle of Joseph touched everything he did so that he used his power wisely, as wisely as it was possible for a human being to do.

When Warren Foote, a miller on State Street in Salt Lake County, heard one of the seven presidents of the seventies find fault with President Young, he didn't know what to believe, and he "felt a little anxiety with regard to these things." Then Foote had a dream: "I thought that I was in a building and Jesus the Savior was there and a few other people were gathered in. When I saw the Saviour, the first thought was to ask him if President Young was leading the people right. I thought that he was free to talk to anyone. I thought that I approached him and asked him with regard to Brigham Young. He gave me to understand that he [Brigham] was doing as well as could be expected of any person in the flesh, clothed in mortality, and like all mankind subject to passionsand imperfections. 'But,' said he, 'when I come all things will be made right.' This dream satisfied my mind, and I have not troubled myself about Brigham and the authorities since. . . . I told [the president of Seventies] that the authorities of the Church were doing the best they could and that their labors were accepted of God."

On August 29, 1877, Brigham died in his Salt Lake City home of the infection produced by a ruptured appendix. He was seventy-six years of age. His story is not the story of a perfect man, but of a good man who, when time after time he was pushed into corners, discovered in himself the grit to do his duty.

SOURCES

The material in this chapter is based upon Leonard J. Arrington, *Brigham Young: American Moses* (New York: Alfred A. Knopf, 1985). Other biographies include Eugene England, *Brother Brigham* (Salt Lake City: Bookcraft, 1980); Preston Nibley, *Brigham Young, the Man and His Work* (Salt Lake City: Deseret Book, 1936); Francis M. Gibbons, *Brigham Young: Modern Moses, Prophet of God* (Salt Lake City: Deseret Book, 1981); Richard F. Palmer and Karl D. Butler, *Brigham Young: The New York Years* (Provo, Utah: Brigham Young University Press, 1982); and Dean C. Jessee, ed., *Letters of Brigham Young to His Sons* (Salt Lake City, Deseret Book, 1974). In some instances, to assure clarity for the reader, the writer has regularized the spelling and punctuation.

LEONARD J. ARRINGTON is Lemuel Redd Professor of Western History and director of the Joseph Fielding Smith Institute for Church History at Brigham Young University. A former Idahoan, he was awarded the Ph.D. at the University of North Carolina. He is author of *Great Basin Kingdom: An Economic History of the Latter-day Saints* (Cambridge, Massachusetts: Harvard University Press, 1958); *Brigham Young: American Moses* (New York: Alfred A. Knopf, 1985); and co-author with Davis Bitton of *The Mormon Experience: A History of the Latter-day Saints* (New York: Alfred A. Knopf, 1979); and *Saints without Halos: The Human Side of Mormon History* (Salt Lake City: Signature Books, 1982).

JOHN TAYLOR
Paul Thomas Smith

In the north of England lies Westmorland County, a wild and beautiful region of lofty mountains, waterfalls, moors and fields, intersected by rugged gorges, deep winding valleys, rushing streams, and enchanting Windermere, the "Queen of English lakes." Remains of Druid castles lie scattered across the landscape. William Wordsworth and other romantic poets drew inspiration for their writings from that extraordinary setting.

On November 1, 1808, a future poet and prophet was born to James and Agnes Taylor in Milnthorpe, a market town and port city on the River Kent. Within a month the Taylors took their infant, the second of ten children, to the Heversham Parish Church where he was christened John in honor of his maternal grandfather. John's godparents vowed that as he matured, he would "renounce the devil and all his works—the pomps and vanity of this wicked world, and all the deceitful lusts of the flesh," that he would "believe all the articles of the Christian faith," and that he would "keep God's holy laws and commandments, and walk in the same all the days of his life."

John's father, James, was well-educated and from a family of some wealth, but under English law an older brother had received the entire family inheritance. Thus, James accepted a position with the British government in the Excise, a department that administered license fees and revenue taxes placed upon the manufacture and sale of articles produced in England.

When John was seven, his father was transferred south to the famous port city of Liverpool, an international manufacturing and business center with seven miles of docks and quays on the Mersey River. Liverpool boasted such industries as rope-makers, distillers, sugar refiners, chemical manufacturers and iron and brass foundries.

In Liverpool John went to school and became a regular church attender, receiving instruction in the catechism and litany of his parents' faith. He memorized and repeated many prayers, such as: "We have erred and strayed from thy ways like lost sheep," and "We have done the things we ought not to have done, and have left undone the things we ought to have done; spare us miserable offenders."

Possessed of a lively and animated personality, John was nevertheless sensitive to the things of the Spirit. He feared God and felt that his occasional lapses offended the Lord, such as once when he slipped on ice on the Sabbath day, and again when his kite was pulled down from the sky by a mischievous boy and John mildly profaned. But his fears were groundless; as a small boy he saw an angel in the heavens, holding a trumpet to his lips, an experience that would have greater meaning later in his life as he became acquainted with the restored gospel of Jesus Christ.

John's father inherited from a kindly uncle a small farm near Hale, Westmorland, so in 1819, when John was ten, James Taylor left government employment for life in rural England. The Taylor children were introduced to the rigors of ploughing, sowing, reaping, and haymaking. For recreation John rode spirited horses and was often bucked off for his efforts.

John attended school at Beetham, a mile's walk from Hale, but he needed a trade, so when he was fourteen, he returned to Liverpool, where an apprenticeship had been arranged with a cooper. There he learned cask and barrel making, but the business failed within a year. He relocated to Penrith, Cumberland, in a beautiful valley called the Vale of Eden for its soaring mountain peaks, flowing river, fertile fields, and luxuriant vegetation. He spent nearly five years in Penrith, learning the vocation of wood turner, crafting furniture and other items on a lathe.

SOON AFTER HIS ARRIVAL in Penrith, John had a religious awakening that changed the course of his life. The empty rationalism of the Church of England had never held much attraction for him, so when he learned of the Methodists, he was attracted to the strong spirit of their sermons, which stressed the strengthening of piety and religious devotion, daily public and private prayer, and visitation of the poor and needy. He joined the Methodists at age sixteen and encouraged his companions to pray with him in the fields each day. His efforts were unsuccessful, but when he began preaching general principles of a Christian life, he found many believers. Within a year he was called to be an exhorter or lay preacher, assigned to a congregation in a village church seven miles away in the countryside.

Spiritual manifestations that had marked his early life continued through dreams, visions, and the "sweet, melodious music" of angelic choirs. One day, while going to fulfill a preaching assignment, he remarked to a companion, "I have a strong impression on my mind, that I have to go to America to preach the gospel." America was then a land about which he knew little. Seven years were to pass before the complete meaning of this impression would be understood, but from that point on his thoughts turned westward.

Once John had completed his apprenticeship in Penrith, he returned to his family in Hale and established his trade. But they were not to remain there long. In 1830 the Taylor family joined thousands of other British families, migrating to Canada to escape the uncertainties of the European economy and hoping for a brighter future on the American continent. Because Edward Taylor, the firstborn son, had passed away,

John, the next in line, was asked to remain behind to sell some properties and conclude his father's business dealings. This took about two years. Then he prepared to emigrate.

As John's ship sailed through the British Channel, severe storms wrecked several nearby vessels, and the captain and officers of his own ship expected that the same fate awaited them. But their anxieties meant little to this Methodist preacher. His belief in the divinity of his call to America had given him absolute faith, even in the face of such extreme danger. "I went on deck at midnight, and amidst the raging elements felt as calm as though I was sitting in a parlor at home. I believed I should reach America and perform my work."

He spent several weeks in Brooklyn and Albany, New York, before continuing his journey to the new family farm near Toronto. He set up his trade in the city and united once again with the Methodist Church. Soon he was preaching on a circuit and found success in winning converts to the doctrines of Christ. He was also successful in winning one of his students to be his bride. But Leonora Cannon, a gentle and refined Englishwoman, rejected his proposal of marriage until a dream offered confirmation that she was to be John's companion.

John's experience in Canada was an invaluable step in his religious destiny, for as he studied and preached, he became convinced of the vast differences between the creeds of Christian churches and the teachings of Jesus Christ. Although he was pleased with his success in leading many to religious belief and practice, he knew that he was not yet serving as the Lord intended. To Leonora he confided, "This is not the work; it is something of more importance."

By 1836 the Taylors had formed a study group of seekers who called themselves the "Dissenters," most of whom were former Methodist lay preachers who rejected existing Christian churches, including their own, and who fasted and prayed to the Lord to send an authorized servant to them with the truth. That spring, Parley P. Pratt was at home in Kirtland, Ohio, burdened with debt and weighted with concern for his tubercular and childless wife, when he was visited by several brethren. Acting as a spokesman, Heber C. Kimball prophesied that Parley's wife would bear a child and means would be provided to meet his debts. For what reason? "Thou shall go to Upper Canada," Heber prophesied, "even to the city of Toronto . . . and there thou shalt find a people prepared for the fulness of the gospel, and they shall receive thee. . . . Many shall be brought to the knowledge of the truth and shall be filled with joy; and from the things growing out of this mission, shall the fulness of the gospel spread into England, and cause a great work to be done in that land." It was a remarkable prophecy made when the very existence of The Church of Jesus Christ of Latter-day Saints was at stake because of widespread apostasy in Kirtland.

Elder Pratt arrived in Toronto in April. He met the Taylors through a letter of introduction, but was coolly received. His attempts to rent halls and preach the gospel met with repeated failure. Discouraged, he prepared to return to Ohio when a Mrs. Walton extended an invitation to preach in her home. This engagement led to an opportunity to explain the message of the restored church to members of John Taylor's study class. After a careful and thorough investigation, the Taylors and many of their fellow seekers were baptized early in May by Elder Pratt. "I was almost immediately ordained an Elder and Brother Parley prophesied concerning me in a manner that almost made my hair stand on my head," wrote John. What he was promised is not known, but he received valuable instruction as Elder Pratt was joined in his Canadian labors by his brother Orson and by Orson Hyde. Guided by the Spirit of the Lord, Elder Taylor and his more experienced companions were successful in teaching and baptizing "a great many people," and he watched as Elders Pratt and Hyde successfully debated ministers and exposed the errors of the ministers' theology. Elder Taylor himself enjoyed "many manifestations from the Lord." He witnessed the power of God in miraculous healings and in the utterance and fulfillment of many prophecies. When the brethren returned to Kirtland in the fall, John Taylor was set apart to preside over several branches of the Church in a newly formed district.

IN MARCH OF 1837, Elder Taylor visited Kirtland and was thrilled to meet Joseph Smith for the first time. However, he had entered in the midst of a crisis. He was shocked to find that Elder Pratt and several other authorities claimed that Joseph Smith was in error in several matters. Elder Taylor offered private reassurance to Parley Pratt: "Now Brother Parley, it is not man that I am following, but the Lord. The principles that you taught me led me to Him and I now have the same testimony that you then rejoiced in. If the work was true six months ago, it is true today. If Joseph Smith was then a prophet, he is now a prophet."

John soon became a public defender of Joseph Smith when, attending a meeting in the Kirtland Temple, he responded to a violent attack by Warren Parrish on the character of the Prophet. By so doing he gained a life-long reputation as a powerful defender of the faith. He compared the murmuring of the Saints to the ancient Israelites who turned from Moses and from the Lord and, "after seeing the power of God manifested in their midst, had fallen into rebellion and idolatry; there certainly was great danger of us doing the same thing." "This was my first introduction to the Saints collectively," he said, "and while I was pained on the one hand to witness the hard feelings and hard expressions of apostates; on the other I was rejoiced to see the firmness, faith, integrity and joy of the faithful, and returned home rejoicing."

But enraged apostates sent one of their number into Canada in an attempt to destroy his influence. In the spring of 1837 Sampson Avard arrived in Toronto from Kirtland and, in the absence of Elder Taylor, immediately assumed leadership of the district, regulating and ordering Church affairs to suit himself. Although the man seemed to be pompous and vain, and boasted of his power, he went unchallenged because of a forged letter of authority, purportedly from his high priests quorum in Ohio. Although John Taylor thought little of Avard, he was obedient to his own apparent release from leadership upon his return, and so he commenced missionary labors with Elder Almon W. Babbitt.

Joseph Smith discovered Avard's deception while visiting

Canada several weeks later. He reinstated Elder Taylor and ordained him to be a high priest, while he severely reprimanded Avard and ordered him to return to his position of leadership in Kirtland. He was later excommunicated for immorality.

Sometime later, Elder Taylor had a manifestation that he would be called to be an apostle, but he feared the impression was from Satan. Now, well into the second year of his ministry in Canada, a messenger arrived from Kirtland with startling news: The Prophet Joseph directed the Taylors to move to Kirtland and then on to Far West, Missouri. Elder Taylor had purchased a home, barn, and five acres of ground near the Kirtland Temple in anticipation of moving to Ohio, but he had not expected to be living in Missouri. In addition, there was greater news—he had also been called, by revelation, to the Quorum of the Twelve Apostles. "The work seemed great, the duties arduous and responsible, but I felt determined, the Lord being my helper, to endeavor to magnify it," he said. "When I first entered upon Mormonism, I did it with my eyes open; I counted the cost. I looked upon it as a life-long job and I considered that I was not only enlisted for time, but for eternity and did not wish to shrink now, although I felt my incompetency."

A 1200-mile journey faced the Taylors. Their finances were nearly depleted, but John set the date for departure and reassured his worried Nora that "God will open out the way." Three days before their scheduled departure, John Mills, learning of the Taylors' need, announced plans to travel with them to Missouri, sharing space in a covered sleigh, with sufficient teams, baggage wagons, and an offer to meet every expense. Other Saints furnished needed provisions and clothing, "enough to last myself and several families for several hundred miles," wrote John. His faith had been amply rewarded.

En route, the Taylors lived and, for two months, worked in Indiana, while awaiting the birth of their third child, Joseph James. Passing through Kirtland deeply saddened the Taylors, for faithful Church leaders had left for Missouri earlier in the year, and only apostates remained in the city.

A few faithful Saints resided in a village just outside Columbus, Ohio, and they arranged for Elder Taylor to speak in a public outdoor meeting. Shortly before the services were to begin, John received word that several men were planning to tar and feather him if he attempted to speak. The members advised Elder Taylor to cancel the engagement, for they lacked strength and numbers to protect him from attack. Although but twenty-nine, Elder Taylor had developed a powerful oratorical and rhetorical style; it was his custom to address the issues without equivocation. Announcing to his friends that he would speak, he made his way through the large crowd and remarked that he had just left Canada, a land ruled by monarchies, but that he now experienced peculiar sensations, standing on free soil among free men:

> Gentlemen, I now stand among men whose fathers fought for and obtained one of the greatest blessings ever conferred upon the human family — the right to think, to speak, to write; the right to say who shall govern them, and the right to worship God according to the dictates of their own consciences — all of them sacred, human rights and now guaranteed by the American Constitution. I see around me the sons of those noble sires, who, rather than bow to the behests of the tyrant, pledged their lives, fortunes, and sacred honors to burst those fetters, enjoy freedom themselves, bequeath it to their posterity or die in the attempt. . . .
>
> But . . . I have been informed that you propose to tar and feather me, for my religious opinions. Is that the legacy you have inherited from your fathers? Is this the blessing they purchased with their dearest hearts' blood — this is your liberty? If so, you now have a victim, and we will have an offering to the goddess of liberty.

Then, in a defiant gesture, he tore open his vest and said: "Gentlemen, come on with your tar and feathers, your victim is ready; and ye spirits of the venerable patriots, gaze upon the deeds of your degenerate sons! Come on, gentlemen! Come on, I say, I am ready!" He paused for a few moments and then launched into a powerful sermon that continued, without interruption, for three hours.

For the Taylors and their friends, the Ohio incident foreshadowed far greater difficulties with anti-Mormons. About the time their party of twenty-four arrived in DeWitt, Missouri, a mob of nearly 150 men threatened the lives of the

Saints living in that community. Elder Taylor found great irony in the fact that Abbott Hancock and Sashiel Woods, Baptist and Presbyterian ministers, led the mob. He recalled:

> This was the first mob I had ever seen . . . and the whole affair was new to me, especially when I considered the kind of officers they had. I had heretofore looked upon the gospel ministers as messengers of peace. Here they came not only in war-like capacity, but as leaders of an armed mob—a gang of marauders and free-booters, with the avowed object of driving peaceful citizens—men, women and children—from their homes. . . .
>
> I had no arms, . . . and heretofore considered that I needed none in a Christian civilized land; but I found I had been laboring under a mistake. The civilization here was of very low order, and the Christianity of a very questionable character. I therefore threw off the sling and bandages from my lame arm (having broken it in an accident while on the way to Missouri), suppressed my repugnance to fighting, borrowed a gun, bought a brace of pistols, and prepared myself at least for defensive measures.

The confrontation produced hot words but no fighting, and the group was able to continue on its journey unmolested.

SOON AFTER JOHN TAYLOR ARRIVED in Far West, his call to the apostleship was confirmed at the October quarterly conference; two months later, at the age of thirty, he was ordained by Brigham Young and Heber C. Kimball, replacing John Farnham Boynton, who had apostatized. For Elder Taylor, the few weeks before that sacred ordinance took place were filled with countless hours of service, as he assisted Saints who were fleeing to Far West from life-threatening persecution in Daviess and Caldwell counties. He personally witnessed several mobbings, and was present when Far West was nearly besieged by hundreds of Missourians. He explained:

> On one occasion, when some thirty-five hundred of the mob forces were approaching Far West, our officer, Colonel Hinkle, sought to betray us, and as a preliminary step, ordered us to retreat. "Retreat!" exclaimed Joseph Smith. "Why, where in the name of God shall we go?" Then turning to our men he said: "Boys, follow me." About two hundred men went out on the open prairies to meet the thirty-five hundred. While these forces faced each other, a flag of truce came in from the

mob bearing the message that it was their intention to destroy Far West; but there was a man and his family – of the name of Lightner – not Mormons, who had friends among the attacking party, and they desired this family to leave the city before it was destroyed. This message was sent to the family. They replied that they had always been treated with consideration by the Mormons, and they would stay with them. This reply the Prophet Joseph Smith took in person to the flag of truce man; and just then a troop of cavalry, two hundred strong, was seen approaching, and Joseph added this to the answer sent by the non-Mormon family: "Go tell your general for me that if he does not immediately withdraw his men, I will send them to hell!"

The mob withdrew.

During the imprisonment of Joseph Smith in Liberty Jail, Elder Taylor assisted in drafting a memorial or statement of facts regarding the persecution of the Saints, seeking justice for their injuries and great loss of property. One such petition was prepared for the Missouri legislature and another for the United States government. The measure was tabled in committee in Missouri and rejected by the federal government as out of its jurisdiction.

A short time after John Taylor's ordination, the Saints were expelled from Missouri by executive order. With Joseph Smith still imprisoned, Brigham Young and Heber C. Kimball evacuated over 11,000 saints across the Mississippi River to safety in Illinois, an invaluable exercise in organization that would aid the Saints immeasurably when they made their way west eight years later.

Soon after Elder Taylor reached Quincy, Illinois, he, four others of the Twelve, and several other brethren recrossed the river to return to Far West, an action that placed their lives in great jeopardy, for Mormons were no longer permitted in Missouri. But they willingly made the journey to fulfill a revelation received by the Prophet Joseph Smith on July 8, 1838, which directed that the Twelve serve a mission in Great Britain – a historic "first" for the Church.

The journey was made doubly difficult because Missouri mobbers were well aware of the revelation and had publicly sworn that it would never be fulfilled. Assembled on the temple site at Far West just after midnight, the brethren held a conference that was marked by the ordination of Wilford Woodruff and George A. Smith to the Twelve. Concluding their business, they offered prayers and then quietly departed to begin their preparations for the long journey abroad.

Three months passed before any of the Twelve could leave for England. By that time the Saints were beginning to settle in and around Commerce, Illinois, a small settlement upstream from Quincy. Elder Taylor's wife and children were housed in a twenty-foot-square room in an abandoned army barracks across the Mississippi River in Montrose, Iowa — less than desirable, but the best they could find at the time.

JOHN TAYLOR AND WILFORD WOODRUFF, both impoverished and in poor health, left their families on August 8. Elder Taylor dedicated his wife and children to the Lord's care. One mile outside Terre Haute, Indiana, he left his wagon, began vomiting violently, and fainted by the roadside. Although he was still quite ill the next morning, the missionaries continued onward, traveling throughout each day and preaching each night. John was finally forced to seek a physician and recuperate in an inn at Germantown, Indiana, while Elder Woodruff was sent on to New York City to await his arrival.

Three weeks of severe illness reduced Elder Taylor in weight and strength, but he valiantly obtained permission to preach in a chapel adjacent to the inn, sitting much of the time as he addressed the audience. His silence regarding his circumstances was unusual for a preacher, and it impressed many who listened. Following one meeting a gentleman approached him with an observation and an offer of assistance: "Mr. Taylor, you do not act as most preachers do; you have said nothing about your circumstances or money, yet you have been here some time sick; your doctor's, hotel and other bills must be heavy. Some friends and myself have talked these matters over and would like to assist you, though we do not wish to give any offense." Thanking the gentleman for the offer, Elder Taylor replied: "I preach without purse or scrip, leaving the Lord to manage those matters you speak of in His own way; and as you have been prompted by the Lord and your own generous impulses, I shall thankfully receive whatever assistance you are disposed to render me."

By the time Elder Taylor arrived in New York City, he had one cent in his pocket. As the time for departure drew near, several individuals donated sufficient ship's passage.

After thirty-one days on the Atlantic Ocean, eight of the twelve apostles arrived in Liverpool, the city of Elder Taylor's youth. This became his base of operations for the sixteen months he would labor in England. His companion was Joseph Fielding, years earlier a fellow seeker in Toronto. Ironically, one of their first opportunities to preach came before a similar group in Liverpool. Preaching in the Hope Street chapel, Elder Taylor said:

> Brethren and friends, we are the humble followers of Jesus Christ and are from America. I lately arrived in this place, and have come five thousand miles without purse or scrip, and I testify to you, my brethren, that the Lord has revealed himself from heaven and put us in possession of those things you are so anxiously looking for and praying that you may receive.
>
> I feel an anxious desire to deliver this testimony. I feel the word of the Lord like fire in my bones and am desirous to have an opportunity of proclaiming to you those blessings that you are looking for, that you may rejoice with us in those glorious things which God has revealed for the salvation of the world in the last days.

During the following weeks, Elder Taylor and his companions were successful in baptizing several former leaders of Non-Conformist denominations.

When Elder Taylor arrived in Liverpool, one-seventh of the population were refugees from Ireland. Thousands were scattered throughout the British Isles, having fled from typhus epidemics, industrial failures, and unconscionably high land rents. Many early converts were natives of Ireland. Following a conference in Manchester in July, therefore, Elder Taylor was appointed to introduce the gospel in Ireland. He was accompanied by two Irish converts and a nonmember who Elder Taylor accurately prophesied would become the first man baptized in Ireland.

The first Mormon sermon in Ireland was preached by Elder Taylor before nearly seven hundred residents of the village of Newry, standing before the courthouse in the early evening. No one responded to the gospel message there, nor did other cities offer positive response to the missionaries, so they departed for Scotland after only ten days on the Emerald Isle. In Scotland the missionaries found Irish immigrants far more receptive to the gospel than in their native land. In the first eleven years of proselyting, eighteen percent of those converted had been born in Ireland. Returning to Liverpool, Elder Taylor preached many sermons before large audiences in the Music Hall, but with much opposition from local ministers.

Elder Taylor went to the Isle of Man, a small island between England and Ireland, in September 1840, and dedicated the island to the Lord for preaching the gospel; then he called upon several of his wife's friends and family members to share his message. Douglas, the capital of the Isle of Man, is located on a beautiful half-moon harbor. On a narrow street, Elder Taylor rented the Wellington Rooms, Douglas's finest hall, which seated a thousand persons. There he presented a series of lectures and debates, including one noted debate with the Reverend Robert Heyes. Heyes quoted three passages of scripture from the Bible purporting to prove that that book of scripture was complete, and that it forbids continuing revelation. Reviewing the passages in question, Elder Taylor showed that the verse in Deuteronomy commanded that no more be added to the Mosaic Law, the passage in Proverbs referred merely to that collection of scripture then in existence, and finally, the express command in Revelation that "if any man shall add unto these things, God shall add unto him the plagues that are written in this book," referred only to the book of Revelation, then existing apart from the other books of scripture. "According to his interpretation of the above scriptures, in quoting from Proverbs, he would reject the New Testament and all the prophets that prophesied after Solomon's Day; and in his quotation from Deuteronomy, he would reject all the Bible but the five books of Moses. But let Mr. Heyes take care that he himself is not incurring the curse by altering the meaning of the words of the very books to which the prohibition positively and particularly refers!"

Despite such opposition, people responded well to Elder Taylor's lively and penetrating replies to his critics. He baptized about forty people and established a branch before the year's end in Douglas. He also found much success in teaching the gospel in towns throughout the countryside.

By the time he returned to Liverpool, more than eight thousand had joined the Church throughout the British Isles. The Prophet Joseph had instructed the brethren to say nothing to new converts regarding gathering with the Saints in America for the time being, but a strong movement developed among many to emigrate. Two female members even dreamed of several ships filled with Saints, en route to an unknown destination. "I find it is difficult to keep anything from the Saints," wrote Elder Taylor, "for the Spirit of God reveals it to them."

Not long afterward he assisted in the emigration of eight hundred converts, organizing them into companies. The brethren then departed from England late in May 1841. They left behind them many notable achievements, including the publishing of a hymnal, The Book of Mormon, and the *Latter-day Saints' Millennial Star*. They had also founded a permanent shipping agency for emigrants, organized branches of the Church in nearly every major city, and witnessed thousands of baptisms. Later, Elder Taylor and the Twelve issued a proclamation to the Saints in Europe, formally inviting them to gather with the Church in Nauvoo.

WHEN ELDER TAYLOR ARRIVED IN NAUVOO on July 1, 1841, he was shocked to find his wife near death, still living in the unhealthful barracks in Iowa. She was gradually restored to health following the administration of several elders in a sacred ceremony.

At general conference in October, John Taylor, Elias Higbee, and Elias Smith were called to compose new petitions seeking reparation for the wrongs suffered by the Saints in Missouri. John's talents as a writer were further utilized four months later when Joseph Smith appointed him associate editor, and Wilford Woodruff, manager, of the *Times and Seasons* newspaper, newly purchased by the Church. Elder Taylor also began the weekly *Nauvoo Neighbor*, his own publication.

Not long after his return to Nauvoo, Elder Taylor learned of the doctrine of celestial marriage from Joseph Smith, a doctrine that included the plurality of wives. "The Prophet was on horseback riding into town, . . . we passed the compliment of the day," wrote Elder Taylor, "when the Prophet said, 'These things must be accepted and entered into, for they cannot be trifled with and the keys will soon be turned unless they are accepted.' These remarks set me to thinking and I soon took steps in accordance therewith."

The new doctrine was not "hailed with delight" by the brethren, for it ran counter to their own concepts of morality and decency. "I had always entertained strict ideas of virtue," wrote Taylor, "and I felt as a married man that this was to me, outside of this principle, an appalling thing to do. Hence, nothing but a knowledge of God, and the revelations of God, and the truth of them, could have induced me to embrace such a principle." Within two years, with Leonora's consent, he married Elizabeth Kaighin, Jane Ballantyne, and Mary Ann Oakley. (He would later marry eleven other wives.)

A key principle in celestial marriage was the eternal nature of the union of husband and wife, as blessed by the priesthood. In 1843 Elder Taylor and all spouses received the endowment preparatory to the marriage sealing ceremony while assembled with the Twelve in the upper assembly room of Joseph Smith's red brick store.

The year 1844 was an election year in the United States. Joseph Smith wrote to the five leading candidates for the office of president, seeking their views on helping the Saints to obtain justice from their enemies in Missouri. The replies were unsatisfactory, so the Prophet determined to present his views to the nation on several major social issues by running for president himself. John Taylor assisted by preparing the Prophet's platform, which was published in a pamphlet and distributed throughout the United States by nearly three hundred Latter-day Saint men, "political missionaries." In a lengthy *Nauvoo Neighbor* editorial, Elder Taylor wrote:

One great reason that we have for pursuing our present course is that at every election we have been made a political target for the filthy demagogues in the country to shoot their loathsome arrows at. And every story has been put into circulation to blast our fame from the old fabrication of "walk on the water" down to the "murder of Governor Boggs." The journals have teemed with this filthy trash, and even men . . . contending for the gubernatorial chair—have made use of terms so degrading, so mean, so humiliating, that a Billingsgate fisher-woman would have considered herself disgraced with them. We refuse any longer to be thus bedaubed for either party; we tell all such to let their filth flow in its own legitimate channel, for we are sick of the smell. . . . Under existing circumstances we have no other alternative (than that of withdrawing from both political parties) and if we can accomplish our object, well; if not we shall have the satisfaction of knowing we have acted conscientiously and have used our best judgment; and if we have to throw away our votes, we had better do so upon a worthy, rather than upon an unworthy individual, who might make use of the weapon we put in his hand to destroy us.

But destruction was to come, not through a candidate or the ballot box, but in mob reaction to the destruction of a newspaper. John Taylor and Willard Richards were the only members of the Twelve in Nauvoo when the city council, of which John was a member, supported Joseph Smith's action, as mayor, in ordering the destruction of the *Nauvoo Expositor*, citing the newspaper as a slanderous and public nuisance. Elder Taylor said that the newspaper "stinks in the nose of every honest man." Its supporters had been previously excommunicated for seduction and adultery.

Charges arising from the destruction of the press were dropped by a circuit court, for the *Expositor*'s editors obtained an arrest warrant in Carthage, charging riot against the city council. Public outcry was so great that Governor Thomas Ford ordered Joseph and Hyrum Smith to appear in Carthage to respond to the charges. Elder Taylor advised that it would be extremely unsafe to go, and that an open confrontation would likely take place between the Mormons and their enemies. He doubted Governor Ford's assurance that they could go unarmed and would be protected.

When the Prophet and his brother Hyrum finally decided to go to Carthage, Joseph asked Elder Taylor and Willard Richards to accompany him. In Carthage, Joseph was charged with treason, arrested, and housed in Carthage jail. Elder Taylor met with Governor Ford but was unable to receive his promised military protection. Governor Ford left for Nauvoo without the Prophet, and the party was left with only such protection as the jailer could provide.

THE WEATHER ON JUNE 27, 1844, was rainy, humid, and depressing. By request, Elder Taylor reluctantly sang "A Poor Wayfaring Man of Grief" twice in his rich baritone voice. Shortly after he had finished the hymn, a mob rushed up the stairs and forced the muzzles of their firearms through the door of their bedroom. Elder Taylor deflected many of them with a walking stick before being hurled toward an open window by a pistol ball that lodged in his left thigh. He was knocked across a windowsill, his fall being checked by a ball from the Carthage Greys outside that struck his vest pocket watch and knocked him backward to the floor. Crawling under a bed for protection, he was struck by three additional balls. One nestled beneath his left knee, a second tore a large piece of flesh from his left hip, and a third entered his left arm and traveled to the palm of his hand. Above all, the lives of Joseph and Hyrum had ended. John later recalled:

When I reflected that our noble chieftain, the prophet of the living God had fallen, and that I had seen his brother in the cold embrace of death, it seemed as though there was a void or vacuum in the great field of human existence to me, and a great gloomy chasm in the kingdom, and that we were left alone. Oh how lonely was that feeling! . . . I thought, "why must the good perish, and the virtuous be destroyed? Why must God's nobility, the salt of the earth, the most exalted of the human family, and the most perfect types of all excellence, fall victim to the cruel, fiendish hate of incarnate devils?

Elder Taylor was taken to the Hamilton Hotel, along with

the bodies of Joseph and Hyrum. There he and Willard Richards managed to prepare an announcement of the tragedy for the Saints while downplaying Elder Taylor's condition:

CARTHAGE JAIL, 8:05 o'clock, P.M., June 27th, 1844
Joseph and Hyrum are dead. Taylor wounded, not very badly. I am well. Our guard was forced, as we believe, by a band of Missourians from 100 to 200. The job was done in an instant, and the party fled towards Nauvoo instantly. This is as I believe it. The citizens here are afraid of the Mormons attacking them. I promise them no!
W. Richards,
John Taylor.

As Willard Richards prepared to return the bodies of the martyrs to Nauvoo the next morning, Elder Taylor asked him to take his watch and purse for safekeeping. It was not until the items were returned to him several days later that Elder Taylor discovered that the watch had deflected a pistol ball and saved his life. "I shall never forget the feelings of gratitude that I then experienced towards my Heavenly Father," he said. "The whole scene was vividly portrayed before me and my heart melted before the Lord. I felt that the Lord has preserved me by a special act of mercy; that my time had not yet come and that I had still a work to perform upon the earth."

Elder Taylor was afterward known and honored by the Saints as a "living martyr." But his suffering continued. Thomas Langely Barnes, a coroner and surgeon in Carthage, operated on Elder Taylor's left palm with a dull pen knife and a pair of carpenter's compasses, a procedure the patient termed "surgical butchery" from a man whose "practice was devilish." Another more competent physician removed the ball from Elder Taylor's hip; the lead in his knee remained in place to his death.

A legal effort was mounted to bring the murderers to justice. Three months after the martyrdom, Elder Taylor swore an oath before Justice of the Peace Aaron Johnson implicating Levi Williams and Thomas C. Sharp. By October 21, Judge Jesse B. Thomas had issued subpoenas for thirty-seven witnesses to appear in Carthage. But John Taylor and other Church leaders

elected to avoid being served with a summons, for they believed that to become a witness was to endanger their lives.
In a *Nauvoo Neighbor* article, Elder Taylor wrote: "Until the
blood of Joseph and Hyrum Smith have been atoned for by
hanging, shooting, or slaying in some manner, every person
engaged in that cowardly assassination, no Latter-day Saint
should give himself up to the law."

AFTER THE DEATH OF THE PROPHET, the two major concerns
of the Twelve were to complete the Nauvoo Temple and to
make successful arrangements to move to the West.

Elder Taylor's fears about the temple were allayed when
on Wednesday, June 18, 1845, he had a marvelous manifestation. He recorded in his journal, "I dreamt that I stood by the
temple and looked up and saw that it was finished. I admired
the elegance and symmetry of the building, and felt animated
in my spirits and rejoiced to see the building finished."

The temple completed, Nauvoo was transformed into a
workshop to build wagons. In February 1846, the Quorum of
the Twelve, the high council, and several hundred families
began the trek across Iowa, battling frost, freezing temperatures, high winds, violent storms, and nearly impassable roads.
Roads were cleared, bridges built, and ferryboats constructed;
and two way-station settlements, Mt. Pisgah and Garden
Grove, were established to provide food and browse for those
who would cross the plains the following spring. "We were
very much exposed, living in tents and wagons," wrote Elder
Taylor, "but . . . we made large fires in the woods. . . . Our
cattle and horses suffered very severely from exposure, and
we ourselves . . . outlived the trying scene—we felt contented
and happy."

As he departed Nauvoo, Elder Taylor composed "In Upper
California," a song about the land that awaited the Saints in
the West:

> We'll reign, we'll rule and triumph
> And God shall be our King;
> The plains, the hills and valleys

Shall with hosannahs ring!
Our tow'rs and temples there shall rise
Along the great Pacific sea,
In Upper California,
Oh, that's the land for me!

Five months after their departure from Illinois, the Taylor families settled in at Winter Quarters, but Elders Taylor, Orson Hyde, and Parley P. Pratt were soon called to England, where they removed from office and membership men who had misappropriated funds from a Church-owned joint stock company. The money was to have been invested and the dividends used to pay the passage of emigrant Saints to America. Having strengthened the Saints, Elder Taylor purchased valuable surveying instruments for the pioneers and received 469 gold sovereigns as tithing from faithful members.

When the brethren arrived at Winter Quarters in April 1847, they were amazed to find that the former tent city had been transformed into a community of 700 cabins, 150 dugouts, and a large log tabernacle. The number of Saints had swelled to nearly 15,000 with 3,000 wagons and 30,000 cattle. Grass now grew on the prairie, and the cattle and horses were becoming sleek and fat. But prosperity belied the tragedies of the past winter. Hundreds had died from cholera, scurvy, and the effects of malnutrition. Ann Pitchforth Taylor, a wife of Elder Taylor and a woman of bearing and refinement, was among those who had lost their lives.

Before Brigham Young left Winter Quarters with his advance company, he placed Elders Taylor and Pratt in charge of leading 1,553 Saints across the plains. But they were delayed, having decided to plow, plant, and fence a large tract of land so that the Saints in Winter Quarters could enjoy an abundance of vegetables. They were further slowed by the 600 wagons, 2,213 oxen, 887 cows, 358 sheep, 716 chickens, and other paraphernalia that the Saints brought with them.

On July 23, 1847, John's young son George was run over by a heavily loaded wagon, but he responded well to medicine and a priesthood blessing. Leonora found the trek no easier—

she suffered from rheumatism in her knees, and promised to sew a dress if one of her daughters would help her.

THE PRATT–TAYLOR COMPANY arrived in Salt Lake Valley on October 5, and the men immediately set to work to provide direction for the Saints and homes for their families. A massive adobe-walled fort stretched across the length of three city blocks. Here the men were instructed to build shelters until the land could be apportioned the following spring. John Taylor wrote:

> Our houses were built on the outside line of the fort in shanty form, with the highest wall outside, the roof sloping towards the interior. The windows and doors were placed on the side facing the enclosure, the outside being left solid, excepting loop holes for protection. Our corrals, haystacks and stables were some distance behind and outside the fort. About Christmas, I had put up, enclosed and covered about ninety feet of building made of split logs, out of which was taken a four inch plank. The plank was used for partitions. . . . In addition to this, I had built corrals and stables behind, and enclosed a garden spot in front, with a board-rail fence. I assisted in all this labor of sawing, building, hauling, enough for one fall.

The lumber was produced in a saw-pit with two men using a long whipsaw, one in the pit and the other standing above.

In December Elder Taylor reported by letter that

> the land is generally rich and fertile, perhaps as much so as any in the world, and our best agriculturists believe that it will yield an abundant increase of every kind of grain. . . .
>
> We have ploughed and sown, since our arrival here, about 2000 acres of wheat, and great numbers of ploughs are incessantly going, and are only prevented by the inclemency of the weather. . . . The climate . . . is beautiful.
>
> Timber in the immediate vicinity is not very abundant, but we have found sufficient for building and fuel for some time to come. . . .
>
> There is sufficient feed for our cattle, sheep and horses, without cutting any hay, during the winter; our cattle are fattening all the time, living alone on the grasses they get, which is highly nutritious. . . .
>
> We have built our houses for the present in the shape of a large fort; but expect as soon as practicable to build our houses on our lots in the city; the houses are now erected and in progress amount to about

700, and are built some of logs, some of sawn timber, and some of [adobe], or sun dried brick.

The city plot is about two miles square; it is laid out in blocks of ten acres, and the streets are eight rods wide, and cross each other at right angles. The lots for each individual are an acre and a quarter, and those that are worthy receive them freely as their inheritance together with what land they can till. We have no land to sell, neither can any other person speculate on their inheritance, for it is the Lord's and while the Lord gives us free possession like the gifts of air, light, water, and life, it is free.

There is a lot set apart for the erection of the temple, containing ten acres, laid out on the bank of a beautiful creek that runs through the centre of the city. . . .

And now, beloved brethren, although I have been writing in a great measure on temporal things, yet my mind dwells not so much on hills, vales, brooks, lakes, houses and land, as it does on things pertaining to the kingdom of God — the building up of Zion — the gathering together of God's elect — the fulfillment of the prophecies — the blessing, glory, and exaltation of His Saints. . . . And as when I was with you, so now when absent, I pray God the eternal Father so to influence the hearts of men in authority, that your way may be opened to gather with the Saints of the Most High, that you may partake of the ordinances of the Lord's house, and finally be counted worthy to possess thrones, principalities, powers, and dominions in the Eternal World.

In building their homes, the men had been misled into thinking that little moisture fell in the valley. They learned differently in April 1848 when snow fell at least a foot in depth. Isaac C. Haight wrote: "Some of our houses, which were flat-roofed, leaked very badly and made it very unpleasant for the occupants." Writing to Brigham Young, who was in Winter Quarters, Elder Taylor half-humorously reported: "We have had a great quantity of rain this spring. . . . Indeed, some people began to pray for rain before they ascertained that their houses were not waterproof, and almost wished that they had deferred their supplications a little longer." He also noted that the wheat harvest would be somewhat less than anticipated, and that "crickets and other insects in some isolated districts have been very destructive to the rising vegetation, . . . but their ranges are limited and their operations not such as to create any general alarm." History records that the Saints survived the onslaught of locusts, not once but several times over the years to come.

Gold was discovered near Sacramento, California, on January 24, 1848, an act that would bring thousands of Forty-niners through Great Salt Lake Valley. Such travelers were typically amazed to find themselves "suddenly and almost unexpectedly in a comparative paradise." One of them wrote:

> Houses of wood and sun-dried bricks were thickly clustered in the vale before us . . . mostly small, one story high. . . . The whole space for miles, excepting the streets and houses, was in a high state of cultivation. Fields of yellow wheat stood waiting for the harvest; and Indian corn, potatoes, oats, flax and all kinds of garden vegetables were growing in profusion. . . . At first sight of all these signs of cultivation in the wilderness, we were transported with wonder and pleasure. Some wept, some gave three cheers, some laughed, and some ran and fairly danced with joy, while all felt inexpressibly happy to find themselves once more amid scenes which mark the progress of advancing civilization.
>
> The Mormons are not dead nor is their spirit broken. And if I mistake not there is a noble, daring, stern, and democratic spirit dwelling in their bosom, which will people these mountains with a race of independent men, and influence the destiny of our country and the world for a hundred generations.

The Great Basin had been a part of New Spain, Mexican Territory, when the Saints arrived, but fifteen months later, in October 1848, the Treaty of Guadalupe Hidalgo was ratified—and much of the West became part of the United States. John Taylor, a British subject, applied on September 5, 1849, to become an American citizen.

AT GENERAL CONFERENCE IN OCTOBER 1849, forty-one-year-old John Taylor received a mission call to open the nation of France for preaching the gospel. He departed with his companion, Curtis E. Bolton, and thirty-four others who had been called to France, the British Isles, and Scandinavia. October was late in the season for departure, and the men experienced rain, frost, and bitter cold. There was little browse for their weakened animals, and many had to be abandoned along the trail.

The missionaries had a good scare as they paused to eat and rest along the banks of the Platte River. Nearly two hundred mounted Cheyenne Indians crested a hill to the east and charged toward them. The missionaries' horses were quickly tied to the wagons, and Jedediah M. Grant formed the men into a line. "The efforts of the Indians were either to break our line or turn our flank," wrote Elder Taylor, "but being repulsed on all points they were brought to a dead halt about a rod and a half in front of us. During all this . . . they were shaking out the priming from their firearms, and priming them anew. Many placed their arrows to their bowstrings — their lances at rest — and were wetting the ends of their arrows with their mouths, that they might not slip from finger and thumb." Just at this crucial moment, the Indian chief revealed that they were merely having a good time at the expense of the white men. Greatly relieved, the missionaries gave the Indians some crackers, meat, and tobacco, and the braves escorted the travelers to a point three miles opposite their village.

While traveling across the plains, Elder Taylor became sufficiently versed in the French language that soon after arriving in France, he was able to write and publish two articles in the *Boulogne Interpreter* newspaper. He and his companions were, however, continually harassed by three ministers who had followed them from England. The ministers challenged them to a public debate on the sincerity of Joseph Smith, the validity of the Book of Mormon, and the authority of their appointments to preach the gospel. The challenge was accepted, and the debate was held on three consecutive evenings. Answering the charge that Joseph Smith was an impostor, Elder Taylor told them, "I was intimately acquainted with the late Joseph Smith. . . . I have traveled with him; I have been with him in public and in private, at home and abroad; I was with him living, and when he died — when he was murdered in Carthage Jail — and I can testify that he was a virtuous, moral, high-minded man."

John Taylor knew personally each of three men who authored anti-Mormon books quoted by the ministers. He reported, "Preying upon the cupidity of the uninformed, they made a very lucrative business of their disgusting traffic, and sold it to the world. . . . Truth has always been opposed by the children of men. It comes in [conflict with] . . . corrupt hearts and wicked practices. . . . When I commenced searching after truth, I did not pursue the same course that you have done — seek to impugn the motives and destroy the characters of the man who made it. . . . I can very soon detect any false system by comparing it with the scriptures; but these gentlemen, having so bungling a counterfeit themselves, of course are not proper to judge, and do not understand the true test."

Based upon the debates, Elder Taylor wrote a tract entitled *Three Nights' Public Discussion . . . at Boulogne-sur-mer, France.* Some 16,000 copies were sold.

Elder John Pack remained in Boulogne while Elders Taylor and Bolton went to Paris. There they were able to establish a branch of the Church. It was an extraordinary achievement, because they were forbidden by the government to preach anywhere in France, to hold large meetings, or to distribute tracts.

Despite such restrictions, the brethren held a conference, and Elder Taylor established a monthly newspaper, *L'Etoile du Deseret* (The Star of Deseret). Elder Bolton translated the Book of Mormon into French, with grammatical revisions made by Louis Bertrand, a new convert and assistant editor of *Populaire,* a militant political newspaper. Elder Taylor supervised the work for doctrinal accuracy, dividing paragraphs when required for easier reading. "The original simplicity of the book is retained, and it is as literal as the genius and idiom of the French language would admit," he said. He later received the assistance of several others in translating the book into German. With help from some professors in Hamburg, the manuscript was complete.

With the French and German texts of the Book of Mormon in hand, a most unusual printing was undertaken, with the German verses published on the left-hand page and the French on the right-hand page. In addition, a monthly periodical was begun in Hamburg, called *Zion's Panier* (Zion's Banner). Elder Taylor also authored *The Government of God,* in which he contrasted the beauty and order of the kingdom of God with the confusion, instability, and discord of earthly governments, and showed what awaited the earth with the establishment of the Lord's kingdom. The short work was later praised by the eminent American historian Hubert Howe Bancroft, who wrote that it had "not its equal in point of ability within the whole range of Mormon literature."

Anxious to promote home manufacture, Brigham Young instructed Elder Taylor to learn how to manufacture sugar and to purchase the necessary equipment and ship it to Utah. Accordingly, Elder Taylor and three other brethren organized the Deseret Manufacturing Company and purchased equipment from a firm in Liverpool for $12,500. They purchased five hundred bushels of sugar beet seed in France and shipped it west as well.

Problems wracked the project almost from the beginning. In New Orleans, a $5,000 duty was assessed on the equipment. A riverboat carrying the machinery was nearly lost in an explosion. Fifty freight wagons and six hundred oxen had to be purchased to carry the equipment across the plains, but many of the wagons proved to be unsound and had to be replaced.

In Salt Lake City, the first sugar manufacturing plant was established on the temple block; later it was moved southeast several miles to an area that became known as Sugar House. The brethren hoped that from 150 to 300 tons of sugar could be processed from the annual fall harvests of sugar beets, but a low quality of sorghum was all that could be produced. It is believed that a high alkaline content in the beets, and perhaps the concealment of a vital step in the sugar production by the Europeans, contributed to the disappointing failure.

While he was in France, Elder Taylor planned to ship from one to two thousand merino sheep to Utah and establish a company for the production of fine broadcloth and women's clothing. In a talk at Carpenter's Hall in Manchester, England, in October 1850, he urged mechanics to immigrate to the Salt Lake Valley and become involved in the venture. The plant was eventually built on Big Canyon Creek and was known as Brigham Young's Woollen and Cotton Factory.

FOLLOWING HIS RETURN to the Salt Lake Valley, Elder Taylor built several adobe homes for his families on portions of two blocks of land a short distance from the temple block. Each home had a garden, an orchard, cows, and chickens. A two-story adobe building was used by all the families, with a blacksmith shop in the basement, a large pantry on the main floor, and a family schoolroom on the upper story.

Among Elder Taylor's offspring were a few mischievous boys who stole some apples and chickens from a neighbor. A family court was convened, and Elder Taylor sentenced the recreant boys to pay back in labor on the neighbor's farm seven times the value of the stolen items. The Taylor children were permitted to play checkers, jackstraws, and other simple games, but they were forbidden to use face cards or read novels. One son won a copy of Jules Verne's *Twenty Thousand Leagues under the Sea* for being the best scholar in the family school. His father, observing the boy reading the book, told him, "It is a novel and you should not read such things." The boy was sent to bed. The next morning the son found his father in the parlor, having stayed up all night reading his novel. "That's a good book, son. You may read it," Elder Taylor admitted.

Elder Taylor enjoyed relating stories from Church history to his children, and he would allow them to feel the bullet lodged beneath the skin of his left leg from his near-death experience in Carthage Jail. One son remembered his home life as "a time of peace, happiness, love, contentment, hard work. There was no jealousy, no backbiting."

A fastidious dresser, Elder Taylor usually wore a dark suit and highly polished boots, shined to perfection by a son. He occasionally wore a red velvet coat for special occasions.

Family members looked forward to his birthday, always held in the evening, with General Authorities invited to enjoy the food, music, and dancing. "He was the king," wrote one child. "We were the princes and princesses because we were helping him gain his and our place in the Celestial Kingdom."

In 1852 Orson Pratt, as spokesman for the Church, made a public announcement of the practice of plural marriage from the newly finished adobe tabernacle on the temple block. Public outcry was so great from politicians and the press in the East that two years later, five of the brethren were called to publish newspapers in New York City, Washington, D.C., Cincinnati, St. Louis, and San Francisco to explain the Church's position. John Taylor was named editor of *The Mormon* in New York, as well as ecclesiastical leader over the Church's eastern branches and emigration agent for Latter-day Saints heading to Utah. He rented rooms for editorial offices on "newspaper row," between the New York *Herald* and the New York *Tribune*, two of the nation's most powerful periodicals. In his first issue he figuratively threw out the gauntlet to the Church's critics: "We defy all the editors and writers in the United States to prove that Mormonism is less moral, scriptural, philosophical, or that there is less patriotism in Utah than in any other part of the United States. We call for proof; bring on your reasons, gentlemen, if you have any; we shrink not from the investigation, and dare you the encounter. If you don't do it, and you publish any more of your stuff, we shall brand you as poor, mean, cowardly liars, as men publishing falsehoods knowing them to be so, and shunting from the light of truth and investigation."

AFTER TWO AND ONE-HALF YEARS in New York, Elder Taylor was called back to Utah to help prepare for the arrival of three thousand troops of the United States Army, sent by President James Buchanan in reply to charges of rebellion, murder, and destruction of court records made against Brigham Young and the Latter-day Saints. The charges had been filed by Judge William W. Drummond, former associate justice of the Utah Territorial Supreme Court. In a talk at a special conference in 1858, Elder Taylor's anger could scarcely be contained: "We have been outrageously imposed upon by United States officials. They send out every rag-tag and bob-tail, and every mean nincompoop they can scrape up from the filth and scum of society, and dub him a United States officer. And are we expected to receive all manner of insults from such men without one word of complaint? They will assuredly find themselves mistaken." Brigham Young reached out and tugged on his garment to calm him down. "Brother Brigham, let go my coat-tail. I tell you, the bullets in me yet hurt!"

The General Authorities had discussed armed resistance to the army but abandoned it in favor of the Sebastopol plan, a technique used by the Russians in the Crimean War wherein they pulled out of the city of Sebastopol but burned it to the ground rather than abandon it to the enemy. Elder Taylor asked the Saints: "Would you, if necessary, put the torch to your houses, and lay the land in waste and go to the mountains?" Four thousand persons sustained the proposal. "I knew what your feelings would be," he said. "We have been persecuted and robbed long enough, and in the name of Israel's God we will be free!"

In the spring of 1858, 35,000 Saints packed their wagons with food storage, clothing, and furniture, and headed to several locations south of Salt Lake City, abandoning their homes to be burned, if necessary. The action elicited a wave of sympathy across the nation and helped in negotiations of peace held with newly appointed Governor Alfred Cumming.

The movement of the army was so effectively stopped that the fiery Elder Taylor was able to exult in the Tabernacle: "I do not remember having read in any history, or had related to me any circumstance where an army has been subjugated so easily, and their power wasted away so effectually without bloodshed, as this at our borders. If this is not a manifestation of the power of God to us, I do not know what it is. Has any man's life been lost in it? No—not one. It is true our brethren have been fired upon; but their balls failed of doing the injury that was expected. Our brethren were told not to retaliate, and they did not do it. Where is there such a manifestation of the power of God?"

The Army remained at Camp Floyd south of Salt Lake City until the outbreak of the Civil War in 1861, when they returned to the East. The strife between the North and South brought forth the wrath of Elder Taylor, who attributed its cause to a gradual decline of "national integrity, [an] increase of crime and corruption, and a want of a proper administration of the laws. . . . Corruption and mob violence began to prevail . . .

[when] the rights of American citizens [the Saints in Missouri] were trampled underfoot, the Constitution and laws desecrated. . . . Joseph Smith then prophesied that mob law would go forth throughout the land. Mob rule commenced by slow degrees at first, but it gained power until like a mighty avalanche it swept through the land. Since then it has ruled rampant. Shall we join the North to fight against the South? No! Shall we join the South against the North? As emphatically, No! Why? They have both . . . brought it upon themselves, and we have had no hand in the matter."

The Saints faced further difficulties from the government when President Abraham Lincoln signed into law an act of Congress that prohibited the practice of plural marriage in the territories, another conflict in which they could not be idle bystanders. "Whence came this law upon our statute books?" challenged Elder Taylor. "Who constituted them our conscience-keepers? Who appointed them the judge of our religious faith, or authorized them to coerce us to transgress a law that is binding and imperative in our conscience? We do not expect that Congress is acquainted with our religious faith; but . . . we do claim the guarantees of the Constitution and immunity from persecution on merely religious grounds."

Six years later, in October 1869, the unyielding stance of the government against the practices of the Saints was brought to their doorstep when Vice-president Schuyler Colfax visited Salt Lake City for the second time and spoke to a crowd from the portico of the Townsend House Hotel. In his opening remarks, he recognized and praised Utah's citizens for the great economic progress made since his first visit. Then he launched into his attack: "I have not strictures to utter as to your creed on any really religious question. Our land is the land of civil and religious liberty, and the faith of every man is a matter between himself and God alone. . . . But our country is governed by law, and no assumed revelation justifies anyone in trampling on the law. If it did, every wrong-doer would use that argument to protect himself in his disobedience to it."

In response to the Church's recent founding of Zion's

Cooperative Mercantile Institution (ZCMI) for economic protection, Colfax said: "You should welcome, and not repel, investments from abroad. You should discourage every effort to drive capital from your midst. You should rejoice at the opening of every new store, or factory, or mechanic shop, by whomsoever conducted."

Elder Taylor read the Colfax speech in the Springfield *Republican* while he was in Boston, Massachusetts, on railroad business. Not one to let such a public scolding pass by, he wrote a response that was published in the New York *Tribune* and reprinted throughout the nation:

Allow me, sir, here to state that the assumed revelation referred to is one of the most vital parts of our religious faith; it emanated from God and cannot be legislated away. It is part of the "Everlasting Covenant" which God has given to man . . . take that from us and you rob us of our hopes and associations in the resurrection of the just.

You do not see things as we do. You marry for time only, "until death does you part." We have eternal covenants . . . visions . . . associations. . . .

It was the revelation . . . that Joseph and Mary had . . . which made them flee from the wrath of Herod, who was seeking the young child's life. This they did in contravention of the law, which was his decree. Did they do wrong in protecting Jesus from the law?

Whose rights have we interfered with? Whose property have we taken? Whose religious or political faith or rights have been curtailed by us? None. . . .

We do acknowledge having lately started cooperative stores. Is this anything new in England, Germany, France or the United States? We think we have a right, as well as others, to buy or sell of, and to whom, anyone we please. We do not interfere with others in selling, if they can get customers. We have commenced to deal with our friends. . . .

"Ours," says Mr. Colfax, "is a land of civil and religious liberty, and the faith of every man is a matter between himself and God alone" — providing God [doesn't] shock our moral ideas by introducing something that we don't believe in. If He does, let Him look out.

"What of your gambling halls . . . gold rings . . . whiskey rings . . . railroad rings, manipulated through the lobby into your Congressional rings? What of that great moral curse of the land, that great institution of monogamy — prostitution? What of its twin sister — infanticide? I speak to you as a friend. Know ye not that these seething infamies are corrupting and destroying your people? . . ."

We have no gambling halls, no drunkenness, no infanticide, no houses of assignation, no prostitutes. . . . There is not, today, in the wide world a place where female honor, virtue and chastity are so well protected as in Utah.

Scarcely had the Colfax incident ended when President Young and others were indicted on unlawful cohabitation by James B. McKean, newly appointed chief justice from New York. When President Young appeared before McKean in his hayloft courtroom, it became evident that McKean was on a vendetta against the Church, for he said: "Courts are bound to take notice of the political and social conditions of the country which they judicially rule. It is therefore proper to say, that while the case at bar is called 'The People versus Brigham Young,' the other and real name is 'Federal Authority versus Polygamous Theocracy'!"

McKean's actions so provoked the anger of the Saints that there was danger of violence. Elder Taylor headed off any demonstrations in counsel given in five published letters: "We now have a reason given for this . . . crusade against the liberties of the citizens of this Territory. . . . There has been an undercurrent that was extremely difficult to comprehend. . . . His honor Judge McKean, however, has dispelled the mist in which it was shrouded, and has plainly given us to understand that it is . . . the United States against the Church of Jesus Christ of Latter-Day Saints. . . . By the unprecedented method of procuring juries, the ignoring of Territorial law and Territorial courts and officers and other outrages, they have evidently been trying to provoke seditions, that a good pretext could be had for calling out troops, that the fires of war might be kindled." Elder Taylor urged moderation and then humorously observed, "The Territorial officials want to pick a quarrel to give them cause of legal action. Don't give it to them. They offer themselves to be kicked. Don't do it. Have some respect for your boots."

Many newspapers around the country sided with Elder Taylor and jumped into the fray against the federal officials. "The whole thing is instigated by a ring of small-fry, popinjay politicians and would-be statesmen who know full well that they will have no show for promotion until the Mormon power is broken," proclaimed the San Francisco *Examiner*. "If they can send Brigham to prison, and induce the people to rise up and liberate him, and thus produce a conflict, Utah will be at once admitted as a state, and under the protection of federal bayonets these mischief-makers can have themselves elected senators, congressmen, etc., just as the thieving carpetbaggers did at the South. The whole affair is a disgrace to the American name."

Public outrage forced Judge McKean from the bench, and President Young was exonerated of the charges against him. For several years afterward, the territory enjoyed a period of peace, as other appointed federal officials were more responsible in their conduct.

During his ministry, Brigham Young was active in directing the establishment of hundreds of new settlements throughout the West. As his health began to fail, he entrusted the task of settling Saints in Arizona Territory to John Taylor, who directed members of the Twelve to seek out five hundred "missionaries" and their families for that purpose. Since the establishment of the United Order was of utmost importance to President Young, Elder Taylor directed the rebaptism of thousands of Saints as a symbolic recleansing and recommitment to their sacred vows in building the kingdom of God.

WITH THE PASSING OF PRESIDENT YOUNG on August 29, 1877, the mantle of leadership fell upon Elder Taylor's shoulders. On September 4, 1877, he was sustained by the Quorum of the Twelve as president of the quorum, to act in place of the First Presidency.

In 1879 an event occurred that was to have far-reaching effects in the spiritual education of the Church's youth. Bishop John W. Hess of the Farmington (Utah) Ward asked his members to help him find a way to reach their boys, many of whom were roaming about, undisciplined, and headed for trouble. Aurelia Spencer Rogers suggested forming a children's organization in which boys could be taught useful skills and good behavior. Eliza R. Snow presented the proposal to Elder Taylor, who approved the plan. Sister Rogers then decided that girls ought to be included, and she wrote to Sister Snow for her opinion. Sister Snow agreed, saying, "I feel assured that the inspiration of heaven is directing you, and that a great and very important movement is being inaugurated for the future of Zion." President Taylor thereafter directed Sister Snow to assist in organizing the Primary Mutual Association in every ward throughout the Church.

April 6, 1880, was the fiftieth anniversary of the organization of the Church, and in celebration President Taylor turned to the example of an Old Testament jubilee celebration to forgive one-half the debts, $802,000, owed by the worthy poor to the Perpetual Emigration Fund Company. In addition, one thousand cows and five thousand sheep were distributed to indigent members to replace some of the thousands lost in the severe winter of 1879-1880. President Taylor also counseled the affluent to forgive the debts of the poor. "It occurred to me," he said, "that we ought to do something, as they did in former times, to relieve those that are oppressed with debt, to assist those that are needy, to break off the yoke of those that may feel themselves crowded upon, and to make it a time of general rejoicing."

Six months later, the First Presidency was reorganized, with John Taylor designated as the president. He chose George Q. Cannon and Joseph F. Smith as his counselors. As part of October conference, a solemn and impressive religious service was held in the Tabernacle, with the general authorities, stake officers, and members of priesthood quorums assembled there to offer a sustaining vote. President Taylor afterward moved into the Gardo House, the Church's new residence for the president and a reception center for visiting dignitaries. He did so with reluctance, for he cared little for such an elegant residence. "I care nothing about the outside show, the glitter and the appearance of men," he commented.

Some time later, President Taylor was visited in the Gardo House by Zina Young Williams, the dean of women of the Brigham Young Academy in Provo and a daughter of Brigham Young. The academy was less than a decade old and was experiencing serious financial difficulties that, if not resolved, would mean its closing. After listening to Sister Williams's plea for help, President Taylor took her hand "in a fatherly way" and said:

My dear child, I have something of importance to tell you that I know will make you happy. I have been visited by your father. He came to me in the silence of the night clothed in brightness and with a face beaming with love and confidence told me things of great importance and among others that the school being taught by Brother [Karl G.] Maeser was accepted in the heavens and was a part of the great plan of life and salvation; that Church schools should be fostered for the good of Zion's children; that we rejoice to see the awakening among the teachers and the children of our people; for they would need the support of this knowledge and testimony of the Gospel, and there was a bright future in store for the preparing for the children of the covenant for future usefulness in the Kingdom of God, and that Christ himself was directing, and had a care over this school.

In a meeting with the Saints in Ephraim, Sanpete County, some years earlier, President Taylor had prophesied: "You will see the day that Zion will be as far ahead of the outside world in everything pertaining to learning of every kind as we are today in regard to religious matters. You mark my words, and write them down, and see if they do not come to pass." Brigham Young Academy (now Brigham Young University) received the funds it needed.

PRESIDENT TAYLOR'S MINISTRY was notable for his work with the priesthood, which underwent significant functional changes with the inauguration of weekly ward priesthood meetings, monthly general stake priesthood meetings, and quarterly conferences for the nineteen stakes. In 1881 he published a pamphlet of instructions on priesthood, and the following year a book entitled *An Examination into and an Elucidation of the Great Principle of the Mediation and Atonement of Our Lord and Savior Jesus Christ*, in which he made clear that Latter-day Saints accept Jesus Christ as the divine Son of God and as the Savior and Messiah of the world.

President Taylor enjoyed a great outpouring of the Spirit regarding the direction and needs of the kingdom of God. On

October 13, 1882, he was directed by the Lord to call George Teasdale and Heber J. Grant to fill vacancies in the Quorum of the Twelve left by the deaths of Orson Hyde and Orson Pratt, and to call Seymour B. Young as one of the First Seven Presidents of the Seventy. Much reorganization proceeded. When President Taylor reviewed what he had done and asked the Lord for counsel, the Lord replied: "What ye have written is my will, and is acceptable unto me. . . . Let not your hearts be troubled, neither be ye concerned about the management and organization of my Church and Priesthood and the accomplishment of my work. Fear me and observe my laws, and I will reveal unto you, from time to time, through the channels that I have appointed, everything that shall be necessary for the future development and perfection of my Church."

On May 17, 1884, President Taylor dedicated the Logan Temple, the second temple in the territory to be completed. (The St. George Temple was the first.) The evening before the dedication in Logan, President Taylor knelt and asked the Lord if the edifice was acceptable to Him. The Lord, by revelation, confirmed His acceptance and blessed all those who would take part in its sacred ordinances, who "act with purity and singleness of heart before me." He then revealed a future function of latter-day temples:

And this house shall be a house of prayer, a house of learning, a house of God, wherein many great principles pertaining to the past, to the present and the future shall be revealed, and my word and my will be made known; and the laws of the Universe, pertaining to this world and other worlds be developed; for in these houses which have been built unto me, and which shall be built, I will reveal the abundance of those things pertaining to the past, the present, and the future, to the life that now is, and the life that is to come, pertaining to law, order, rule, dominion and government, to things affecting this nation and other nations; the laws of the heavenly bodies in their times and seasons, and the principles or laws by which they are governed, and their relation to each other, and whether they be bodies celestial, terrestrial, or telestial, shall be made known, as I will, saith the Lord, for it is my will and my purpose to place my people in closer communion with the heavens, inasmuch as they will purify themselves and observe more diligently my law; for it is in mine heart to greatly bless and exalt my people, and to build up, exalt and beautify my Zion, inasmuch as they shall observe my law.

Among the first ordinances performed in the Logan Temple were the marriage ceremonies performed by President Taylor for two of his sons and their brides.

In 1882 Congress passed the Edmunds Act, a law that provided stringent penalties for so-called unlawful cohabitation. In general conference that April, President Taylor said: "Let us treat it the same as we did this morning in coming through the snow storm—put up our coat collars (turning up his own) and wait until the storm subsides. After the storm comes sunshine. While the storm lasts it is useless to reason with the world; when it subsides we can talk to them." The Edmunds Bill, signed into law, not only defined polygamy as unlawful cohabitation—a misdemeanor—but also disfranchised polygamists from holding public office, serving on juries, or exercising the right to vote. The latter privilege was determined by the federally appointed "Utah Commission," a five-man board under whose direction test oaths were administered by qualified registrars in political districts throughout the territory.

The Church vigorously opposed all such legislation, arguing in the courts that the Bill of Rights protected the Latter-day Saint practices as a matter of religious belief. In a lengthy revelation to President Taylor, the Lord said that through this type of legislation, Satan was seeking "to take away the free agency of man [as] in the beginning . . . and has sought to introduce the same principles upon the earth, which principles are opposed to me, to my institutions and my laws, and to the freedom, the welfare and happiness of man, and by which principles the Government of the United States has sought to deprive my people of their free agency."

Federal prosecutors now began to indict Latter-day Saint leaders. In 1884 Rudger Clawson (who later became an apostle) was given a sentence of three and one-half years in the Utah

Territorial penitentiary, and as other men were indicted, the First Presidency determined that it was wise to withdraw from public view.

On February 1, 1885, President Taylor addressed the Saints for the final time in the Salt Lake Tabernacle. He advised them not to retaliate against federal officials, despite their many acts of provocation — "no breaking of heads, or bloodshed, rendering evil for evil. Let us try to cultivate the spirit of the gospel, and adhere to the principles of truth. . . . While other men are seeking to trample the Constitution under foot, we will try to maintain it. . . . And as I have said before I say today, — I tell you in the name of God, WOE! to them that fight against Zion, for God will fight against them!"

President Taylor, George Q. Cannon, and other prominent Church leaders no longer lived in their homes, but stayed for a few days at a time in a succession of Mormon residences located in communities throughout Salt Lake Valley and elsewhere. Although telephone service was now available to a number of homes, President Taylor conducted the affairs of the Church through correspondence that was picked up and delivered to a "safe house" after nightfall each evening. During this period on the "underground," he encouraged missionary work among the Indians, recommended the establishment of settlements in southern Colorado, Arizona, Mexico, and Canada, and otherwise directed the financial, organizational, and spiritual work of the Church in fairness and wisdom. Not all was stress, however. For example, President Taylor enjoyed pitching quoits with his security guard Samuel Bateman.

The final eight months of President Taylor's life were spent in the comfortable farm home of Thomas F. Roueche, mayor of Kaysville, Utah, a few hundred yards from the shores of Great Salt Lake. As the president's health deteriorated, Wilford Woodruff, senior apostle, dreamed that Brigham Young handed the keys of the Salt Lake Temple to him (Wilford Woodruff), with instructions to open the doors and admit the Saints. Elder Woodruff felt impressed that this meant President Taylor would not live to dedicate that temple. His counselor Joseph F. Smith was notified of President Taylor's condition by letter in the Sandwich Islands, where he was laboring, and arrived in Kaysville on July 18, 1887. One week later at 7:55 p.m. on Monday, July 25, 1887, President Taylor died. Present were several family members, his counselors, the Roueches, and men who had served as security for him.

JOHN TAYLOR'S LIFE AND BACKGROUND were markedly different from those of his predecessors Joseph Smith and Brigham Young. By birth he was English, while they were Americans. He enjoyed a formal education, while they briefly attended frontier common schools. His language and demeanor were correct, reserved, and cultivated, while their manner of expression reflected the self-confident, unpolished enthusiasm and determination of those who were subjected to a rugged, hard-scrabble existence. His dress was that of a gentleman, while theirs was often homespun. The style of each man was different, yet each was needed and welcomed, for each lent strength and power to the youthful and rapidly expanding church.

Frederick W. Taylor, a son of President Taylor, wrote to his fiancée, "We all dearly loved him who gave us life, through the instrumentality of God and provided well for our wants, never neglecting to sow in our hearts love for the Creator of the Heavens and Earth and all that in them is and the truths which have been revealed in this our day. . . . He was one of the great spirits of this world, spending most of his days in the service of God endeavoring to establish truth and righteousness upon the earth, promulgating the plan of salvation whereby we may be saved."

The son concluded, "When I think of his useful life and noble example he placed before us I feel like praying that we may follow in his footsteps and prove faithful to ourselves and fellow man. . . . [I am sure that] his work goes on in the sphere where he is, his knowledge and intellect are utilized and the work of God goes on until the accomplishment of all his purposes."

SOURCES

Letters and papers of John Taylor in the LDS Church Archives; Francis M. Gibbons, *John Taylor: Mormon Philosopher, Prophet of God* (Salt Lake City: Deseret

Book, 1985); Samuel W. Taylor, *The Kingdom or Nothing: The Life of John Taylor, Militant Mormon* (New York and London: Macmillan Publishing Co., 1976); B. H. Roberts, *The Life of John Taylor* (Salt Lake City: George Q. Cannon & Sons, 1892); Samuel W. and Raymond W. Taylor, *The John Taylor Papers: Records of the Last Utah Pioneer, Volumes I and II, The Apostle and The President* (Redwood City, California: Taylor Trust, Publisher, 1984-1985); Samuel W. Taylor, *Family Kingdom* (New York and London: McGraw-Hill Book Co., 1951); Preston Nibley, *The Presidents of the Church* (Salt Lake City. Deseret Book, 1971), pp. 69-100; and Richard L. Jensen, "The John Taylor Family," *Ensign* 10 (February 1980): 50-56.

PAUL T. SMITH is instructor at the Institute of Religion at the LDS Business College in Salt Lake City. A graduate of Brigham Young University with a master's degree in education, he previously taught at institutes of religion in California and Florida and served as a curriculum writer for the Church Education System. He has been working for several years on a biography of President John Taylor, and has published articles in *New Era* and in church manuals.

WILFORD WOODRUFF

Dean C. Jessee

The life story of Wilford Woodruff began on March 1, 1807, in the hinterland near Hartford, Connecticut, on his father's farm, which contained a sawmill, flour mill, carding machine, and a herd of cattle. Wilford was one year old when his mother died, and nearly four when his father remarried. He spent the early years of his life attending school and fishing and trapping in the streams that fed his father's millpond. It was here that he gained a love for the outdoors that remained with him throughout his life. As a matter of record, he and his brother Thompson were considered the best fishermen of any who visited the streams in that neighborhood. "My mind was rather more taken up upon these subjects in my boyhood than it was in learning my books at school," he wrote, "for in those days parents did not feel the importance of looking after the education of their children any more than merely to send them to school, considering that the education of their children was wholly depending upon the school master."

Beyond his juvenile interests, Wilford's early life became a consuming quest for religion and meaning. As a child he witnessed a religious revival in the community, during which his stepmother, two brothers, and several other relatives professed religion. He too attended the meetings, prayed with the young people, "and tried to get religion. But it soon wore off from my mind," he later recalled.

At age fourteen, Wilford took up residence with a local farmer, attending school during the winter and working on the farm in the summer. With his friends he "attended enquiring meetings and prayer meetings among the Presbyterians; they being the only religious society in the town." He also attended Sunday School and diligently searched and prayed in an effort to obtain salvation, but something in the teaching and exhorting people to give their hearts to God, without telling them what to do or pointing out the way so they could understand, left an emptiness. The preaching, he remembered, "created darkness and not light, misery and not happiness and their teachings did not seem to enlighten my mind or do me good, although I laboured hard to obtain benefit from it." While others around him were professing religion, Wilford "did not wish to make a mock of those things, or profess to be converted and have religion unless I could be made sensible that I had received light and truth and something tangible that would be of benefit to me. I did pray and labor hard to obtain religion but did not feel that I obtained any special light, truth, or benefits in trying to follow the teachings given me at that time."

Three years later, Wilford's father made arrangements for the young man to attend school at West Hartford, doing chores for an acquaintance in exchange for room and board. Here Wilford suffered through the "distressing disease" of home-sickness, which eventually weaned him of his domestic attachment. At age twenty he began life on his own, leaving his father's home, never to return except for an occasional visit. As he pondered his situation, he saw the period of his existence between eighteen and twenty-five as the formative years of his character and felt that the principles and sentiments he attained during those years would control his destiny. He wrote:

I felt to say how cautious I ought to be how I pass this link in the chain of my existence. I felt that I needed caution, prudence, circumspection, and wisdom to guide my footsteps as I step forth to act for myself. I reflected upon the days of my youth which were gone and the speed of time which had flown like an arrow to return no more forever. While walking in a rapid stream we cannot tread twice in the same water, neither can we spend twice the same time; then how ought we to prize the golden moments of time and measure it out with our talents to the honor and glory of God and for the salvation of our souls so that when the Lord comes he may receive his own with usury. In trying to comprehend the fleetness of time I asked myself the question where is the old world? Where are the Prophets and Apostles? Where are the millions of the inhabitants of the earth, including my fathers and where are the days of my youth? Gone, gone, all gone, into the boundless ocean of Eternity where I shall soon find myself.

ABOUT THIS TIME Wilford took employment working on shares at his aunt Helen Wheeler's flour mill at East Avon, Connecticut. While there he befriended many of the prominent young men of the community and sought to satisfy his inner spiritual hunger in a social way. He occasionally mingled in parties and dances, and in several instances took a hand at the card table. Although he felt a hesitation to engage in such activities, his consolation was that his associates were the best young men of the community. But in all his seeking he came away empty. "I felt that the hand of the Lord was over me in this thing," he noted,

for whenever I . . . yielded to the enticement of my associates to stake any thing at the card table I had the good fortune in almost every instance to lose it . . . until I made a strong resolution that I would entirely forsake this vice . . . before I gained much of a taste or desire for it. . . . There was a spirit at work with me in all recreations—the card table, ball room, or any party of pleasure that drew my mind away. I took no pleasure in those things whatever my anticipations were. They all fled when I arrived at the spot. I seemed to be as a speckled bird in the midst of my associates. They all seemed to enjoy themselves except me.

Finally, unable to find satisfaction in his social contacts and desirous of not wasting the leisure hours available to him each day, Wilford turned to reading and study, a discipline that had eluded him during his early years. But what should he read? He did not like to read novels, "because it was a fiction and did not store the mind with truth or knowledge." Then one day he came across the statement "He that will spend his life in that manner which is most excellent will find that custom will render it most delightsome." These words made a strong impression upon his mind, he recalled:

I soon found I gained a taste for reading history. I obtained an interest in it which grew upon me. While perusing history we hold converse with men of judgment, wisdom, and knowledge; and by pursuing this course we can lay up an extensive fund of valuable information. I commenced by reading the history of the United States, of England, Scotland, Greece, Rome, Rollins's Ancient History, Josephus, and others which I took much interest in. And finally I took hold of the Bible for history, and I never have found as interesting a history as the Bible.

At this time, Wilford found his only consolation in the Bible, and he became a keen student of its precepts. As he surveyed the various denominations in his searching for the meaning of existence, he measured all that he heard and saw by the standard of the divine word of scripture.

Wilford managed his aunt's flour mill in East Avon for three years, all the while continuing to wrestle with his feelings and ponder the complexities of life. He observed another religious revival, listened to the preachings of the ministers, and attended the gatherings of the people. "But the teachings and principles were not such as I believed in or such as I believed should belong to the Church of Christ." Up to this time (age twenty-three), he saw his existence as "a little like a ship tossed upon the waves of the sea, up and down, unstable and unsettled." At times he had tried to worship the Lord and live a Christian life and at other times he had sought pleasure "in the things of the world." He continued:

I sensibly realized and deeply felt that my youth had gone to return no more forever to me, and I felt that I had spent a good deal of my time in a manner that was not profitable to me, not that I had been guilty of committing any heinous or outbreaking sins such as murder, theft, adultery, fornication or blasphemies, yet I had spent a good deal of my youth in vanity and folly giving way at times to many idle words and vain and foolish recreations which did not store my mind with knowledge or produce any profitable fruit. At this time I reflected deeply upon the past and I became thoroughly convinced that there was no real peace or enjoyment in any thing except the service of God or in those things, which the Lord would approbate.

Continuing his quest, Wilford resolved to diligently seek the Lord, follow the dictates of the Holy Spirit, "and do the will of God as far as I could learn it." On May 14, 1830, he took employment in the flour mill of Samuel Collins at Collinsville, Connecticut. When he found that most of the thirty men he boarded with were "of a vain worldly turn of mind," he withdrew from the boardinghouse and cloistered himself in a private home. About this time a reformation among the Methodists at Farmington attracted his brother Asahel. Wilford also attended the meetings. He reflected,

I had a great desire to do the will of God and to know what to do to be saved. I prayed night and day as I had an opportunity, and the Lord blessed me with much of his Holy Spirit and I was happy. All things to me seemed to praise the Lord — the sun, moon and stars, sky, air land and water, mountains hills rocks and dales, forests groves meadows & grain — all things seemed to praise the Lord. It began to me to be the happiest period of my life. I had often heard those feelings expressed by individuals but to me it was a blind story until now. . . . These feelings is enjoyed more or less at times by all who are governed and controlled by the Holy Spirit. I felt to resolve more and more that I would spend my whole life in the service of the Lord.

My work was very light in the mill and I had much leisure time for reading, meditation and prayer, and I began to read the Bible with a more prayerful attention than ever before in my life and I found it to be a new book to me. It contained truths of the most glorious and sublime nature. If I wish[ed] for history I could find it there. If I was cast down or tried or tempted I there found a remedy in connection with the spirit of God. . . . The more I prayed and searched the word of God the more I felt my own weakness and dependence upon the Lord. I felt to pray that the Lord would enlighten my mind, enlarge my heart and give me wisdom and understanding.

Not far from the mill where Wilford worked was an island surrounded by a rapid stream of water. The banks were "thickly studded with tall waving pines," he remembered, but inland from its shore was "an open level field covered with wild flowers of various kinds." This isolated retreat became his personal cathedral:

> I chose this island day and night as my place of retirement for prayer, praise and meditation before the Lord. I spent many a midnight hour alone upon that island in prayer before the Lord and the many happy hours in sweet meditation which I spent in my lonely walks upon that pleasant retreat I shall never forget.
>
> The roaring waters, the waving pines, giving room to the passing winds, the field of flowers crusted with the silver rays of the moon, being all open to the eye and ear while the curtain of heaven decked with the stars and moon mingling with the survey. These things resting upon my mind as the handy work of God in connection with prayer and meditation accompanied by the Holy Spirit gave unto me a peculiar charm, sensation, joy, and happiness which I had never before enjoyed and experienced in my life.

Because of his searching of the Bible and meditation, Wilford felt the need to attend to certain requirements of the gospel, and he sought for someone like the prophets of old who could administer them. He turned to a local Baptist priest, a Mr. Phippen, from whom he requested answers to three pressing issues: the absence of spiritual gifts that had been in the ancient church, the correct day for Sabbath observance, and the importance of baptism. On the subject of spiritual gifts, Wilford wrote Mr. Phippen:

> . . . while perusing the sacred volume of inspiration I find many wonderful works were performed by our Savior and likewise by the apostles . . . and if I mistake not when Christ first sent his disciples to preach the gospel . . . he commanded them to heal the sick, cleanse the lepers, raise the dead, cast out devils. . . . Again in the last chapter of S[aint] Mark Christ appeared to the eleven as they sat at meat and gave them a many forcible command to go into all the world and preach the gospel to every creature. He that believeth and is baptized shall be saved and he that believeth not shall be damned and these signs shall follow them that believe. . . . This apparently was the last command given by our Saviour before he ascended to heaven. Now the question that arises in my mind is when and where were those gifts done away . . . ? I find no scripture satisfactory to prove that they ever were done away. Therefore I am led to believe that God is the same today as in ancient days, and likewise should people at this day live as did the apostles and exercise the faith that did Abraham in offering up his son Isaac, that these gifts

might again be on the earth, and in case of sickness we might look to the Lord for deliverance in preference of trusting to an arm of flesh.

With respect to the Sabbath day, Wilford continued his letter:

. . . we almost universally regard the first day of the week as the Sabbath, but when God appeared to Moses on the mount he commanded him to keep the seventh day as the sabbath and not to labor on that day, so it appears that if there has not been a change of the sabbath we as a body are not keeping the day that we were commanded to keep. . . .

Finally, he turned to baptism, a subject "that has long lain with weight on my mind":

I think it not only our duty but our highest privilege to take the word of God and make it the man of our counsel and form our principles thereby. . . . I for one consider myself transacting business for eternity and I believe that Jesus Christ set the example for the pilgrim to follow and I believe that the Christian ought to strive to imitate his example as near as possible . . . I at times have been almost overwhelmed in astonishment while meditating upon the difference[s] of opinion and principle that exist in our land upon religious subjects when we have all the same bible to read . . . but more especially upon the subject of baptism. . . . I had the ordinance of infant baptism administered to me but it does not answer my mind for I have not found any scripture to support it from Genesis to revelation and if I may be allowed to use the expression it has been a mystery to me how so many great divines that have been so long taking up the light of the gospel and still continue in so gross an error with respect to baptism. For if I am not greatly mistaken I find no account of John or any of the apostles administering the ordinance of baptism until they become believers in Christ . . . and respecting the mode of baptism it appears plain to me that there is no room for one moment to doubt but that our Saviour was buried in baptism in the river Jordan, and that all that the apostles baptised was buried with Christ. . . . And setting aside every other example but the one that Christ left us, that alone ought to be sufficient to convince mankind that immersion was the right and only mode of baptism.

Then came the main point of Wilford's inquiry. Convinced that immersion was the correct mode of baptism and believing it essential to his "prosperity and happiness," he asked the Reverend Phippen if it would be against his principles and discipline to baptize someone without their joining the Baptist church, "for I at present am not prepared to join with any Church. Still I feel it my duty to be baptised." At first, Mr. Phippen refused to separate the baptismal ordinance from Church membership, arguing that it was "against the rules." But after repeated urgings, he relented to his persistent inquirer.

So on March 5, 1831, the Reverend Phippen preached a discourse on the subject of baptism, then went into Farmington River and baptized Wilford Woodruff and his brother Asahel, as a large congregation looked on. "We went on our way rejoicing thinking we had done the will of God. . . . hands was not laid upon me for the Holy Ghost for it was not practiced but I had peace of mind because I acted up to the best light I had at the time," Wilford later reflected.

SHORTLY AFTER HIS BAPTISM, Wilford began working at the flour mill of Richard B. Cowles in New Hartford, Connecticut. While there he attended meetings of the different churches in the area and gained two friends — kindred spirits in the search for religious understanding. "We visited each other much and prayed together often and spent many a good hour together in prayer and conversing upon the things of God." Of this time Wilford noted,

I did not join any church but I gave myself constantly to prayer, reading the Bible, and meditation and I called upon the Lord earnestly to lead and guide me. I spent many hours in the woods among the rocks and in the mill at midnight calling upon the Lord to teach me what to do. I finally made the following prayer and petition unto the Lord with a determination to ask until I obtained an answer. "O Lord are the priests and people who profess thy name and who appear zealous in thy cause by holding many meetings and call[ing] upon thy name with a loud voice and who labour hard to make many proselytes, are they thy people? Are they and their works accepted at thine hand? If so O Lord why am I separated from them in spirit? Why cannot I feel at home with them and worship with them? Why am I left alone like a speckled bird of the forest? Why do they oppose me in those things which the spirit and word of God teach me is true? And again if they are not the people of God and are not accepted of thee why do they prosper? Why do they gather many souls unto their churches who appear sincere? And if they are not the people of the Lord where shall I find thy people? O Lord, show me these things and teach me what to do and I covenant to obey thy voice and do thy will."

While praying earnestly in his mill one night, imploring God for an answer to his prayer, Wilford felt prompted to go to the Bible. He opened the book randomly, "praying the Lord in my heart to direct my mind to that portion of his word which would answer my prayer and show me the truth." His eyes settled upon the 56th chapter of Isaiah, which he became satisfied was the answer he sought; he believed that "the salvation of God was about to be revealed," and that he should "live to see the people of God gathered, and . . . should be with them and . . . should have a name and a place in the House of God with his sons and daughters."

During the spring of 1832, while working at the Cowles mill, Wilford wrote his brother Asahel:

I am resolved by the grace of God assisting me that neither things present nor things to come, heights nor depths, riches nor favours Presbyterians nor Methodists, male nor female, shall be able to hinder my obeying the calls of God or keeping his commands as far as I think it be my duty. I have too long been a slothful and unworthy servant. I have too long conferred with flesh and blood. I almost wonder that I am a spared monument of the mercy of God. But he is good to me far above my desserts. I am determined to serve him more faithful the remainder of my days.

A short time later, Wilford saw a newspaper reference to "a new sect," professing to be a restoration of the ancient gifts of the gospel. Within two years he had moved to New York with his brother Azmon, bought a farm, and cast his lot with the new religion, convinced that it was the answer to his years of searching. Wilford was baptized by Latter-day Saint missionaries on the last day of December 1833. At one moment his mind had been "flushed with the idea of accumulating something of this world's goods that [he] might enjoy the society of [his] parents in their decline of life with other friends." Then suddenly the scene had changed. He had found the answers he had searched for for so long, and he was called to forsake parents, brethren, sisters, houses, and lands, "to assist in pruning the vineyard for the last time . . . to visit foreign climes and the islands of sea," and to endure the perils of "an indignant wicked generation" for what he regarded as "the testimony of Jesus Christ."

Less than four months after his baptism, Wilford met Joseph Smith, whom he soon regarded as much a prophet as any about whom he had read in his study of the Bible. He reflected upon the meeting in his personal writings:

> My first introduction to him . . . might have been calculated to have tried the feelings and faith of some men who had formed in their own mind how a Prophet would look and act. For when I first saw him and his brother they were shooting at a mark with a brace of pistols. When they stopped shooting I was introduced to them. Brother Joseph shook hands heartily with me and invited me to go to his house and make his habitation my home while I stayed in Kirtland. I gladly accepted the invitation and went home. In a few moments he brought into the room a wolf skin and said come Brother Woodruff, I want you to help me tan this wolf skin as I want to put it on my seat while I go my journey to the west. So I pulled off my coat, rolled up my sleeves, and went at it and soon tanned it over a chair post. While employed at this I smiled at the appearance of my first labour with the Prophet.

The following Sunday Wilford heard the Prophet preach, and he confided in his diary that "there was more light, knowledge, truth and good sense made manifest in this meeting respecting the gospel and kingdom of God than I had ever received from the whole sectarian world during my life. I rejoiced much in being made acquainted with a Prophet of God and the Saints of God. I felt that it was a fulfillment of the promises of God to me in former days. It was what my soul had desired for many years. And I had now found the people, Church, and Kingdom of God, and I was satisfied."

Once baptized by Mormon missionaries, Wilford never looked back, nor did he waver in his commitment. "I feel like living my religion and dying for it if necessary," was his conviction. "Life is of no value to me at the sacrifice of salvation and the favor of God in the eternal world. I know the cause that we are engaged in is good." His faith was such that he

saw the hand of God in everything from a stormy ocean crossing to the darkest hours of the government crusade against
polygamy. To him the events of the earth were of cosmic
importance, and he was glad to be a participant in them.

THE MISSIONARY JOURNEYS of Wilford Woodruff are reminiscent of the travels of the Apostle Paul. Having a great desire
to preach the gospel, but reticent to make his wants known
to his associates, he retired into the woods alone one Sunday
evening and petitioned the Lord in earnest prayer to open the
way for the desire of his heart. "I arose from my knees happy,
and walked some forty rods and met Elias Higbee, a High
Priest, with whom I had stayed a number of months. As I
approached him, he said 'Br. Wilford, the Spirit of the Lord
tells me that you should be ordained and go on a mission.' I
replied, 'I am ready.' " This incident was the beginning of a
long missionary career. A short time later he was among the
first to take the message of the restoration into the Southern
States, proselyting in Arkansas, Tennessee, and Kentucky in
1835-36. While there he established several branches of the
Church and organized the first company of Saints to emigrate
from the South to the body of the Church in Missouri.

In 1837 he traveled to the Fox Islands, off the coast of
Maine, becoming one of the first to introduce Mormonism
upon the islands of the sea. His mission there ended with news
that he had been named to the Quorum of Twelve Apostles,
whereupon he led a company of fifty-three converts in ten
wagons nearly two thousand miles from Maine to western
Illinois. During this trip his wife, Phebe, a native of Maine
whom he had married in Kirtland shortly before embarking
on his mission, nearly died of "brain fever." Her life was spared
through her husband's faith and prayers.

Elder Woodruff was among those who introduced Mormonism in England. He traveled there twice, first with other
members of the Twelve in 1839, and then as president of the
mission in 1844. During his first mission he witnessed a veritable pentecost when some eighteen hundred people, includ-

ing two hundred ministers, followed him to the waters of baptism. A young investigator, Mary Ann Weston, told of his coming to her house in Worcestershire: "He sat by the fire and soon commenced singing . . . . Br. Jenkins had told us that he had left his home in America crossed the sea and come to preach this gospel to the people in England. While he was singing I looked at him. He looked so peaceful and happy I thought he must be a good man and the gospel he preached must be true." A short time later, because of the persecution that was raging against him, Wilford baptized Mary and two others at midnight in a pond in the center of the village.

During this mission, antagonism seemed to grow in proportion to his success. After preaching to a "vast mass of human beings" in April 1840, Elder Woodruff was petitioned by many of his listeners for baptism, but this was prevented by a large, unruly crowd of antagonists. Some, however, insisted upon baptism in spite of the persecution and the late hour. Thus, Wilford went into the water about midnight surrounded by a "desperate mob" and commenced baptizing amid a shower of stones. One rock hit him on the head and nearly knocked him senseless, but he was able to complete the baptisms.

Like Paul, Wilford Woodruff attested to the administration of angels. While proselyting in the Southern States in 1835, one evening he went into a small back room of the place where he was staying in Kentucky, and during his contemplations he was "overwhelmed with joy" at the appearance of a heavenly messenger. The heavenly visitor unfolded a marvelous panorama before him. "He told me he wanted me to see with my eyes and understand with my mind what was coming to pass in the earth before the coming of the Son of Man," he later wrote.

In London one night, while meditating upon the things of God and after determining to carry the gospel to the people of that city, "a person appeared unto me which I considered was the Prince of Darkness or the Devil. He made war with me and attempted to take my life. He caught me by the throat and choked me nearly to death. . . . As he was about to overcome me I prayed to the father in the name of Jesus for help. I then had power over him and he left me though much wounded. Three personages dressed in white came to me and prayed with me and I was immediately healed and delivered from all my troubles."

On numerous occasions Elder Woodruff attributed the preservation of his life to a kind Providence and his heeding the promptings of the Holy Spirit. One time as he was about to board a river steamer at Pittsburgh with a hundred Latter-day Saints en route to the West, he was suddenly impressed to withdraw his passage with that particular steamer. The ship started out. "It was a dark night, and before the steamer had gone far she took fire, and all on board was lost. We should probably have shared the same fate, had it not been for that monitor within me."

Another time, en route to the East with his family, he drove his carriage into a dooryard, tied his mules to an oak tree, and had just retired for the night when "the Holy Spirit told me to get up and move my carriage. I got right up. My wife asked me what I was going to do. I said I was going to move the carriage. She wanted to know what for. I told her I did not know. I moved the carriage about fifteen rods, looked around, and then went to bed again. The Spirit told me to get up again and move my mules. I did so. In twenty minutes there came up a whirlwind that blew that oak tree down and laid it right across where my carriage had been."

Repeatedly throughout his life Elder Woodruff was, as he described it, miraculously preserved from accidents in which he nearly lost his life. "It seemed as though some invisible power or fate was watching my foot steps in order to find some opportunity to take my life." These occurrences were so frequent and of such a profound nature to him that he devoted a chapter of his autobiography to the subject. On several occasions he had broken bones in his arms and legs. He split his foot with an ax; was bitten by a mad dog in the last stage of hydrophobia; was battered by falling trees; nearly died of blood poisoning when he accidentally inoculated his arm while skinning an ox that had died from poison; survived the wreck of a train going full speed; was nearly drowned, frozen, and scalded; and suffered several forms of severe illness, any one of which could have taken his life.

He ultimately explained his preservation as a divine sanction upon his record keeping: "I know ever since I was born the devil has tried to kill me. . . . I have wondered why it was the devil was after me all my life, and why he hadn't killed me. I have prayed over it. . . . The only answer I could ever get, in the world, was: 'The devil knew you would write, if you lived'—and I guess he did." Yet, in spite of the physical beating he took during his lifetime, his body was strong and sound, allowing him to endure hard physical strain. On many occasions during his travels he walked forty or fifty miles, and once, sixty miles in one day.

WILFORD WOODRUFF REJOICED in the spiritual gifts he had so earnestly sought before his conversion. On many occasions he saw the sick healed under his touch. Shortly after he arrived in Manchester during his first mission to Great Britain, he was called with his companion to visit three sick people "and administer to them according to the order of the gospel"; one of them presented a "very distressing" case. "We found the Sister possessed of the Devil and a burning fever. . . . She was raging and trying to tear herself, although in the hands of three or four men. We laid hands upon her and commanded the devil to depart, and the fever to stand rebuked in the name of Jesus Christ and it was done, though not without a great struggle, and we left her calm in her mind and principly delivered of her pain."

During his mission in the South, while traveling on horseback in a wilderness during a heavy rainstorm amid rising creeks and fallen timber, he and his companions were suddenly surprised by an inexplicable bright light that saved them from falling into a precipice and illuminated their way to a friendly house.

Beyond this, Wilford Woodruff's experience was diverse and expansive. His travels, which he calculated at more than 175,000 miles, took him to Great Britain, Canada, and twenty-three of the United States. He crossed the Atlantic Ocean four times; participated in the march of Zion's Camp in 1834; and was a member of the pioneer company that arrived in Salt Lake Valley in 1847. His labors for church and community were varied. He assisted in the publication of the *Times and Seasons*, and *Nauvoo Neighbor* in Illinois, and the *Millennial Star*, and Doctrine and Covenants in England. He was a member of the city council in Nauvoo, Illinois, and chaplain of the Nauvoo Legion. He sat with the Utah Territorial Legislature twenty-two years and the Territorial Council twenty-one. He served on the board of directors of Zion's Co-operative Mercantile Institution (ZCMI); was a member of the Council of Fifty; was foreman of a Salt Lake City grand jury in 1867; served as president of the Cooperative Stock Company Association; was president of the Universal Scientific Society; and was chairman of the Medical Board of Examiners. He was the clerk and historian of the Council of Twelve, and Church Historian for more than thirty years. He also directed the completion of the Salt Lake Temple and presided at its dedication in 1893.

A CAREFUL OBSERVER of the drama in which he participated, Elder Woodruff kept a diary where he wrote his thoughts, feelings, and observations with candor and dedication. He commenced his journal writing shortly after his conversion, and his prose reveals a man of faith and commitment. It was said of him that he was "not a very humorous man and always too hard at work and too serious to notice jokes or silly things." His writings and discourses reflect a certain mildness and solemnity. But while his speech was generally sober, it contained food for thought. On one occasion when several sacks of grain were stolen from his premises, he stood up in the Tabernacle the next Sunday, announced the theft, and told his listeners that if the thieves "would ask a blessing on the food when they made the flour into bread," and return his empty grain sacks, he would forgive them. The next morning he found the sacks on his doorstep.

Wilford Woodruff's life spanned practically the entire nineteenth-century years of Mormonism and reveals a wide range of experience. At one end of the spectrum, one finds an industrious man who loved the outdoors and procured his living by hard manual labor; at the other was a thoughtful, contemplative man with deep sensitivity for spiritual things.

Wherever he settled, he was engaged in tilling, planting, and harvesting to support his family. "I spent the day . . . setting out strawberries and getting out manure and sawing wood." "I spent the day at the farm shucking corn." "I set out $24 worth of trees shrubbery strawberries &c. I was very weary come night."

While these references are typical of his domestic labor, Wilford was more than an average farmer. On his Salt Lake City land which consisted of a farm, garden, orchard, and herds of cattle and sheep, he developed skill in cultivating and improving a variety of vegetables, nuts, and fruits. During the beginning years of the settlement of the Great Basin, he lectured his brethren one time "on the propriety of introducing the diascorea batatas or chinese potatoe." For fourteen years he presided over the Deseret Agricultural and Manufacturing Society, which sponsored the annual territorial fair, and in 1855 he was appointed president of the Utah Territorial Horticultural Society.

He exchanged information and samples with horticulturists in the United States and Europe, seeking to improve a species of tree or crop and to develop plants best suited to the arid climate and conditions in the Great Basin. In 1857 he wrote his brother Thompson that he had successfully grafted and budded seventeen different kinds of apples that he had received from the eastern states and California. To a gentleman in New York he sent a variety of insects, including a tarantula, scorpions, and grasshoppers. He corresponded with William Hooker, director of the Royal Gardens in London, and on one occasion he sent Mr. Hooker seed of the "wild Utah mountain currant," the "Utah sarvice berry," and samples of the mesquite bush found in southern Utah.

In 1861 he wrote a cousin in Connecticut that his land produced "all that I need of this worlds goods to make me and my family comfortable. . . . I have one acre of orchard and vineyard by my residence here in Salt Lake City that will yield me $1000 dollars worth of fruit annually with a fair season, besides what we want to use in the family. I have a farm that produces 40 bushels of wheat to the acre upon an average and the best wheat I ever saw in my life. I never saw such vegetables in any country as these we raise here, on an average 300 bushels potatoes, 600 of Beets, & 1000 of carrots to the acre. . . . This sounds like a great story in Connecticut, but not here. . . ." In 1860 Woodruff informed his brother Ilus that he had produced 1500 gallons of syrup from his three acres of sugar cane.

Products from his soil repeatedly won awards at the territorial fair. In 1860 he received first prize for the best fenced and cultivated farm of not less than twenty acres; best fenced and cultivated garden; best acre of sugar cane; best three acres of squash; the best six acres of sugar beets; best bush beans; best three cantaloupe; best apples; and best grapes. He took second prize in competition of wooled French Merino buck sheep and watermelon.

Throughout his life Wilford Woodruff was known as a hard worker; he continued tilling the soil, when not absent on church assignments, until he was almost ninety. A man who, in the prime of his youth, labored with him in harvesting potatoes and binding wheat and oats, wrote that although Wilford Woodruff was fifty years his senior, he was "too many for me in a hard days work." Another acquaintance wrote of him:

I have seen him feed a threshing machine with bundles from a stack, when three ordinary men complained of the task. He was never particular where he worked, usually he got in the most disagreeable place about a thresher in order to favor those with whom he worked. When he might have chosen his place, he went to the chaff-pen where the smut and dirt were almost unbearable. I never knew a harder worker than Wilford Woodruff.

At one time as Elder Woodruff prepared to embark on a new church assignment, his thirteen-year-old daughter expressed relief that "the president has appointed you to go on a mission so that you will not have to work so hard as you have done."

Elder Woodruff was an experienced outdoorsman in other ways besides farming. He enjoyed fishing from the early days at his father's Connecticut millpond until his later years in the Great Basin, and he excelled in that sport. Writing to the editor of *Forest and Stream* magazine in August 1892, shortly after returning from a fishing and hunting trip to the headwaters of the Weber River in Utah's Uintah Mountains, he reflected upon the wildlife population of pioneer Utah and related an incident from his own experience. He told of catching twenty trout, four of which weighed over four pounds each, in four hours with a rod and reel, and losing one ten-pounder because the perpendicular bank prevented him from landing it.

While on the underground in southern Utah during the height of the antipolygamy campaign in the 1880s, Elder Woodruff caught fifty trout, some of which weighed two pounds, in Pine Valley after a forty-mile hike over a "very rough rocky road," and in a place where it had been supposed there were no trout larger than four ounces. "The brush caught my line several times and 3 times [I] got the hook into my hand. I had to cut it out twice with a jack knife out of the ball of my thumb and out of one finger. I found it hurt to cut into the flesh with a knife. But we have to endure such things or not ketch fish."

Periodically throughout his writings the reader finds references to hunting and fishing. One December day in 1867 he went shooting ducks with friends near the mouth of the Jordan River. He carefully recorded the event in his diary:

We rowed our boats into the rushes where we could hide ourselves and as the ducks would fly over or around us we would shoot them on the wing. We stayed till dark then rowed back to our wagon, drew our boats up on to dry land, made up a fire, cooked a duck pot pie, eat our supper, made our beds in the boat and slept all night. The wind blew very hard. We got up before daylight . . . and took our boats and went back to our shooting place. On the way down a flock of geese came over us. I shot into the flock and hit them but the shot was too fine to kill them. The wind blew very hard most of the forenoon. We shot till the middle of the afternoon then we . . . loaded our boats in to the wagon and returned home. . . . We counted our game and found we had 40 ducks and 3 geese.

A MAN OF HUMILITY, Wilford Woodruff became president of The Church of Jesus Christ of Latter-day Saints at general conference in April 1889, in his eighty-third year. Upon hearing of the death of his predecessor, John Taylor, he was awed by the responsibility he then faced. He wrote:

This places me in a very peculiar situation, a position I have never looked for during my life, but in the providence of God it is laid upon me. And I pray God my Heavenly Father to give me grace equal to my day. It is a high and responsible position for any man to occupy and a position that needs great wisdom. I never expected to outlive President Taylor . . . but it has . . . come to pass and I can only say marvelous are thy ways O Lord God Almighty. For thou hast certainly chosen the weak things of this world to perform thy work on the earth. May thy servant Wilford be prepared for whatever awaits him on earth and have power to perform whatever is required at his hands by the God of Heaven. I ask this blessing of my Heavenly Father in the Name of Jesus Christ the Son of the Living God.

Wilford Woodruff's ascendance to the presiding office of the Church came at a crucial time in its history. He had been in hiding on the underground, to avoid imprisonment under the provisions of federal antipolygamy legislation, when word came of President Taylor's death. During these years he had spent much of his time away from his family in southern Utah and Arizona, as his letters, signed "Lewis Allen," attest.

By the summer of 1890 federal antipolygamy legislation had almost totally restricted the effectiveness of the Church in its mission. For weeks President Woodruff "wrestled mightily with the Lord." Finally, on September 25, 1890, he issued his now-famous Manifesto, which brought an end to the practice of plural marriage. On the eve of that event he wrote in his diary, "I have arrived at a point in the history of my life as the president of the Church . . . where I am under the necessity of acting for the temporal salvation of the Church."

But the trials of the aging prophet did not end with the

Manifesto. The financial burden incurred by the polygamy crusade, the completion of the Salt Lake Temple, the demands of Church education, increased welfare expenditures due to the 1893 depression, and costs of funding local industries— these all placed the Church in what seemed like a hopeless situation. To a friend in St. George in 1893, President Woodruff noted that he had been busy meeting with presidents of stakes in contemplation of asking the Saints to lend the Church from one to a thousand dollars for a year, "to help us pay the debts of the Church which are now due which we cannot pay, for we cannot collect what is due us. The U.S. has taken $1,000,000 of our real estate, $500,000 of our money, we have had to back up the sugar factory which cost $600,000 and owes $300,000. . . . We have had to help so many things and times so hard to collect anything the Church today cannot pay its notes. . . . Now if you or any one else can help us to any money let us know. . . . It is getting close times with us at present. . . . I never saw a day in my life when I was so overwhelmed in business care and responsibility as I am today. . . ." A year later he wrote, "We are passing through a great financial diffi-culty, the Lord alone can help us out. . . . Our debts are very heavy . . . money matters are crowding hard upon us."

Although over ninety years of age, President Woodruff noted to a friend that he was at his office every morning of the week, "crowded all day in meeting & councils until my brain aches." He added that he had been ill for a year, suffering from insomnia and asthma, during which time he had hardly slept two hours a night, "so I set up to my table nearly all night and read books and papers because I cannot sleep."

Besides his church calling and labors, which took him away from home much of the time, Wilford Woodruff raised a large family. He lived during the years when the practice of plural marriage was an authorized institution of the Church, and his family consisted of five wives and thirty-three children. Nor was he immune from the heartaches and frailties of domestic life. One marriage ended in divorce, and another wife and fourteen of his children preceded him in death.

President Woodruff's writings to his family reveal the anxiety and concern he had for them during the months and years he was absent from home in church service. "I prize the love of my family and want to do what I can to make them comfortable but being called of God and the president of the Church to officiate in the spiritual things of the Kingdom it of course deprives me of laboring all the time for my family and spending my time with them." To a nine-year-old daughter, he wrote from St. George where he was engaged in the work of the temple in 1877: "I hear a very bad report of many young people in Salt Lake City. I hope my boys and girls will be good. I shall feel very bad to have them do wrong, to swear, steal, and become wicked." He expressed his philosophy of family life to a nineteen-year-old daughter a few years before his death: "We are expecting to live together forever after death. I think we all as parents and children ought to take all the pains we can to make each other happy as long as we live that we may have nothing to regret."

President Woodruff's family provided his greatest comfort. He was overjoyed upon returning to his ancestral home in Connecticut a few years after joining the Church; there he was successful in baptizing his father, his stepmother, his half-sister, and several other relatives. Like the ancient patriarchs, he felt it part of his covenant with God to preserve and unite his family, whether in life or death, "that when the trump shall sound and the graves be opened that they may have the privilege of first striking hands with their fathers and their children." From Nauvoo Wilford urged his father to come west: "I do not know that you have any son that will render you assistance should you need it, in the decline of life without I do it myself and . . . I have no desire to be liberated from the obligation which the Law of God, of nature, and of reason hath laid upon me towards my fathers." He subsequently brought his father to the Salt Lake Valley, and throughout his life he maintained correspondence with other relatives in the East.

A crowning point of President Woodruff's life was the work he performed in the St. George Temple for many of his relatives who had passed on. "Through the blessings of God I have been enabled in connection with my family of being baptized for about 3000 of my dead relatives and also through the assistance of friends I have been enabled to get endowments in the Temple . . . for about 2500 of my relatives."

AN IMPORTANT PART OF THE LEGACY of Wilford Woodruff was the diary he kept during his lifetime. The significance of his writing lies in his having preserved important historical data at a time when that function of the Church was in its formative years. Although the members' consciousness of record keeping commenced with an 1830 revelation, the record-keeping process developed slowly because of limiting obstacles. In reconstructing and interpreting events of the early decades of Latter-day Saint history, the Woodruff diary has supplied information recorded nowhere else. President Woodruff regarded his "journalizing" almost as a religious sacrament that occupied all of his free time. He explained:

I have been inspired and moved upon to keep a Journal and write the affairs of this Church as far as I can. . . . You may say that this is a great deal of trouble. Very well it has been. . . . It has occupied nearly every leisure moment of my time. . . . But what of it? I have never spent any of my time more profitably for the benefit of mankind than in my journal writing, for a great portion of the Church History has been compiled from my journals and some of the most glorious Gospel sermons, truths, and revelations that were given from God to this people through the mouth of the Prophets Joseph, Brigham, Heber, and the Twelve could not be found upon the earth on record only in my Journals.

In 1861, in a letter to an uncle, he explained his record keeping as a gift from God:

I write all my daily journals in this hand and I do all my reporting in phonography [shorthand]. I have reported more sermons and done more journal writing than any man in the Church, and a great deal of the Church History is made from my journal. I have kept a daily journal for twenty-five years and I have recorded in my journal many of the sermons and teachings that I have heard Joseph Smith the Prophet and Brigham Young [deliver], and it has been a gift bestowed upon me that I could hear half a dozen sermons delivered in succession and go to my office and sit down next day and write most of them sentence by sentence as they were delivered, and it is in consequence of this gift that I have been employed as the Assistant Historian of the Church. I have a great anxiety to preserve the History of the Church & Kingdom of God established upon the earth in the last dispensation and fulness of times for it is destined to become a mountain and fill the whole earth as Daniel saw it.

For Wilford Woodruff, the responsibility for writing a diary was inherent in his ordination to the priesthood. And although some of his colleagues in the Quorum of the Twelve considered him "rather enthusiastic" on the subject, he could point to Joseph Smith for his precedent: "When the Prophet Joseph organized the Quorum of Twelve he commanded them to write and keep a Journal of History of their lives and gave his reasons why they should do it." President Woodruff felt that "when men are called to stand at the head of a great dispensation like this and to build up the kingdom of God on the earth . . . they of all men on earth ought to compile a true and correct history of the rise and progress of that kingdom." Yet he saw his literary output as "only a limited account of the labors of one man out of thirty Apostles, one hundred and fifty Patriarchs, some five hundred High Priests, five thousand Seventies, and twenty thousand Elders, besides the Lesser Priesthood, and two hundred thousand members of the Church."

President Woodruff regarded his journals as more than a personal record. Following a forty-four-year synopsis of his labor in the ministry, he wrote that if a future historian wished to record or publish his synopsis, it would be necessary to blend his 1879 summary with the one of 1880. And in his will, he designated that his journals be filed in the Church Historian's Office "for the benefit of the History of the Church," and also that his family have "free access" to them in case his heirs should wish to publish a biography of his life. After marking another anniversary as a diarist, he implored God "that the many hours and days which I have spent in this way may prove a blessing to future generations."

Wilford Woodruff's devotion as a chronicler brought his colleagues to his door to seek his service. Following the death of Joseph Smith, Brigham Young encouraged Wilford to "keep an account of things" as he would "look to me for his journal some day." In 1852 he was appointed clerk and historian of the Twelve Apostles. Beginning in 1856 he commenced thirty-three years of service as Church Historian. After nearly a half century he wrote confidently of his efforts: "I will here say God has inspired me to keep a Journal and History of this Church and I warn the future Historians to give credence to my History of this Church and kingdom for my testimony is true, and the truth of its record will be manifest in the world to come."

Among those who have served Mormon history, none have exceeded Wilford as an advocate of record keeping. He told a company of missionaries in 1856:

> We are not apt to think of the importance of events as they transpire with us but we feel the importance of them afterward. We are living in one of the most important generations that man ever lived on earth and we should write an account of those important transactions which are taking place before our eyes in fulfillment of the prophecies and the revelation of God. There is a great flood of revelations fulfilling in our day and as they are transpiring before our eyes we want a record made of them. . . . If there was no other motive in view only to have the privilege of reading over our journals and for our children to read it would pay for the time spent in writing it.

In addition to his public exhortations on record keeping, President Woodruff urged his family to write their daily experience. During an extended absence from home in 1885, he directed one letter to a ten-year-old daughter: "You are old enough to begin to keep a journal. It will be very interesting to your grandchildren to read what their grand mother done when she was a little girl . . . now begin while you are young and you will make a very interesting History by the time you are 50 years Old."

The Woodruff diary is but a portion of his total literary output. Besides his diaries and autobiographical writings, he kept careful records of personal and family finances and was engaged in extensive correspondence that, if measurable, would probably exceed his journal keeping in volume. By his own calculations, he wrote some twelve thousand letters during his lifetime. In numerous observable instances he not only wrote the original, but also retained a longhand copy for his file.

Something of the Woodruff literary tenacity is seen in an incident that occurred in 1879, while he was living in the remote wilderness of Arizona, 165 miles from a post office. After an absence from his place of residence for a few days, he returned to find forty-one letters and two months of newspapers. Persuading the mail carrier to wait for him to read and answer his correspondence, he embarked on a writing marathon during which he produced thirty-six letters in three days and nights of almost uninterrupted writing, "until my hand and arm became numb and brain ceased to act," and he was forced to stay in bed in great pain for four days with what he called bilious cramps. "I had 10 turns during the night of cramp of the stomach and vitals, the last one at day light. It entirely took away my breath. My friends thought I was dead and [I was] only restored by the administration of the Elders. I could not have lived through another turn. For 48 hours I could no more stand on my feet than a new born infant."

Wilford Woodruff launched his diary keeping when he began his proselyting mission to the Southern States in January 1835. References to writing letters, studying English grammar, journalizing, and copying his journal are found throughout his writings. By 1835 he had become skilled enough in Taylor shorthand to add this cryptic element to an occasional diary entry, complicating an already difficult process of deciphering his handwriting, especially the cursive. It was said that he vied with Horace Greeley for illegibility of handwriting. And his brother Ozem, who himself excused poor writing because he had no thumb with which to steady his pen, pled with Wilford in 1857 "to write a little more plain," as it took "some time" to read his letters. Recognizing the problem of his cursive, Wilford printed by hand most of his journal entries.

For Wilford Woodruff, his writing was as necessary as his life. His perception of Joseph Smith and the Prophet's mission brought significance to every aspect of living.

"When in the course of human events has there ever been a more important period than at the present day and age of the world?" he wrote. "It is at once beneficial and instructive to the reflecting mind to review the past with candour and rightly consider the present and be in perfect readiness for that which is to come." And he regarded it as not only a privilege, but also a duty "to keep an accurate account of our proceedings." He kept his personal record so that when required, he could give a minute account of his stewardship. He listed miles traveled, letters written and received, church ordinances performed, meetings attended, and other data. For example, in his 1840 year-end summary, while proselyting in England, he noted that he had traveled 4,469 miles during the year; held 230 meetings; established and organized forty-seven branches of the Church consisting of 1500 Saints; baptized 336 people, including 57 ministers; blessed 120 children; administered to 120 sick people with oil and the laying on of hands; assisted in collecting 1000 pounds sterling for church publication projects; and assisted 200 Saints to emigrate to America; and had been beset by four mobs.

President Woodruff died on September 2, 1898, at the age of ninety-two in San Francisco, California, where he had occasionally gone to seek relief from the ailments of old age. Among the multitude of his writings were instructions he had written in 1882 concerning his death and burial: "I do not wish my family or friends to wear any badge of mourning for me at my funeral or afterwards, for, if I am true and faithful unto death, there will be no necessity for any one to mourn."

SOURCES

The major source of information on the life of Wilford Woodruff is his diaries and papers filed in the LDS Church Archives, Salt Lake City. In addition, the following are informative: Wilford Woodruff, "History of Wilford Woodruff," *Deseret News* 8, nos. 18-22 (July–August 1858); "Autobiography of Wilford Woodruff," *Tullidge's Quarterly Magazine* 3 (October 1883); Wilford Woodruff, *Leaves from my Journal: Third Book of the Faith-Promoting Series* (Salt Lake City: Juvenile Instructor Office, 1881); Thomas G. Alexander, "Wilford Woodruff and the Changing Nature of Mormon Religious Experience," *Church History* 45 (March 1976): 56-69; Scott G. Kenney, ed., *Wilford Woodruff's Journal 1833-1898*, 9 vols., Typescript (Midvale, Utah: Signature Books, 1983); and Matthias F. Cowley, *Wilford Woodruff* (Salt Lake City: Bookcraft, 1964). In the quotations from his diaries and letters, I have supplied necessary punctuation and corrected the spelling.

DEAN C. JESSEE is associate professor of history and church history at Brigham Young University and research historian with the Joseph Fielding Smith Institute for Church History. A graduate of Brigham Young University, he has authored or edited *Brigham Young's Letters to His Sons* (Salt Lake City: Deseret Book, 1974); *The Personal Writings of Joseph Smith* (Salt Lake City: Deseret Book, 1984); and many articles in professional and church journals.

LORENZO SNOW
Heidi S. Swinton

The determinative event in the life of Lorenzo Snow occurred when he was twenty-two years old. He had been born
on the American frontier in Mantua, Ohio, the oldest son and
fourth child of New England parents who had gone from Massachusetts and Connecticut to Ohio shortly before his birth.
His experience laboring on the family farm, his personal drive
for excellence, and his intensive reading, studying, and schooling suggested a future filled with success and accomplishment.
When he joined The Church of Jesus Christ of Latter-day
Saints, his life took on exceptional dimensions and directions
as promised by Joseph Smith, Sr., in a patriarchal blessing
given six months after Lorenzo was baptized. Lorenzo was
told in the blessing:

Thou hast a great work to perform in thy day and generation. God has
called thee to the ministry. Thou must preach the gospel of thy Savior
to the inhabitants of the earth. Thou shalt have faith even like that of
the brother of Jared. . . . There shall not be a mightier man on earth
than thou. . . . The diseased shall send to thee their aprons and handkerchiefs and by thy touch their owners shall be made whole. Thou shalt
have power over unclean spirits — at thy command the powers of darkness shall stand back and devils shall flee away. If expedient the dead
shall rise and come forth at thy bidding. . . . Thou shalt have long life.
The vigor of thy mind shall not be abated and the vigor of thy body
shall be preserved.

As Lorenzo's life unfolded, each promise in his patriarchal blessing was fulfilled, one by one. The Lord had great purpose for Lorenzo Snow, and this valiant disciple followed the Lord's guidance without wavering. Trial and disappointment were heaped upon him, yet he methodically responded to all with total faith in the Lord and in his responsibility to his Father in heaven.

As president of the Church, he was described by a prominent writer as "a cultured man, in mind and soul and body. His language is choice, diplomatic, friendly, scholarly. His mannerisms show the studied grace of schools. The tenor of his spirit is as gentle as a child. You are introduced to him. . . . You are pleased with him. You converse with him. You like him. You visit with him long, you love him. And yet, he is a 'Mormon!' " Lorenzo was truly a Mormon. The last prophet to have been taught, counseled, and led by Joseph Smith, he served for fifty years as an apostle, president of the Quorum of the Twelve, president of the Salt Lake Temple, and finally president of the Church.

LORENZO SNOW WAS BORN April 3, 1814, following four sisters, Leonora, Eliza, Percy Amanda, and Melissa. Two brothers, Lucius and Samuel, trailed Lorenzo, making a family of seven for Oliver and Rosetta Snow. As the eldest son, Lorenzo assumed a great deal of responsibility for running the farm. The Snows were hard-working settlers, well-to-do by local standards. Oliver was one of the township's most prominent citizens, serving as county commissioner and justice of the peace.

The pressures of the farm did not deter Lorenzo from becoming well read. After he was twelve, most of his schooling came during the winter months. He completed the requirements of elementary school and enrolled for one year at the high school in Ravenna, Ohio, where he studied for one term under a professor of Hebrew. Fond of books, he was often found reading when his chores were finished, and he, like his sister Eliza, was noted for his love of literature and curiosity about history. Lorenzo's frontier experience set a pattern for hard work and industry that would benefit him all his life.

The Snows were active Baptists, and their home was a forum for religious teachings. Reading the scriptures and daily prayer set the tone for much spiritual discussion, and they opened their home to intelligent representatives of any denomination. Joseph Smith, Jr., visited their home in the winter of 1831 and told them about the restoration of the Church of Jesus Christ. The eldest daughter, Leonora, and her mother, Rosetta, were most receptive and were baptized into the new church that year. Eliza and Lorenzo were less eager to embrace the teachings, though they both shared a sincere interest in the gospel. Eliza joined the Church in 1835, Lorenzo in 1836.

As Lorenzo matured, he favored a military life over one of farming. Both of his grandfathers were patriot soldiers in the Revolutionary War, and Lorenzo was attracted by the glittering uniforms of those in service to their country, as well as enthusiastic about the stirring martial music and the accompanying pageantry. He was so consumed by his goal to join the military that he persuaded his devoted sister Eliza to tailor his first military uniform. The suit was magnificent; though only five foot six and one hundred forty pounds, he was striking and convincing in this new role, and he went on to receive a lieutenant's commission from the governor of Ohio.

Lorenzo soon realized that to attain any position in the military, he needed a college education. He disposed of his share of his paternal estate and set out in September 1835 for Oberlin College, twenty-five miles east of Mantua. At this point, his life began turning in a new direction, though it would be some time before he recognized the shift. On the journey, he met David W. Patten, who only seven months before had been ordained as one of the original Twelve Apostles of The Church of Jesus Christ of Latter-day Saints. Elder Patten, who was returning home after having completed a mission to Canada, took advantage of the long ride to discuss Mormon doctrine with his young companion. Never before had Lorenzo heard anyone speak with such certainty about the premortal existence and celestial life for those who live God's commandments.

Lorenzo was well read, but not in subjects of religion. The

profound logic of this godly man relative to man's relationship to his Father in heaven made a tremendous impact on this young scholar. That Elder Patten was not college bred and spoke with some difficulties in grammar did not diminish Lorenzo's interest in his message. He records:

> I seemed unable to resist the knowledge that he was a man of God and that his testimony was true. I felt pricked in my heart. This he evidently perceived, for almost the last thing he said to me after bearing his testimony was that I should go to the Lord before retiring at night and ask him for myself. This I did with the result that from the day I met this great Apostle all my aspirations have been enlarged and heightened immeasurably. This was the turning point of my life.

Lorenzo's academic pursuits at Oberlin were successful, and he distinguished himself, finding favor with his professors and his classmates. However, he found religion sorely lacking at Oberlin, a Presbyterian institution, commenting, "If there is nothing better than is found here in Oberlin College, good-bye to all religions."

Eliza presented an alternative academic course. She suggested that he come to Kirtland, Ohio, where she made her home with the family of Joseph Smith and was engaged as the teacher of the Prophet's family school. A Hebrew scholar was opening a school to teach the Hebrew language, she said, urging Lorenzo's attendance. Mormon leaders, including the Prophet, were enrolled in the course. Upon the conclusion of his term at Oberlin, Lorenzo accepted her invitation and moved to Kirtland. He met the Prophet frequently in his home as well as in the school for Hebrew studies.

Lorenzo reflected upon the time when he had seen Joseph Smith three years earlier at the Johnson farm just four miles from the Snows'. Many years later he described his first impressions of Joseph: "The Prophet was talking to an audience of about 250 persons under a bowery. I had heard something about the 'Mormon' prophet. I felt some anxiety to see him and judge for myself as he was generally believed to be a false prophet. . . . Joseph Smith was not what would be called a fluent speaker. He simply bore his testimony to what the Lord had manifested to him. . . . As I looked upon him and listened, I thought to myself that a man bearing such a wonderful testimony as he did and having such a countenance as he possessed could hardly be a false prophet."

Lorenzo felt impressed to determine for himself whether Joseph Smith, Jr., was a true prophet of God. He attended a "patriarchial blessing meeting" in the Kirtland Temple, presided over by Patriarch Joseph Smith, Sr. At the end of the spiritually enlightening meeting, Eliza introduced Lorenzo to the Patriarch. The Prophet's father counseled Lorenzo to talk to the brethren, study, pray about the matter, and compare the scriptures with the teachings. "After a time you will be convinced that Mormonism is of God and you will be baptized," he advised.

Heeding this counsel, Lorenzo studied the principles and listened to the Prophet. "Speaking as with the voice of an archangel and filled with the power of God, his whole person shone and his face was lightened until it appeared as the whiteness of the driven snow. . . . Finally my prayers were answered and I was convinced of the truth sufficiently to want to be baptized to get a knowledge for myself of the testimony that Joseph Smith had seen God."

IN JUNE 1836, Lorenzo Snow was baptized in the Chagrin River by John F. Boynton, one of the Twelve Apostles, bringing to fruition the feelings that had been planted by David W. Patten. Coming out of the water, Lorenzo reported he felt very much the same. He had expected a significant witness from the Lord on this momentous occasion, but he was not a "new" man. This troubled him, for others who had joined the Church had reported of angels singing and a change of heart and spirit immediately after baptism.

Depressed and disconsolate, Lorenzo headed for a nearby grove of trees, where he had communed each evening with his Father in heaven. At first he felt no desire to pray. He forced himself to go through the motions, though, and then the "heavens seemed like brass over my head." He heard a "rustling of silken robes" over his head, and "immediately the Spirit of God descended upon me, completely enveloping my whole person filling me from the crown of my head to the soles of my feet and Oh, the joy and happiness I felt! No language can describe the instantaneous transition from a dense cloud of mental and spiritual darkness into an effulgence of light and knowledge. . . . I received a perfect knowledge that God lives, that Jesus Christ is the son of God, and of the restoration of the Holy Priesthood, and the fulness of the gospel. It was a complete baptism — a tangible immersion in the heavenly principle or element, the Holy Ghost and even more real and physical in its effects upon every part of my system than the immersion by water." After the same divine manifestation recurred for two or three successive nights, Lorenzo concluded that God had conferred upon him "that which is of greater value than all the wealth and honors worlds can bestow."

It was clear to Lorenzo that many of the things he had prized in his youth were a far cry from the richness and rewards of living a godly life. This revelation was a confirmation of the new direction he had chosen for his life, and he pursued the Lord's will from this point on with great fervor.

In addition to his testimony of spiritual principles, Lorenzo received several personal spiritual confirmations that reinforced his responsibility to serve as a missionary. He offered himself to the Lord's church, submitting a request to be ordained an elder and enter the mission field. His desire to preach the gospel and the truths of salvation to a world faltering with false religions was so real that he abandoned any further educational pursuits. In the spring of 1837, he "went forth . . . to the neighborhood that gave [him] birth" to teach former friends, relatives, and neighbors. Without purse or scrip, he embarked on this new endeavor with confidence in his work but without the comforts he had always known. This was not unusual for missionaries of the Church in the early days; for the most part, they followed the pattern of the apostles of old, relying upon the benevolence and charity of those they contacted to house and feed them. But to Lorenzo, who was used to paying his way and living comfortably, the new conditions proved the first challenge to his commitment. Describing his travel plans to his aunt on his first night in the field, he spoke matter-of-factly about the hostility encountered by many of the elders who were "turned out of doors." "I do not expect to be treated any better than my brethren," he added. He was right. He approached nine homes the first night before finding a floor to sleep on, and he was sent off in the morning with no breakfast.

His first meetings were attended by his grandfather, uncles, aunts, numerous cousins, and school friends to whom he "felt he owed a duty . . . to preach." But he did not sway his friends. "I thought I was going to convert them all but after I got through talking and bearing testimony all I could get from them was, 'Well, Lorenzo is an honest boy, but he is deceived.' I baptized a few, very few, of my classmates."

Lorenzo's labors continued to meet with closed doors and closed minds. The Lord prepared him for trouble and in one case foreshadowed a mob attack with a dream showing the violence. While he was teaching the gospel to friends, the following evening, two well-dressed men approached the door and asked Lorenzo to join them in visiting the schoolhouse, where a crowd had gathered to hear his message. Recalling his recent dream, he declined. They pressed the invitation, but he refused again and again. They finally left, but not without angry shouts and bellows. He later learned that a mob had gathered at the school, not to hear his words but to cause him harm.

Before leaving the area, Lorenzo finally succeeded in converting a number of people, including his aunt and uncle and several cousins. One of the converts was his cousin Adaline, who later became his wife. This first mission set the stage for many more to follow. He had learned firsthand the rigors of missionary work and found himself closer to the Lord as a result. He had also found his life's work in his short Ohio mission. That devotion to preaching the gospel dominated his endeavors for all his years to follow.

Returning home, Lorenzo found Kirtland in turmoil from

persecutions of the Saints and accusations against Church leaders by some of the Saints themselves. Unlike the early leaders of the Church who later fell away, Lorenzo was not swayed by these accusations or intimidated by the anger thrust at the Saints. He supported the Prophet Joseph Smith and had an unshakable knowledge of God and his teachings. For Lorenzo, that was paramount in his life.

The Snow family left Kirtland in the spring of 1837 and followed the Prophet Joseph Smith to Far West, Missouri, hoping to leave the detractors and dissidents behind. During the journey, Lorenzo became very ill with a fever, which caused terrific head pains. So severe were the pains that his sister, Eliza, cradled his head in her lap to cushion it from the rocking and lurching of the wagon. He was forced to stay at Sidney Rigdon's home to convalesce while the family moved on to Adam-ondi-Ahman.

IN THE FALL OF 1838, Lorenzo, though still recovering from ill health, desired again to serve in the mission field. Believing that his health would benefit from missionary labors, he set off with another elder for southern Missouri. After meeting with little success and a great deal of animosity, they decided to separate. Lorenzo headed for Illinois and Kentucky, where, through the winter, he preached to people whom he found to be generally indifferent to the gospel. Sometimes he was treated with kindness, civility, and every courtesy; at other times, mobs and disbelievers forced him to fear for his life. At the close of a meeting in Kentucky, he learned a mob was gathering. Some of the malcontents were warming themselves at the fire near Lorenzo and accidently brushed against his jacket. They felt the scriptures, a gift from Joseph Smith, Sr., that he carried in his breast pocket, and mistook them for a concealed weapon. The mob dispersed into the darkness.

By February 1839, Lorenzo was prepared to return to Ohio to preach, visit family members, and take care of personal affairs. The 500-mile walk home in the rough winter weather took its toll on him. When he reached his destination, he was initially denied entrance to the home of a relative because he was so haggard and emaciated. After a bout of violent fever and delirium, he finally recovered.

Lorenzo rejoined his family in May 1840 at LaHarpe, thirty miles from Nauvoo, Illinois, where they had settled after being driven from their home in Far West. There he received a spiritual manifestation that was one of the most significant of his life and has since touched the lives of thousands of members of the Church as well. Visiting at the home of Elder H. G. Sherwood, he listened to a description of what was meant by "laborers in the vineyard." In the scriptures, the Savior depicts the husbandman calling servants in the vineyard at different hours of the day. As Lorenzo listened to an explanation of this scripture, the Spirit of the Lord rested mightily upon him and a spiritual illumination filled him. "I saw as clear as the sun at noonday . . . the pathway of God and man." Afterward, he formed a couplet to express what he saw:

> As man now is, God once was.
> As God now is, man may be.

The magnitude of the doctrine, which was far beyond the scope of what was currently being preached in the Church, amazed Lorenzo. He kept the experience to himself, sharing it only with his sister Eliza. Later, however, while he was in England on his first foreign mission, he discussed the experience with Brigham Young, who advised him, "That is new doctrine; if true, it has been revealed to you for your own private information, and will be taught in due time by the Prophet to the Church; till then I advise you to lay it upon the shelf and say no more about it." Three years later, Lorenzo mentioned the experience to the Prophet, who confirmed that it was "true gospel doctrine and a revelation from God."

IN THE SPRING OF 1840, Lorenzo again left his home, family, and friends to serve as a traveling missionary. The call this time was to the British Isles, where many of the apostles and Church leaders were laboring. With little money, he was able to cross the Atlantic only as a steerage passenger on a small sailing vessel that was filthy and overcrowded. His limited personal belongings included a blanket, a buffalo robe, and scanty provisions. For six weeks the small vessel rocked and creaked amid tremendous storms and crescendoes of waves. Despite the miserable conditions, Lorenzo kept his trust in the Lord. "I did not feel surprised that men, women and children who had not learned to trust in God, wrung their hands in an agony of fear, and wept. My trust was in Him who created the seas and designed their bounds. I was on His errand—I knew that I was sent on this mission by the authority He recognizes, and, although the elements raged and the ship swayed and trembled amid the heaving billows, He was at the helm and my life was safe in His keeping."

Elder Snow's missionary work began in Birmingham, an industrial city of about 300,000. During a three-month period, he brought more than thirty people into the Church. The mission in the British Isles was much more structured than the previous areas where Lorenzo had labored. His leadership qualities as well as his effectiveness in preaching the gospel distinguished him, and he was soon appointed to take the "superintendency" of the Church in London. Near the conclusion of his mission, he served as a counselor to Thomas Ward, president of the British Mission, which included by that time a membership of more than ten thousand.

As they had with other church leaders, evil spirits sought to confound Lorenzo in his efforts. One night in his London apartment, he was awakened by loud noises. "It seemed as though every piece of furniture in the room was put in motion, back and forth against each other in such terrible fury that sleep and rest were utter impossibilities." Accompanying the commotion was an oppressive feeling that filled the whole room. The disturbance came again the next night, and several more nights after that, until Lorenzo determined something had to be done. In prayer and fasting, he awaited the evening; then, as the room again filled with disruption, he read aloud from the Bible and in a voice with authority rebuked the evil spirits and "commanded them to leave the house." Calm and tranquillity enveloped the room, and Lorenzo retired for the night with "no more disturbances." From his patriarchal blessing, the promise had been fulfilled: "at thy command, the powers of darkness shall stand back and devils shall flee away."

On April 6, 1841, to commemorate the eleventh anniversary of the organization of the Church, the missionaries gathered in Manchester under the direction of Brigham Young. Present were several hundred church leaders and members, including nine members of the Quorum of the Twelve, three of whom—Brigham Young, John Taylor, and Wilford Woodruff—would eventually become presidents of the Church. The meetings were filled with earnest preaching and a spirit that gave strength and renewed purpose to the Lord's servants.

Elder Snow was very successful in building the congregation in London. "I baptized seven yesterday, making nine that I have baptized in London since Elders Woodruff and Kimball left and making eleven that have received the gospel in this city since conference," he wrote. When he prepared to leave for home, the London Conference was in a strong position with more than 400 Saints. One of the highlights of his mission was a personal audience with Queen Victoria and His Royal Highness Prince Albert. Elder Snow was privileged to present them with two specially bound copies of the Book of Mormon prepared by Brigham Young before he left the country. With Lorenzo's refined background and extensive education, he was perfectly suited for the task and thoroughly enjoyed the experience. The Queen autographed his album, which was one of his most treasured possessions.

He left from Liverpool in 1843, directing a company of 250 converts destined for Nauvoo. The voyage was far more pleasant than his trip to Britain. Lorenzo and the Saints discussed the gospel, sang hymns, and even preached to the crew. The first mate was baptized in New Orleans along with several others. During the voyage, the steward of the vessel, a favorite among the crew and particularly with the captain, became ill and lingered close to death. One Mormon sister implored the captain to let Elder Snow administer to the young man. The captain did not discourage the woman from sending for Elder Snow, though he had no faith in such actions. After offering a silent prayer, Elder Snow laid his hands upon the steward's head and in the name of Jesus Christ commanded the disease to leave him. In a short time, the steward was up walking about the deck, thanking and praising God for his miraculous recovery. The blessing of Patriarch Smith was once again fulfilled that Lorenzo would have the power to heal the sick.

AT AGE TWENTY-NINE and home from his third mission, Lorenzo took a post as teacher in Lima, Illinois, a small settlement about thirty miles from Nauvoo. He found the seventy students to be "roughnecks," proud of the difficulties they caused their teachers and exhibiting little interest in scholarship and learning. But he was undaunted. Recognizing that he was no match for them physically, he set out to win their respect by treating them with kindness and concern. He ultimately won their confidence and produced a well-mannered and scholarly schoolroom.

The Church was growing and changing as the Lord revealed new doctrines to the Prophet. Eliza Snow, who had been a lifelong confidante of Lorenzo's, felt uncertain how to tell him of the newly revealed commandment of plural marriage by which she had become the wife of the Prophet. She told Joseph of her concerns, and one day on the banks of the Mississippi, he explained the doctrine of plural marriage to Lorenzo. Lorenzo, with faith that the Lord spoke through the Prophet, accepted the new principle without wavering. He later recounted: "I was an unmarried man and to this day would have remained so had I not received an understanding of the law of Celestial Marriage—its object and necessity in securing eternal glory and exaltation. My heart and soul and all my energies and ambition were enlisted in the service of God and I thought I could not better please or serve Him than by employing my entire time, unburdened by family cares in the great field of missionary labor. Joseph pointed out to me clearly my duty and privileges in reference to the law." Two years later, in 1845, Lorenzo embraced the doctrine at the altar in the Nauvoo Temple, taking two wives, Charlotte Squires and Mary Adaline Goddard. He wed Sarah Ann Richards and Harriet Amelia Squires in another ceremony that same year.

The fury against and condemnations of the Church and its

leaders, particularly Joseph Smith, were reaching a feverish pitch in Nauvoo. The Prophet had appealed to President Martin Van Buren and to the U.S. Congress, but no relief was forthcoming. The Mormons were told to work out their difficulties with local leaders, all of whom held great animosity for the Church. Joseph Smith began investigating migration to the West, where, he explained to the apostles, the Latter-day Saints could "have a government of their own."

An exploratory party was called to search for a settlement site, with Lorenzo as a member of the team. However, the Prophet's entry into the race for U.S. president resulted in Lorenzo's energies, like those of many of the Church leaders, being directed to campaigning on Joseph's behalf. Lorenzo was responsible for the campaign in his native Ohio, though he, like most of his co-workers, recognized that Joseph's candidacy was basically a vehicle to bring the plight of the Mormons to the public, to promote Mormon principles, and to influence government policies. Lorenzo was actively campaigning when he received news of the martyrdom of the Prophet Joseph and his brother Hyrum Smith. Feeling a tremendous loss for these two leaders, he left for home to be with the Saints and comfort his sister Eliza.

At home, he found that the tenor of the members had changed from one of fear and defense in the days before the martyrdom to one of responsibility to carry on the work and hope for the future. The Twelve had taken charge under Quorum President Brigham Young, with the first order of business to complete the Nauvoo Temple for performance of sacred ordinance work. However, animosities again swept the communities and the Mormons were forced to speed up their exodus, which had been planned for the following spring. In the winter of 1846, Lorenzo and his family filled two wagons with belongings suitable for the trip and took their one milk cow. He would be responsible on the journey for ten families including those of Parley P. and Orson Pratt.

In mid-May, these pioneers reached Pisgah, a settlement about 175 miles from Nauvoo. Soon after arriving, Lorenzo was taken seriously ill with a burning fever that, he said, "so affected my brain that I was delirious many days, lying at the point of death." His life was saved, he recorded, by kind brethren who wrapped him in a sheet, "placed [him] in a carriage and drove to a stream of water and baptized [him] in the name of the Lord for [his] recovery. The fever immediately abated," and Lorenzo credits the kind attention and care of his wives and sister Eliza with nursing him back to full health.

Lorenzo was called to preside over the Pisgah community, succeeding Elder Charles C. Rich. He immediately set to work, organizing the brethren into cooperatives to produce goods and services. Committees were organized for every possible purpose, from repairing broken wagons and farming tools to manufacturing furniture and household accessories that could be marketed in nearby communities. Lorenzo's tenure was also marked by his efforts to brighten the lives of the Saints by encouraging frequent gatherings for the people with a host of recreational activities. Usually they came to his home, a fifteen-by-thirty-foot log cabin with dirt roof and floor and lit by candles in scooped-out turnips. A dish of succotash was often served for refreshment. Pleasant evenings featured "composed short speeches full of life and sentiment, appropriate songs, recitations, toasts, conundrums [riddles], exhortations, etc." Lorenzo learned early the necessity to keep the Saints' spirits high when their mortal circumstances were marked by disease, death, poverty, and discouragement. He used these forms of diversion and enlightenment many times as a leader of the Saints.

With the coming of spring in 1848, Lorenzo received a call from Brigham Young to lead a large group to Zion. Just before they departed, Lorenzo was sealed to Eleanor Houtz, "belle of Pisgah," in a ceremony performed by President Young. His company included quite an assemblage: 321 persons, 99 wagons, 20 horses, 3 mules, 388 oxen, 188 cows, 38 loose cattle, 139 sheep, 25 pigs, 159 chickens, 10 cats, 26 dogs, and 2 doves. They crossed the plains with few difficulties, ample food, good weather, a well-marked trail, and little trouble with the Indians, and arrived in the Salt Lake Valley September 22, 1848. Lorenzo settled temporarily with his family in a cabin in the Old Fort.

A NEW ERA WAS BEGINNING for the Saints and for Lorenzo as well, as he was called to the Council of the Twelve Apostles soon after his arrival in the Salt Lake Valley. Also called at the same time were Charles C. Rich, Erastus Snow, and Franklin D. Richards. Lorenzo was astonished by his call to this important responsibility but committed himself to serve the Lord and assist Brigham Young and his brethren. He pledged himself, with his brethren, to "be one and to be inspired by the same Holy Ghost . . . that we may echo the same feeling and intelligence unto the people that exists in brother Brigham, that we may be one with him in all things . . . and be bound together by the principle of love that binds the Son of God with the Father."

Lorenzo's selection as an apostle followed years of faithful service in the Lord's church. He responded without question to the Spirit's promptings and callings, following a pattern in his life that he described in an early address to the Saints where he talked of the necessity of always doing "what is required." He told the audience assembled in the Tabernacle, "We have to look at things, calmly, cooly, seriously and firmly, and to live in a way to get righteousness incorporated in our systems. We are placed under certain regulations, certain restrictions, that we may get the notion of acting from practice."

Lorenzo had distinguished himself in Pisgah as an organizer, which resulted in a call from Brigham Young to supervise the festivities for the second Pioneer Day celebration. The event began in the early morning with a martial and military band, followed by speeches, shouts, choruses, toasts, and parades throughout the day. It was a gala affair that took advantage of Lorenzo's flair for production. He was assigned with other apostles to build up the Perpetual Emigration Fund, and the group raised more than five thousand dollars the first season. The fund allowed for a gathering of the Saints in Zion, which boosted the strength and growth of the Church in its new home.

At general conference in October 1849, the first missionaries to leave from the Salt Lake Valley were called to Europe, with Lorenzo Snow and fellow apostles John Taylor,

Erastus Snow, and Franklin D. Richards among the group. Lorenzo was called to Italy, with Joseph Toronto, who had family ties to Italy, as his companion. Though Lorenzo had strong ties to "the exiled Saints now struggling for subsistence in a wild recess in the Rocky Mountains," he took up the Lord's call, declaring, "We knew that the work in which we were engaged was to carry light to those who sat in darkness and in the Valley of the Shadow of Death and our bosoms glowed with love and compassion toward them."

Again, as his patriarchal blessing promised, Lorenzo Snow was a missionary for the Lord. This trip across the Atlantic to England was far more pleasant than the trip nine years before. In England, the missionaries visited many of the great landmarks in the country and several of the Church conferences. Most significant was Lorenzo's visit to London, where he "shook hands with hundreds who looked upon [him] as having been the means of leading them to the light of the gospel." He noted, "When I received my appointment to that city, I found 30 or 40 members; now 1500 and many had emigrated."

Elder T. B. H. Stenhouse, president of the Southampton Conference, joined Elder Toronto and Elder Snow, who reflected as they sailed for the Continent, "I am sent by the revelation of the Lord to proffer the gospel to Italy. If her people receive my testimony, they receive the word of the Lord— rejecting it they reject the gospel of eternal life."

In Italy the missionaries found a people whose "self esteem, joined with deep ignorance, presents a formidable opposition to the progress of the gospel." Barriers of language, social customs, and cultural background made the missionary effort a slow process. After eleven months, Elder Snow directed his companions to pursue teaching among the Protestant people in the Piedmont region. He confided to Elder Richards in a communication that the Lord "had hidden up a people amid the Alpine Mountains" and that the elders would "commence something of importance in that part of this dark nation."

The door was opened for the work by a blessing to a critically ill child, Joseph Guy, who appeared to be on the verge of death. His body was emaciated and his skin a "pale marble hue." His family had given him up for dead with his father whispering, "He dies, he dies." Recognizing this as an opportunity to show the strength of the gospel, Lorenzo and the elders beseeched the Lord in private prayer to spare the child. Then at his bedside, they administered to the boy. They left immediately and learned later that not only did the child sleep peacefully that night, he was much improved the next day. Elder Snow had been right. When word of the miraculous healing spread, doors opened to the missionaries and they had increased opportunities to teach the gospel.

One morning the elders retreated to a mountain they designated "Mount Brigham" and sat on a ledge that they called "The Rock of Prophecy" to organize the Church in Italy and sing praises and offer up prayers. Elder Snow was named president of the organization in that country. That day was the beginning of success in proclaiming the gospel to the Italian people. Soon after, the first convert was baptized and that "opened a door no man can shut."

With the work underway, Elder Snow felt inspired to go to London to arrange for the translation of several pamphlets and the Book of Mormon into Italian. Prior to leaving, he and his companions climbed their summit once again and sang the praises of the Lord. Lorenzo spent eleven months in England overseeing the translation and publishing of the Book of Mormon in Italian. In his free time, he assisted in the missionary work, preaching of a life to be continued through the eternities and emphasizing the message that "we suffer in all things, that we may be qualified and worthy to rule and govern in all things, even as our Father in Heaven and His eldest Son, Jesus."

Visiting Wales, Lorenzo and his companions retired to a hotel after a meeting and found their room appeared to have a defective lock. Thinking little of it at the time, they retired quickly, only to be awakened later by three "savage looking fellows" who ordered them from bed. In the scuffle that followed, the intruders' light was extinguished and the hoodlums left to get another. The elders barricaded the door. When the men returned, the noise and uproar was so great that the land-lord, who had assisted them in entering the room, "quelled the disturbance by requesting the ruffians to retire." Years later, Elder Snow saw the retribution of those who mistreat the Lord's servants. The hotel "was being used as a common stable for the accommodation of horses and the landlord had been signally reduced to beggary, and was a vagabond upon the earth."

Inspired to continue the spread of the gospel, Lorenzo sent missionaries to Malta and to India. He then returned to Italy, where he found the work progressing so well that he went on to Malta. He had hoped to return home by way of India, but because of difficulties with the steamships heading there, he was stymied in his efforts to visit this new land where the gospel was beginning to grow. That 189 persons had joined the Church in India was, he reported, "cheery intelligence from my Indian missions." Satisfied that the gospel would go forth in the new mission, he prepared to return home by way of England, where all the Italian publications and translations were close to completion.

The Twelve had been called to assemble in Salt Lake City for general conference in April 1853. Arriving in Salt Lake late in the summer of 1852, Lorenzo learned his wife Charlotte had died while he was abroad. He mourned her loss, "yet there was consolation in the thought that her pure spirit was mingling with holy beings above." One of the faithful Saints in London, a Sister Woodward, later told Lorenzo of "an open vision in which she saw a beautiful woman, the most lovely being she ever beheld, clothed in white robes and crowned with glory. This personage told her that she was a wife of Lorenzo Snow."

The enthusiasm of his children for his return helped to soften his grief. One "little prattler" named Sylvia, born a short time after Lorenzo left for Italy, was as thrilled as the other children that her father had finally returned. But, she asked the other children first, "Is that my favvy?" Prompted by their positive replies, she approached Lorenzo with "Is you my favvy?" He replied, "Yes, I am your father." She then said, "Well then, if you is my favvy, I will kiss you."

REUNITED WITH HIS FAMILY, Lorenzo realized that their log home was most inadequate. Not only was it too small, it was also in severe disrepair, particularly the roof, which leaked everywhere. Though he had no financial reserves, he began constructing a new home. Like every other undertaking, he took his newest venture to the Lord. He frequently knelt within the home's foundation, entreating the Lord that the small means he could command "might be blest and multiplied in its use." The Snows moved into their new home, a two-story adobe home with nine rooms, and Lorenzo thanked the Lord as "the Giver of all good for the blessing of a comfortable and respectable habitation."

In addition to providing a home for his family, Lorenzo took up his duties with the Quorum of the Twelve. Brigham Young had called them home to help lay the cornerstone of the Salt Lake Temple. The members assembled on April 6, 1853, the twenty-third anniversary of the Church, for a historic event that was accompanied by bands, speeches, and prayers.

It was at this time that Lorenzo, like his father, began years of public service in addition to his ecclesiastical roles. He was elected to the territorial legislature and named a regent of the newly established University of Deseret. Anxious to help expand the minds, culture, and creativity of the Saints in the Salt Lake Valley, he founded a "Polysophic Society," which met Wednesdays to share music, poetry, essays, and often presentations in foreign languages. The program flourished and soon moved to Social Hall Avenue to accommodate all the participants. The society was the framework for the mutual improvement associations later instituted as part of the main structure of the Church organization.

The pace changed again for the Snows when Lorenzo was called to preside over and strengthen the settlements in Box Elder, sixty miles north of Salt Lake City. He later gave the community the name Brigham City. He described the conditions in the settlement "unprosperous," adding that "even the big meeting house with its ground floor and earth roof was more extensively patronized as a receptacle for bed bugs than for the assemblage of the Saints." About two hundred people were living in Brigham City when Lorenzo arrived there. He called an additional fifty families to join him in the colony to solidify the settlement.

Though Lorenzo's task was enormous, he methodically tackled the needs of the settlers. He established the Dramatic Association of Brigham City to raise the cultural level of the community, instituted a public school system, and organized programs to provide for the needs of all the settlers, including a monthly fast to aid the destitute. Distinguished visitors were greeted by parades, martial music, flags, banners, and cheering throngs lining the streets.

Under Lorenzo's direction, Brigham City became a model colony. He continued to rely on the Lord, believing that "men change and circumstances alter, but the Lord is always the same, kind, indulgent and affectionate Father, and will bless those that will, in childish simplicity, humble themselves before him and ask for what they want." Though he was living in Brigham City, he traveled frequently to Fillmore, the state capital, since he represented the northern communities in the legislature, and to Salt Lake City to fulfill responsibilities as a member of the Quorum of the Twelve.

Lorenzo Snow's influence continued to be felt by Saints throughout the Church. In England he had shared his patriarchal blessing with a sister who had since immigrated to Davis County. Distraught over her husband's serious illness and concerned that he had not responded to any priesthood blessings, Sister Smith recalled the Lord's promise to Lorenzo, that "the diseased shall send to thee their aprons and handkerchiefs and by the touch their owners shall be made whole." She sent a beautiful silk handkerchief to Elder Snow in Brigham City and asked for a blessing for her husband through the handkerchief. Elder Snow consecrated perfume and sprinkled it on the cloth. "I bowed before the Lord and in earnest supplication besought him to remember the promise he made through his servant the Patriarch, whom he had now taken to himself, and let the healing and life inspiring virtues of this Holy Spirit be imparted to this handkerchief and thence to Brother Smith," he later wrote. When the handkerchief was placed over the patient's face, his return to full health was instantaneous, a "surprise and astonishment" to all who witnessed the healing. In 1864, Lorenzo, along with Elder Ezra T. Benson and missionaries Joseph F. Smith, Alma Smith, and William W. Cluff, accepted an assignment to travel to the Hawaiian Islands. A missionary to Japan, Captain Walter M. Gibson, had misinterpreted his calling, taken control of the Hawaiian Mission, assumed Church land holdings for his purposes, and organized a new church in which he sold rights to priesthood offices.

Arriving at the island of Lanai, the group encountered stiff winds and turbulent seas in the harbor with "surf, thirty or forty feet high, rushing toward us swifter than a race horse," capsizing the craft and flinging the men in all directions. Lorenzo "felt confident that there would be some means of escape and that the Lord would provide the means, for it was not possible that my life and mission were thus to terminate. This reliance on the Lord banished fear and inspired me." He, however, could not swim. The other members of the craft were either experienced swimmers or were able to grab the overturned craft. When Lorenzo was finally dragged from the water, his body was stiff and lifeless. The elders administered to him, pleading with God "to spare his life that he might return to his family and home." Working feverishly, they tried every technique they knew to get him breathing, including pouring camphor over his face. Finally they were impressed to breathe into his mouth to inflate his lungs, alternating blowing in and drawing out the air. As they labored, they noticed a slight wink from Lorenzo, and his lifeless body began to respond. It was close to an hour before he finally revived, but he suffered no ill effects from the ordeal.

After locating Captain Gibson, they found circumstances even worse than their reports. Gibson was a convincing and impressive leader with a strong hold on the people. He was currently raising a militia to take control of the neighboring islands. The apostles finally excommunicated him after all attempts to get him to abandon his ways failed. However, the action was not supported by Gibson's congregation. Elder Snow prophesied that the captain would eventually be rejected by those supporting him. Twenty years later, he was driven from the islands; he died in San Francisco.

Turning his attention again to Brigham City, Elder Snow realized the community needed a stronger economic base. Familiar with the principles of consecration and stewardship as explained to him by the Prophet Joseph, he instituted a cooperative enterprise called the Brigham City Mercantile and Manufacturing Association, whose aim was "to furnish every person employment, wishing to work; and pay as high wages as possible — mostly in home products." In the beginning, all profits were put back in the business and dividends were given in commodities sold by the store. In only four years, the venture of "home industries" expanded, with the construction of a $10,000 tannery to produce shoes, saddles, boots, and harnesses for local use. By 1870, the cooperative added a $35,000 water-powered woolen factory employing 32 persons running 200 spindles. Workers continued to be paid in kind, and by 1874, forty branches or departments had been clustered under the program, including millinery and tailor shops; a horticulture department to supervise orchards, vineyards, and flowers; a blacksmith shop; a dairy; sawmills; masonry, broom, and brush factories; a public works department; and even a "tramp department" that provided work for passing hoboes. The profit or loss of each department was shared equally by the stockholders. The employees were paid weekly in two kinds of scrip, one for the mercantile department and one for manufacturing. Checks were printed "on good, strong paper in the form of bills from five cents up to twenty dollars and constitute the principal currency in circulation."

Brigham City was recognized as one of the most prosperous and progressive settlements in the territory. The Saints could provide for almost all their essentials and their luxuries from their own industries. Elder Snow was invited to many communities to explain how the system worked. Brigham Young recognized the significant achievements of the northern Utah settlement and heralded Lorenzo, saying, "Up there in Brigham City Brother Snow has led the people along and got them into the United Order without their knowing it."

LORENZO HAD TRAVELED over the United States and to several foreign lands during his ministry, but now a new assignment came: he was to accompany President George A. Smith to the Holy Land. This proved to be one of the most memorable journeys of his lifetime. Few had the intense devotion to the Savior and His Father as did Lorenzo. To ask him to make such a pilgrimage was to ratify his entire life and commitment and provided yet another witness to his powerful testimony. The call to visit Palestine, issued in October 1872, was specifically to "dedicate and consecrate the land to the Lord, that it may be blessed with fruitfulness, preparatory to the return of the Jews, in fulfillment of the prophecy and the accomplishment of the purposes of our Heavenly Father." In addition, the group was counseled to make contacts "with men in position and influence in society" wherever possible in order to introduce the gospel. The party of seven included President Smith, Elder Snow, Feramorz Little, George Dunford, Paul A. Schettler, Eliza R. Snow, and Clara Little. They were joined in the Holy Land by Elder Albert Carrington of the Quorum of the Twelve, who had been serving in England.

This trip was quite a contrast to Lorenzo's usual forms of travel. The group crossed country in luxurious train cars and the Atlantic in an up-to-date steamer. In England, they visited many of the landmarks, with the Tower of London and its grisly history of imprisonment of English notables making the strongest impression on Lorenzo. In Europe, they toured Amsterdam, Brussels, the Hague, Paris, Marseilles, Milan, Venice, and Rome and were impressed with the historical buildings and museums, cultural activities, and industrialization, as well as religion. Lorenzo and Eliza kept serious notes and recorded their travels in a booklet, "Correspondence of

Palestine Tourists," which outlined populations, architecture, foliage, landmarks, climate, cultural events, and hospitality of the people.

Alexandria, the Delta of the Nile, and Cairo held a special fascination for the travelers, prompting Lorenzo to laud the Egyptian journey, "which in many respects has proved the most agreeable and interesting of any country we have visited in regard to its physical appearance and the character, religion, customs and manners of its inhabitants."

The party arrived at the Holy Land in February. Their arrangements for touring there included a chef, an interpreter, good horses, saddles, plenty of servants, and a camp inventory with three large circular wall tents to serve as sleeping quarters for the sisters and two for the brethren, with another sleeping tent doubling as a dining room and one as a kitchen. The tents were furnished with tables, camp stools, washbowls, iron bedsteads, bedding, mattresses, and "clean white sheets."

The Saints' journey began at Jaffa and wove toward Jerusalem. Wrote Lorenzo, "We felt that we were passing over the land once occupied by the children of Abraham, the plains once trod by the Kings of Israel with their marshalled hosts, the land of the Apostles and Prophets. We were in Palestine! The Holy Land!" As they approached Jerusalem, Lorenzo exclaimed, "Yes, there is Jerusalem! Where Jesus lived and taught and was crucified, where He cried 'It is finished' and bowed his head and died."

On March 2, 1873, the three apostles, in a simple, yet significant ceremony at the Mount of Olives, dedicated the land of Palestine for the gathering of the Jews and gave "heartfelt thanks and gratitude to God for the fulness of the Gospel and the blessing bestowed on the Latter-day Saints." To Lorenzo, "it seemed the crowning point of the whole tour, realizing as I did that we were worshipping on the summit of the sacred Mount, once the frequent resort of the Prince of Life."

LORENZO CAME HOME TO A NEW CALL, to serve as one of the five counselors to President Brigham Young. This responsibility would take advantage of his special expertise in cooperative systems as well as his almost twenty-five years of experience in Church leadership.

In 1874, when the first official United Order community was established in St. George, the Brigham City cooperative was used as its model. Soon the Brigham City cooperative was converted to the United Order with a council of sixty citizens overseeing the efforts under Lorenzo's direction. With less administrative responsibility, he was able to participate in other Church matters. The difficulty the Saints experienced throughout the Church in living the United Order, coupled with the frequent absence of their great leader Elder Snow, resulted in a gradual decline and dismantling of the Brigham City cooperative system in the late 1870s.

In the spring of 1877, Lorenzo joined Brigham Young and the other apostles in St. George for the dedication of the St. George Temple. Before the April 6 dedication, President Young introduced a new plan for realigning stakes along county lines and calling new stake presidents. Lorenzo was replaced as stake president in Box Elder County by his son Oliver, though he continued to have substantial influence among the Saints there for many years.

The Saints were again under fierce persecution, this time for the practice of plural marriage. Federal officers stalked the territory, enforcing the "laws of the land," and Church leaders were forced to flee their homes to keep from being thrown in prison for a practice basic to their religious beliefs. Lorenzo's responsibilities had imposed many pressures upon his home and family. Referring to the strength and determination of his wives, he said, "They have proven themselves superior to the hardships, privations, poverty and even perils which the Saints in the earlier periods of the history of the Church experienced." He credited them with possessing "that rare gift—the gift of sound common sense, my wives all acted in concert, mutually assisting each other; and with all the inconveniences, hard work, and privations, to which while raising children, they have experienced, through my frequent and at times long absence, they scorned to complain and never have they at any time, sought to detain me or prevent my fulfillment of public duties; but on the other hand, have been and are co-laborers with me in the great work of the last days."

Lorenzo was in the San Francisco Bay area when President John Taylor called him to embark on a new missionary opportunity. The words of his patriarchal blessing, "Thou must preach the gospel of thy Savior to the inhabitants of the earth," took on new significance as he was asked to teach a group of native Americans. Given the latitude to determine which tribe, Lorenzo selected the Nez Perce Indians in northwestern Idaho and immediately traveled to that area. Securing a guide near the reservation, he reviewed the circumstances and interest of the Indians. He determined that the best forum for the gospel message would be an agency in the vicinity of the reservation that allowed easy access for the Indians and the missionaries. He planned to include the Umatilla tribe in the mission as well, since they were close neighbors.

His last missionary venture was to the Wind River Reservation in Wyoming, where Chief Washakie and his family of seventeen had been baptized four years earlier and had then been left without care or additional teaching, as "wandering babes in the woods" with little grasp of the fulness of the gospel. Lorenzo's persuasions with the tribe and the Church authorities resulted in a mission being established for the Shoshones and Arapahoes at the reservation.

The Edmunds Act, which outlawed polygamy and made its practice punishable by law, was passed by Congress in 1881. Lorenzo, who had nine wives, had scarcely returned from his mission to the Indians in 1885 when he was arrested by the U.S. Marshal. On January 16, 1886, he was sentenced to serve three six-month terms and pay a fine of three hundred dollars on three indictments of plural marriage. He was the only apostle in office to serve a prison term for polygamy. Appeals were denied, and on March 12, at age seventy-two, Lorenzo Snow became a prisoner. Two prominent physicians appealed on his behalf, noting that because of his age and "delicate condition," his health "would be seriously jeopardized by depriving him of his hair and beard" which he had worn for sixteen years.

The authorities granted the request for this special consideration, allowing him to keep his distinctive white hair and beard. He did, however, wear the regulation horizontally striped uniform.

In his first letter to his family, he showed that his spirits were high and his sense of humor still apparent. "In a general sense, we are here as the invited guests of the nation, boarded and lodged all at Government expense, a remarkable instance illustrating in a striking manner that spirit of philanthropy pervading the bosom of our mighty republic."

Amnesty was promised if Lorenzo would renounce plural marriage, but his reply was "thank you, but having adopted sacred and holy principles for which we have already sacrificed property, home and life on several occasions in their defense we do not propose, at this late hour, to abandon them because of threatened danger." He wrote to his brethren in the First Presidency, "If I can serve the Holy Cause, which is dearer to me than life, and promote the glory of God by passing through the ordeal of incarceration in a penitentiary, I am perfectly willing."

During his incarceration, he introduced a school to teach reading, writing, math, and bookkeeping; organized activities for the prisoners; engaged in gospel study; and held church meetings. He was a model prisoner and an inspiration to those who shared his plight. The Supreme Court reversed the Snow decision on February 7, 1887, and he was released the following day to a cheering crowd, with members of the Twelve, the Seventies, his family, and hundreds of friends assembled.

April Conference was held in Provo that year, with Elder Snow conducting. With many on missions or in exile, only a handful of the apostles and other Church authorities were present. Elder Snow called attention to the difficulties that the followers of Jesus Christ had always experienced and that the members of the Church had faced from the beginning. Noting that the difficulties would continue, he emphasized that members must "pass through the narrows and learn by sacrifice." Following his conference duties, Elder Snow toured the settlements of Southern Utah, holding meetings in Deseret, Fillmore, Scipio, Salina, Richfield, Monroe, Circleville, Panguitch, Orderville, and St. George, where he and President of the Twelve Wilford Woodruff met in the temple and exchanged experiences since they were last together. His return followed a similar pattern of meeting and counseling with the Saints; he also reorganized the Sevier Stake under the direction of President Taylor.

NOT LONG AFTER LORENZO'S ARRIVAL HOME, President Taylor died, as did Lorenzo's dear sister Eliza, who had brought him to the gospel. At the ensuing conference, Wilford Woodruff became the president of the Church and Lorenzo Snow the president of the Twelve. He was seventy-five.

Lorenzo's patriarchal blessing had foretold of great responsibilities the Lord had in store for this righteous son: "if expedient the dead shall rise and come forth at thy bidding." A young woman severely ill with scarlet fever sensed that her time of passing was near and prepared for death by combing and washing her hair and bidding farewell to her loved ones. Her spirit left her body, and her narration of what followed described a beautiful place with everyone clothed in white and Eliza Snow teaching Sunday School. The young woman was with her relatives who had passed on when she heard Elder Snow administer to her and call her back. "For a long time afterwards I had a great desire to go back to that place of heavenly rest," she said.

Lorenzo Snow had lived a "long life" as promised in his blessing. But the Lord had additional responsibilities for him to fulfill. The Salt Lake Temple was ready to be dedicated, bringing great jubilation and celebration to the Saints. Ceremonies to lay the final cornerstone drew more than 40,000 people to Temple Square. It was appropriate that so many were able to witness the completion of the temple, which stood as a reminder of the cornerstone of the latter-day religion as well and visibly tied the Saints to all who had passed on before them.

Leading the Hosanna Shout for the dedication of the Salt Lake Temple was Lorenzo Snow, president of the Quorum of the Twelve and soon to be named president of the temple as well. No better selection could have been made, because Lorenzo had been prepared for such a call. He had been closely associated with Joseph Smith, who had revealed the temple ordinances, and had received his own endowments from the Prophet. He had lived a life of total dedication to the Lord's work and added this dimension to his tenure as a willing and able servant of the Father. So loved and respected was he by the temple officials and workers that on his eightieth birthday, they presented him with an ebony cane with a handle wrought in gold and personal inscriptions to him.

LORENZO WAS IN THE TEMPLE when he learned of the Lord's desire to have him serve as president of the Church. One evening, knowing of the frail health of President Woodruff and aware of the grave responsibilities of directing the Church that might fall upon him were President Woodruff to be taken, Lorenzo retired in private prayer in the temple. Earnestly he asked the Lord to extend the life of the President beyond his own. He concluded with, "Nevertheless, thy will be done. I have not sought this responsibility but if it be Thy will, I now present myself before Thee for Thy guidance and instruction." The Lord Jesus Christ appeared to him, as he later testified, and presented him with the procedures for reorganizing the First Presidency when the mantle of prophet of The Church of Jesus Christ of Latter-day Saints was his.

Not long after this, President Woodruff died while in California and the First Presidency, in accordance with the instructions previously given in the temple, was reorganized before the next conference. Lorenzo Snow was sustained and ordained by the Twelve as president, prophet, seer, and revelator, and George Q. Cannon and Joseph F. Smith were named as his counselors. The *Deseret News* heralded the new prophet with these words: "He has been identified with the Church since 1836—ever faithful, ever active, constantly laboring for the benefit of his fellowmen at home and abroad. He has been one with the Saints in their trials and triumphs; he has performed his part of the labor necessary for the temporal and spiritual advancement of the people and borne with the faith and fortitude of a martyr his share of the persecutions they have suffered. His entire life has been a school — God's school — fitting him for the exalted position he now occupies among his brethren. . . . His long experience in the service of the Church, his intimate acquaintance with the founder thereof and above all his integrity and Apostolic zeal qualify him for the position he has been called to occupy as the fifth president of the Church of Jesus Christ of Latter-day Saints." Lorenzo was fulfilling that final calling illuminated in his patriarchal blessing: "There shall not be a mightier man on earth than thou."

The Church was again not without its trials. Years of persecution, unjust legislation by critics and enemies, expensive litigation had caused such severe financial pressures that the Church was facing financial bankruptcy. Turning to the Lord in prayer, President Snow was told to make a trip to St. George, visiting the principal settlements on the return trip. Though the purpose of the visit was not clear in light of the plea for assistance in the financial crisis, Lorenzo and selected brethren left for the southern Utah settlement. There they were greeted by a huge crowd from St. George and the surrounding communities, who lined the streets to welcome the prophet for a special conference. At the opening session held on May 17, 1899, President Snow revealed to the Saints a vision that was before him being manifested at that very moment.

His son LeRoi recorded the experience: "He told them that he could see, as he had never realized before, how the law of tithing had been neglected by the people, also that the Saints themselves were heavily in debt, as well as the Church, and now through strict obedience to this law — the paying of a full and honest tithing — not only would the Church be relieved of its great indebtedness, but through the blessing of the Lord this would also be the means of freeing the Latter-day Saints from their individual obligations and they would become a prosperous people."

President Snow indicated that the Lord was irritated with the Saints' lax adherence to the principle of tithing, and that the continued drought in Dixie was evidence of His displeasure. He then promised that if the people would turn to the Lord and fill their storehouses with their tithing, the drought would end and the fields would again become fruitful. He repeated what was "required of the people under the peculiar conditions in which the Church is now placed": "The time has now come for every Latter-day Saint, who calculates to be prepared for the future and to hold his feet strong upon a proper foundation, to do the will of the Lord and to pay his tithing in full. That is the word of the Lord to you and it will be the word of the Lord to every settlement throughout the land of Zion."

The return home was characterized by twenty-four meetings in sixteen towns. President Snow carried his theme throughout the region in the months to come. Records showed that during a four-month period in 1898, $65,000 in total tithing had been paid by the membership of the Church. For three and a half months in 1899, following President Snow's revelation on tithing, tithing receipts totaled $137,000. The Lord's message had been received.

Referring to the significant financial achievements of President Snow, Elder Heber J. Grant said: "In three years this man, beyond the age of ability in the estimation of the world, this man who had not been engaged in financial affairs, who had been devoting his life for years to laboring in the temple, took hold of the finances of the Church of Christ, under the inspiration of the living God and in those three years changed everything financially from darkness to light." President Snow had truly prepared the Church to enter the twentieth century, lifting it from financial ruin and serving as an inspiration to the members.

That he was responsible for bringing the message of Christ to all people was a major focus of Lorenzo Snow's administration. In a greeting published to the world reflecting his spiritual convictions and his understanding of the coming challenges for the new century, he called for monarchs, workers, the rich, the poor to work together, to honor Him who sent them, and "to make others happy." In conclusion, he proclaimed, "May the twentieth century prove the happiest, as it will be the grandest of all the ages of time and may God be glorified in the victory that is coming over sin and sorrow and misery and death. Peace be unto you all!"

Having turned the attention of the Saints to their financial responsibilities, he now moved ahead in the missionary effort, calling elders to serve in the stakes of Zion and opening Japan for the word of the Lord.

At general conference in October 1901, President Snow suffered from a cold in his lungs and was able to speak at only the closing session. His condition quickly deteriorated, and on October 10, he laid his mortal mission aside. His funeral in the Salt Lake Tabernacle, prior to his burial in Brigham City, was one of the largest ever attended, with scores of faithful Saints having to stand outside to witness the event. The services were opened with the hymn "O My Father," written by his sister Eliza, and many of the apostles elaborated on the testimony, spirituality, and example of this great and noble leader. President Joseph F. Smith concluded the remarks and paid final tribute to President Snow, stating firmly that with the exception of the Prophet Joseph, he didn't believe any man on earth ever bore "a stronger more clear-cut testimony of Jesus Christ."

SOURCES

Papers and letters of Lorenzo Snow, LDS Church Archives, Salt Lake City, Utah; Thomas C. Romney, *The Life of Lorenzo Snow* (Salt Lake City: Sugarhouse Press, 1955); Preston Nibley, *The Presidents of the Church* (Salt Lake City: Deseret Book, 1974), pp. 137-78; Eliza R. Snow Smith, *Biography and Family Record of Lorenzo Snow* (Salt Lake City: Deseret News, 1884); Leonard J. Arrington, *Great Basin Kingdom* (Lincoln: University of Nebraska Press, 1966); Clyde J. Williams, ed., *The Teachings of Lorenzo Snow* (Salt Lake City: Bookcraft, 1984); Francis M. Gibbons, *Lorenzo Snow: Spiritual Giant, Prophet of God* (Salt Lake City: Deseret Book, 1982); and Maureen Ursenbach Beecher, "Leonora, Eliza, and Lorenzo," *Ensign* 10 (June 1980): 64-69.

HEIDI S. SWINTON, a teacher of writing at Utah Technical College in Salt Lake City, is former director of public relations for Sweetwater Corporation and co-author of a history of the Westin Hotel Utah. A graduate of the University of Utah and Northwestern University, she has written articles appearing in *Utah Holiday* and in various trade journals.

JOSEPH F. SMITH

Scott Kenney

Joseph F. Smith was born in 1838, the most strife-torn year in the Church's history. The apostasy that had begun the year before in Kirtland spread to Missouri, where Oliver Cowdery, David Whitmer, and Lyman E. Johnson were excommunicated. A few weeks later Sidney Rigdon publicly intimated violence against apostates, and a letter circulated warning the dissenters to leave the county. Rumors spread that "Danites" would handle those who remained. Non-Mormons, long apprehensive about the influx of large numbers of Mormons in Missouri, agitated for their removal. On the Fourth of July, Joseph Smith and the Saints cheered when Sidney Rigdon declared, "That mob that comes on us to disturb us, it shall be between us and them a war of extermination; for we will follow them till the last drop of their blood is spilled, or else they will have to exterminate us."

Blood was soon shed on both sides. The Prophet was charged with insurrection, and the governor instructed the state militia to put down civil disturbances. Thomas B. Marsh, president of the Quorum of the Twelve, and Orson Hyde, one of the Twelve, accused the Prophet of inciting violence, and the governor ordered the militia to exterminate the Mormons or drive them from the state. Three days later, seventeen Saints were massacred at Haun's Mill.

On October 31, betrayed by a Mormon militia officer, Joseph Smith and several others were taken prisoner. The next day, Joseph's brother Hyrum was taken and, with the other prisoners, sentenced to death. Only the courage of a non-Mormon officer, who refused to carry out the order, saved their lives. When the prisoners were brought to Far West to obtain clothing, Hyrum recalled, "We were not permitted to speak to any one of our families, under the pain of death." Hyrum's wife, Mary Fielding Smith, expecting their first child, was given two minutes to get his clothing, "and in a moment [I] was hurried away from them at the point of the bayonet." As the prisoners' wagon started for Independence — and eventually Liberty Jail — a guard warned Mary she would never see her husband alive again.

As Joseph and Hyrum were being tried for treason, murder, and other crimes, Mary gave birth to Joseph Fielding Smith on November 13, 1838. Far West was an open city. Gangs of thugs and thieves roamed the streets, occasionally breaking into shops, ransacking homes, and terrorizing the people. Overcome by the strain and a severe cold, Mary was unable to nurse Joseph F. or care for her five stepchildren. Fortunately, her sister Mercy Rachel Fielding Thompson, already nursing her five-month-old Mary Jane, was able to nurse both babies and care for Mary and the children. One day men entered the home, broke open Hyrum's trunk, and stole his papers and other valuables. In the commotion bedding was thrown on top of little Joseph F., who was discovered almost suffocated when the men left.

On January 21, 1839, Mary was laid in a wagon bed with her new baby, Joseph F., and traveled with Mercy and Mary Jane, and the Prophet's wife, Emma, and six-year-old Joseph III to visit the prisoners in Liberty. The families spent a sleepless night in the crowded cell and began the forty-mile journey home the following morning.

In mid-February, with Mary in a wagon bed, the Saints crossed Missouri to Quincy, Illinois, where the citizens welcomed them. Mary's family, in addition to the children, included the elderly George Mills, "Aunty" Hannah Grinnel, and Jane Wilson, a younger woman disabled with fits. Joseph and Hyrum were permitted to escape in April and within a few days they were reunited with their families. For the next five years Hyrum would never be long from home, except for two brief trips to the East in 1841 and one in 1842.

In May 1839 Hyrum Smith moved his family to Commerce, soon to become Nauvoo, where he was elected to the first city council and later became vice-mayor. He was never long absent from the side of his younger brother the Prophet. He had been one of the eight witnesses of the Book of Mormon and one of the original six members of the Church. He had helped lay the cornerstone of the Kirtland Temple and had been captain of the Prophet's bodyguard in Zion's Camp. He had been named assistant counselor to the First Presidency in September 1837 and second counselor two months later. In January 1841 he was called by revelation as Patriarch to the Church, to give patriarchal blessings, to be, the Lord said, "a prophet, and a seer, and a revelator unto my church," and "to hold the sealing blessings of my church, even the Holy Spirit of promise, whereby ye are sealed up unto the day of redemption." (D&C 124:91-95, 124.) With the Twelve Apostles abroad on missions, First Counselor Sidney Rigdon living in Philadelphia, and Second Counselor William Law conspiring against the Prophet, Joseph relied on Hyrum for support and counsel.

Joseph F. was five and a half years old when his father was murdered. He would never forget the weeping and anguished cries of grief of that day. The memory of being lifted up to look into the coffins and peering into the lifeless faces of his father and uncle would always be with him.

AS THE SAINTS PREPARED to leave Nauvoo, many widows were married as plural wives to Church leaders. Mary married Heber C. Kimball and became one of thirty-eight women for whom he assumed responsibility. But she made her own way. She sold her property for provisions, and seven-year-old Joseph drove their ox team. From the fall of 1846 to the spring of 1848, the family lived in Winter Quarters, where Joseph tended cattle.

During the winter of 1847-48, many of Mary's cattle and horses died. By spring, Joseph F. recalled, "Winter Quarters was a most sickly hole, and was being deserted by the Saints." Not having sufficient oxen, the Smiths hitched some of their seven wagons to cows and calves, which slowed their progress to Elkhorn. When they finally arrived, Elder Kimball assigned Mary to Cornelius Lott's fifty. Lott declared it would be folly for her to attempt the journey in such a condition. "Go back to Winter Quarters and remain till another year," he insisted, "for if you start out in this manner, you will be a burden on the company the whole way, and I will have to carry you along or leave you on the way." Mary replied, "Father Lott I will beat you to the valley and will ask no help from you either." Joseph F. was struck both with the harsh treatment of his mother and her determination to provide for the welfare of her family. She traded some provisions for new oxen and resumed the journey.

Several weeks later, Joseph F. recalled, "one of our best oxen laid down in the yoke as if poisoned and all supposed he would die. Father Lott now blustered about, as if the world was about at an end. 'There,' said he, 'I told you you would have to be helped, and that you would be a burden on the company.'" But after the ox was anointed with oil and blessed, it got up and resumed its labors. A short distance later another ox fell, was blessed, and recovered. And a third time the process was repeated, "to the astonishment of all who saw and the chagrin of Father Lott." Eventually one of Mary's oxen died; soon after, three of Lott's best oxen and one of his mules died — a great loss. Joseph recalled: "[He] insinuated that somebody had poisoned them through spite, all of which was said in my presence and for my especial benefit, which I perfectly understood, altho' he did not address himself directly to me. . . . My temper was beyond boiling; it was 'white hot,' for I knew his insinuation was directed or aimed at my mother. . . . At this moment I resolved on revenge for this and the many other insults and abuses this old fiend had heaped upon my mother, and should most certainly have carried out my resolution had not death come timely to my relief and rid the earth of so vile and despicable an encumbrance while I was yet a child. One cause of his spite at mother was that she would not allow me to stand guard of nights, and perform all the duties of a man."

The death of his father and the hardships of Winter Quarters (359 died while the Smiths were there) had robbed Joseph of his childhood. At nine he was struggling with anger not easily suppressed, an anger that rose to the surface quickly throughout his early years. He wanted desperately to be a man.

The Smiths arrived in the Salt Lake Valley on September 23, 1848 — ahead of Cornelius Lott. After a few weeks at the fort, they moved six miles southeast to Mill Creek, where they spent the winter in their wagons and tents. In the spring they built a fourteen- by twenty-eight-foot log cabin consisting of two rooms and an attic, where Joseph F. and his half-brother John slept. When the crops began to appear, Joseph F. recalled, "they were besieged by vast hordes of black crickets which seemed to devour everything before them. Our grain fields soon began to vanish from view, when, suddenly, the gulls, in numberless flocks, lit upon the fields and devoured the crickets. These birds would gorge themselves with crickets to the utmost, and then would line up on the water ditches and disgorge them, and begin their work of devouring the crickets again. ... We were literally preserved from starvation by ... these beautiful winged saviors, which we esteemed as the providence of God. ... From year to year for many years we were visited by large flocks of gulls in search of crickets, until the latter seemed to have been almost entirely, if not entirely extinguished."

Joseph F. tended the cattle and sheep, cut wood, and hired out at harvest time. Through hard work and frugality, the family's welfare gradually improved, but in the summer of 1852 Mary was taken ill. She passed away on September 21. Joseph F. was thirteen years old. Years later he wrote, "I have never met her equal in some respects; her faith in God and the holy gospel was implicit, boundless, sublime. Her patience in trials, her unwavering fidelity to her husband's family through all the persecutions and drivings, her endurance in poverty and hardships, and her perfect integrity to every good word and work were beyond anything I have ever seen in womankind. For her sake alone I love her sex, and all the more those of them in whom I see many of her precious traits of character."

To Joseph F. and his twenty-year-old half-brother, John, fell the full responsibility for themselves, Hannah Grinnels, sixteen-year-old Jerusha, fourteen-year-old Sarah, and nine-year-old Martha Ann. When crops and livestock were secured, Joseph F. and Martha Ann attended school. The teacher imposed discipline with a leather strap. On one occasion, Joseph F. recalled, the teacher brought out his leather to discipline Martha Ann. "I just spoke up loudly and said, 'Don't whip her with that,' and at that he came at me and was going to whip me, and instead of him whipping me, I licked him good and plenty."

The incident ended Joseph F.'s formal education, and he was called on a mission at the next Church conference, April 1854. The Sandwich Islands (Hawaiian) mission was the fastest-growing mission in the Church. George Q. Cannon and four other missionaries had baptized "upwards of 4,000" in three and a half years, and Joseph F. was one of twenty-one called to continue the work. He was only fifteen.

ARRIVING IN HONOLULU on September 27, Joseph F. was assigned to Maui. After a few days of recovering from a fever in the Lahaina home of President Francis A. Hammond, the young missionary attended the dedication of the city of Joseph ("Iosepa"), a gathering place for the native Saints on the neighboring island of Lanai. Then he was assigned to Kula in the center of Maui. "I felt for him," President Hammond wrote, "knowing what he has to undergo in preaching and in residing among the people. . . . Brother Joseph is the son of Hyrum Smith, the martyred prophet. He is not yet 16 years old, but bids fain to make a mighty man in this Kingdom." President Hammond blessed Joseph F. that "a mighty man in council should he be, and the spirit of his father Hyrum the martyr should rest upon him."

Joseph F. learned the language quickly. In six months he was called to preside over three districts, and three months later, over the entire island. At age sixteen, he was responsible for two other missionaries and twelve hundred Saints. Later he presided over the island of Molaki and the Hilo and Kohala conferences on Hawaii.

Food was always scarce, and though the natives were usually willing to share what they had, it was not uncommon for the missionaries to go several days at a time without food. Poi and sweet potatoes were the staples, occasionally enriched with fish, pork, or dog meat. Receiving no funds from home, Joseph F. relied on the impoverished Saints to provide clothes. On March 5, 1856, he wrote, "I tended no meetings as I had no clothes to ware or coat to put on. Brother Simpson begged 25 cts. towards getting me a coat. Hard times. Nearly got the bleues, not quite tho. The Saints are poor but I am poorer."

Of course, there were bright spots too. On May 1, 1857, he wrote, "In the evening we seen a sight that was worth all other 'sights' that I ever seen. It was composed of three native girls engaged in a hawaiian dance. It is more than I can describe." Joseph F. attended Simpson Molen's school and worked on vocabulary and reading—newspapers, Benjamin Winchester's *History of the Priesthood*, Lucy Mack Smith's *Biographical Sketches of Joseph Smith the Prophet*, *Uncle Tom's Cabin*, and juvenile novels.

Joseph F. prized righteousness, obedience, and diligence, and he had difficulty reconciling them with Hawaiian attitudes. On May 4, 1857, his physical and spiritual resources strained to the breaking-point, he poured out his frustration and anger:

I have ate enough dirt and filth, put up with anough inconveniances slept sufficiently in their filth, muck & mire, lice and everything else. I have been ill treated, abused, and trod on by these nefarious ethnicks just long anough. I believe it is no longar a virtue, if they will not treat me as I merit, if they will not obey my testimony, and my counsels, but persist in their wickedness, hard heartedness and indifference, their lyings, decietfulness, & hard hearted cruelty as regards the servents of the Lord, I will not stay with them, but leave them to their fait. . . .

This evening we had a pint of poi each & with it I ate 6 chile pepers and retired, more to alleviate the gnawing of a hungry gut than to seak repose and rest.

Of course, he did not abandon the "ethnicks" at all, but grew to love their simple faith and childlike character. In return, they lavished love on him as perhaps on no other *haole*. It was to the Hawaiians that he would flee for refuge in the 1880s, and for relaxation and pleasure in his later years.

Forged in adversity, Joseph F.'s testimony was strong and powerful, a testimony that endured with the same passion and commitment to his dying day. Near the end of his mission, he wrote his favorite childhood cousin Josephine Donna Smith (Ina Coolbrith):

Do you not know that Mormonism is the foundation upon which I have built? The Life of my soul, the sweetest morsal of my existance, the highth of my pride and ambition? *it is*! *Tuch* it, and you tuch the apple of my eye, the fiber of my existance! — because I *know*, — hear it ye worlds! — I KNOW IT IS TRUE! . . . Mormonism I love. Not with that "Boyish love" that lasts for a time, and changes with each new phase, but with the devotion of Man-hood! . . . Let me expire in and for the Cause, for which my Fathers died. I love their hallowed names, and cherish in honor the remembrance of their Noble Spirits. . . . A radiant smile from the Parants who gave me Birth, will thrice pay me for an hundred deaths!

When word arrived in Salt Lake City on July 24, 1857, that two thousand federal troops were en route to Utah to put down a "Mormon rebellion," Brigham Young ordered the missionaries home. Joseph F. took the first available passage to San Francisco, then worked his way to home as a teamster, arriving February 24, 1858. The next day he reported to Brigham Young and joined the militia. As thirty thousand Saints evacuated northern Utah, Joseph F. patrolled the area between Fort Bridger, Wyoming, and Echo Canyon, Utah. In June the troops passed through abandoned Salt Lake City, monitored by, among others, Joseph F. and his cousin Samuel H. B. Smith. The two cousins then helped their families to return to the city from Provo.

On April 5, 1859, Joseph F. married Samuel's sixteen-year-old half-sister, Levira. Brigham Young performed the ceremony in his office. A year later, on April 27, 1860, Joseph F. and Samuel left Salt Lake City on a mission to Great Britain. At the Mississippi they made a side trip to Nauvoo. "I could pick out nearly every spot that I had known in childhood," Joseph F. wrote, "the Office, the Barn, and the little Brick Out house where I shut myself up to keep from going to prison as I supposed." At the home of the Prophet Joseph, they found "young Joseph," who greeted them warmly. "After chatting a few minutes we went over to the mansion, where we found Frederick and Allicksander who greated us cordially. . . . After dinner Frederick took us in to his mother [Emma]. She appeared to have forgotten Samuel but *me* she said she would have known anywhere because I *looked so much like father!!*"

Young Joseph had been blessed by the Prophet to "be my successor to the Presidency of the High Priesthood: a Seer, and a Revelator, and a Prophet, unto the Church, which appointment belongeth to him by blessing, and also by right." But being only eleven when the Prophet died, the youth was not eligible to lead the Church. The Prophet had also conferred the keys of the kingdom on the Twelve, who were sustained as the presiding authority of the Church in August 1844. Joseph F. and Samuel H. B. bore their testimonies to young Joseph, but if there ever had been any question in his mind that the "Utah church" might be the rightful successor, the practice of plural marriage had long since induced him to take his own course. It was a difference that would divide the two branches of the family and their respective churches for generations to come.

In England, Joseph F. got a haircut and purchased a new wardrobe. "You had ought to see me now," he wrote Levira. "You would hardly know whether it was Joseph or not. Let me discribe him as he sits. Here he is, hair 'shinggaled,' tall 'stovepipe' hat, stiff collar & in full English Style, all set & in full trim to go forth a regular english mormon preacher! . . . We stand quite a show even if they did take us to be wilde beasts & monkeys when we first came."

Joseph F. and Samuel were assigned to Sheffield, where Samuel had labored during his first mission. After five months in England, Joseph F. was appointed president of the "Sheffield Pastorate," including the Sheffield, Bradford, Hull, and Lincolnshire conferences.

In 1862 Elder George Q. Cannon of the Quorum of the Twelve replaced Amasa Lyman and Charles C. Rich as mission president. He invited Joseph F. to accompany him on a tour of Germany and Denmark, starting a relationship that would endure forty years. The following year Joseph F. toured Scotland and, with Brigham Young, Jr., visited Paris. He was given charge of the emigration of four thousand Saints who left Europe for Utah that year, requiring much correspondence with local church leaders, government officials, and steamship lines.

The mission to Great Britain gave Joseph F. ample opportunity to develop administrative skills and leadership abilities, but his long absence was a heavy price for Levira. Chronically ill, she lived with relatives, then took in wash and made rag carpets to support herself and her widowed mother. Anxiously she awaited Joseph F.'s return. In March 1862 he wrote that he might be home in six weeks. However, he stayed to supervise emigration though the fall, then until April, May, and finally June of 1863. The disappointments of each delay were heartrending, and by the time he reached the Salt Lake Valley in late August, Levira was on the verge of a complete breakdown.

Before the mission she had been unable to conceive. No doubt Joseph F. believed that adopting a four-year-old boy, Edward, in England would be good for her, but Levira was unable to care for herself, let alone Edward, and he was sent to live with Joseph F.'s cousin Rachel Fielding Burton. "For six weeks after my arrival," Joseph F. wrote, "I did not go to bed, nor take off my clothes to rest. Nor did I have an hour's unbroken rest or sleep during that whole six weeks night or day, but my struggles and faith prevailed. The Lord raised her up."

Six months later, Joseph F. was off on a mission to correct

irregularities in the Church in Hawaii. Traveling with Ezra T. Benson and Lorenzo Snow of the Quorum of the Twelve, William W. Cluff, and Alma L. Smith, Joseph F. arrived at Lahaina on March 29. The delegation found the Saints confused and disturbed over the claims of Walter Murray Gibson. Gibson, an adventurer who had persuaded Brigham Young to send him on a mission in 1860, had mixed LDS teachings with native traditions to win popular support and set himself up on Lanai as the supreme authority. All church property and livestock were registered in his name. Church services were conducted with extraordinary pomp and ceremony. The natives went to work when Gibson rang the bell and quit when he sounded it again. He claimed the right to ordain his own bishops, apostles, and temple priestesses, and sold church offices for personal gain. The apostles excommunicated him and returned to Utah, leaving Joseph F. as the presiding authority, with William Cluff and Alma Smith to assist. The three rallied the members, baptized new converts, and selected the site for a Church plantation at Laie.

His assignment complete, Joseph F. sailed for San Francisco, arriving on November 5, 1864. There he met Levira, who had been staying with their Aunt Agnes, Don Carlos Smith's widow; her divorced daughter, Ina Coolbrith; and other relatives. Joseph F. was anxious to return to Salt Lake City. They set off in late November, but Levira grew increasingly ill. At Dutch Flats they parted. She returned to San Francisco, where she later miscarried, and he continued on to Salt Lake City, where he boarded with his Aunt Mercy. Levira remained under a physician's care for another year, complaining of headaches, nervousness, and depression. Ina wrote Joseph F., "It appers to me Levira is something of a hypochondriac."

IN JANUARY 1865 Brigham Young called Joseph F. to replace Thomas Bullock as a clerk in the Church Historian's Office. He worked closely with the Church Historian, George A. Smith, who had been like a father to Joseph F., and Assistant Church Historian Wilford Woodruff. From them Joseph F. learned not only the names and dates, but the personalities and issues of the Church's earliest days.

Joseph F. was elected to the first of seven consecutive terms in the Territorial House of Representatives in August, and in February 1866 he was elected to the Salt Lake City Council. He continued to serve on the stake high council and attended prayer circles organized by the First Presidency and Twelve.

Levira returned to Salt Lake City in the fall of 1865, but their two-room home was confining and Salt Lake life dull compared with San Francisco. Then, on April 3, 1866, Julina Lambson, sixteen-year-old daughter of Alfred B. and Melissa Bigler Lambson, moved into the living quarters of her Aunt Bathsheba and Uncle George A. Smith in the Historian's Office.

Joseph F. "did not lose any time," Julina recalled. "He had never paid any special attention to me, and I do not think that he had any thought of getting another wife, but President Young advised him and he had told him a number of times, so he thought he should obey." Julina's mother cautioned, "Joseph has a wife whom he loves and he is not marrying you for love," but Julina replied, "Mother, I love him and if I am good, he will learn to love me. He is the only man I have ever seen that I could love as a husband." They were married by Heber C. Kimball on May 5, with Levira's permission and in her presence.

A few weeks later, Joseph F. was invited to speak in the Salt Lake Tabernacle. "The power of God was upon him," wrote Wilford Woodruff, "& he manifested the same spirit that was upon his Uncle Joseph Smith the Prophet & his Father Hyram Smith."

On the following Sunday, July 1, at the conclusion of a prayer circle attended by Brigham Young, George A. Smith, John Taylor, Wilford Woodruff, George Q. Cannon, and Joseph F. Smith, President Young suddenly stopped and exclaimed, "Hold on, shall I do as I feel led? I always feel well to do as the Spirit Constrains me. It is my mind to Ordain Brother Joseph F. Smith to the Apostleship, and to be one of my Councillors." After receiving the endorsement of the apostles present, President Young ordained Joseph F. Smith an apostle and a counselor to the First Presidency. The ordination was kept private, even from First Counselor Heber C. Kimball, for more than a year.

In the meantime, Joseph F. fulfilled his usual responsibilities, including an assignment to northern Utah in the fall. He returned to find Levira had returned home to her mother, and on June 10, 1867, they filed a legal separation that ended in a bitter divorce. This was perhaps the most painful period of Joseph F.'s life, for family was second only to God in his life, and he knew that his quick temper had played a part in the failure of his first marriage. "My greatest difficulty has been to guard my temper—to keep cool in the moment of excitement or trial," he later wrote his son Alvin. "I have always been too quick to resent a wrong, too impatient, or hasty. I hope you will be very careful, my son, on these points. He who can govern himself is greater then he who ruleth a city."

The trauma of the separation was broken for Joseph F. on August 14, 1867, by the arrival of Mercy Josephine, the first of Joseph F.'s forty-three children (in addition to five adopted children). "Oh! How good and kind the Lord has been to me and mine in this regard!" he later wrote. "It seems to me I could endure anything, if only I could feel that all was well with those I love. . . . My children . . . are all the wealth I have, or cherish as of immortal worth. Even when I have passed beyond I would live in my children, if I could, and although generations may come and go, not one shall be so distant or remote that my interest shall cease in them."

THREE WEEKS AFTER JOSEPHINE'S BIRTH, Joseph F. replaced Amasa Lyman in the Quorum of the Twelve. He was set apart by Brigham Young on October 6 in the upper room of the Endowment House and sustained two days later in the first conference to be held in the new Tabernacle. The members of his quorum included Orson Hyde, Orson Pratt, John Taylor,

Wilford Woodruff, George A. Smith, Ezra T. Benson, Charles C. Rich, Lorenzo Snow, Erastus Snow, Franklin D. Richards, and George Q. Cannon.

In December 1867, Brigham Young reconvened the School of the Prophets, which met weekly in Salt Lake City to receive instruction in doctrine, church administration, history, and temporal affairs. At a meeting of the school in January, President Young nominated Abraham O. Smoot to go to Provo as "President, Mayor, and Bishop," with John Taylor as judge, and among others, Wilford Woodruff and Joseph F. Smith as city councilors. It was felt that their presence would tend to suppress the rowdy element in Utah County. After he was elected on February 10, 1868, Joseph F. moved to Provo, where he worked in a cabinet shop for two dollars a day. He married seventeen-year-old Sarah Ellen Richards, daughter of Willard Richards, on March 1. They would have eleven children.

In 1869 Joseph F. returned to Salt Lake City, resuming his work in the Historian's Office and beginning to work regularly in the Endowment House, giving endowments, sealing couples, and performing ordinances in behalf of the dead. On January 1, 1871, he was sealed to Julina's nineteen-year-old sister, Edna Lambson. They would have ten children.

The completion of the transcontinental railroad in 1869 facilitated the gathering of the Saints and lowered the cost of imported goods, but it also brought non-Mormon businessmen, miners, and adventurers to Utah. To conserve their social values and economic interests, the Saints pooled their agricultural and mercantile resources in cooperatives and boycotted non-Mormon businesses. The young women were organized into Retrenchment Societies to combat worldly fashions and ideas. Julina was the president of her ward Retrenchment Society.

Objecting to these isolationist measures, William S. Godbe and E. L. T. Harrison established the Salt Lake *Tribune* and, in cooperation with non-Mormons and anti-Mormons, organized Utah's Liberal Party. In response, Mormons organized the People's Party. Joseph F. took an active role in the People's

Party and drafted resolutions for a mass meeting to protest anti-polygamy legislation in 1870.

On February 28, 1874, one week after concluding his responsibilities as a member of the Territorial Legislature, Joseph F. left for England to preside over the European Mission. His cousin Francis M. Lyman, son of Amasa Lyman, was already serving in England. He would later be called as an apostle and serve thirteen years as president of the Council of the Twelve under Joseph F. Smith. Soon they were joined by another cousin, John Henry Smith (who would serve as a counselor to Joseph F. in the First Presidency), and L. John Nuttall, clerk of the Utah Legislature (later secretary to the First Presidency). With Elder Nuttall in charge, the mission office ran smoothly, and Joseph F., John Henry, and Francis M. Lyman toured Germany, Switzerland, and Denmark together.

Conditions in the mission were trying. The Saints were poor, and few paid tithing. Joseph F. had only a couple dozen missionaries to cover all of England, and he rarely received counsel from Brigham Young. On September 1, 1875, George A. Smith died. Joseph F. grieved for weeks, unable even to write his regular editorial for the *Millennial Star*. "I cannot tell with what terrible weight this melancholy intelligence fell upon my soul," he wrote. "My whole being seems oppressed with a sense of lonliness. . . . O! how I loved him! How I honor his memory!" Within days Joseph F.'s replacement, Albert Carrington, arrived and Joseph F. returned home.

THOUGH HE HAD BEEN GONE less than two years, conditions in Utah had changed dramatically. Utah's economy had not recovered from the depression of 1873, and United Orders were being established throughout the territory. Joseph F. was appointed to preside over the Saints in Davis County and was elected president of the Davis County Cooperative Company, which consisted of several small cooperatives, including a tannery, shoe shop, cattle, horse and sheep herds, and other projects. In addition, he worked in the Endowment House, served on the Salt Lake City Council, and supervised the calling of families to settle Arizona.

General conference in 1877 was held in conjunction with the dedication of the St. George Temple, the first temple completed since Nauvoo. At that conference Joseph F. was called to return to the presidency of the European Mission in Liverpool. This time he was permitted to take Sarah and four-year-old Joseph Richards with him. Joining him was Charles W. Nibley, who became Joseph F.'s closest friend, confidant, financial adviser, and eventually Presiding Bishop of the Church.

Joseph F. found the British Mission "flat as a pancake, broke entirely." There was no money from the Perpetual Emigrating Fund to help the Saints emigrate, and tithing had dropped to half of the 1875 level. Despite his lumbago and eyestrain, he maintained a steady, demanding pace to inspire proselyting among the missionaries and faithful living among the Saints. In August, Orson Pratt arrived to consult with British phoneticists and shorthand experts to develop a new system of spelling and to publish the standard works, primers, and grammars. But the work was soon interrupted by news of the death of Brigham Young on August 29, 1877. The apostles returned to Salt Lake City, arriving on September 27.

For three years the Church was directed by the Quorum of Twelve. One of the most urgent matters facing them was the Brigham Young estate, which was intertwined with church property. Wilford Woodruff, Erastus Snow, Franklin D. Richards, and Joseph F. Smith were appointed to unravel the problem along with George Q. Cannon, Brigham Young, Jr., and Albert Carrington, executors of the estate. Over a period of two years Joseph F. put in many long hours, painstakingly going over financial records and correspondence. At the same time he continued to work in the Historian's Office and, with Daniel H. Wells, superintended the Endowment House.

In September 1878, Joseph F. Smith and Orson Pratt went east to visit historic sites and interview former Church leaders. In Independence, Missouri, they spoke with William E. Mc-Lellin, one of the original members of the Twelve. In Richmond they interviewed David Whitmer, one of the three witnesses to the Book of Mormon. "I always knew that David

Whitmer's testimony was true," wrote Joseph F., "since I received the witness myself, but now I know that David Whitmer is as conscious of the truth of that testimony as he is of his own existence. No man can hear him tell his experience in these matters but he can see and sense that he is conscientiously telling the truth of his own knowledge." In Far West, the two apostles visited the temple site and, across the street, the spot where Hyrum Smith's home once stood. They also visited acquaintances of Joseph and Hyrum in Kirtland, Ohio, and Palmyra, New York. For four weeks Joseph F. visited the sites of his childhood memories and learned of his father and uncle from those who had known them personally, especially Orson Pratt and David Whitmer. It was an invaluable experience, one that Joseph F. detailed in articles and sermons through the ensuing years.

On October 10, 1880, John Taylor was sustained as president of the Church, with George Q. Cannon as first counselor and Joseph F. Smith as second counselor in the First Presidency. At fifty-three and forty-one respectively, George Q. Cannon and Joseph F. Smith were relatively young and vigorous. Their years of dedicated church and civic service qualified them well for their high callings. President Smith had served years in local and state government, and President Cannon was well respected as a delegate to Congress. Both were experienced missionaries and Church administrators, well versed in church history and doctrine.

THE LATE 1870s AND 1880s saw mass rallies held throughout the country protesting the Church's practice of plural marriage. In 1882 the Edmunds bill was enacted, providing for imprisonment of those convicted of polygamy or "unlawful cohabitation." Over the next ten years more than a thousand men were fined and sentenced to six months or more in prison. Polygamists were barred from public office and from jury duty, and a federal election commission barred them from voting. As a polygamist, George Q. Cannon was expelled from the House of Representatives.

Rather than submit to unjust laws, the First Presidency

and Twelve chose civil disobedience. "When I entered into celestial marriage with my first wife," Joseph F. wrote, "I solemnly covenanted and agreed, and so did my wife 'to observe and keep,' not a part but 'all the laws, rites' &c appertaining unto the new and everlasting covenant of matrimony. I understood and still do that the eternity of the marriage covenant includes a plurality of wives, that the marriage of one wife in the new and everlasting covenant is the beginning of the law to be kept in righteousness, and that plural marriage is another part of the same law in the same covenant." On December 16, 1883, he married twenty-five-year-old Alice Ann Kimball, daughter of Heber C. Kimball, and adopted her three children. They would have four more of their own. Finally, on January 13, 1884, he married eighteen-year-old Mary Taylor Schwartz, niece of John Taylor. They would have seven children.

Joseph F. spent much of 1883 and 1884 in seclusion. In September 1884 he and Edna accompanied Erastus Snow on a tour of Mormon settlements in Colorado, New Mexico, and Arizona. The following January the First Presidency and four apostles toured the same region. Joseph F. and President Taylor continued on to Mexico and then to San Francisco, where they consulted with California Governor Leland Stanford. When word arrived that warrants had been issued in Utah for the arrest of the First Presidency, President Taylor advised Joseph F., who was most familiar with plural marriages performed in the Endowment House, to go to Hawaii. Julina and a daughter were soon on a train to San Francisco, where they joined Joseph F. on a voyage to Honolulu. For the next two and one-half years, the Church plantation at Laie was home for "J. F. Speight."

Sitting on the sidelines was agonizing to Joseph F. Smith. Thousands of miles from four wives and fourteen children, he could do little to provide for their physical or emotional needs. In March 1887 Julina returned to care for the children, and soon after, Edna wrote, "We are living at our poorest now. No butter, no meat, but imported bacon, and we women folks cannot eat that. . . . Some of us are almost starved. . . . The most of Ina's talk is about Papa. . . . She said, '. . . When he comes back I'll hold him just as tight as tight, so he cannot leave us anymore.' Oh! My Papa I can only think of you in that lonesome room all alone. The silent tears have wet my pillow at night, when I have been thinking of you, my sorrow seems greater than my joy. For when oh when will we ever meet again?"

In June, Joseph F. was called home. President Taylor was on his deathbed. Joseph F. arrived at the President's hiding place in Kaysville on July 18, and a week later President Taylor passed away.

In Joseph F.'s absence, the government had disincorporated the Church and confiscated all of its property in excess of $50,000; women's suffrage had been abolished in the territory; and no one could vote, serve on a jury, or hold public office without taking an oath in support of antipolygamy laws. The Church faced financial ruin and its members complete disfranchisement.

Shortly before his death, President Taylor had endorsed a state constitution prohibiting polygamy. Once statehood was achieved, local citizens, not federal appointees, would legislate and enforce the laws. The antipolygamy constitution was ratified by a vote of the people one week after President Taylor's death.

In February 1888 the Twelve appointed Joseph F. to oversee the Church's lobby in Washington. He was to be assisted by Charles W. Penrose, whom Joseph F. would later call to the apostleship and eventually to the First Presidency. They proceeded to the nation's capital immediately, returned in June when Congress adjourned, then resumed their post in Washington from January to March of 1889.

Ultimately, however, resolution of the conflict between the Church and the government would not take place in Washington but in Utah.

THE FIRST PRESIDENCY WAS REORGANIZED at the April 5 meeting of the Twelve, with Wilford Woodruff as president and George Q. Cannon and Joseph F. Smith as counselors. Still subject to arrest, Joseph F. was unable to attend general conference or live in his own home. Instead, he remained in the Gardo House across the street from the Beehive House and Lion House, and ventured out only in disguise.

After a series of defeats at the polls, a decision by the Supreme Court upholding Idaho's test oath, and the threat of even more stringent federal legislation, the First Presidency, on June 30, 1890, formulated a new policy regarding plural marriage. "The times have changed," Joseph F. wrote to Charles W. Nibley. "The conditions are not propitious and the *decrees* of the 'Powers that be' are against the move [for Nibley to take another wife]. I do not care so much for the outside *powers* as I do those within, although common prudence would suggest that deference should be paid to both. The *decree* now is that there shall be no p----l m-------s in the United States, and that there shall be none anywhere else unless *one* or both of the parties remove beyond the jurisdiction of this government to make their home. This comes to within one of being absolute prohibition. How long this condition of things may last no man knoweth, but for the present it is the 'law'."

Although the action was not publicly announced, it was hoped the government would respond favorably. But reports continued to come that the temples would soon be confiscated unless plural marriage was publicly disavowed. In early September the First Presidency went to San Francisco to confer with politicians, railroad and newspaper officials and leaders of the Republican Party. Shortly after their return to Utah, President Woodruff issued the Manifesto advising the Saints "to refrain from contracting any marriage forbidden by the law of the land."

The Manifesto achieved the desired effect. Prosecution of polygamists was relaxed, and the way was opened for Utah's statehood and the return of Church property in 1894 and 1896. Joseph F. appealed to President Harrison for amnesty in August 1891, and it was granted the next month. In October, Joseph F. was able to attend a general conference of the Church for the first time in seven years. "The house was full to the gallery," he wrote. "I spoke briefly, for I was so overcome by my feelings that I could scarcely restrain them. . . . I shook hands with my friends until my hand and arm felt lame. . . . This is a memorable day for me, and no words at my command can express my gratitude to God." At last Joseph F. Smith was free to associate with the Saints and resume a normal life with his family, which now numbered five wives and twenty-six children.

Three weeks later Joseph F., with Presidents Woodruff and Cannon, was called upon to testify before the master in chancery to obtain a return of Church property. They were required to state that the Manifesto was intended to apply universally, not just in the United States, and that it included a prohibition on cohabitation in existing plural marriages as well. Their testimony created great controversy, but as President Woodruff told the Saints in Logan, "The Lord . . . has told me exactly what to do, and what the result would be if we did not do it. . . . I saw exactly what would come to pass if there was not something done. I have had this spirit upon me for a long time." As far as the general membership of the Church was concerned, plural marriage had ended, though exceptions were granted until President Smith ended the practice in 1904.

The other major impediment to statehood for Utah was the charge that Church leaders dictated the political life of its members. From the days of the Prophet Joseph Smith, Latter-day Saints had looked to the president of the Church for temporal as well as spiritual guidance, including counsel regarding those best suited to govern civil affairs. "Theodemocracy," it had been called during Brigham Young's administration. But to non-Mormons, religious "interference" in politics was un-American. Therefore, in early 1891 the First Presidency concurred in the recommendation of People's Party officials to disband the party and encourage the members to divide along national party lines. Since the Republicans had been in the forefront of the antipolygamy campaign, most Mormons favored the Democratic Party. But a mass exodus from the People's Party to the Democratic Party would preserve the appearance of Church-dominated politics. In addition, statehood for Utah would require the support of the Republican Party. Thus, the First Presidency assigned Joseph F. Smith and Elder John Henry Smith to stump for the Republican Party.

Campaigning for the Republicans was an uphill battle. They were defeated in the 1891 election, and the following year Joseph F. published *Another Plain Talk: Reasons Why the People of Utah Should Be Republicans*. In January 1893, Republican President Benjamin Harrison granted amnesty for those "who since November 1, 1890, have abstained from unlawful cohabitation," and in 1895 Republican John Henry Smith presided over Utah's constitutional convention. Just before the 1895 election, Joseph F. created a considerable stir by suggesting in a church meeting that Elders Moses Thatcher and B. H. Roberts were out of favor for not obtaining permission of the First Presidency before accepting nominations from the Democratic Party for the U.S. Senate and House of Representatives. The Republicans swept the election. Non-Mormon Clarence E. Allen was elected to the House of Representatives, and Arthur Brown, a non-Mormon attorney, and Frank J. Cannon, son of George Q. Cannon, became Utah's first senators.

In 1898 B. H. Roberts obtained permission from the First Presidency to seek the Democratic nomination for the House of Representatives. He won the election, but the House refused to seat the polygamist representative; William H. King, a Mormon Democrat, later filled the vacancy.

WILFORD WOODRUFF PASSED AWAY on September 2, 1898, and the new First Presidency—Lorenzo Snow, George Q. Cannon, and Joseph F. Smith—was sustained eleven days later. The greatest problem facing the Church was economic. First undermined by the government's 1887 confiscation of property, the treasury had been depleted by the legal defense fund, completion of the Salt Lake Temple, and establishment of a churchwide education system. The Panic of 1893 had virtually ruined the Church financially, and when the escheated property was returned, it was found to be substantially less than had been taken. Finally, in December 1898, the First Presidency decided to issue two bond series of $500,000 each, redeemable in five years. Senator Frank Cannon believed he had the agreement of the presidency to sell the bonds in the East, for a substantial commission. But Joseph F. eventually prevailed, insisting that the bonds be sold to the Saints without a commission. It was a bitter defeat for Cannon, one he would never forget.

George Q. Cannon died April 12, 1901, and Lorenzo Snow on October 10. At the next regular meeting of the Twelve in the temple on October 17, the First Presidency was reorganized with sixty-two-year-old Joseph F. Smith as president and John R. Winder, then second counselor in the Presiding Bishopric, and Anthon H. Lund of the Council of the Twelve as counselors. Joseph F. departed from tradition by asking to be set apart by his half-brother John, who had been called as Patriarch to the Church by Brigham Young in 1855. Joseph F. noted "that the Lord had given the patriarch Hyrum Smith first and then the presidency." (See D&C 124:124.) He proposed that in the future the Patriarch be sustained in general conference before the Twelve, but concerns expressed by President Lund and members of the Twelve induced him to table the proposal.

On October 24, President Smith submitted the name of his twenty-nine-year-old son Hyrum Mack Smith to fill the vacancy in the Twelve. The calling was approved, and at a special conference of the Church on November 10, the appointments were sustained by the membership.

In his initial address, President Smith sounded the theme of his presidency: "We have been looked upon as interlopers, as fanatics, as believers in a false religion; we have been regarded with contempt, and treated despicably; we have been driven from our homes, maligned and spoken evil of every where, until the people of the world have come to believe that we are the off-scourings of the earth and scarcely fit to live. . . . The Lord designs to change this condition of things, and to make us known to the world in our true light—as true worshippers of God . . . and that our mission in this world is to do good, to put down iniquity in the hearts of the people, and to establish in the minds of our children, above all other things, a love for God and His word . . . making them firm believers in the word of the Lord, in the restored Gospel and Priesthood, and in the establishment of Zion, no more to be thrown down nor given to another people."

Joseph F. saw that his twofold mission was to convince the world that the principles taught by the Church were the true gospel of Jesus Christ, and to pass on to the next generation a testimony that the faith received of their fathers remained in fact the kingdom of God on earth.

THE MOST SERIOUS CHALLENGE to the first part of President Smith's goal began with the election of Elder Reed Smoot as Republican Senator from Utah. Contrary to the counsel of many political and religious advisers, President Smith had endorsed Elder Smoot's candidacy, and the election of a Mormon apostle by Utah's Republican legislature set off a storm of protest. Nineteen citizens of Salt Lake City demanded his expulsion from the Senate, alleging that Elder Smoot was a member of a ruling body that continued to promulgate plural marriage.

A Senate committee appointed to consider the protest commenced hearings on January 16, 1903, and continued until June 1906. The high point of the hearings was the appearance of President Joseph F. Smith on March 2 to 4, 1904. On the central question, much in the vein of his father's and uncle's statements in Nauvoo, President Smith denied any knowledge of new plural marriages. He did, however, acknowledge that his continued marital relations with plural wives were in technical violation of the law and Church rules.

At the April 1906 general conference of the Church, President Smith issued an "Official Statement," endorsed by the conference, prohibiting new plural marriages, with excommunication for those who persisted. President Smith was sympathetic with those who had entered plural marriage in good faith after the Manifesto, but those who refused to acknowledge the authority of the president to withhold permission in the future would be excommunicated. At least six apostles had taken post-Manifesto plural wives, but only John W. Taylor and Matthias F. Cowley would not endorse the policy. They resigned from the Twelve in April 1905. Elder Taylor was excommunicated in March 1911; Elder Cowley was disfellowshipped in May; his membership was restored in 1936.

The Smoot hearings had an unsettling effect on the Saints. The anti-Mormon American Party gained control of Salt Lake City from 1905 to 1911. Ex-Senator Frank J. Cannon, editor of the *Tribune*, frustrated by the lack of support for his political ambitions, mounted a scathing attack on President Smith, calling him "a liar," "a sorcerer," and "a maker of evil." President Smith, he proclaimed, "will not need to wait to be cast down to hell in the next world, for he will get some of the condemnation here." For years Cannon seemed intent on playing the devil's role, making President Smith's life as uncomfortable as possible. President Smith felt betrayed by one who knew the truth. "Furious Judas" was his nickname for Frank J., but he made no response to the outrageous charges except to say, as in 1906, "I do not care for and don't want to pay any heed to the ridiculous nonsense, the foolish twaddle, and the impious slurs that are being cast on me and my people, by wicked hearts and perverted minds. Let God deal with them as seemeth Him good."

Of President Smith's many contributions, perhaps none is more important than the final resolution of tension between the Church and the federal government. During his administration the hostilities ended and Latter-day Saints were accepted as loyal, law-abiding citizens whose contributions to the nation and the world would become even more apparent as the years passed.

With his Senate testimony behind him, President Smith was able to give more attention to other matters. In May 1905 the Smith homestead in Sharon, Vermont, was purchased and President Smith attended the dedication of the monument at the Prophet's birthplace on the hundredth anniversary of his birth, December 23, 1905. The return trip included stops at the Sacred Grove, Palmyra, and Kirtland, reinforcing the sense of continuity with the past for the modern church. President Smith also approved the purchase of the Smith farm at Palmyra, property at Adam-Ondi-Ahman, Carthage Jail, and property adjacent to the Independence temple lot in Missouri.

In addition to the acquisition of historic sites, the Church in 1905 appropriated $175,000 for completion of the LDS Hospital in Salt Lake City; $105,200 for Brigham Young University in Provo, LDS University in Salt Lake City, and Brigham Young College in Logan; $104,000 to the poor; $99,000 for the Cochran Ranch in Alberta, Canada; and $61,000 for sixteen stake academies. Half of all Utah secondary-school students were enrolled in LDS academies. The purchases and funding of expanding educational programs were made possible by the substantially improved financial situation of the Church. At the April 1907 conference President Smith announced that the 1898 bonds had been retired. The Church, he reported, "owes not a dollar that it cannot pay at once. At least we are in a position that we can pay as we go."

In addition to the administration of Church affairs, President Smith was president or board member of dozens of businesses in which the Church had a significant interest, such as ZCMI, Beneficial Life Insurance, Utah-Idaho Sugar, and Zion's Savings Bank. The demands placed on him were great. Fortunately, he was well suited for the calling. "President George Q. Cannon is the only man I ever met to whose capacity for endurance I had to bow," he wrote, "and he possessed one gift — a rare one too, which I, unfortunately, did not possess. It was this, at night when the toil of the day was done and we laid ourselves down for rest, the moment his head pressed his pillow he slept and snored, and snored and slept, while I would toss and roll and sigh for sleep and rest but like the will of the wisp it would mockingly dance before my o'er wraught nerves and perhaps for hours when most I needed it, elude me. And then I never failed to hear or sense the slightest sound or stir. I have carried this nervous temperament for more than 66 years and still I live! but it is due to kind providence, to the mercy and love of God."

President Smith, wrote Charles W. Nibley, "was a most strenuous worker and never considered saving himself at all. You could go up to his little office in the Beehive [House] most any night when he was well, and find him writing letters or attending to some other work. Perhaps some dear old soul had written him a personal letter, and he would work into the night answering it with his own hand."

In July 1906 President Smith and Edna made a trip to Europe with Charles W. Nibley and his wife. Four of President Smith's sons were serving missions there at the time, and no other president of the Church had toured Europe. In August and September they visited the Saints in the Netherlands, Germany, Belgium, Switzerland, France, and England. On the return trip, Elder Nibley raised the sensitive issue of an apostle in the Senate. He suggested that "it would be unwise for Reed Smoot to be re-elected to the United States Senate. I was con-scientious in my objection, and I had marshaled all the facts, arguments, and logic, that I could. . . . I could see [Joseph F.] began to listen with some little impatience, and yet he let me have my say, but he answered in tones and in a way that I shall never forget. Bringing his fist down with some force on the railing between us, he said, in the most forceful and posi-tive manner: 'If ever the Spirit of the Lord has manifested to me anything clear and plain and positive, it is this, that Reed Smoot should remain in the United States Senate. He can do more good there than he can anywhere else.'" Elder Smoot retained his Senate seat for a total of thirty years, serving many years as chairman of the powerful Senate Finance Committee.

In December 1907, President Smith named Charles W. Nibley as Presiding Bishop of the Church. Bishop Nibley chose as his counselors Orrin P. Miller and President Smith's son David A. Smith. On April 7, 1910, President Smith ordained his son Joseph Fielding Smith an apostle. Other apostles or-dained by President Smith were Elder John Henry Smith's son George Albert Smith (1903), Charles W. Penrose (1904), Elder Franklin D. Richards's son George F. Richards (1906), Orson F. Whitney (1906), David O. McKay (1906), Anthony W. Ivins (1907), James E. Talmage (1911), Stephen L Richards (1917), and Elder Francis M. Lyman's son Richard R. Lyman (1918). Patriarch John Smith died in November 1911, and his grandson Hyrum Gibbs Smith was ordained a high priest and Presiding

Patriarch by President Smith in May 1912. Three of the apostles called by President Smith eventually served as counselors in the First Presidency. Joseph F. Smith served seventeen years as president; the three called by him who became president led the Church for twenty-seven more years.

PROGRAMS AND POLICIES INITIATED during the Joseph F. Smith administration included weekly priesthood quorum meetings, standardized lesson manuals, seminary, adult Sunday School classes, the *Children's Friend*, affiliation of the Relief Society with the National Council of Women, adoption of the Boy Scouts of America program, and a boarding home for working girls in Salt Lake City.

Significant doctrinal pronouncements and applications included statements on war, evolution, the Godhead, the resurrection, and the plan of salvation. The First Presidency justified military service of Church members on both sides of World War I. When some BYU professors were dismissed for their insistence on teaching higher criticism of the Bible and evolution, President Smith explained, "In reaching the conclusion that evolution would be best left out of discussions in our Church schools we are deciding a question of propriety and are not undertaking to say much of evolution, or how much is false. ... The Church itself has no philosophy about the *modus operandi* employed by the Lord in His creation of the world." A statement on "The Father and the Son" delineated the roles of Jesus as Jehovah, as Creator or Father of the earth, as Father of his disciples, and as one invested with the authority of God the Father while on earth.

In July and August 1910, President Smith and his wife Mary again toured Europe with the Charles W. Nibleys. Over the next several years, President Smith undertook numerous trips to visit the Saints throughout the United States, particularly in the West. On a trip to Canada in July 1913, he dedicated the site for the Alberta Temple. In 1914 he purchased a vacation home dubbed "Deseret" in Santa Monica, California.

In May 1915, after the death of his wife Sarah, President Smith and Julina took a trip to Hawaii with the Nibleys. At

Laie, President Smith dedicated the temple site. On his return he met with the First Presidency and the Twelve and, he said, "I sprung the proposition to build a small temple at Laie ... and it met with a warm approval by the entire council."

President Smith, always intrigued by politics, took a special interest in the 1916 presidential election. U.S. President Woodrow Wilson had reduced tariffs sharply, adversely affecting home industry, and had instituted a federal income tax to compensate. President Smith attended Republican rallies but did not speak. When Wilson was reelected, he wrote, "A pall of gloom hangs over the city and the Republican party of Utah." Four days later President Smith experienced severe chest pains that put him to bed.

President Smith's heart continued to trouble him through 1917, causing restless nights and uncomfortable days. Still he maintained a relentless schedule of meetings and correspondence. In April he moved into the new Church Administration Building at 47 East South Temple, next door to the president's residence in the Beehive and Lion houses. The following month, he visited Hawaii, "perhaps for the last time," he noted.

On January 23, 1918, President Smith's son Hyrum M. died from complications of appendicitis. The unexpected death was a terrible shock to President Smith, and his physical health began to fail. "I may have physical ailments," he told the Saints in April, "but it appears to me that my spiritual status not only remains steadfast as in times past, but is developing, growing, becoming more thoroughly established in the faith of the gospel, in the love of truth, and in a desire to devote all the energy, time, wisdom and ability the Lord may give me to build up Zion in these latter days." He spent much of his time in prayer and meditation.

At the October conference he said, "I have not lived alone these five months. I have dwelt in the spirit of prayer, of supplication, of faith and of determination; and I have had my communication with the Spirit of the Lord continuously." Just the day before, he reported, he had been reading First Peter as he prepared his address. "The eyes of my understanding were opened, and the Spirit of the Lord rested upon me, and I saw the hosts of the dead, both small and great." He reported seeing the Lord during his mission to the spirits of the dead, and saw that righteous spirits were appointed to minister to them as well. He saw his father Hyrum, the Prophet Joseph, and others, and learned "that the faithful elders of this dispensation, when they depart from mortal life, continue their labors in the preaching of the gospel."

This vision was presented to the Quorum of the Twelve Apostles and Presiding Patriarch on October 31, and was accepted as a revelation from God. It was initially published in the *Improvement Era*, and in 1981 it was published as section 138 of the Doctrine and Covenants.

On November 17, 1918, President Smith had an attack of pleurisy, which developed into pneumonia, and he passed away on November 19. As Salt Lake City was under quarantine because of the influenza epidemic, no public funeral service was held. But as the cortege passed from the Beehive House to the City Cemetery, his son Joseph Fielding wrote, "thousands of people thronged the streets with bowed heads."

Born in persecution and turmoil, Joseph F. Smith died in peace and tranquility, his bitterest enemies deceased or won over. "In his earlier days," editorialized the Salt Lake *Tribune*, "he was fiery, fearless, impetuous and uncompromising, and was therefore looked upon as a fanatic, intolerant of moderation and irreconcilable to opposition. But with the coming of age, the assumption of authority, the increase of responsibility and the consequent contact with his fellow men, came a broadening of vision and a softening of his nature which gained for him a recognition of those sterling qualities for which he will be remembered longest and best. . . .

"Even those who differed radically from him in the past have doubtless forgotten it in the presence of death, if it had not already passed from their memories in close acquaintance through mutual interests and activities of later years."

NINETEENTH-CENTURY MORMONISM witnessed extraordinary transformations. Latter-day Saints were called upon to consecrate all their property to united orders, then embrace capitalism; to put aside traditional family values and even endure imprisonment for plural marriage, then espouse monogamy; to maintain a united political system directed by prophets and apostles, then divide between national parties dominated by non-Mormons; to defend the kingdom of God against a nation bent on its destruction, then send their children off to die in that nation's wars.

Continuity amid such radical change was crucial, and the living witness of President Joseph F. Smith was of the greatest significance. Through his veins flowed the blood of prophets. He had passed through the violence of the early decades, the deprivation of the pioneer period, and the prosecution of the territorial years. His passion for the restoration was unquestioned, his loyalty to the kingdom unexcelled. His presence alone was reassuring, his affirmations compelling. He was, in word, in action, and in being, a link with the past, a bridge over troubled waters.

SOURCES

This essay has been written from the diaries, letters and other documents in the Joseph F. Smith Collection, LDS Church Archives, Salt Lake City. The standard biography is Joseph Fielding Smith, *Life of Joseph F. Smith* (Salt Lake City, 1938). See also Hyrum M. Smith and Scott G. Kenney, eds., *From Prophet to Son: Advice of Joseph F. Smith to His Missionary Sons* (Salt Lake City, 1981); Joseph F. Smith, *Gospel Doctrine* (Salt Lake City, 1971); Leonard J. Arrington, "Joseph F. Smith: From Impulsive Young Man to Patriarchal Prophet," *The John Whitmer Historical Association Journal* 4 (1984): 30-40; Don Cecil Corbett, *Mary Fielding Smith, Daughter of Britain, Portrait of Courage* (Salt Lake City, 1966); and Pearson H. Corbett, *Hyrum Smith, Patriarch* (Salt Lake City, 1963).

SCOTT KENNEY, a native of Salt Lake City, is a graduate of the University of Utah and the Graduate Theological Union in Berkeley, California. He is director of Eden Hill Publishing Company and has done historical research for the LDS Historical Department. He has published on historical and theological topics in a variety of church and professional journals, and is co-author of *From Prophet to Son: Advice of Joseph F. Smith to His Missionary Sons* (Salt Lake City: Deseret Book, 1981).

HEBER J. GRANT
Ronald W. Walker

Not since the double deaths of Joseph Smith and his brother Hyrum had the Saints mourned so openly. Salt Lake City's doors and windows were draped in black. The Territory's flags stood at a respectful half-mast, their bottoms striped with a swath of sable crepe. City councilmen placed somber bands on their left arm. They would continue the gesture for a month. Commerce ceased, and in preparation for the obsequies, military commanders ordered outlying regiments to the city. "The notice is short," admitted one officer, "but by prompt action you will be able to . . . be on hand." Come "without fail, even if it takes you all night, hard riding."

Forty-year-old Jedediah Morgan Grant — President Young's counselor, Salt Lake City's first mayor, and a general of the Territory's Nauvoo Legion — was dead. "Lung disease," apparently a combination of typhoid and pneumonia, had taken him on the first day of December 1856.

The funeral proceeded with elaborate formality. The uniformed Legion formed a block-long aisle from the Grant home to Temple Square. A solemnly decorated spring wagon served as a hearse, and most dramatic of all, a solitary groom led a fully caparisoned and riderless horse. When the cortege finally reached the Old Tabernacle, the formalities had caused almost a two-hour delay. As a result, President Young spoke briefly.

Jedediah had been "a great man, a giant, a lion," Brother Brigham eulogized. But even the magnetic Jedediah Grant was not irreplaceable. Attempting to still the congregation's grief, President Young promised the Saints even greater leaders for the future. There are "young whelps . . . growing up here who will roar louder than ever he dare[d]."

Sometime that morning, four-year-old Tony Ivins played on the Grants' second-story balcony, overlooking the crowds and ceremony below. His mother had already told him about the death of his distinguished uncle. While he hardly understood her words, they frightened him and fixed in his mind a few random events that became his earliest memory. He would later remember seeing Aunt Rachel, Jedediah's seventh wife, still bedridden from her difficult birthing. Out on the adjoining porch, he also would remember finding a crib, which he pulled close to him. Looking inside, he found little Heber, Rachel's child, his thirteen-day-old cousin who had been born on November 22. Unbeknown to little Tony, Rachel Grant, and probably President Young himself, here was one of Brother Brigham's prophesied "whelps," ready for the making.

FROM THE BEGINNING Rachel's young son seemed a child of promise. When Bishop Edwin Woolley christened him Heber Jeddy Ivins Grant, the spirit of the occasion was unusual. "I was only an instrument in the hands of his dead father . . . in blessing him," Bishop Woolley later remarked. Heber Grant "is entitled to be one of the Apostles, and I know it."

There were other stirrings of the future. Once Rachel took the child to a formal dinner at the Heber C. Kimball home. After the adults had finished, the children were invited to eat what remained. Little Heber was thoroughly enjoying himself when President Kimball, who had served with Jedediah in the First Presidency, suddenly lifted the boy atop a table and began prophesying. The boy understood nothing of President Kimball's words, but he long remembered his coal black eyes, which unsettled him.

Too, there was a Relief Society meeting in William C. Staines's home in the Twelfth Ward. Eliza R. Snow and Zina

D. Young were speaking and interpreting in the "unknown" tongue. Blessing each of the women present, they eventually turned to Rachel. Heber, who played on the floor, recalled hearing something about his becoming "a great big man." His mother's understanding, however, was more accurate. "Behave yourself," Rachel knowingly told him as he grew to maturity, "and you will someday be one of the apostles in the Church."

Heber's progenitors had laid the foundation for such service. Both Joshua and Athalia Howard Grant, Jedediah Grant's father and mother, came from families that had farmed Connecticut's stony soil for at least four generations. When the Mormon missionaries found them, they had twelve children. "Jeddy," as their son was usually known, was their seventh.

Seventeen-year-old Jedediah quickly took to Mormonism. When he was baptized in a river near his home, the winter temperature was so biting that his clothes froze. A year later he marched with Zion's Camp to Missouri. At nineteen he began the first of four proselyting missions, which won him a reputation for wit, eloquence, and successful baptizing. In 1843 he received the appointment of presiding elder of the Philadelphia Branch, and soon thereafter he became a member of the First Council of Seventy and of Joseph Smith's General Council at Nauvoo. When the Saints went west in 1847, Jedediah captained the "Third Hundred" pioneers across the plains and into the valley.

Once settled in Salt Lake City, Jedediah Grant found that church and public duty again dominated his life. Twice President Young called him to the East on church assignments. Then in quick succession he became Salt Lake City's first mayor, Speaker of the Territorial House, and an apostle and second counselor in the First Presidency. Because of his Indian-fighting heroics, open-handed charity, and preaching zeal, there grew around Jedediah a folklore that lost nothing in the telling. To the Saints he was a Mormon Sam Houston or Andy Jackson.

Jedediah M. Grant died as dramatically as he lived. Sensing President Young's displeasure with the Saints' lack of spiritual and temporal progress, Jedediah began in September 1856 the grand climax of his career, the famed Mormon Reformation. He swept through the Territory preaching repentance and social improvement. His "words flowed from his mouth like a great river," the Saints recalled. "We have never heard a man, before nor since, who spoke with greater power." Preaching as many as three one-hour sermons during a single evening, Jedediah pushed himself beyond his limits. While visiting the Historian's Office on November 19, he was noticeably ill. Less than two weeks later, he lay dying. "Diffuse the spirit," he whispered. Diffuse it "under the earth, through the earth, and over the earth." They were his last words.

Heber's quiet and prim mother, Rachel Ridgeway Ivins Grant, was a marked contrast to the high-spirited Jedediah. She was the sixth of eight children born to Caleb and Edith Ridgeway Ivins. Both parents died before she was ten, and Rachel was raised by a succession of New Jersey relatives, who instilled within her the family virtues of hard work, neatness, discipline, and Christian kindness.

The Ivinses and Ridgeways were similar. They were serious-minded and prosperous merchants who had migrated to America in the late seventeeth century. Many of the family branches were Quaker. Rachel, however, found the Friends' seriousness burdensome. For instance, she liked to sing. While living with a straight-laced cousin who banned music from his home, the orphan would steal off to a small grove of trees, where she'd sing as she sewed for her dolls.

When at eighteen years of age she first met the dashing Jedediah Grant, still in his early twenties, she at first wondered if he might be one of the "false prophets that the Bible speaks of." She returned home after one Mormon preaching session, knelt down, and pleaded for the Lord's forgiveness for deliberately listening to false doctrine on the Sabbath. But more searching prayer and study convinced her otherwise. In 1840 she was baptized into The Church of Jesus Christ of Latter-day Saints, and two years later, with relatives who also had accepted the faith, she traveled to Nauvoo.

The well-bred Rachel Ivins must have turned more than one head in Nauvoo. A friend later described her: "She was dressed in silk with a handsome lace collar, of fichu, and an elegant shawl over her shoulder, and a long white lace veil thrown back over her simple straw bonnet. She carried an elaborate feather fan. . . . One could easily discern the subdued Quaker pride in her method of using it, for sister Rachel had the air, the tone, and mannerisms of the Quakers."

After the death of Joseph Smith, Rachel at first did not follow the Saints west. Disturbed by the doctrine of plural marriage (rumors circulated that Joseph Smith himself sought her hand), she returned to New Jersey and her family for half a dozen years. However, with her faith rekindled, she joined a pioneer company in 1853. Doctors warned that the journey might turn a persistent cough into something dangerous—her family had a medical history of "consumption," or tuberculosis. Most of Rachel's relatives also attempted to dissuade her. They offered a lifetime annuity if she would remain.

When the New Jersey pioneers arrived in Salt Lake City, they turned up Main Street and found temporary lodging with their old friend, Jedediah Grant. Two years later, Rachel returned to the home as Jedediah's wife, the couple having been married in the Endowment House "for time [in mortality] only." Apparently to satisfy any obligation that might be owing Joseph, President Young suggested that she first be "eternally sealed" by proxy to the Prophet.

JEDEDIAH'S DEATH left Rachel and her only child without a tangible source of security. Her plentiful cache of New Jersey "store goods" had long since been personally used or given to those around her, while Grant's small estate proved unequal to the needs of Rachel and her sister-wives. The New Jersey Ivinses and Ridgeways promised that the latchstring would always be out for Rachel—but only if she would renounce Mormonism. However, this was no longer an issue.

President Young offered a solution. If the Grant wives would remain as a unit on Main Street and accept George Grant, Jedediah's brother, as their new husband, the President believed little Heber and his half-brothers and -sisters would have ample security. Rachel complied, but the marriage was difficult. Once a faithful churchman, Indian fighter, and hero of the 1856 handcart tragedy, George was, unbeknown to Church leaders, struggling with alcohol. When his behavior became more immoderate and erratic, President Young dissolved the two-year marriage. "It was the one frightful ordeal of my mother's life, and the one thing she never wishes to refer to," Heber remarked in later years.

Of course, the little boy knew nothing of his mother's struggle. His memories of pioneer Main Street were happy. Homes like the Grants' sat on a spacious acre and a quarter. This permitted smokehouses, orchards, and truck gardens of cabbage, corn, and tomatoes. Hogs rooted in backyard pens and chickens announced the dawn. The Grant homestead, located on the site of today's ZCMI department store, was one of the city's finest. Out front, where the property met the street, Jedediah had placed some incipient shade trees, and behind them a decorous "quaken-asp-pole" fence. The home itself, which eventually grew to three sections, had as its centerpiece a two-story Greek revival-like structure, complete with a colonnade and a colonial "widow's watch" balcony.

Heber remembered boyish things. There was the hole in the stone fence that separated the Grant property from General Daniel H. Wells's land to the north. The hole was originally built to allow a meandering fork of City Creek to flow behind the two homes, and the lad found he could crawl through the opening and escape his own backyard to the Wells property. Heber also recalled Joe Elder's fifteen-by-twenty-foot cooper shop located a block south down on Main Street. The boy often visited Elder at this shop, where he liked to watch him work and hear him talk. And located across the street from the Grant home were two attractions bound to claim a boy's attention. These were the Globe Bakery and the Livingston-Kincaid store, the city's first eatery and mercantile establishment.

Heber best remembered the community leaders who befriended him. The kindly Daniel Wells often acted like a father to him. Presiding Bishop Edward Hunter, whose property lay just south of the Grants, frequently invited the boy to climb into his buggy and bring a bucket. Traveling south, the two went to Bishop Hunter's farm and gathered sweet or pop corn, some of which Heber was allowed to put in his bucket and bring home. A northern course took them to Bishop Hunter's Warm Springs orchard. Again, the result was food for the Grants' larder. Once while at Warm Springs, the boy fell into a pond. His life was probably saved by the quick action of several companions who pulled the foundering youth from the water, though the incident cost him his first pearl-handled pocket knife, lost in the pond's depths.

Then there was Brigham Young, who lived just around the corner from the Grants. One day the President's sleigh slowed at the corner of South Temple and Main Street before heading south, and six-year-old Heber jumped on behind. He planned to hold on for a block's free ride and then walk home. But President Young enjoyed a swift team, and soon the sleigh was traveling at what seemed to the little boy to be a terrifying pace. Not knowing what to do, he fastened his grip. Within moments the coach, the Church President, his driver, and the frightened boy were out of the city and flying through the countryside.

Finally, when Heber must have assumed his life was at peril, the coachman slowed to navigate a creek and President Young spotted the stowaway. The sleigh quickly stopped, and Brigham wrapped the freezing lad in the buffalo robe and placed him beside him on the front seat. They drove on for a few minutes in silence.

"Are you warm?" the President asked. "What is your name?"

Heber's answer set the older man thinking about past times with Jedediah, whom he described as "one of his nearest and dearest and most beloved friends." It also elicited an invitation. "You tell your mama that in about six months . . . she is to send you up to have a visit with Brother Brigham."

After the prescribed interval, the youth entered the presidential office, probably as frightened as before.

President Young recognized him instantly. "So you have come to have a visit with Brother Brigham, have you?"

After the two got better acquainted, the President asked if Heber might like to join the Young family's evening prayers.

Thus began another of Heber's rituals. Often on hearing the Youngs' prayer bell, he'd hurry through the rear gate behind his home, turn left on the footpath next to George A. Smith's home, and scurry across South Temple Street and into the Youngs' parlor. He learned to call the President's wives by their familiar family title "aunt." He also learned something about prayer. So fervent were President Young's petitions, Heber once opened his eyes in hopes of seeing the Lord himself.

There were other legacies. His General Authority neighbors gave the fatherless boy strong male models to pattern his life after. Because of them, he found it easy to be around "important" people. They, in turn, became his later advocates, solicitous of his welfare and aware of his character and talent.

HEBER'S HAPPY DAYS ON MAIN STREET lasted until he was about seven years old. Then, despite taking in boarders, Rachel and the other widowed and now divorced wives found it impossible to meet expenses. They consequently broke up their extended family and sold their Main Street property. Rachel took her $500 share of the transaction and purchased a cottage on Second East Street.

The new home had no luxuries. Rachel at first had only six dining plates, two of which were cracked, an occasional cup and saucer, her bed and bedding, and several chairs. There were blustery nights with no fire and a meager diet that allowed only several pounds of butter and sugar for an entire year. One Christmas she wept because she lacked a dime to buy a stick of candy for her son's holiday.

Poverty, or at least scarcity, was a part of pioneer living, and the Grants' situation differed from many others only in degree. Yet, being accustomed to comfortable circumstances and to giving rather than receiving, the mother and son must have found these trials poignant. Once while visiting her sister in St. George in southern Utah, Rachel firmly declined President Young's offer of Church aid. Instead, she supported herself and Heber by sewing, at first by hand in the homes of others and later with a Wheeler and Wilcox sewing machine in her own house. "I sat on the floor at night until midnight," Heber remembered many evenings, "and pumped the sewing machine to relieve her tired limbs." The machine's constantly moving treadles became a symbol of the Grant family's stubborn independence.

Despite their financial distress, the Grants found money for the things that seemed most important. A willing hostess, Rachel often subjected Heber and herself to a diet of fried bread (warmed slices of bread in a greased frying pan) so she could splurge on entertaining her friends. She also highly valued schooling for her son. Without modern state-supported education, most pioneer parents sent their children to rudimentary cottage or ward schools. In contrast, whenever Rachel could afford the fees, Heber went to the best schools in the city.

First there was the Doremus School, located on Union Square near present-day West High School. There, Heber's keen sense of justice brought him some grief. When asked about one boy's conduct, Heber told the truth — and as a result later received a backyard thrashing from the misbehaving boy. Professor Doremus also used physical force. After one whipping that Heber believed was undeserved and being sent upstairs for another, he bolted for home, sure that Doremus and his intimidating willow were behind him every step of the way. But not all of Heber's memories of the school were unhappy. In praise of his character, Mrs. Doremus gave him a small piece of paper with TRUTH written in bold, blue lettering. Heber saved the token until after his marriage, and in later years he regretted its loss.

He also attended Brigham Young's private school, just east of Eagle Gate. Brother Brigham's teachers used the *Wilson* and *National* readers, which spoke of duty, success, and moral truth. So influential were these elementary-school texts in forming the boy's character that Heber quoted from them the rest of his life.

Heber was good at math, memorization, and recitation but less gifted in grammar, spelling, and especially foreign languages. He was, he believed, a quick study, better at mastering an immediate lesson than in later remembering it. Orson F. Whitney, a classmate and later a member of the Quorum of Twelve Apostles, recalled that young Grant was "a persevering sort of chap whose chief delight seemed to be in overcoming obstacles. He did especially well with the Deseret Alphabet, a phonetic system that Church leaders tried to establish but later abandoned." "I believe he could have recited the Deseret Alphabet backwards," Elder Whitney said. "To look at it was enough for me."

Mary and Ida Cobb were eastern-educated schoolmarms with an eye for up-to-date methods and curricula. Mary handled the preparatory course at the Social Hall, while Ida ran the "university" held at the Council Hall across the street from Temple Square. Despite his weak orthography (Heber wondered if his marks hadn't been adjusted to his advantage), he was advanced to the university, where the strong-willed boy and the arbitrary Miss Ida were often at odds. After a playground fracas with one of his best friends, Heber was temporarily expelled. This caused Rachel such remorse that the boy promised to do better.

At first his behavior was exemplary. "For three or four months I never whispered once," Heber recalled. "Then one day Miss Ida kept the whole school in for whispering and told us to study. I was so mad to be kept in when I hadn't whispered at all that I didn't study; I just sat there. She saw me sitting there. Finally some of the boys lifted their hands and asked to go out, and she let first one and then another go. Finally, I lifted my hand. She said: 'You keep your seat.'

"I said: 'If others can go out, so can I.' I got up to go and we met at the top of the stairs. She grabbed me by the collar, and I stepped two or three steps down, she still holding on to my collar. I lifted my feet: I knew she couldn't hold my weight. Then she moved to go around me and I made a bound and lit on the bottom of the first platform, and she lit on top of me . . . [but] never let go of her grip. Just then Mary Cook came in and said: 'Expel him from school.'"

Heber's temper quickly cooled. Recalling his unequivocal

promises to his weeping mother, Heber broke down. He tear-fully pled for forgiveness and as a result was allowed to stay in the school.

A VERY CLOSE BOND EXISTED between Rachel and her son. After Jedediah's death and her divorce from George, Rachel's overriding concern became Heber. She lavished love and con-cern on him and sometimes indulged him. She talked to him about adult concerns and frequently reminded him of his pre-ordained mission. While he did not at first understand and pay much attention to the latter, the boy responded with his own deep love and by trying to fulfill her wishes.

Nothing pleased Rachel more than to see her son involved with the Church. Fortunately she had the Thirteenth Ward, the Grants' home congregation, to help her. Bounded on the east and west by Third East and Main streets and on the north and south by South Temple and Third South streets, the ward ranked among the best in pioneer Utah. Its congregation was filled with capable people—General Authorities, prominent merchants, and prominent women. Morever, it had the re-sources to fund programs. One observer thought it "was richer than all the Saints at Kirtland when the Temple was built." Indeed, it may have enjoyed the highest income level of any ward in the Church.

Moreover it had two unusual assets. First, there was Bishop Edwin D. Woolley. A bluntly speaking and sometimes contrary-minded merchant (if he ever drowned, Brigham Young suppos-edly said, don't look for Bishop Woolley's body downstream; look upstream, for he always goes against the current), Woolley was one of the ablest bishops in the city. His three-decade service more than spanned Heber's youthful years. Second, the ward had the "Assembly Rooms." By all accounts one of the Church's most beautifully decorated meetinghouses, its pulpit and windows were draped in crimson, two bronze chan-deliers hung from the ceiling, and a stucco cornice framed the interior. More important to the younger generation, the build-ing had space for youth meetings and parties.

Some of Heber's fondest memories centered on Bishop

Woolley and the Assembly Rooms. He was present at the ward, for instance, when the bishop organized the first modern Sunday School in the Church. A few scattered and short-lived Sunday Schools had been organized earlier, but Bishop Woolley's was the first since the city's bishops agreed to make wide use of them. Typically, the children met at the Assembly Rooms, where as a group they listened to short talks, sang, and recited inspirational prose and poetry. Leaders might also "catechize" the children with questions drawn from the Bible, Book of Mormon, or LDS history, giving prizes for correct answers and proper conduct.

Heber was often at front stage. With his ability to memorize, he quickly mastered the Articles of Faith, the first pages of John Jaques' *Catechism*, and Joseph Smith's health revelation, the Word of Wisdom. "You were our prize Sunday School boy," recalled a classmate. "Bros. Musser and Maiben predicted great things for you." On one occasion Heber pitted his declamatory skills against those of Orson F. Whitney, whose rendition of "Shamus O'Brien" proved superior to Heber's "The Martyrdom of the Prophet and Patriarch." But "Heber had another card up his sleeve," Elder Whitney remembered. "He answered more questions from the *Catechism* than any other student in school, and won a prize equal to mine, which was the *Autobiography of Parley P. Pratt.*"

Despite his outward confidence, young Heber actually was shy and uncertain. When first asked to pray before the Sunday School, he trembled "like a leaf." President Young's visit brought similar results. Unnerved by his presence, Heber stumbled badly when he tried to give his usually pat recital of the Word of Wisdom, a performance that brought laughter from his classmates. Thoroughly confused, the school's star performer began his recitation anew and somehow labored through it. Brigham Young later salved the incident by highly complimenting him. "I was my father's own son by not being discouraged [and quitting]," Heber remembered Brother Brigham telling him, "but demonstrated a true spirit of determination to accomplish the task given me."

Heber attended more than Sunday School meetings at the

Assembly Rooms. He was also present during the afternoon preaching sessions. Bishop Woolley didn't like meetings to last longer than two hours, and he usually warned preachers to limit their sermons to a single hour. Heber normally positioned himself in the northeast corner of the chapel, where, after the obligatory hour, he would periodically snap his watch crystal as a reminder of the hour's lateness. The act usually was unnecessary. From his vantage point, Heber could witness the bishop's surreptitious hand reach out and tug a long-winded preacher's coattails. But Bishop Woolley's behavior was not automatic. A spell-binding speaker like John Morgan, fresh from his Southern States mission, received *carte blanche.* "Bishop Woolley knows whose coat to pull," Heber observed.

Heber learned other lessons from attending the preaching meetings. One Thirteenth Ward elder never used a simple word when several larger ones might do. After delivering a fulsome sermon, he was followed to the speaker's stand by the ungrammatical Millen Atwood. During the first sermon, Heber, who was studying English at the time, penciled on his removable cuff a long list of unfamiliar words that required study. Eyeing Atwood, he proposed to continue his self-improvement by listing a few solecisms. "I did not write anything more after that first sentence—not a word," Grant remembered sixty-five years later. "When Millen Atwood stopped preaching, tears were rolling down my cheeks. . . . [Atwood's] testimony made the first profound impression that was ever made upon my heart and soul of the divine mission of the Prophet [Joseph Smith]."

His testimony grew when he first read the Book of Mormon. Anthony C. Ivins, his uncle, played a key role. Pitting the fourteen-year-old Heber against his own son, Elder Ivins promised the first boy to finish the book a pair of buckskin gloves, a wild frontier extravagance. After the first day, Heber's hopes were virtually dashed. Young Ivins stayed up most of the night to read 150 pages, while Heber, hoping to read the scripture thoughtfully, amassed only 25 pages. The incident, however, had a "Tortoise and the Hare" ending. "When I finished the book," Heber remembered, "I not only got a testimony [of it] but . . . the gloves as well." After a fast start, his cousin never read another page.

HEBER'S TEENAGE YEARS did not pass without the usual jars and struggles. One episode involved President Young himself. Calling the seventeen-year-old into his office, President Young talked about the responsibility of Heber serving a mission. Despite his initial hesitation, Heber finally took to the idea. After all, Patriarch Perkins had already promised that he would "begin the ministry when very young." Excited by the prospect, he began reading of the youthful missionary exploits of George Q. Cannon, Joseph F. Smith, and Erastus Snow, perhaps comparing his skills and sinew with the young heroes who had preceded him. He paid his debts and prepared for an early departure.

According to the custom of the time, missionary calls were formally announced during the proceedings of general conference, and Heber entered the Tabernacle in April 1876 confidently expecting to hear his name read. When the clerk failed to do so, he was devastated. During the next several days, his work associates at the Wells Fargo office noticed his emotional distress. Disappointed and apparently embarrassed at his failure to receive a missionary call, the young man frequently wept. Years later he learned why his name had not been read. When the list of prospective missionaries had been submitted for General Authority approval, both Erastus Snow and Daniel Wells had objected to his call. The boy, they claimed, was already performing "a very splendid mission" in providing for his widowed mother.

The wound was slow to heal. Unbeknown to his closest friends and even to his mother, in whom he often confided such things, the episode haunted him during the next four or five years. "I was tempted seriously for several years to renounce my faith in the Gospel because this blessing was not fulfilled," he later admitted. "The spirit would come over me . . . that the patriarch had lied to me, and that I should throw the whole business away."

Uncertain of his inherited faith, the young man became

interested in the writings of Robert G. Ingersoll, nineteenth-century America's anti-Christian curmudgeon. Moreover, his circle of friends expanded to include several of questionable reputation. They "smoked a little, and did things they ought not to do," he remembered, "but I liked them, they were jolly fellows." He later realized his error. "I stood as it were upon the brink of usefulness or upon the brink of making a failure of my life."

He credited the Thirteenth Ward for his salvation. Bringing his Sunday School experience to full circle, the twenty-one-year-old Heber was appointed a Sunday School teacher. He now stood before the congregation of young students, teaching, catechizing, praying, and serving as a role model — just as Benjamin Goddard, John Maiben, and Milton Musser had done many years earlier for him. After he had served for several years, his responsibilities were expanded to include assistant secretary and eventually secretary of the school, a position usually reserved for one of the leading members of the ward.

The ward's Mutual Improvement Association, the first organized in the Church, also gave him a chance for introspection and growth. MIA exercises included self-study and the giving of speeches, though the minutes of the organization suggest that their services were at times informal. "Bro. H. J. Grant said he like the rest who had spoken before him was unprepared," the secretary once recorded, "but according to the Book of Mormon he was satisfied that this was the Gospel of Christ restored."

Heber first served in the ward YMMIA presidency. Later he acted as a Salt Lake Stake YMMIA officer and as a Mutual "missionary" in the emerging churchwide youth organization. The latter required him to speak before various Utah congregations. His first effort was a halting, two- or three-minute affair that probably drew beads of perspiration. His early Mutual service culminated with a call to serve as secretary to the general MIA superintendency of the Church, consisting of Elders Wilford Woodruff, Joseph F. Smith, and Moses Thatcher, members of the Quorum of Twelve Apostles.

"You must know and I am the only person who would tell

you so," Heber somewhat facetiously wrote a friend attending college in the East, "I have got to be a very good boy. I attend meetings Sunday, generally twice a day, [and] go to the Elders Quorum [and my] Young Men's Mutual Improvement Asstn." Clearly, his Church commitment was deepening.

Somehow he found time for youth activities, like baseball. Lacking natural coordination and a strong physique ("sissy" and "ramrod" were his playground epithets), he resolved to master the game that had become Utah's passion. The Territory's teams were divided into three groups, and at first Heber endured the indignity of playing with the worst. Nevertheless, he "practiced, practiced, practiced," throwing his ball on Bishop Woolley's neighboring barn when no available "baseballist" could be found to join him. And to improve his catching, he hired the hardest thrower in school to pitch "bullets" at him.

As a baseball player, he had several advantages. His height and long arms helped with fielding. Moreover, he proved a surprisingly quick runner. "That grasshopper dude," said one begrudging opponent, "gave three hops and a jump and he was at the first base before the ball got there." But more than natural ability, he had perseverance, which came to be widely admired. "You will see Heber in the Quorum of the Twelve," said one father to his son as they observed him play. The father no doubt was as pleased with the second baseman's character as his actual playing skills. Before abandoning his baseball compulsion ("I am not sure that there ever has been an American youth more enthusiastic over baseball than I"), Heber played on the team that won the territorial championship and consequently became a local hero.

HEBER'S SOCIAL ACTIVITIES centered around the high-spirited Wasatch Literary Association. With its sixty members drawn from the ablest young people in the city, the society met each Wednesday evening for cultural exercises. These might include declamations, lectures, debates, readings, musical renditions, and even small-scale theatrical productions. In reality, "Wasatchers" often used culture as an excuse for good-natured fun. When Heber forgot where the society was meeting one week, Jim Ferguson sent him to Kittie Heywood's home high on a Salt Lake City hill. "It was a good joke on me walking so far for nothing," Grant admitted after the wild-goose chase, "and I think I shall try & get even with James for playing me so."

Rumors of the "Wasatchers" love entanglements were a society staple. Several squibs were read detailing an alleged romantic interlude between Rob Sloan and the popular Emily Wells on her distinguished father's front porch. They graphically continued with the reactions of her distraught admirers, Billy Dunbar, Orson Whitney, and Heber Grant. "I would [have] given a dollar if you could have been there to hear them," Heber reported the episode to a friend in the East. The readings "were too good for anything."

There was more than rumor connecting Heber and Daniel Wells's daughter. From his Main Street days, Heber could not remember a time when he wasn't drawn to Emily. As they reached maturity, however, he questioned their compatibility for marriage. He felt that he should be "sealed" by his twenty-first birthday. Emily seemed unhurried. Moreover, Heber was bothered by her outspoken opposition to plural marriage. Believing the practice central to Mormonism, he prayed for direction. The answer, that he should give up Emily, presented him with "one of the greatest trials of my life."

At length he turned to Lucy Stringham, a Thirteenth Ward neighbor whose arduous life differed from the carefree routine of many "Wasatchers." Since the death of her father, Briant Stringham, when she was thirteen, Lucy had managed the Stringham household and even helped to educate her younger brothers and sisters. Heber found her "very forceful," yet "happy and cheerful." Because of her rounded features, large dark eyes, and luxurious hair, Heber thought her to be "one of the handsomest girls in our Ward." When she at first seemed unresponsive to the young man's courting, Heber resolved on an expedient. Along with his friend Frank Kimball, who also had chosen a prospective bride, Heber hired Sister Holbrook, a "splendid English cook." "We decided to see if we could catch the girls in the same way as the girls catch the men, that is, via the stomach," he explained. "So we would take the girls home to lunch nearly every day." The plan was successful. Heber and Lucy were married in the St. George Temple on November 1, 1877, three weeks before the groom's twenty-first birthday.

Heber's financial situation allowed for an early marriage. He had left school at fifteen to take a series of office jobs, and from the first he found the world of insurance and finance to be exciting. He mastered each job easily and was often left with free time on his hands. While working with H. R. Mann and company, which occupied the front basement portion of the banking firm A. W. White and Company, he would complete his normal work and then wander back into the bank looking for additional tasks. He offered "to do anything and everything I could to employ my time, never thinking whether I was to be paid for it or not, but having only a desire to work and learn." In turn, Mr. Morf, the bookkeeper, tutored his penmanship. Soon Heber's Spencerian had allowed him to earn more after office hours writing cards and invitations than he gained from his insurance salary.

FOR A YOUNG MAN still in his teens, Heber's success at H. R. Mann and Company was remarkable. Three or four years after first coming to the company, Heber assumed the "entire charge of the business," with the exception of writing an occasional letter and actually signing the policies. This was only the beginning. At the age of nineteen, he bought the company after Rachel mortgaged her home to provide the necessary five hundred dollars.

Heber found admiring friends for his venture. "Few young men here are held in higher esteem by all classes than he," the Salt Lake *Herald* wrote in praise of Heber and his new business. Prominent bankers Horace S. Eldredge and William S. Hooper signed his insurance bonds, while businessmen Hiram Clawson, W. S. McCornick, and Thomas Webber vouched for his ability and integrity. Bishop Edward Hunter did not care for Heber's initial business advertisement and taught him a lesson in public relations. "H. J. Grant, H. J. Grant, insurance agent, insurance agent," Bishop Hunter spoke in his customary staccato echoes. "Who is he? Thought I knew all the Grants, thought I knew all the Grants." When told that H. J. Grant was none other than Heber J., Jedediah's son, he commented in his terse double-speak, "Why don't he say so, why don't he say so? . . . Might mean Helen J., might mean Helen J." When informed of the bishop's views, Heber immediately changed his business name to Heber J. Grant.

Insurance success, then as now, was a slow accretion, so Heber looked for supplemental income. He peddled books, sought Utah retailers for a Chicago grocery house, did odds and ends for the Deseret National Bank, and taught penmanship and bookkeeping at the University of Deseret. With Brigham Young's support, he was also appointed assistant cashier of Zion's Savings and Trust Company. The position was literally a one-man show: cashier, bookkeeper, paying and receiving teller, after-hours note collector, and janitor. Heber confessed that he took the job because it gave him the chance to sell insurance on the side to Zion's customers.

His hard work began to pay dividends. A typical Utah wage earner of the time might make annually five hundred dollars. In contrast Heber, still in his early twenties, was earning ten times that amount. In short order he opened another insurance agency in Ogden and began to fulfill his hope of furthering home industry. With a partner, he purchased the Ogden Vinegar Works.

His frantic activity told a great deal about the young man's dreams. Rachel might periodically remind him of his church destiny, but for the moment that seemed far away. "I had other plans," he admitted. By the age of thirty he hoped to be a director of Zion's Cooperative Mercantile Institution, Utah's largest wholesale and retail outlet. Then he might found a local insurance company, preside over a Utah bank, and sit on the board of one of the transcontinental railroads. Politics also had appeal. Mightn't he succeed his father as Salt Lake

City mayor, sit in the Governor's chair, or even occupy a seat in the United States Congress?

Events, however, led in another direction. On October 30, 1880, the twenty-three-year-old Heber found himself in Tooele, twenty-five miles west of Salt Lake City, addressing a stake conference. In a seven-and-a-half minute speech that "told everything I could think of . . . and part of it I told twice," the young man accepted the call to be president of the Tooele Stake. On hand were President John Taylor; his counselors, George Q. Cannon and Joseph F. Smith; former Tooele Stake president Francis M. Lyman, recently called to the Quorum of Twelve Apostles; and Bishop Edwin D. Woolley, who wanted to assure the local Saints that they were "getting a man and not a boy."

Some stake members remained doubtful. While few actually voted against the young Salt Lake City import, Heber noticed that many abstained. And after the meeting he overheard comments that were possibly meant for his hearing. "It is a pity that if we have to have a boy preside over this Stake of Zion," said one, "the Authorities . . . could not find one with sense enough to talk ten minutes." Heber had a strong contrary view. "There was only one living person who had any right to complain about my being made the president of that stake," he remembered thinking, "and that person was Heber J. Grant." As the Saints raised their hands to sustain him, he quietly said goodbye to many of his financial and political ambitions.

The new assignment was difficult and trying. For one thing, Heber's finances deteriorated badly. His new ecclesiastical duties required a great deal of time, and his insurance business declined proportionately. To his dismay and chagrin, his Ogden Vinegar Works burned to the ground, and he found himself professionally embarrassed by being underinsured. He was confronted also by a series of unexpected expenses. He had to keep a team and buggy for official church travel. There were the costs of his frequent commuting between Salt Lake City and Tooele. And as a leading citizen in both communities, he was expected to donate freely in each.

These financial problems probably weighed on him less than his private concerns. After a week in their Tooele home, the Grants' second daughter came close to dying and Lucy began to suffer from a serious, long-lingering illness. Moreover, Heber himself "felt mightily" his weakness as Tooele's spiritual leader and most prominent citizen. To meet his church and business duties, he drove himself mercilessly. He worked most nights until midnight, often past two in the morning. Finally his slight 140-pound frame could endure no more. In January 1882 he was seized by a series of "nervous convulsions," and an attending doctor warned that if the young man did not slow his pace, he should certainly have a "softening of the brain." So severe was his illness that nervousness and insomnia would plague him the rest of his life.

Yet there were also benefits coming from his Tooele service. As the Saints increasingly recognized his common sense, ability, and performance of duty, his own confidence grew. Likewise there were moments of spiritual deepening. He enjoyed traveling throughout the stake, especially when the ebullient Elder Francis M. Lyman joined him. Such service brought "the sweet and comforting influences of the Good Spirit." And when Patriarch Rowberry blessed him, he felt a special spiritual feeling that suggested a future far surpassing the actual words of his blessing. Someday, the Spirit seemed to whisper, he would become the president of the Church.

That he now sensed a future so different from his earlier ambitions indicated a deep change growing within him. Heber himself felt it. Fourteen months after his call to Tooele, he attended a reunion of the old "Wasatch crowd." "They are all good hearted [w]hole souled people & strictly honest," he reflected, "but I am sorry to say [that they] have but a little faith. . . . I take greater joy in associating with men that love to talk of the principles of the Gospel than I do in dancing with my old friends." Clearly he had taken a different path.

THE MORNING OF OCTOBER 16, 1882, less than two years since his call to the stake presidency, Heber J. Grant received a telegram asking him to attend a 3:30 P.M. council meeting in

President John Taylor's office. Arriving, he listened as the President read a revelation announcing his appointment to the Council of Twelve. Two weeks before, just prior to a general conference session, he had had a premonition of such a call, but he had tried to suppress the idea from his mind. Not quite twenty-six years old, he was the first native Utahn to be called to the Twelve.

Heber would serve as an apostle for the next three and a half decades. The first period, 1882-1901, allowed considerable flexibility. At the time the duties and routines of an apostle were not clearly defined, and members of the Quorum were expected to do both church and personal work. For Elder Grant, these were years of inward searching, rapid-paced business and financial activity, and varied ecclesiastical assignments. It was also a time when his family grew to include two other households, and he briefly once again considered the possibility of political office.

From the announcement of his apostolic call, there were whispers and innuendoes about his selection. While his closest associates welcomed his appointment, Elder Grant was painfully aware that it had taken President Taylor's written revelation to convince others that he was apostolic timber. No one doubted his integrity — only his preparation for the calling and what some saw as his preoccupation with business.

Heber himself was probably his toughest critic. "I must say that I consider my position much in advance of my knowledge," he wrote to a friend. "I regret very much that I have not a better knowledge of grammar. . . . My orthography is perfectly [lacking]. . . . I have not a good memory, or if I have it[,] it has been so badly neglected that I have not found out that it is good. . . . I know little or nothing of History — and were it not that I have from 15 to 25 years in which to study to overtake such men as [Elder Francis M.] Lyman, [Elder] Jos. F. Smith and others, and knowing that I have the right to call upon our Heavenly Father for assistance[,] I assure you that I should feel almost like backing out."

During the next few months he experienced a "dark night

of the soul" as he continued to question his ability and preparation. His gloom did not lift until, traveling on the Navajo Indian Reservation near Canyon Diablo in Arizona, he had a comforting spiritual experience. Separating himself from the main party and dismounting his mule, he pondered once again his apostolic calling. As he did so, he "*seemed* to see and *seemed* to hear" ("I really saw and heard nothing," he later explained) a heavenly council. Jedediah Grant and Joseph Smith, his adopted father by sealing, were discussing the long-standing vacancies in the Quorum of the Twelve. "Why not choose the boy who bears my name and who belongs to you?" he sensed Jedediah saying. At the end of his experience, Elder Grant took from his pocket his well-worn copy of President Taylor's revelation calling him to the Twelve and wept. He never doubted his "proper place" again.

Still unresolved was his future role in the Twelve. At first he planned to follow the example of the impecunious Elder Erastus Snow, who labored tirelessly in the service of others. At other moments, his self-denial wavered. Must not he be himself? He knew that he had a rare gift for business, and he enjoyed making money. Couldn't his talents be used, as President Young had long urged, to build Mormon-owned "home industries"? The profits could help the Saints instead of enriching their enemies.

The next decade saw Heber J. Grant involved with a flurry of businesses, each designed to assist the kingdom. Because "almost the entire control of the wagon and implement business was in the hands of men whose interests were inimical to our people," he helped found the hugely successful Consolidated Wagon and Machine Company. He also mounted a public subscription campaign that saved the pro-Mormon Salt Lake *Herald* and managed the sale of the Church-owned ZCMI wholesale and retail business on terms favorable to the Church after the Federal Government demanded its sale. In another effort, he established Grant Brothers Livery Company with its magnificent forty-passenger Raymond Coach and "great West Temple Street stables," described in the local press as the largest west of Omaha. He entered the livery business because "anti-Mormon cabbies" often told scurrilous tales about the Church as they drove out-of-town visitors through the city.

There were other pro-Mormon business activities. To plug the drain of insurance premiums from the territory and provide money for local investment, Elder Grant organized Home Fire of Utah and Home Life of Utah. In 1889 he secured control of the majestic but unprofitable Salt Lake Theatre in order that the LDS community might enjoy uplifting and popular entertainment. A year later, when he sensed that the Church-owned banks inadequately served their Mormon clientele, he founded the largest capitalized bank in the territory, the State Bank of Utah. And to provide a cash crop for Utah farmers, at the request of President Woodruff he raised capital and helped found the Utah Sugar Company.

Elder Grant was also busy with church activities. He was a member of the Church Salary Committee, the Sunday School general board, and the Mutual Improvement Association general superintendency. And he traveled extensively. Twice he proselytized among the dangerous Yaqui Indians in Mexico. His tours in the Southwest earned him the title of "the Arizona Apostle." Indeed, at a time when General Authorities volunteered to visit and supervise outlying stake conferences, Elder Grant believed that with the exception of Elder Francis M. Lyman, no quorum member did more traveling to stakes than he. Occasionally such visits brought drama. When John Dalton was gunned down by an antipolygamist deputy marshal in Parowan, Elder Grant's telegram from neighboring Cedar City probably averted vigilante justice. "Do not, for Heaven's sake, allow your friends to take the law in their own hands," he implored the local Saints. "Such a course would only bring condemnation upon them and our whole people."

DURING THESE YEARS, Elder Grant was also busy with his large family of three wives and twelve children. His method of choosing his second wife was unusual. After fervent prayer on the subject, he penciled the names of several prospective mates on separate slips of paper, and on another slip he wrote

234

"NEITHER." He then put the pieces of paper in his pocket and, after once again praying earnestly, drew the slip inscribed with the name "Miss Winters." Huldah Augusta Winters, in fact, became his wife, but only after a ratifying seven-month courtship.

His third wife was Emily Wells, who, upon her conversion to the idea of plural marriage, readily accepted Heber's offer of marriage.

The three Grant wives were similar in many ways. They were well educated for the times. All had taught school. Augusta had conducted classes ten years before her marriage and was reputed to be one of the ablest and highest-salaried schoolmarms in the Territory. In addition, each of the women bore a quiet belief in her religion, and all descended from pioneer families.

These three women, their husband, and Rachel, who lived into her eighty-eighth year, set the tone for the Grant family. Church activity always was stressed. As one daughter said of the family's commitment to the Church: "We early became aware that the best way to show our love and appreciation for our parents was to do our best to help in Church organizations." The children were also introduced to cultural influences. Because of Elder Grant's controlling interest in the Salt Lake Theatre, the children attended its weekly performances. Following the play the children were asked to discuss the production at the family dinner table, a practice that led one Grant child to count the theater second only to her schooling in educational value. Books also had a high place among the Grants. Like the morality plays of the Salt Lake Theatre, emphasis of the Grant library was on Victorian didacticism — "right and wrong" — rather than great works.

The dictum "spare the rod and spoil the child" never had much of a place in the rearing of the Grant children. "They will only be children once," Elder Grant explained, "and I want them to get as much pleasure as they can out of life as they go along."

The Panic of 1893 removed the possibility that the children might be spoiled. The financial storm caught both Elder Grant and the Church badly overextended, largely because of efforts to fund the fledging Sugar Company. As credit began to contract in the spring of 1893, Heber J. Grant, as the Church's "financial apostle," was dispatched to the East to renew its short-term credit. "This is the most difficult mission bro. Heber has ever undertaken," one apostle observed, "now that financial affairs are tumbling in all directions."

During the summer Elder Grant was able to renew financial note after financial note, often despite difficult odds. But by autumn the situation looked impossible. Many more loans were about to mature. Worse, depositors were making a run of the Mormon banks in Salt Lake City. Arising on the morning of September 2 in New York City, Elder Grant knelt at morning prayers and, with the specter of another Kirtland-like bank disaster before him, offered to forfeit his life in exchange for a way of preserving the Church's finances. Experiencing a calming assurance, he bathed and breakfasted deliberately and then, without a destination in mind, boarded an elevated railway train. Eventually he found his way to Blake Brothers, where he met John Claflin, a longtime acquaintance and prominent New York merchant. Claflin offered what only a few hours before seemed improbable—a large loan that allowed the Church to navigate one of its most difficult hours.

Wealthy before the Panic's onslaught, Elder Grant was left with crushing debts that he shouldered for the rest of the decade. Nickels now seemed worth dollars. Domestic help, once a Grant family expectation, became an unaffordable luxury. Faced with hard times, the older Grant children helped with household chores and even with their father's debts. "As soon as we were old enough," one remembered, "we started to work in his office, and it was the greatest satisfaction of our young lives to feel that we were helping him by caring for ourselves and in that way sharing his heavy burden of debt."

Elder Grant might have supplemented his income with a political office. When Utah Territory entered the Union as a state, Elder Grant believed he could have had the Democratic Party's nomination for governor for the asking, and subsequent election seemed likely. For a moment his youthful political hopes flickered anew. "I wanted to be the first Governor of the State of Utah as much as I ever wanted anything in my life," he frankly admitted.

Several years later he also believed he could have been elected to the United States Senate. With the Utah legislature hopelessly deadlocked over several hotly contesting candidates (prior to the Eighteenth Amendment, Senators were elected by state legislatures), a majority of representatives seemed willing to turn to Elder Grant as a compromise.

Heber asked for ten minutes to consider the offer and, as was his custom when making an important decision, retired to his office to think out aloud his options.

"Why would you like to be Senator?" he asked himself.

"From pride," came the response.

"Because you think you can do more good as a Senator?"

"No, from pride, because I do not believe I can do more good as a Senator. I do not like that kind of work; it is not in my line. But I do love to mingle among the people and preach the Gospel of life and salvation. I would not do credit and honor to my people as a Senator; I do not care for that kind of work."

"Then, what is the main incentive why you would like to be a Senator?"

"To lay my card down on the desk of my cousin William M. Ivins, in New York—'Heber J. Grant, U.S. Senator from Utah.'" Ivins, who wanted a Senate seat himself, had repeatedly received Heber's courtesy calls with slightly concealed contempt.

After a few minutes of such candid soliloquy, Elder Grant had his answer. As with his earlier refusal of the governorship, he concluded that he could do "more good for the Latter-day Saints" by not diluting his ministry with politics. Consequently, he advised his friends that he was not available for the "Senatorship" and did not want to be troubled by such matters in the future. His response permanently closed the political door.

As UTAH AND THE CHURCH entered the twentieth century, Elder Grant's ministry changed. The old Mormon and non-Mormon commercial and political rivalry began to diminish. Too, the growing church required more and more time and service from its leaders. Elder Grant's work from 1901 to 1918 reflected these events. He filled two foreign proselyting missions during this period. When in the United States, he spent increased time at Church headquarters or on official assignments. However, there were opportunities for special projects, such as helping the cause of Prohibition or directing bond drives to finance World War I. Finally, his long-time service and seniority brought him to the position of president of the Quorum of the Twelve Apostles.

For years the First Presidency deemed Elder Grant's activities in Salt Lake City too important to permit a foreign mission call. But in 1901 he was asked to open the Japanese Mission. Initially two phases were considered. First, Church leaders hoped that he and several accompanying elders would proceed to Japan to look over the country and dedicate the land for missionary work. Later, additional missionaries could be dispatched, a formal home or headquarters established, and actual proselyting begun. Both phases would likely require that Elder Grant stay in Japan for five years.

To Elder Grant, the dedicatory prayer he offered just south of Yokohama was "the greatest prayer of my life." One companion recalled that "every word penetrated into my very bones and I could have wept with joy." Another companion thought that the ground shook as the new mission president spoke. Yet, after so auspicious a start, the missionaries found progress to be intolerably slow. The Americans issued two tracts and commissioned a scholarly book on Mormonism, but the Japanese seemed more interested in the commercial value of learning the English language than in listening to the missionaries' religious message.

Elder Grant had no reciprocal feeling about the Japanese tongue. He found its syntax complex and difficult to learn. Most vocabulary words slipped through his mind as quickly as he memorized them. And what he did learn was of little use. "The Japanese could not understand their own language when I spoke it," he said with some edge. Isolated by his inability to master Japanese and frustrated by the coolness of his reception, Elder Grant grew restive. "Feeling that I was not accomplishing anything, I went out into the woods and got down on my knees, and told the Lord that whenever He was through with me . . . [in Japan], where I was accomplishing nothing, I would be very glad and thankful if He would call me home and send me to Europe to preside over the European missions." Several days later he received a cable from Salt Lake City asking him to return immediately to Church head-quarters, where his call to the presidency of the European Mission was confirmed.

His new assignment included almost a dozen continental missions but principally the large British Mission head-quartered in Liverpool, England. After the futile and difficult days in Japan, he at last found an assignment in which he could release his energy. Missionaries found him to be "a veritable dynamo of enthusiasm," with a philosophy "to push and keep pushing." He systematized the missions' reports and called for the distribution of more and more Mormon pamphlets, which quickly exceeded previous totals by two hundred percent.

There were also deeply spiritual times, like the pentecostal Bradford Conference, the first modern British-wide assembly of elders. Young Hugh B. Brown described its proceedings as "the best and most spirited . . . I have ever attended. Pres[ident] Grant spoke with great power. . . . Most every elder wept with joy." Others confirmed the extraordinary spirit. "Some [missionaries] whose testimonies were weak said, 'Now I know.' Many even of the most energetic Elders were heard to say that they had received a great awakening touch." After the conference, the monthly total of distributed tracts leaped to an unprecedented 450,000, more than five hundred for each missionary. An increased number of conversions followed.

President Grant's three European years were, for the most part, happy. "I got nearer to the Lord and had more joy in the mission field than ever before or since," he later reflected. He especially enjoyed the young missionaries, who in turn found him to be open, frank, and unpretentious. In fact, in Liverpool he often joined his busy elders for a game of tennis behind the mission home ("how you used to whack 'em over the netting with the speed of a Colt .45," one elder recalled). And despite his working longer hours than at any time previously, his health improved. Since his illness in Tooele, he had constantly felt weary, and often "only a matter of will" propelled him on. Now he felt "a new lease on life" and placed twenty additional pounds on his slender frame.

He traveled widely. He visited each British missionary conference four times, the Holland branches five times, and the German and Scandinavian Saints three times. Like his young missionaries, his railroad accommodations were usually an unpretentious third class. ("You know, people ask why 'Mormons' always travel third class," he once joked. "The answer is 'Because there is no fourth class.'") At first there was little time for sightseeing, but with the culturally minded Emily at his side, in London he eventually toured St. Paul's Cathedral and the British National Art Gallery, where he found himself particularly drawn to the works of Murillo and Reynolds. At the end of his mission term, he and Emily embarked on a month of Continental sightseeing. He thought the paintings of Florence to be "magnificent," while his day at Pompeii was "one of the most intensely interesting of my life." St. Peter's Cathedral in Rome was "more wonderful than any building I have ever seen." Yet Europe's brilliant sights also increased his appreciation for his own heritage. "The simplicity of the Gospel in comparison with the display [of Europe] has never been made so forcible to my mind," he reflected in his diary. He also wondered about the practicality of the ostentation that he saw everywhere. Might not the jewels of St. Mark's Cathedral in Venice, he asked himself, be better used to fund "manufacturing institutions to furnish the poor people employment?"

Soon after he returned to America, the European mission years assumed an unexpected poignancy. Elder Grant learned that Emily was severely ill with stomach cancer and that their happy years together in Europe would be among their last. Thus he was again faced with the torturous prospect of watching one of his immediate family members die. His only two sons, Daniel and Heber, had both died while yet children. His first wife, Lucy, "a sufferer for many years . . . with but little hope of . . . recovery," had passed away in 1893. When Emily died in May 1908, she scarcely weighed fifty pounds.

Like many living during the progressive decades of the early twentieth century, Elder Grant embraced good causes. "I would gladly *work* and also take fifty dollars in tickets," he typically responded when asked to aid a proposed benefit concert for an aged and needy citizen. In addition, he raised funds for the Salt Lake City's Deseret Gymnasium, supported Utah's anti-tuberculosis campaign, and served as a director of the Utah Health League, which sought improved milk and public health standards. He believed "decency in our [social] dancing" to be a "burning" issue, and worked to discourage and prohibit use of tobacco and liquor. The latter he labeled "the greatest financial [and] . . . moral problem" facing Utahns and Americans generally.

Elder Grant was especially forceful during the five Liberty Bond drives of World War I. Appointed as Utah's chairman during the third drive, he worked indefatigably. One day he signed 2,400 personal appeals for bond purchases, as three assistants hovered about him shifting papers, blotting ink, and enclosing his signed letters in envelopes. In order to set a proper example, he personally bought at a level far beyond his means and then was forced to sell the bonds on the open market at a loss. "We are not doing very much compared with the men who are fighting for us in the trenches," he reminded his fellow citizens. Under his leadership, Utah became the fifth state in the third drive to oversubscribe its allotment as Utahns purchased one bond for every five men, women, and children in the state. His motto, "A Liberty Bond in Every Home," became a virtual reality.

Most of Elder Grant's post-European mission time was devoted to his increasing duties as a senior apostle. He continued his stake and mission tours, served as a Genealogical

Society director, increased the circulation and influence of the *Improvement Era*, and helped to manage the educational activities of the Church. In 1916, thirty-four years after his apostolic ordination, he became president of the Quorum of the Twelve. "I do not think I have ever in my life felt my weakness more than I do today," he commented after his ordination, "or that I have had more of the spirit of humility than I have this day."

SINCE HIS TOOELE BLESSING so many years before, Elder Grant had periodically felt the impression that someday he might preside over the Church. Each time, however, he dismissed the idea or placed it in the distant future. Now as he assumed his duties as president of the Twelve, the office next in seniority and in line of succession to the presidency, his premonitions returned—but he again postponed them to the indefinite and remote future. Certainly, he thought, President Joseph F. Smith would live to preside over the Church's centennial anniversary in 1930.

This hope, however, proved illusory. In November 1918 President Smith's health deteriorated rapidly, and when Elder Grant stopped at the Beehive House, President Smith's residence, to ask about his condition, he was stunned by his reception. "You would better wait and see him," an attendant warned, "as it may be your last chance to speak to him."

Ushered into President Smith's room, Elder Grant was greeted feebly by his longtime friend, who reached out for his hand.

"The Lord bless you, my boy," President Smith said. "You have a great responsibility. Always remember that this is the Lord's work, and not man's. . . . He knows whom He wants to lead His Church, and never makes any mistake. The Lord bless you."

Less than a week later, President Grant was set apart as the Church's seventh prophet, seer, and revelator.

At first some Latter-day Saints seemed uncertain about their new leader. His brisk and informal ways were in marked contrast to President Smith's conservative style. "Some of our wisest and most faithful and diligent Latter-day Saints . . . felt that it was almost a calamity when I came to the Presidency," he ruefully remarked many years later.

Some doubters received an immediate reassurance. Reminiscent of one of the Church's most cherished traditions surrounding President Brigham Young's succession to leadership, many Saints testified that as they first saw President Grant address them, his face seemed to be transformed into President Joseph F. Smith's visage. Others claimed that they viewed President Smith's figure standing next to their new president. Most Saints, however, were simply satisfied by his commanding mien. Wrote one: "Your fine voice, the dispatch with which you do things, and your clear announcements of all the features of the occasion . . . , these things have all brought forth very favorable comment."

During his twenty-six-and-a-half-year administration — the Church's second longest — Church members grew familiar with the hardy, pioneer themes of President Grant's extemporaneous preaching. The Saints were told to avoid debt, gambling, state welfare, big government, and such modern notions as evolution and labor unionism. Using personal anecdotes drawn from his long experience, he spoke of the need for charity, duty, honor, service, and work. He chastened the Saints to live modestly and to observe the prohibitions of the Word of Wisdom. Above all, he repeatedly testified to the divine mission of Joseph Smith and to the divinity of Jesus Christ. For Saints disoriented by the century's rapid social and cultural changes, President Grant's firm voice, ramrod-straight posture, and forceful and sometimes sharp-tongued delivery conveyed strength and ballast. Here was a dependable voice speaking of time-tested values.

Non-Mormons particularly found President Grant's lively, homespun speeches to be delightful. As he concluded his remarks before San Francisco's prestigious Commonwealth Club, he was greeted with cries of "Go on! Go on!" In Boston a Rotarian jumped on a chair when President Grant ended his speech and led the audience in the enthusiastic chant, "Heber Grant, Heber Grant, Heber Grant." The national media reported his several addresses before the Second Dearborn Conference of Agriculture, Industry, and Science. There the "Chemurgicians" twice gave him standing ovations, and the convention's main sponsor, Henry Ford, sought out his views. "Mr. Grant and Mr. Ford hit it off splendidly," reported *Time Magazine*.

Whenever possible, President Grant used these occasions to talk about his faith. After the sponsors of Kansas City's Knife and Fork Club asked him to avoid religious themes, he only briefly referred to Joseph Smith and Mormonism. But these passing comments piqued the interest of members of the city's Chamber of Commerce, who asked President Grant to deliver a second address dealing with the Church's beliefs. This speech in turn was so well received that the chamber mailed a copy of Mormonism's Articles of Faith to each of its six thousand members.

President Grant's speaking to non-Mormon audiences reflected a major aim of his administration. After years of adverse Church publicity and misunderstanding, he was determined to place a more positive image of Mormonism before the national public. To do so, he personally guided nationally prominent business and political leaders through Salt Lake City and Utah, introducing these men to both the beauties of the West and Mormonism. He quietly assisted such pro-LDS Hollywood movies as *Union Pacific* and *Brigham Young*. He promoted national tours by the Tabernacle Choir. He supported the political activity of Utah's U.S. Senator and LDS apostle Reed Smoot, whose growing national influence increasingly brought favorable comment to Utah and Mormonism. In addition, President Grant cultivated the friendship of such national opinion-makers as perennial presidential candidate William Jennings Bryan; Charles G. Dawes, later U.S. vice president; Harry Chandler, publisher of the Los Angles *Times*; and Eugene Meyer of the Washington *Post*; and he visited U.S. Presidents Warren G. Harding, Calvin Coolidge, Herbert Hoover, and Franklin D. Roosevelt at the White House. These activities increasingly gave both Mormonism and President

Grant a favorable press image, including cover treatment in *Time Magazine*. While believing his *Time* cover portrait looked like "Abraham, Isaac, and Jacob, rolled into one," President Grant nevertheless judged the accompanying article to be "very fair."

ALMOST FROM THE OUTSET, the Grant administration was beset with hard times. Farming and mining, two of Utah's main industries during the first half of the twentieth century, slumped badly after World War I. Less than a decade later, the American economy entered the Great Depression. During these difficult years, President Grant carefully conserved Church finances, trimming expenditures and construction projects, yet trying to provide the necessary means for the still growing Church. When one anxious stake presidency sought money to build a seminary building, President Grant typically explained that the Church had no available money. Projects from the preceding year, he told the disappointed local leaders, had yet to receive funding. Could the Church assist them by helping them secure a loan for their project?

During this time of financial difficulty, President Grant repeatedly used his contacts with national business and political leaders to keep key Utah- and Church-owned banks and businesses afloat. A prominent Salt Lake City banker knew something of this and noted that "over the years he has either organized or saved in some panic period many of the great institutions" of the city, including ZCMI, Utah-Idaho Sugar Company, Beneficial Life Insurance Company, the Home Fire Insurance Company of Utah, the Hotel Utah, the Utah State National Bank, Zion's Savings Bank and Trust Company, and others. "All this statesmanlike work was done for the good of the people and not one cent of remuneration [went] to himself." Those who were close to President Grant had no doubt about the importance of his personal role. He was "a man who [was] endowed with a mind to be matched with the best financiers of the country," wrote a former Utah governor, and who had "a courage, tact and perseverance to overcome obstacles which would frighten and dismay any ordinary negotiator."

President Grant's administration was also concerned with helping the individual Saint to get through the Depression. After four years of discussion, he unveiled in 1936 the "Church Security program"—later renamed the Church Welfare Program. The New York *Tribune* correctly noted its noneconomic dimensions. "Men are being encouraged to support themselves," the newspaper informed its readers, "not alone for economic reasons but because of the spiritual and moral advantages of standing on their own feet instead of being what the people of Utah call 'leaners.'" While at first President Grant seemed staggered by the project's magnitude, he continued to support the plan that President J. Reuben Clark, his first counselor, had designed, and later pronounced it to be his "first love." To help the program succeed, he donated his large dry farm in western Utah in which he had invested more than eighty thousand dollars.

The Saints grew accustomed to Heber J. Grant's expansive ways. Until his mounting administrative burdens and his declining health finally intervened, his office door was open to General Authorities, stake and local leaders, and even to ordinary Saints afflicted with problems. The peripatetic church leader traveled widely throughout America, and in 1937 he marked the Church's European centennial by touring the missions of Great Britain and western Europe. He thereby became only the second president of the Church to venture across the Atlantic Ocean. Standing before a congregation, he often sang as well as preached. The former activity, he explained, showed the virtues of industry and perseverance. Born tone-deaf and consequently forced to learn a hymn by memorizing its vibrations, he spent scores of hours mastering a single melody.

President Grant gave generously of his time and substance. Recalling his mother's struggles, he took particular delight in helping widows. Finding one elderly woman ill and a half year behind in her house payments, he characteristically paid her bills and enclosed enough additional money for a small, personal Christmas gift. He and Augusta frequently invited widows to join them for an automobile ride. "That he gave freely of his means is well known," recalled one, "but I think his considerate sharing of his automobile with others who would be made happier by such attention is evidence of his understanding heart." His kindness was also manifested by his large-scale giving of books. To express his friendship and appreciation to the Saints, he gave away whole editions of such high-toned books as N. C. Hanks's *Up From the Hills*, William Jennings Bryan's *The Prince of Peace*, or Edgar A. Guest's *Heap o' Living*. These he personally autographed, and when time permitted, he marked or underlined them to highlight his favorite passages or verses. The volume of this book-giving was prodigious. When the Heber J. Grant Library at Brigham Young University was dedicated, he estimated that he had given away more books in his lifetime than were housed in the new facility.

Declining health marked his last years. While visiting southern California in 1940, he suffered a series of strokes, which greatly slowed his tempo. Yet even during this final period, he maintained a daily schedule at Church headquarters, signing documents and giving his approval for projected programs. There was an Indian-summer quality to these long months of semiconvalescence. "I find that as the years mature with me," he wrote shortly before his death, "the mellowing influences of time soften down whatever was rough and jagged in life and leave me with recollections that are sweet beyond measure. . . . The past becomes as gloriously colored a reality as the visions of the future." He died on May 14, 1945, at the age of eighty-eight, as his physician held his wrist and monitored his fading pulse. It was a peaceful, almost indiscernible passing.

During his administration Church membership had almost doubled. He had traveled more than 406,000 miles and filled 1,500 appointments, including 1,250 sermons and 28 addresses to state, national, civic, or professional groups. But his achievement lay in something larger than the hurried pace that these statistics suggested. "He was a valiant pioneer and a great fighter," eulogized a friend. "He wrote his own epitaph in the achievements that caused the desert to blossom as a rose."

Fittingly, he was interred in Salt Lake's city cemetery near the remains of the father whom he had never known. The site overlooked much of the city and culture that he had helped to mold.

SOURCES

The sources of this essay were drawn largely from President Grant's personal diaries and correspondence, which are housed in the Library-Archives of the Church in Salt Lake City. Additional material was taken from such printed sources as the *Improvement Era*, oral history interviews, and Salt Lake City and national newspapers.

RONALD W. WALKER, a native of Salt Lake City, received degrees from the University of Utah and Stanford University. He is associate professor of history at Brigham Young University, senior historian with the Joseph Fielding Smith Institute for Church History, and assistant editor of *BYU Studies*. He has contributed many articles to the *Ensign, BYU Studies, Arizona and the West, Dialogue, Sunstone,* and other periodicals. He is presently working on a major biography of President Heber J. Grant.

GEORGE ALBERT SMITH

Merlo J. Pusey

George Albert Smith brought some unique distinctions to the presidency of The Church of Jesus Christ of Latter-day Saints when he succeeded Heber J. Grant in that position in 1945. A grandson of George A. Smith, who was a cousin of the Prophet Joseph Smith, George Albert was the third member of George A.'s family to serve in the First Presidency. In his later years George A. had been a counselor to Brigham Young, and his son John Henry had served in a similar capacity to President Joseph F. Smith. By heritage and training as well as by temperament, therefore, George Albert was well prepared for the great responsibility that came to him at the passing of President Grant.

In some other respects, however, he was under a handicap, being probably the frailest man who has ever occupied the office and a victim of what many regarded as a series of misfortunes. Yet he was a man of great tenacity, unshakable faith, and devotion to duty, which, combined with a truly unique capacity to love his fellowmen, made his relatively brief occupancy of the office a truly memorable period.

GEORGE ALBERT SMITH was born in Salt Lake City on April 4, 1870, the second of eleven children of John Henry and Sarah Farr Smith. Educated in the district schools in Salt Lake City, he took one year at the Brigham Young Academy in Provo (now Brigham Young University), where his schoolmates included Reed Smoot, later United States Senator; George Sutherland, later United States Supreme Court Justice; and Richard R. Lyman, later a distinguished engineer and member of the Council of the Twelve Apostles. George Albert was always grateful to have had Karl G. Maeser as a teacher at BYA, and spoke often of the inspiration Dr. Maeser provided.

Coming from a poor family, although with an illustrious name, George Albert went to work early. Because his father's house had no front lawn, he labored to put one in, toting water from an irrigation ditch every night. He went to work making overalls in a factory operated by Zions's Cooperative Mercantile Institution (ZCMI), a church-owned department store. He then completed a year at the University of Deseret, now University of Utah, and took correspondence courses in law. During the summers he worked as a farm implement salesman and as a surveyor. In the latter capacity he sustained an eye injury that permanently impaired his sight, and he left school without graduating.

In view of George Albert's later career, it sometimes seems incongruous that he first came to the notice of his associates as a comedian strumming a guitar and singing funny songs along with a youthful companion. Beneath his levity, however, he felt a deep sense of commitment to God. He had been much impressed with his grandfather's admonition that there was a sharp and well-defined line between the devil's territory and the Lord's, and if he kept on the Lord's side of the line, he would be in no danger. Another factor was an accident suffered by his mother when she accidentally tipped a cupboard on herself and lay unconscious on the floor. In desperation George prayed for her restoration and, in return for the blessing he asked, pledged that he would devote his life to God's service. One other factor was impressive. A patriarchal blessing given him by Zebedee Coltrin contained a promise that he would become "a mighty apostle in the church and kingdom of God upon the earth, for none of thy father's family shall have more power with God than thou shalt have, for none shall excel thee."

The strong sense of principle that guided his life was demonstrated during a stormy love affair. As a young man, George fell in love with Lucy Woodruff, a granddaughter of President Wilford Woodruff, who lived nearby with her grandparents because of the death of her mother. An attachment grew between them, but while George was poor—a struggling salesman for ZCMI—Lucy was almost swept off her feet by a rival suitor who seemed to have class, wealth, and a dashing personality. George struggled to hold Lucy to her promise of marriage, but he was less persistent than his rival because he sincerely wanted her to be happy in the choice she made. When she finally honored her former commitment to marry George, she was still unhappy, but in later years when the more dashing suitor turned out to be chiefly a windbag and George, out of his limited resources, helped the former rival save his home from mortgage foreclosure, Lucy would exclaim to her children, "I nearly made a terrible mistake."

Shortly after their marriage in 1892, George was called on a mission to Chattanooga, Tennessee, and his bride was almost devastated from loneliness. When her former unsuccessful suitor began seeking her company again, George's father arranged to have her sent to Chattanooga, where she joined George in missionary work. Their joint labors were both fruitful and adventurous. At the conclusion of their mission, they spent a belated but happy honeymoon at Niagara Falls before returning to Salt Lake City and settling down in a rented house on north West Temple Street.

An able salesman, George had no difficulty in returning to ZCMI, despite the hard times in the middle 1890s. At the same time he played an active role in the Church auxiliaries of the Seventeenth Ward and in the Utah National Guard. This latter activity is significant largely because of a single incident. George aspired to an office in the National Guard and lost, he believed, because a rival spread ugly rumors about him. George's anger mounted to a point where he felt like thrashing his rival, and he refrained from renewing his covenants in church because his heart was filled with hatred. But he prayed for guidance and felt impressed to take the initiative in seeking a reconciliation. Calling on his rival, who tried to shield himself from an anticipated attack, George merely sought forgiveness for the hatred he had been harboring. The rumormonger was deeply chagrined, begged for forgiveness for what he had done, and promised to make amends. The result was a lasting friendship between the two men.

Along with his father, George was an active supporter of President William McKinley in 1896 and was rewarded by an appointment as receiver of public money and special disbursing agent of the Land Office of the Department of the Interior. After a second appointment to this office from President Theodore Roosevelt, it began to appear that George would make a career of public service, and several attempts were made to groom him as a candidate for Congress. He resisted these suggestions because of the feeling that he could not afford a congressional campaign, and a bid for election by the Utah legislature as United States Senator would have implied an alliance with Senator Thomas Kearns, who was seeking a candidate to beat Reed Smoot.

WHILE HE WAS STILL DEEPLY IMMERSED in his responsibilities at the Land Office, on October 6, 1903, George experienced the greatest surprise of his life. Leaving his office that Tuesday about 3:30 P.M. he crossed Temple Square, where general conference was in session; but, finding the Tabernacle too crowded to get in, he continued across the street to his own home. There he found a great deal of excitement, the house filled with friends who were kissing and congratulating Lucy on some great good fortune.

"What is all this about?" he asked.

"Don't you know?" Nellie Colebrook Taylor asked incredulously.

When she informed him that his appointment as a member of the Quorum of the Twelve Apostles had just been announced in the conference, George Albert didn't believe it.

"That couldn't be right," he insisted. "There must be some mistake." Fearing that she might have misconstrued what she had heard, Nellie Taylor rushed back to the Tabernacle, where her original report was fully confirmed. George Albert Smith had indeed been named to the second highest ruling body in the Church without consultation with or even advance notice to him.

Confronted by this momentous *fait accompli*, George Albert was more depressed than elated. At the age of only thirty-three, he felt unprepared and unworthy to assume the heavy responsibilities the apostleship would entail, and he dreaded the charges of nepotism that would flow from the fact that his father was a member of the First Presidency. John Henry Smith was also highly conscious of the family tradition of opposing nepotism, and his words to his son when the two first met after the appointment had been announced were, "George, I didn't have anything to do with it." The initiative had come entirely from President Joseph F. Smith. As George Albert was cordially welcomed into the Quorum of the Twelve by all of his brethren, he was consoled by the thought that his extraordinary moral strength would go a long way toward balancing his limited experience and other deficiencies.

Actually he was well adapted to the new role that had been thrust upon him. Since he loved people, he had a great capacity for mingling with them and lifting them up to a new sense of responsibility toward their fellowmen and the Church. Reminding his audiences that "we are all the children of God," he admonished everyone who would listen to let the love of Christ drive bickering and animosity from their hearts. By his understanding and compassion, he developed a remarkable capacity for rewarming disgruntled members and creating goodwill for the Church.

His sermons were always spontaneous, although they reflected both study and prayer. His heavy reliance on inspiration was reflected in his frequent comments to speakers using manuscripts: "Brother, why don't you give the Lord a chance." Yet his sermons were filled with practical advice as well as spiritual admonitions. Parents should be good examples to their children, beautify their homes, be good neighbors, get out of debt, observe the Sabbath day, avoid profanity, and improve their places of worship, and husbands should treat their wives with kindness and respect. George Albert's high-pitched voice, his enthusiasm, and his great emphasis on the theme of love usually brought warm responses from his audience.

Despite his optimism, good will, and general enthusiasm, Elder Smith was critical of deficiencies where he found them. After a tour of the missions in several of the southern states, he reported to the First Presidency that there was much evidence of faith, humility, and industry on the part of the mission presidents and some of the missionaries. Yet there were other elders, he reported, who failed "to grasp the importance and dignity of their calling," displayed poor manners, and lacked "an intelligent apprehension of the gospel they are required to teach." His own exuberance did not lead him to gloss over weaknesses where they existed. His report contributed to many changes that would strengthen the missionary system in the future.

As THE YEARS PASSED, Elder Smith developed a creed that was designed as a guide to his own conduct, but since it was published in the *Improvement Era* in 1932, it stands as a useful summary of the principles that he associated with leadership in the Church. Some have called it "The Creed of a Saint":

I would be a friend to the friendless and find joy in ministering to the needs of the poor.

I would visit the sick and afflicted and inspire in them a desire for faith to be healed.

I would teach the truth to the understanding and blessing of all mankind.

I would seek out the erring one and try to win him back to a righteous and happy life.

I would not seek to force people to live up to my ideals, but rather love them into doing the thing that is right.

I would live with the masses and help to solve their problems that their earth life may be happy.

I would avoid the publicity of high positions and discourage the flattery of thoughtless friends.

I would not knowingly wound the feelings of any, not even one who may have wronged me, but would seek to do him good and make him my friend.

I would overcome the tendency to selfishness and jealousy and rejoice in the success of all the children of my Heavenly Father.

I would not be an enemy to any living soul.

Knowing that the Redeemer of mankind has offered to the world the only plan that will fully develop us and make us really happy here and hereafter, I feel it not only a duty but a blessed privilege to disseminate this truth.

George Albert Smith's creed is indicative of how fully he had dedicated his time, talents, and energy to the ministry. Despite his frailty, there seemed to be no limit to his devotion. In the early years of the twentieth century, travel in many parts of the West was still rather primitive. Elder Smith often drove to stake conferences through raging blizzards. On many of his longer trips, he encountered hazards that were nerve-racking. At home his responsibilities had been magnified by the birth of three children—Emily, a youngster of strong will and keen intellect; Edith, a placid and especially lovable child; and George Albert, Jr., a youngster of great promise who in many respects shared his father's temperament and talents.

While the children were a real joy to him, their involvement in a series of accidents, illnesses, and the vicissitudes of growing up added to his worries. Although he was well aware of the fact that he was overtaxing his physical resources, he held to a rigorous schedule of conferences, funerals, extended tours, and occasional business trips until his strength gave way. On February 25, 1909, he recorded in his journal: "Spent a miserable night and in the morning found that I was unable to get up. My strength was gone, and I was in pain from head to foot. La Grippe and general collapse was my trouble as diagnosed by Dr. Gamble. I spent the following week in bed trying to get well."

Discouraged by the slowness of his recovery, George Albert sought recuperation in California, where he stayed with John and Lucy Acomb, Lucy Smith's uncle and aunt. By fall he appeared to have made some progress, but one day as he sought relaxation in the surf, he was caught in a powerful wave and barely escaped drowning. The result was a "bad sinking spell" that kept a doctor and the missionaries at his bedside all night. His new aversion to the sea induced him to return to Salt Lake City, where his doctor ordered complete rest in the quiet environment of his Uncle Acomb's home. Although he tried to resume a few activities, his doctors insisted that his strained heart muscles would require a year of absolute rest. With great difficulty the family went to St. George to spend the winter, and George Albert was unable to leave his bed for five months.

Discouraged by his incapacity and worried about his inability to discharge his apostolic duties, George began to suspect that his work was finished. Could God be displeased with what he had been doing? In the midst of his distress, he dreamed one night that he met his grandfather, George A. Smith, on a trail in the woods. As George ran forward to greet him, the grandfather stopped him with a question: "I'd like to know what you have done with my name." A kaleidoscopic review of his entire life seemed to race through George Albert's mind. "Grandfather," he replied, "I have never done anything with your name that you need be ashamed of."

Awakening with tears of joy because he had been able to report that he had been true to his heritage, George Albert felt some relief. It was difficult to believe that God was punishing him with this affliction because of any failure or misconduct on his part. Perhaps God was only calling him to a new assignment. As this thought became lodged in his mind, the frail apostle asked his wife, Lucy, to join him in praying for restoration or for release from mortal life, if that were God's will. Devastated by the thought of losing him, Lucy refused. But as he grew weaker and emphasized the futility of clinging to a shadow, she relented and they prayed together. "Thy will, O Lord, not mine be done."

Gaining some strength after this experience, George Albert returned home, but his recovery was painfully slow. Finding quiet relaxation on the shore of the Great Salt Lake, he spent most of the summer in an improvised retreat at Saltair. After treatments in a sanitorium, he returned to the Acombs' home and concentrated on walking to regain strength. By the beginning of 1911 he was able to resume meeting with the Quorum of the Twelve. Yet another setback came when Lucy had to spend four weeks in a hospital following an operation. The death of his father was another blow, but at the same time he firmed up his resolution to shake off his ailments and look after the family of which he was now the head.

His strength gradually returned, and Elder Smith resumed his travels and other activities. Some years previously, in 1907, he had been agent for the Church in acquiring the Joseph Smith farm and the Sacred Grove, where the Father and the Son had appeared to Joseph Smith, and had sought to purchase also the Hill Cumorah, where the plates from which the Book of Mormon was translated had been found. The owner of the hill, Pliny Sexton, had cagily refused to sell at that time, but as Elder Smith resumed his travels, he made a practice of calling on Sexton with the object of warming him to the idea of selling the famous hill. Ultimately these efforts were successful, and with the great annual pageants on the Hill Cumorah every summer, it has become one of the best-known historical sites associated with the Church.

New business responsibilities came to Elder Smith. He served as a director of ZCMI, the Utah National Bank, the Home Fire Insurance Company, and the Heber J. Grant Company, and had some interests in the oil and gas industries and the Mutual Creamery Company. He was a trustee of the Groves LDS Hospital in Salt Lake City. Because of his special capacity for making friends, he became associated with a number of national organizations, especially the Sons of the American Revolution, which showered him with high honors and responsibilities. The Boy Scouts of America also held his lasting interest, and he would ultimately be recognized as one of the most influential and respected leaders of the national organization. He was also an influential member of the international farmers movement, serving as president of the International Irrigation Congress (1916), the International Dry Farm Congress (1917), and the International Farm Congress (1918).

WHEN PRESIDENT JOSEPH F. SMITH died during the influenza epidemic of 1918, George Albert Smith felt that he had "lost another father." The new president, Heber J. Grant, was a practical man involved in many enterprises as well as a notable spiritual leader. Although Elder Smith's relations with the new president had always been close and cordial, his first assignment under the new administration was somewhat jarring because of his continued lack of vigor. He was asked to go to London and reinvigorate the European Mission, which had been closed during World War I. Despite misgivings in his family, Elder Smith responded without a murmur. In London he found it a major undertaking to get permission for the admittance of 175 missionaries to Great Britain. After visits to Dublin and Glasgow, he was caught in a railroad strike and had to return to Liverpool on a freight motor lorry. The experience sent him to bed "too weak and nervous to do anything," and for some time he had to direct the mission's activities from his bedside.

As his strength returned, Elder Smith went to London several times to press for the admittance of missionaries. The government's resistance seemed to be related to antagonism aroused by some American soldiers stationed in Britain during the war and to an anti-Mormon propaganda crusade then at its height. The persistent apostle exerted himself to counter these prejudices by the presentation of facts and a persistent manifestation of good will. At last the ban on the admittance of the missionaries was lifted, but not until May 31, 1920. Previously he had obtained permission for missionaries to resume their labors in Switzerland. With the wartime restrictions thus easing, he toured Norway, Sweden, Denmark, Holland, and Germany, holding conferences and striving to reinvigorate long-neglected church activities. On the return trip, his son, George Albert, Jr., induced him to cross the English channel in a bouncy little airplane. The apostle's reaction during the flight was, "If I ever get out of this thing alive, I'll never get into another one." But he seemed to suffer no ill effects, and later he became an enthusiastic patron of the airlines.

In England as well as in the United States, George Albert Smith made a persistent practice of talking religion as he traveled. When he conversed with a Presbyterian minister in a compartment one day, he encountered some sharp criticism. "Why do you Mormons come here and divide our families and our churches and lure people to leave this good land for America?" he was asked. Elder Smith replied, in effect, "If you have not converted them, you have little ground for complaint when we come and help you." Then he expounded a thesis that he often used in appealing to other Christians: "We are asking you to keep the truths you have acquired in your churches, from the scriptures and your educational institutions. Keep also the fine characters you have developed and the love and beauty that are in your hearts from having lived in this wonderful land. Keep all this. It is part of the gospel of Jesus Christ. Then let us sit down and share with you some of the things that have come into our lives that have enriched our lives and made us happy. We offer these things without money and without price."

One other incident is indicative of Elder Smith's capacity to turn animosity to good advantage. Having agreed to represent ZCMI in a tour of England and Scotland with the American Dry Goods Association, as guest of the British Chamber of Trade, he seemed to become a special target of a pompous Englishman who repeatedly made belittling remarks about the Mormons, apparently intended to alienate the apostle from the other guests. Reporting these incidents to the chairman, George Albert volunteered to withdraw if his presence was causing any embarrassment. The chairman begged him to stay, but that did not end the hazing. One day the pompous dignitary, his jacket almost covered with garish medals, flipped Elder Smith's lapel, on which was pinned an emblem of the Sons of the American Revolution. "I say, Mr. Smith," he gloated, "what is that funny little button you are wearing?"

George Albert raised his voice to a triumphant ring as he replied, "That little button, my friend, represents the time when my great-grandfather whipped your great-grandfather." Some bystanders burst into applause, and the baiting was at an end.

Relieved of his duties as president of the mission by Orson F. Whitney, with all of his major objectives accomplished, George Albert Smith returned with his family in time to celebrate Utah Pioneer Day, July 24, at the Joseph Smith farm in Vermont. He reached his home in Salt Lake City in August 3, after an absence of twenty-six months.

As he resumed activities on the home front, his principal assignment was the general superintendency of the Young Men's Mutual Improvement Association, a responsibility for which he was admirably qualified. He surrounded himself by vigorous and devoted leaders of youth and launched a new era in warming young people to the Church and alerting them to their opportunities in life. At the same time he intensified his activities in the Sons of the American Revolution, of which he was vice-president general. He often toured different parts of the country with other general officers of the SAR, and supervised that organization's national convention in Salt Lake City in June 1924. His intensified activities on behalf of the Boy Scouts of America brought him the Silver Beaver Award in 1932. New business responsibilities that came his way included a vice-presidency in Utah-Idaho Sugar Company and the chairmanship of the executive committee that supervised operations of the *Deseret News*.

More important was an assignment to direct the Church's observance of its centennial on April 6, 1930. Because of his great interest in Church history and the preservation of memorials associated with the past, George Albert Smith was the logical choice for this responsibility. He headed a committee that included David O. McKay, Joseph Fielding Smith, and Melvin J. Ballard of the Council of the Twelve; B. H. Roberts and Rulon S. Wells of the First Council of Seventy; Presiding Bishop Sylvester Q. Cannon; and LeRoi C. Snow. Long in advance of the great occasion, they laid plans for four days of

pageantry, oratory, rejoicing, and an outpouring of thankful-
ness for the growth of the Church and the fully established
intermountain empire. This assignment greatly stimulated
Elder Smith's interest in the history of the Church and the
memorable trek to the West and launched him on a career of
marking trails and historic landmarks in cooperation with the
Oregon Trail Memorial Association and similar groups. For
the remainder of his life he found special satisfaction in recap-
turing the drama and heroism of the past, which he saw as
the fulfillment of divine purpose.

THE DEEPENING PROBLEMS OF THE DEPRESSION of the 1930s
brought new problems to the Smith family. Not only was
there a reduction of family income, but differences also arose
over how Church agencies should respond to the squeeze of
the depression, especially when Elder Smith resisted President
Grant's insistence that ZCMI would have to reduce pensions
it had previously indicated it would pay. While details of the
controversy have never been fully disclosed. Elder Smith resigned from the board out of a feeling that faithful, long-time
employees were being unfairly penalized at a time when they
most needed funds to meet their obligations.

The still fragile apostle suffered more severe psychological
jolts when his eldest daughter, Emily, was dismissed from the
general board of the Primary because of a controversy with
the general president of that organization. When he seemed
to find no relief for his daughter's grievances in the Quorum
of the Twelve, his diary records that he was frequently unnerved and again found it necessary to take to his bed to cope
with worry and weakness. He wrote in his diary, "My nerves
are nearly gone but am holding on the best I know how."

It was a case in which family loyalty outran the discretion
of a great Church leader. All possibility of reconciling the
quarreling sisters had long since passed, and the Quorum of
the Twelve was under severe strain from the continued agita-
tion of the issue. President Grant finally put an end to the
controversy with some stern admonition to George Albert to
drop it. The devoted apostle did so, with a complete reversion

to his customary habit of cultivating goodwill. He was soon able to say to those who wanted to continue talking about the controversy: "Now, brother, we must forgive and forget all about it."

Despite the goodwill that persisted between President Grant and Elder Smith, other intellectual differences arose. In November 1934, the First Presidency decided to release all apostles from presiding over Church auxiliaries because of the pressures of their quorum assignments. It was a logical and essential transition in a rapidly expanding organization, but it came as a blow to Geoge Albert, who was loath to be disassociated from the Young Men's Mutual Improvement Association. The new policy coincided, moreover, with a move to release two University of Utah professors from the YMMIA general board on grounds of unorthodoxy and excessive emphasis on recreational activities in the organization. Elder Smith had welcomed the professors because of their links to education and their appeal to youth, and he resisted any action that might reflect on the services they had rendered. When the controversy was finally resolved by release of the superintendency and the general board from further duties in January 1935, George Albert recorded in his journal: "Ill at home the remainder of the month."

His health seemed to be substantially improved on a trip to Hawaii, where he mingled with many friendly Saints, but on his return home he was again depressed by Lucy's deteriorating health. Because of his eloquence and his faith in life after death, he was much in demand to speak at funerals, and he was speaking comfort to the survivors of James B. Wallace in the Yale Ward on November 5, 1937, when he was informed of the death of his own wife. It was a crushing blow, but at home he promptly went onto his knees and thanked God for their many happy years together, for the good things they had shared, and for their children.

To assuage his grief, Elder Smith's brethren prescribed for him an extended trip to the South Seas. There he mingled with the Saints, preached frequently, visited royalty, and even rode a bicycle on fascinating tropical trails. Returning much rejuvenated, he resumed his trail-marking activities, helped to direct the Nauvoo centennial, intensified his work in behalf of the blind, labored persistently with his kinsmen in the Reorganized Church of Jesus Christ of Latter Day Saints, and intensified his charities despite limited resources.

HEAVIER RESPONSIBILITIES fell on George Albert Smith with the death in February 1941 of Reed Smoot, veteran apostle who had also served as a United States Senator for thirty years. With the president of the Twelve, Rudger Clawson, too ill to provide more than nominal leadership, Elder Smith inherited the active directing role within the quorum. President Grant, too, was seriously incapacitated, and most of the work of directing the now large and flourishing Church rested on the shoulders of his counselors, J. Reuben Clark, Jr., and David O. McKay.

The Japanese attack on Pearl Harbor on December 7, 1941, brought new worries and responsibilities, and the death of President Clawson a year and a half later thrust George Albert into the presidency of the Quorum of the Twelve at the age of seventy-three, at a time when he was still afflicted by high blood pressure and a variety of physical weaknesses. Because of President Grant's continued illness and the strongly entrenched tradition that the president of the Twelve would succeed to the presidency of the Church, it was highly probable that George Albert Smith would soon stand at the pinnacle.

Meanwhile, Elder Smith continued to help the troubled, the poor, and the underprivileged. He was particularly supportive of the Society for Aid to the Sightless, a Church organization formed in 1904 to publish literature for the blind and aid in their education and general welfare. He served as its president for sixteen years. He organized classes at the Utah State Prison, went to see countless persons in pain or distress, and visited isolated Indian villages, while at the same time entertaining and visiting with world-famous dignitaries.

Although they occasionally differed on matters of Church policy, George Albert had a good working relationship with President Grant. After the funeral services for Rudger Clawson,

President Grant ordained George Albert president of the Quorum of the Twelve with these words: "I bless you for your devotion. No more devoted and splendid worker has ever been among the leaders of the Church than yourself, excepting, of course, the Prophet Joseph Smith."

In his relatively brief tenure as president of the Twelve, the frail apostle encountered many new responsibilities and managed to respond to most of them despite continued weakness. With the world at war and the possibilities of calamity ever present, his preaching gained new intensity. "If civilization is to live at all," he warned, "we must turn to the Lord and keep his commandments."

As the new president of the Twelve, Elder Smith plunged into the work of guiding his fellowmen through the trauma of World War II. In a Church of the Air address on April 8, 1945, he declared: "With our sons and daughters pouring out their blood like a river on the battlefields of the world to save us from destruction, surely the most praiseworthy and effective thing we can do to show our appreciation of their sacrifice will be to repent of our sins and set our lives and our homes in order so that we can worthily ask our Heavenly Father to restore peace to the earth and bring our loved ones back to us again."

A few weeks later, he was on a train en route to New York to negotiate for a monument site when a porter awakened him at 2:00 A.M. with a message that President Heber J. Grant was dead. This meant that he was immediately de facto head of the Church and would soon find it necessary to reorganize the First Presidency with himself at the head. Leaving the train at Buffalo, he hastened to return to Salt Lake City but had ample time to contemplate the new responsibility that had fallen upon him. Never had he regarded the presidency of the Church as an object of ambition. Rather it was an awesome obligation now thrust upon him. Although he felt personally inadequate, he would not shrink from its responsibilities because of his firm conviction that God would be with him.

After greeting his family and various Church leaders at the train depot in Salt Lake City, George Albert went straight to the Grant home to comfort the President's widow and then sought out his brother Winslow, a confidant who would understand his humility in facing his new responsibilities. At the Grant funeral, George Albert Smith was wholly unstinting in his praise of President Grant's great qualities and then expounded his boundless faith in the certainty and the glories of the resurrection.

WHEN THE APOSTOLIC COUNCIL met on May 21, 1945, to choose a new president of the Church, fourteen members were present (David O. McKay and J. Reuben Clark had resumed their places in the quorum, after being automatically released from the First Presidency). Tears flowed as all the members welcomed the new president and George F. Richards ordained him. The big question of the hour was whether President Smith would then ask Elders Clark and McKay, who for some years had been directing the affairs of the Church because of President Grant's illness, to resume their places as counselors. The new president heartily responded to what he regarded as the will of God and summoned the two former counselors to his side. It was a dramatic illustration of his determination to "seek . . . first the kingdom of God and his righteousness."

The new president was soon in charge. He drew heavily on the advice of his brethren, especially J. Reuben Clark, Jr., a tower of strength and experience. If an initial discussion of a problem did not bring full agreement among the brethren, he would bring the matter up for further discussion, but his lifelong habit of resolving problems in a spirit of love, tolerance, and goodwill bridged many gaps. His dominant admonition to his brethren was to "love the people into living righteously."

Great events demanded response befitting the head of a large and alert religious organization. In September President Smith directed an emotional and enthusiastic mass meeting in the Salt Lake Tabernacle in celebration of the end of World War II. Then, after fasting to attain spiritual dedication, he spent three exhilarating days dedicating a new temple at Idaho Falls. The president, now seventy-five, felt encouraged and blessed because he was able to meet his responsibilities with what appeared to be a new flow of strength. In his first general conference as president of the Church, where he was unanimously sustained by all the priesthood quorums, he even waxed boastful over the achievements of the Latter-day Saints, who, he said, had the lowest death rate and highest birth rate of any people in America while finding joy and exultation through walking in obedience to the commandments of God.

The major emergency the Church had to meet was getting food to the starving Saints in postwar Europe. President Smith went personally to Washington to see what could be done. In a conference with President Harry Truman, he was warned that the money of the wartorn European countries "isn't any good." The response was that the Church was more interested in getting food to the hungry than in money. The Church had plenty of food available, he reported, because while the government was slaughtering pigs and advising farmers to reduce output, the Church was building warehouses and storing supplies. President Truman good-naturedly promised his full cooperation in getting these supplies to hungry people. President Smith named Elder Ezra Taft Benson of the Council of the Twelve to head the relief mission, and 127 carloads of food, clothing, quilts, and other supplies, as well as substantial sums in cash contributions, were soon on their way to relieve the distress in wartorn lands.

On the domestic front, responsibilities multiplied as President Smith took over the presidencies of several Church enterprises, made a special point of stimulating the work projects at Welfare Square, and at the same time continued to find time to visit many sick and homeless people. Recruiting able leaders to head the Church's expanding missions proved to be a major task. The importance he attached to carrying the gospel to the Indians is illustrated by his early appointment of Spencer W. Kimball to oversee the Navajo-Zuni Mission. He also appointed Elder Matthew Cowley to head up the Pacific Mission, encompassing seven missions.

In May 1946 President Smith went to Mexico with the

special objective of bringing back into the Church about twelve hundred dissidents who had broken away because they had felt neglected during the war and had formed a separate "convention" of their own. Since feelings among the loyalists and the dissidents still ran strong, it seemed highly questionable, when President Smith succeeded in getting them together into a joint conference, whether a reconciliation would be effected. Many questions were raised and the discussion was often animated. After President Smith warmed his audience with anecdotes, stories, and faith-promoting incidents, and then poured out an emotional appeal for love, brotherhood, and loyalty to Jesus Christ, all but a few of the dissidents voted to come back to the fold.

THE CENTENNIAL YEAR OF 1947 brought a fitting zenith to George Albert Smith's presidency. As a grandson of George A. Smith, who had entered the Salt Lake Valley with the first company of Mormon pioneers a century earlier, and as the outstanding leader in marking pioneer trails to commemorate historic events, he had had the advantage of personal identification with the history being celebrated. In July 1946 he led a party of historians, writers, and personal friends over the old pioneer route from Nauvoo to the Salt Lake Valley, celebrating events and installing new markers as they went. Since 1946 was the fiftieth anniversary of the admission of Utah to the Union, patriotic enthusiasm was mingled with religious zeal in reliving the past. George Albert Smith's tender feelings for his native state and for the United States as a whole were closely bound up with the feeling that God had raised up the Founding Fathers to establish a political atmosphere where freedom could flourish and the full gospel of Jesus Christ be restored.

Proud of what had been accomplished, President Smith invited many special guests to come to Utah in 1947. The National Conference of Governors assembled in Salt Lake City that year, and forty-three governors and their wives, along with more than five hundred other officials and guests, swarmed through the Smith home on Yale Avenue, with its charming canyon retreat and garden, for a buffet dinner and reception. The climax of the centennial celebration came when 50,000 persons witnessed a spectacular parade and the unveiling of the impressive Pioneer Monument at the mouth of Emigration Canyon. More than a million people visited Temple Square in 1947.

In his efforts to keep abreast of his responsibilities, President Smith often rested at home for a couple of hours in the afternoon. Considerable relief from his burdens came when he named D. Arthur Haycock as personal secretary and administrative assistant. Sometimes he discussed with his son, Albert, a professor of the Harvard School of Business Administration and an expert in the field, the advisability of introducing modern administrative techniques into the Church organization. Aware of his limited strength, however, he undertook no major steps in that direction, although he did oversee the beginning of major changes and phenomenal growth in the Brigham Young University, under the direction of President Ernest L. Wilkinson.

The electoral campaigns of 1948 brought a succession of eminent political leaders to Salt Lake City—President and Mrs. Harry S Truman, Governor Thomas E. Dewey of New York, and Governor Earl Warren of California among them. President Smith greeted them all cordially and listened to their oratory without being drawn in any way into their political rivalries. His position as the unquestioned leader of the Latter-day Saints was everywhere recognized, but it was a leadership strictly confined to spiritual advancement and the extension of goodwill to all people.

A break in the rigorous pace he was following finally came when he went to Los Angeles in January 1949 to clear the way for construction of the Los Angeles Temple. Following a series of conferences, personal visits, and official entertainment, he became exhausted and had to go to a hospital; there it was found he had suffered a slight thrombosis. After three weeks in the hospital and a further period of recuperation, he returned home and sought to resume his activities. He was able to address a session of the general conference in April but went home exhausted. He suffered impairment of hearing and other ailments as he valiantly struggled to resume normal activities. Nevertheless, he managed to go to California to celebrate the achievements of the Mormon Battalion, and to Vermont and Washington, D.C., to dedicate two monuments to Brigham Young. His eightieth birthday on April 4, 1950, was an occasion for a gala celebration, and two days later he rejoiced in reporting to the general conference that the Church, which had been organized 120 years earlier with six members, now had a membership of more than a million.

When he journeyed to Hawaii to celebrate the centennial of Mormonism in the islands, new stimulation seemed to keep him in motion, although he found it necessary to miss part of the ceremonies. Back home, he was able to address the general conference, dedicate a chapel in Denver, and receive various official visitors, but through the late fall and winter months he was confined to his home with illness that simply would not yield to the exuberance of his spirit. After a period in the hospital, he began to feel that his time had come. Still, it was God's will that should prevail.

After a few more struggles to fulfill his presidential duties, the flesh would no longer respond. When asked if he had anything to say as he lapsed into unshakable weariness, he would reply: "Yes, I know that my Redeemer lives." He died on April 4, 1951, his eighty-first birthday. Consciousness gave way to oblivion seemingly without pain, a fitting end for one who had labored so valiantly to relieve others of suffering.

Thousands gathered, high officials as well as humble workmen and children, to pay him honor. There seemed to be general agreement with the tribute of Elder Matthew Cowley at the funeral service: "To be in his presence was to be healed, if not physically, then indeed spiritually." Many other tributes reached for the superlative: "A man of God if there ever was one." "A kinder man never lived." "He was loved by everyone who knew him." "I shall always think of him as the most

Christ-like man I have ever known." "If ever a man walked the streets of this world who was fit to walk and talk with God, it was George Albert Smith."

SOURCES

The most complete information on George Albert Smith is in Merlo J. Pusey, *Builders of the Kingdom: George A. Smith, John Henry Smith, George Albert Smith* (Provo, Utah: Brigham Young University Press, 1981), pp. 201-361. This biography made extensive use of George Albert Smith's journal and private papers, which are in Brigham Young University Library. Other treatments of George Albert Smith's life include Leonard J. Arrington, "George Albert Smith," in *Dictionary of American Biography*, Supplement Five, 1951-1955, John A. Garraty, ed. (New York: Charles Scribner's Sons, 1977), pp. 639-40; Preston Nibley, "Eighth President: George Albert Smith," in *The Presidents of the Church* (Salt Lake City: Deseret Book, 1974), pp. 265-304; James B. Allen and Glen M. Leonard, *The Story of the Latter-day Saints* (Salt Lake City: Deseret Book Co., 1976), esp. pp. 548-59; and Joseph Fielding Smith, *Essentials in Church History* (Salt Lake City: Deseret Book, 1973), pp. 532-36.

MERLO J. PUSEY was born in Utah and graduated from the University of Utah. He spent most of his professional life in Washington, D.C., as an editorial writer and associate editor of the Washington *Post*. He was author of a biography of Chief Justice Charles Evans Hughes, which won the Pulitzer and Bancroft Prizes, as well as of biographies of Dwight D. Eisenhower and Eugene Meyer. He also wrote *Builders of the Kingdom: George A. Smith, John Henry Smith, George Albert Smith* (Provo, Utah: Brigham Young University Press, 1981) and *Ripples of Intuition* (Salt Lake City, 1984), a book of poems. He died in the fall of 1985.

DAVID O. MCKAY

James B. Allen

Centuries ago in the Scottish highlands, chieftains of Clan McKay wore an impressive crest badge inscribed with the motto "manu forti," meaning "with a strong hand." Few expressions could describe more appropriately the leadership of David O. McKay, a modern descendant of that clan and ninth president of The Church of Jesus Christ of Latter-day Saints. As a missionary, teacher, husband, father, school administrator, church leader, and in many other capacities, this remarkable man was an example of both love and firmness in all he did. It was his lot to lead the Church into the last half of the twentieth century, when rapid change in the world around it called for a strong hand in meeting new challenges and promoting important new developments within the Church itself. He became president at age seventy-eight, and by the time he died, at ninety-six, the Church had nearly tripled in size, the number of stakes had grown more than two and a half times, the number of missions had more than doubled, and the missionary force had expanded six times.

DAVID O. MCKAY'S FAMILY ROOTS in the Church extended back to his grandparents on both sides, all of whom joined the Church in the year 1850. William McKay, a contractor, and his wife, the former Ellen Oman, were living in Thurso, Scot-

275

land, when they were contacted by Latter-day Saint missionaries. Readily accepting the restored gospel, they and their three oldest children were baptized on November 3, 1850. In less than two years, William was ordained an elder and made president of the branch at Thurso. In South Wales, meanwhile, Thomas and Margaret Evans also accepted the message of the missionaries and were baptized in May 1850. Thomas was soon ordained an elder and made president of his branch. They lived near Merthyr Tydfil, where all eleven of their children were born.

Both families endured the classic tests of discipleship that required difficult decisions and sacrifices. Members of Ellen McKay's family refused every effort she made to teach them the gospel, and decried her decision to emigrate to America as a "mad adventure." Thomas Evans's family was so irate with him for joining the Mormons that he was disinherited, and he never saw the family again.

In 1856 the McKays of Scotland and the Evanses of Wales joined over forty-three hundred European Saints who decided to sell all they had and emigrate to America. On May 4 the McKays were among 764 Saints, under the leadership of James G. Willie, who left Liverpool aboard the ship *Thornton*. Unfortunately, when they arrived in New York City they were unable to find a friend who had borrowed money from them in Scotland and promised to return it in America. This forced the family to remain in the eastern states in an effort to earn enough money to continue their journey. In the meantime, nearly nineteen hundred of the immigrants, in five different companies, followed the newly suggested plan of crossing the plains to Utah on foot, pulling or pushing their belongings in handcarts. About five hundred members of Willie's group became the fourth handcart company that year, and one of two ill-fated companies caught in an early snowstorm. Sixty-seven souls were lost in the tragedy. The McKays moved to Iowa in 1858, and in 1859 they joined a company at Florence, Nebraska, headed westward under the leadership of Captain James Brown. They arrived in Salt Lake City on August 29, but soon moved north to Ogden. Later they moved to Huntsville, where they took up farming.

The Evans family left Liverpool on May 25, 1856, among the 856 Saints under the leadership of Edward Martin aboard the ship *Horizon*. Ironically, about six hundred of this group became the second handcart company to be caught in that terrible early storm of 1856, and some 145 of them perished. The Evans family, however, had decided not to travel all the way to Utah that year and, instead, remained in Iowa for three years. Finally, in 1859, they obtained wagons, teams, and an extra cow and joined Philip H. Buzzard's Utah-bound company. They arrived in Salt Lake City four days ahead of the McKays, and two weeks later they moved to Ogden.

In spite of their surprisingly parallel experiences, the two families never met until, shortly after the Evanses' arrival in Ogden, fifteen-year-old David McKay spotted the beautiful nine-year-old Jennette Evans sitting on the tongue of a wagon. They soon became well acquainted, and eight years later David persuaded Thomas Evans to let him marry his daughter, even though she was not yet eighteen. David was already a successful farmer, and the young couple settled in a log cabin in Huntsville, where their first two daughters were born. Later they moved into a larger and more comfortable rock house, still known affectionately by the McKay family as "The Old Home." It was there that the third of their ten children, David Oman McKay, was born on September 8, 1873.

As DAVID O. GREW UP IN HUNTSVILLE, he learned the lessons of industry and hard work, the reality of tragedy, and the implications of church service. He was only six when, in the spring of 1880, his two older sisters died within a week of each other and were buried in the same grave. Just a year later, David McKay, the youth's father, received a call to go on a mission to his native Scotland. "Impossible," he told his wife, for another child was on the way and all his responsibilities at home and on the farm seemed too overwhelming. "You must accept," she replied. "David O. and I will manage things nicely." After much discussion with friends and family, David accepted the call. "Take care of Mama," he told his seven-year-old son the day he left, and at that point young David O. began to assume responsibilities that soon matured him beyond his years. They also, no doubt, helped prepare him well for the heavy church responsibilities that came to him in his early thirties.

Her husband was gone for two years, but Jennette McKay, her two sons, a two-year-old daughter, Jeanette, and the baby daughter born ten days after David left survived well enough. David O. and his younger brother, Thomas E., quickly learned even more about farm work and household chores, though, of course, friends and neighbors helped out considerably. Priesthood quorums did the spring planting, and by summer a good crop of hay and grain was ready for harvest. But grain prices were low that year, so Jennette, with the advice of her family, stored her grain until spring, when she realized an unusually high profit. Encouraged, she and her sons worked even harder the next season, and before her husband returned in 1883, she built the addition to her house that the two of them had planned before he left. She told the children to keep it a secret, however, so they could surprise their father when he returned. Jennette also kept her sons in school, held regular family prayer with them, and continued their training in all the virtues expected of good Latter-day Saints.

David O. turned eight in the fall of the year his father left, so it was probably a disappointment that he could not be baptized by his father. Nevertheless, he was baptized on his birthday by Peter Geertsen and confirmed a member of the Church by Bishop Francis A. Hammond. When their father returned, one of the children asked if he had seen any miracles while he was gone, and he replied by putting his arm around his wife and saying, "Your mother is the greatest miracle that one could ever find." Little wonder that David O. spent so much time in later years giving honor to her. As he wrote on one occasion:

> My Mother! God bless you!
> For your purity of soul,

Your faith, your tenderness,
Your watchful care,
Your supreme patience,
Your companionship and trust,
Your loyalty to the right,
Your help and inspiration to father,
Your unselfish devotion to us children.

After their father returned from his mission, David O. and Thomas continued to work with and learn from him on the farm. David O. also took a summer job carrying the daily paper, the *Ogden Standard*, to LaPlata, a mining town not far away. He rode horseback all the way, and the round trip took him from seven to five each day. He spent much of the time reading, and in the process he memorized excerpts from great literature that, in later life, added interest and color to many of his sermons. He also learned in these years to bring timber out of the mountains. Beyond all that, life in Huntsville included horseback riding, swimming in Spring Creek, baseball, dramatics, debating, and glee clubs. David O. was involved in all of them, and also played the piano with the town's dance orchestra.

Young David grew up in a period of stress as well as great achievement for the Church. The transcontinental railroad was completed just four years before he was born, bringing greater opportunities to the Church so far as immigration and economic development were concerned, but also creating more opportunity for conflict with incoming gentiles. Brigham Young was still president of the Church in 1873, and was engaged in a struggle to maintain religious instruction or, at least, keep teachers who had religious commitments employed in Utah schools — a problem David O. McKay would also wrestle with during the years of his church leadership. Brigham Young Academy (forerunner of Brigham Young University) was founded in 1875. This decade saw the blossoming of more conflict with the national government, particularly over the issue of plural marriage. It also saw the expansion of church settlements, the establishment of the United Orders in Utah, the dedication of the St. George Temple, and a tightening up of church administrative practices in a great priesthood reform movement begun by Brigham Young shortly before his death in 1877.

One of President Young's objectives was to bring more young men into the Aaronic Priesthood. As a result of this move, more were ordained than ever before. David O. became a deacon on December 14, 1885, three months after his twelfth birthday, and eventually he became a member of the presidency of both his deacons and teachers quorums. Activity in these quorums meant cleaning the chapel, chopping and hauling wood for the chapel stoves, and chopping wood for widows. As early as age thirteen, David O. was bearing his testimony in quorum meetings. According to the "Minutes of the Teachers and Deacon's Quorums" of Huntsville Ward, on November 13, 1886, "David O. McKay bore his testimony and said he felt pleased at coming to meeting."

Gaining an abiding testimony of the gospel, however, was by no means easy or automatic. Even though he firmly believed in the reality of Joseph Smith's visions and in the Book of Mormon, young David did not receive the confirming spiritual manifestation he wanted to have. He learned that the testimony of the Spirit is something that must be sought after and worked for, and as a young man he tried vainly to have it come to him. He often prayed secretly, "on hillside and in meadow," but the desired manifestation did not come. On one occasion, he reported, while he was hunting cattle, he stopped to rest his horse and

there, once again, an intense desire came over me to receive a manifestation of the truth of the Restored Gospel. I dismounted, threw my reins over my horse's head, and there under a serviceberry bush I prayed that God would declare to me the truth of his revelation to Joseph Smith. I am sure that I prayed fervently and sincerely and with as much faith as a young boy could muster.

At the conclusion of the prayer, I arose from my knees, threw the reins over my faithful pony's head, and got into the saddle. As I started along the trail again, I remember saying to myself, "No spiritual manifestation has come to me. If I am true to myself, I must say I am just the same 'old boy' that I was before I prayed."

280

He remained true to his beliefs, however, and in 1899, while he was on his mission, that longed-for manifestation finally came.

In the meantime, David O.'s father was ordained a bishop and assigned to preside over the ward in nearby Eden. In 1885 he was sustained as bishop of his home ward in Huntsville. Two years later the Patriarch to the Church, John Smith, visited Huntsville and accepted Bishop McKay's request that he give blessings to his children. David O.'s blessing was particularly impressive because of its solid wisdom and prophetic nature. "Brother David Oman McKay," the patriarch said, "thou art in thy youth and need instruction, therefore I say unto thee, be taught of thy parents the way of life and salvation, that at an early day you may be prepared for a responsible position, for the eye of the Lord is upon thee.... The Lord has a work for thee to do, in which thou shalt see much of the world, assist in gathering scattered Israel and also labor in the ministry. It shall be thy lot to sit in council with thy brethren and preside among the people and exhort the Saints to faithfulness."

Young David's continuing church activity included a call, at age fifteen, to serve as secretary of the Huntsville Ward Sunday School. In 1893 he became a Sunday School teacher. Also in 1893 he was ordained to the office of priest. In the meantime, he completed the eighth grade in Huntsville and entered Weber Stake Academy in Ogden. At the end of two years he was pleased to accept an offer to return to Huntsville as principal of the school. After a year, however, he decided to continue his education and prepare himself more fully for a professional career in teaching. It was about this time that his mother received a gift of twenty-five hundred dollars from her own mother. Her brother and sister urged her to invest it, but, instead, she said simply, "Every cent of this goes to the education of our children." David O., Thomas E., and two sisters, Jeanette and Ann, all benefited from their mother's sacrifice by attending the University of Utah. In June 1897 David O. graduated as president and valedictorian of his university class. His life-long quest for learning was beautifully symbolized in the theme of his "oration" which, according to the *Deseret News*, was "that an unsatisfied appetite for knowledge means progress and is the state of a normal mind."

David also received his teaching certificate and was offered a position in Salt Lake County. He eagerly accepted but, as had happened to his father and grandfather before him, the Church suddenly changed his well-laid plans. In July he received a mission call to Great Britain. Most such calls in those days were surprises, and his was no exception. He did not hesitate to accept, however, and on August 1, 1897, he was ordained to the office of seventy and set apart for his mission by President Seymour B. Young of the First Council of the Seventy.

ELDER MCKAY ARRIVED in Liverpool on August 25. The mission president immediately assigned him to the Scottish conference. There he literally followed in the footsteps of his father as he labored first in the Lanark District, then in Glasgow and Stirling. In December 1898, like his father before him, he was appointed to preside over the Scottish Conference.

While serving in this capacity, Elder McKay received the special manifestation that he had longed for since childhood. It finally came, he later said, "as a natural sequence to the performance of duty." As exemplified in his life, this could be an important lesson for many Latter-day Saints: powerful testimonies and spiritual confirmations of testimony usually do not come by simple request. Rather, they are the result of seeking the Spirit through obedience, love, service, and personal sacrifice.

Elder McKay's experience was not outwardly dramatic, but it was so profoundly real to him that throughout his life he considered it a milestone. It came at a special priesthood meeting of the Scottish Conference, presided over by James L. McMurrin of the European Mission presidency. As David O. McKay himself recounted the story:

> I remember as if it were but yesterday, the intensity of the inspiration of that occasion. Everybody felt the rich outpouring of the Spirit

of the Lord. All present were truly of one heart and one mind. Never before had I experienced such an emotion. It was a manifestation for which as a doubting youth I had secretly prayed most earnestly on hillside and in meadow. It was an assurance to me that sincere prayer is answered "sometime, somewhere."

During the progress of the meeting, an elder on his own initiative arose and said, "Brethren, there are angels in this room." Strange as it may seem, the announcement was not startling; indeed, it seemed wholly proper, though it had not occurred to me there were divine beings present. I only knew that I was overflowing with gratitude for the presence of the Holy Spirit. I was profoundly impressed, however, when President James L. McMurrin arose and confirmed that statement by pointing to one brother sitting just in front of me and saying, "Yes, brethren, there are angels in this room, and one of them is the guardian angel of that young man sitting there," and he designated one who today is a patriarch of the Church.

Pointing to another elder, he said, "And one is the guardian angel of that young man there," and he singled out one whom I had known from childhood. Tears were rolling down the cheeks of both of these missionaries, not in sorrow or grief, but as an expression of the overflowing Spirit; indeed, we were all weeping.

Such was the setting in which James L. McMurrin gave what has since proved to be a prophecy. I had learned by intimate association with him that James McMurrin was pure gold; his faith in the gospel implicit; that no truer man, no more loyal man to what he thought was right ever lived; so when he turned to me and gave what I thought then was more of a caution than a promise, his words made an indelible impression on me. Paraphrasing the words of the Savior to Peter, he said: "Let me say to you, Brother David, Satan hath desired you that he may sift you as wheat, but God is mindful of you." Then he added, "If you will keep the faith, you will yet sit in the leading councils of the Church." At that moment there flashed in my mind temptations that had beset my path, and I realized even better than President McMurrin, or any other man, how truly he had spoken when he said "Satan hath desired thee." With the resolve then and there to keep the faith, there was born a desire to be of service to my fellow men, and with it a realization, a glimpse at least, of what I owed to the elder who first carried the message of the Restored Gospel to my grandfather and grandmother who had accepted the message years before in the north of Scotland, and in South Wales.

Elder McKay had another experience that he remembered throughout his life. In Stirling, Scotland, he and his companion spent half a day walking around Stirling Castle but also feeling depressed, and a little homesick, because of the unfriendliness of the people. As they walked back to town, Elder McKay noticed an unfinished residence with an unusual stone arch over the doorway. Even more unusual, the arch bore an inscription, and he was curious enough that he went over to read it. He later reported, "This message came to me, not only in stone, but as if it came from One in whose service we are engaged: 'Whate'er Thou Art, Act Well Thy Part.'" The message struck deep and stirred within him an even greater resolve to act well his part as a missionary of The Church of Jesus Christ of Latter-day Saints. Over half a century later, in 1955, he visited Scotland as president of the Church, found the same spot, and repeated the story for those who were with him. Later the inscribed stone was obtained by the Church and displayed in the David O. McKay exhibit in the Church's Museum of History and Art in Salt Lake City.

Elder McKay was released from his mission in August 1899, and on August 26 he sailed for home. He had with him a letter inviting him to become a teacher at Weber Stake Academy. So far as he was concerned, his direction in life was set, and he eagerly looked forward to a productive and enjoyable career in education.

AT THE UNIVERSITY OF UTAH, David had become acquainted with Emma Ray Riggs, daughter of the landlady from whom he and Thomas E. had rented a house. Though no serious courtship took place at the time, the two became good friends, and he even invited her, along with her aunt, to attend his missionary farewell activities in Huntsville. Ray, as he always called her, looked forward to his coming home, but when she got word he was about to arrive, she was visiting relatives on a cattle ranch on Antelope Island in the Great Salt Lake. She was determined to meet him when he got to Salt Lake City, but she learned that the passenger boat from the island simply would not reach the mainland on time. Nothing would do, therefore, except for her and her cousin Belle to rig a sail on an old rowboat and row across the lake in order to be there the day he arrived. Their friendship soon blossomed into serious courtship, as David taught at Weber Stake Academy and

Ray, after graduating from the University of Utah, took a job at Madison School in Ogden, across the park from the academy. It was in the park that he finally proposed, and on January 2, 1901, David O. McKay and Emma Ray Riggs had the distinction of being the first couple married in the Salt Lake Temple in the twentieth century.

The newlyweds made their home in Ogden, where their seven children were born. Very quickly they learned how to adjust to the rigors of a busy professional life overlaid by heavy church responsibilities. David was a member of the Weber Stake Sunday School board and later became a member of the superintendency. About two weeks after their first baby was born and the nurse had been discharged, David kissed his wife goodbye one evening and left for a board meeting. Ray was distressed, and at first she could not believe that her husband would leave her alone with the baby and the dishes. As she started to cry, she remembered her mother's advice: "Don't cry before you're hurt" and "Don't cry over spilt milk." Well, she had asked her mother, "If I can't cry before I'm hurt and I can't cry after I'm hurt, when can I cry?" The obvious answer: "Don't cry at all." Ray told herself not to be foolish, and she quickly vowed that she would never feel bad when David had to leave on a church assignment.

Sunday School work continued to be David's main church assignment in Weber Stake. In 1900 he became a member of the stake superintendency and was given the responsibility of revitalizing classwork. His innovations in outlining courses of study and in helping teachers with lesson planning not only succeeded in Ogden, but eventually they were adopted by all the Sunday Schools of the Church.

In the meantime, David O. McKay continued in his impressive career at Weber Stake Academy, where, in 1902, he became the principal. He was a popular and effective teacher, and as principal he was well liked by students, board members, and townspeople alike. He instituted several important innovations, including a student newspaper, a special lecture series, a Domestic Arts Department, a Domestic Science Department, two women's literary clubs, and an improved student-body organization. He also recognized the need for a school band, and when he could not find a teacher, he organized and directed it himself. One day a musician, Ernest Nichols, was passing and heard the band practicing. The discordant notes coming from the window so disturbed him that he went inside, told Principal McKay that he needed a band leader, and was hired on the spot.

Principal McKay's most outwardly visible contribution was the addition of a new wing to the academy's Moench Building. Student-body growth was rapid in those years, and the building became so crowded that the only place for the principal's office was the space between the two front doorways. Some classes were forced to meet in hallways and on the stairs. The board of trustees could do little, for some members had even mortgaged their own homes in order to raise money for the original building, but the determined principal proposed to the teachers that they join him in a personal fund-raising program. They visited every ward in the stakes affected by the academy, solicited funds from members and nonmembers of the Church alike, and even put up money of their own. Principal McKay was especially delighted when Samuel Newhouse, a non-Mormon, gave him five thousand dollars. Eventually the $60,000 addition was built, providing the school with additional classrooms, chemistry and geology laboratories, space for a vocational training shop, and an auditorium.

DURING THE YEARS OF TRANSITION between the nineteenth and twentieth centuries, The Church of Jesus Christ of Latter-day Saints continued to expand its worldwide vision and adjust its programs to the needs of the new age. In the 1890s, when David O. McKay served his first mission, the Church's missionary force nearly tripled, and between 1888 and 1900 eleven new missions were opened. Areas of new missionary activity included the South Pacific. Japan was opened for missionary work in 1901, and missionaries were also sent to Mexico and South Africa. In addition, the Church provided funds for meetinghouses and mission headquarters outside the United States. The time for immigration to Utah was over, and church leaders were encouraging members to stay and build up the kingdom of God in their homelands. "We desire it to be distinctly understood that 'Mormonism,' as it is called, has come to the world to stay," declared President Joseph F. Smith in 1903. In less than two decades David O. McKay, as an apostle, would make some important contributions to that vision.

In order to meet the challenges of secularized education, the Church expanded its own church school and academy program, and by the time David began attending Weber Stake Academy, at least thirty-one such institutions had been established in Utah, Idaho, Arizona, Canada, and Mexico. The greatest spiritual symbol of the decade was the dedication of the Salt Lake Temple in 1893. About this time also, the Church began to place increased emphasis on genealogical research, urging the Saints more strongly than ever to seek after their dead in order to perform the sacred temple ordinances in their behalf. Not many years later, in 1918, President Joseph F. Smith received his important vision in which he saw the Savior's visit to the spirit world and the organization of missionary work among the dead. (See Doctrine and Covenants, section 138.) All this and more represented the continuing spiritual vitality of the church that David O. McKay was being prepared to lead.

The Church also faced some serious challenges in these decades, one of which would have an impact on the timing of his call to the apostleship. In 1890 President Wilford Woodruff issued, by revelation, his famous Manifesto, which officially announced the end of plural marriage in the Church. This important announcement quickly paved the way for reconciliation between the Church and many Americans who had disapproved of some of its practices, and also for Utah statehood. The unfortunate aftermath of the Manifesto, however, was that some Latter-day Saints could not find it in their hearts to follow its intent, as explained by President Woodruff, and continued to enter into new plural marriages. Two apostles, John W. Taylor and Matthias F. Cowley, even continued to authorize and perform such marriages, without official church sanction. Eventually they were asked to resign from the

Quorum of the Twelve and their resignations were officially announced in general conference on April 8, 1906. Another vacancy had occurred earlier, with the death of Marriner W. Merrill, and the three new apostles chosen were George F. Richards, Orson F. Whitney, and David O. McKay.

The shock that came to the thirty-two-year-old principal of Weber Stake Academy when he received the call must have been profound. He and his family were in Salt Lake City for the conference meetings and were having lunch with relatives when a call came for him to come immediately to the office of the Council of the Twelve. Surmising that he might be asked to serve on the Church Board of Education, David O. was ushered into the office of Council President Francis M. Lyman. "So you're David O. McKay," said President Lyman. "Well, David O. McKay, the Lord wants you to be a member of the Quorum of Twelve Apostles." The stunned young man could say nothing until, after some urging by President Lyman, he humbly and sincerely replied, "I am neither worthy nor able to receive such a call." "Not worthy? Not worthy? What have you been doing?" President Lyman asked, and Elder McKay could only explain that he had done nothing in the sense that he was afraid President Lyman might have understood. "Well then, don't you have faith that the Lord can make you able?" "Yes, sir, I have that faith," was the reply. President Lyman then instructed him not to tell anyone about the call until his name was presented in conference that afternoon.

If the call was a surprise to David O. McKay, it was at least as much so for his faithful wife. True to his instructions, he told no one, not even her. She heard it first, along with everyone else, when the names of the three new apostles were presented for the sustaining vote of the conference. She burst into tears, and her husband heard someone behind them saying, "There's one of them. See, his wife is crying." With this high and holy calling, the direction of both their lives was changed forever.

Immediately Elder McKay's schedule became busier than ever. Attending meetings of the Council of the Twelve, visiting stakes and missions throughout the Church, and attending to all the other duties that come with the apostleship were becoming increasingly time-consuming as the Church grew in numbers and confronted the new challenges of the twentieth century.

Elder McKay was not immediately relieved of all of his other responsibilities, however. The addition to the Moench Building was not complete, and he was allowed to remain as principal at Weber Stake Academy until the building was dedicated in 1908. His work with the school did not end there, however, for he was immediately made president of the board of trustees, a position he held until his European mission in 1922.

For several years the new apostle and his family continued to live in Ogden. This meant commuting regularly between Ogden and Salt Lake City, and often he was seen running down 24th Street in Ogden to catch the "Bamberger" commuter train that ran between the two cities. On more than one occasion some good Samaritan rescued him by giving him a ride to the train station in a car or on horseback. His work as an apostle also kept him away from home much of the time. Members of the family accepted it in the patient, good-natured way they had been trained, however, and even learned to joke about it. One evening, after an extended absence, he gave his wife a special compliment on the fine dinner she had prepared. Ray thanked him, whereupon his four-year-old daughter chimed in with "Come again sometime!" The children were learning, as had David and Ray very early, of the sacrifices as well as the blessings associated with church leadership.

One of Elder McKay's first important assignments as a General Authority was with the Sunday Schools. He was already a member of the Deseret Sunday School Union general board, and in October 1906 he became second assistant to the superintendent. Three years later he became first assistant, and in 1918 he became the superintendent, a position he held until 1934. Also in 1918 his book *Ancient Apostles* was published. It was prepared as one of the early official Sunday School manuals of the Church.

In these positions, because of his love of teaching and his

years of preparation, Elder McKay continued to have an effective influence on the teaching programs of the Church. One important reform, for example, instituted churchwide in 1906, was the introduction of the parents' class. This was the result of a successful two-year experiment in certain stakes, including Elder McKay's own Weber Stake, in which classes centered around the topic of child rearing. This was actually the beginning of a regular adult program in the Sunday Schools.

Elder McKay also continued to exert influence in another area where his background and training were especially useful: the Church's education program. In 1919 he became the first Church Commissioner of Education. He held the post for only two years, but during that time he made some decisions and recommendations that had far-reaching consequences. Public schools had become so well established that there were serious questions about whether the church academies were economically viable. Church members could hardly afford to support two school systems at the same time: one with their taxes and the other with tuition and other donations. One alternative was to open seminaries near high schools attended by LDS students, which would allow them to continue to get daily religious instruction and yet would save the Church and its members considerable money. Already the experiment begun at Granite High School in 1912 was proving successful, and in 1920 Commissioner McKay recommended that several academies be eliminated in favor of the seminary program. By 1924 all church academies, except the one at Colonia Juarez, had been closed or turned over to the states to be operated as secondary schools.

At the same time, Elder McKay took a hard look at the several colleges owned by the Church. Besides Brigham Young University, these included Brigham Young College in Logan, Utah; Dixie College at St. George; Weber College, David O. McKay's former Weber Stake Academy; Snow College at Ephraim; and Ricks College in Rexburg, Idaho. After considerable study, he recommended in 1920 that Brigham Young University should develop a full college curriculum leading to a four-year degree, while the others should establish two-year courses for the training of teachers. That way the Church would not be duplicating its efforts in promoting several four-year schools, but it would produce many well-trained teachers with basic religious values who would no doubt take their places in the school systems of Utah and surrounding states. The commissioner's proposals were readily accepted, though at the end of the decade most of the Church's colleges in Utah were turned over to the state.

DESPITE HIS HEAVY SCHEDULE, David O. McKay found time for his family. The amount of time may not have been as great as other men had, but the quality of that time was of the highest order. "Papa Dade" and "Mama Ray" were the affectionate names the children often called their parents, and they suggest the impressive closeness enjoyed by the McKays. Ray, of course, had the major responsibility for the children, and she carried it out by being not only a mother in the traditional sense, but also a companion. "There was no generation gap," her son David Lawrence said later. She took her family to movies and even persuaded her husband that there was humor in the famous Mack Sennett comedies. She read good literature to her children, told them stories, sang songs, and played games. Rook, Pit, and backgammon were among the most popular games in the McKay home, and frequently the busy father shared evenings of such enjoyable activity with his family.

As parents, David and Ray made it a point never to disagree in front of their children. On one occasion there seemed to be a difference of opinion when Lawrence wanted to subscribe for certain magazines and his mother told him to ask his father, who said no. His mother simply looked at him but said nothing. A few days later, however, his father quietly told him it would be all right. Whatever differences David and Ray had in such matters, they were never made a point of controversy before the children, and such exemplary public unity provided important lessons.

Both parents were good disciplinarians, but their discipline consisted of praises and smiles. Neither believed in spanking or scolding, yet the children obeyed. Their method of using gentle firmness was displayed on one occasion when the family was riding together in a surrey on the way to Huntsville. Two boys were scuffling in the back seat, and their father asked them to stop. They kept on, however, and, as one of them remembered later, "the next thing I knew I was walking, watching the surrey getting farther and farther away up the hill as I trudged along behind. I started running for Huntsville. Fortunately, Father and the surrey were waiting for me at the top of the hill." Needless to say, there was no more scuffling for the remainder of that trip. Family outings were also regular affairs, and the children could always count on two special trips each summer: one to Yellowstone National Park and the other to the Lagoon amusement park in Farmington, Utah. The fun and family closeness enjoyed by the McKays served well to demonstrate the seriousness with which their father took one of his own oft-repeated sayings: "No other success can compensate for failure in the home."

David O. McKay was also known for his love of animals, and his kindness to them became legendary. He kept various kinds of animals as a youth, and as an adult delighted in playing with animals, and especially in breaking and riding horses. It was not uncommon, even when he was a General Authority, for him to leave home early in the morning, drive to Huntsville to help break a colt, then be back by the time the office was open.

If anyone was exemplary in his love of good literature, it was David O. McKay. From his youth he read voraciously and widely; as one of his children remarked, "A good book is father's friend." He took natural delight in the writings of the Scotsman Robert Burns, and his trips through Scotland were augmented by recitations of Burns's poetry. Shakespeare, Sir Walter Scott, and Charles Dickens were also among his favorite writers. His sermons were augmented with quotations from fine literature, and his companions on his world travels were delighted with his ability to quote many passages memorized from great authors. As one national columnist said in 1952,

"The writer has never met a more interesting person than David O. McKay. . . . Mention Robert Burns, and Mr. McKay can quote poem after poem by memory. The spirit and philosophy of Shakespeare still live in the mind of David O. McKay and can be quoted by memory. The rhythmic lines of Longfellow can pour in an unbroken stream from his storehouse of memory. Five years of literature in two different universities did not bring the writer in contact with a teacher as well versed in literature as Mr. McKay."

Beyond all that, David O. McKay had a sense of humor. "Don't be afraid to laugh," he said. "A person without a sense of humor misses much of the joy of living."

Even as an experienced apostle, David O. McKay continued to learn some personal lessons about the promptings of the Spirit. A miraculous healing in 1916 illustrated this for him, just as it demonstrated the reality of the healing power of the priesthood. It was about the middle of March, and the flooding Ogden River raged through the canyon narrows, washing out the road. Elder McKay drove three of his children to the narrows to show them the destructive torrent.

That evening his brother Thomas stopped at David's home and called his wife to ask her to arrange for the road supervisor to bring a horse through the canyon the next morning so he could get through. He wanted one of David O.'s sons to drive him to where the road was washed out, but, having seen the danger earlier in the day, the apostle volunteered to drive him himself. He only wanted to be back in time to catch his train to Salt Lake City for an important meeting that morning.

After some unforeseen delays the next morning, they were finally on their way about seven o'clock, and the train was due to leave at eight. At that point, Elder McKay received a strong impression that he should "go to the bridge and back," which meant he should not drive all the way to where the road was washed out. As they rushed toward the canyon in the little Ford, his brother suddenly said, "I think you had better not attempt to cross the bridge." "Notwithstanding these two warnings," Elder McKay recalled later, "as we approached the bridge I thought I could spend another five minutes and take him as far as I had taken the children the day before." Anxious to help his brother as much as possible, he assumed that the bridge was still intact and decided to cross. What he had missed seeing was a rope stretched across the road by the watchman who had gone off duty the night before. "Look out!" Thomas shouted, but too late. Before David could stop the car, the rope smashed through the window, catching him on the chin and gashing his lip, knocking out his lower teeth, and breaking his upper jaw. Thomas, who somehow escaped injury, moved his unconscious brother from the driver's seat and drove him to the hospital. After the doctors sewed his jaw in place and took fourteen stitches in his lip and cheek he heard one of the attendants remark, "Too bad. He will be disfigured for life." And a nurse attempted to console him by reminding him that he could wear a beard to hide the scars.

It was not long, however, before Bishop A. E. Olson and two other close friends appeared in his hospital room and administered to him. As Bishop Olson sealed the anointing, Elder McKay heard him say, "We bless you that you shall not be disfigured and that you shall not have pain." It was then that the power of faith came clear. By Saturday evening the doctor was amazed that his patient no longer felt any pain. The next morning the president of the Council of the Twelve, Heber J. Grant, came to visit, in spite of the "Visitors Not Allowed" sign on the door, and told him, "David, don't talk. I'm just going to give you a blessing." The blessing included the words "I bless you that you shall not be scarred," but David's face looked so bad at the moment that even President Grant wondered if he had made a promise that could not be fulfilled. Seven months later the General Authorities were attending a banquet at the Hotel Utah, and Elder McKay noticed President Grant looking at him most intently. "David," he said, "from where I am sitting I cannot see a scar on your face." "No, President Grant, there are no scars," the younger apostle replied. "Your blessing was realized completely."

IN 1920-21 DAVID O. MCKAY took an assignment that dramatically symbolized the growing worldwide commitment of the Church. He was appointed by the First Presidency to tour the missions of the Church around the world. Accompanied by Hugh J. Cannon, a former European Mission president, he left home on December 4, 1920, and returned on December 24, 1921. Traveling about 56,000 miles, the two men visited such places as Japan, China (which Elder McKay dedicated for the preaching of the gospel), the islands of the South Seas, Australia, Egypt, Jerusalem, Europe, and Great Britain. A General Authority had never before visited some of these areas, and the stream of love from the local Saints was overwhelming.

While the entire trip was an inspiration to Elder McKay as well as the people he visited, it was in the South Seas that he seemed to be blessed with a special outpouring of spiritual experiences. At Laie, Hawaii, after an impressive flag-raising ceremony by a group of small children, he was inspired by the Spirit to prophesy that this spot would someday become an important religious and educational center for the Church. The Hawaiian Saints saw the fulfillment of that prophecy as they continued to visit the Hawaiian Temple, dedicated in Laie in 1919, and witnessed the dedication of the Church College of Hawaii in 1958.

In New Zealand, Elder McKay had a deeply moving spiritual experience. At the village of Peketapu, hundreds of native Saints assembled to see and hear the first apostle ever to visit their land. "I realized," he reported later, "how inadequately I might satisfy the ardent desires of their souls, and I yearned most earnestly for the gift of tongues that I might be able to speak to them in their native language." Elsewhere he had spoken through an interpreter, but this time, after praying deeply for divine assistance, he told his local interpreter not to translate sentence by sentence. "Oh, how I wish I had the power to speak to you in your own tongue," he told his audience, "but since I have not the gift, I pray, and I ask you to pray, that you might have the spirit of interpretation, of discernment, that you may understand at least the spirit while I am speaking, and then, you will get the words and the thought when Brother Meha interprets." His sermon went on for forty minutes, and as it proceeded, he recognized, from the tears in many eyes, that many, if not most, were actually receiving the gift of interpretation. When, at the end, Brother Meha began to translate the address, some of the Maori Saints even corrected him on a few points. The gift so longed for by Elder McKay had been given, for the benefit of the Saints. The same gift would come to him again on this trip, and at least once more later in his life.

When Elder McKay visited Samoa, he experienced a particularly touching outpouring of love as he took his leave from the Saints at the village of Sauniatu. Three times he returned to say goodbye, and finally he pronounced a remarkable apostolic blessing on the group. A year later a stone monument was dedicated to commemorate the visit and blessing. It was inscribed: "A Fitting Climax to a Perfect Visit." With such experiences as these to remember, this apostolic journey became one of the high points in the life of David O. McKay.

Soon after he returned home, Elder McKay was appointed to the board of regents of the University of Utah. In less than a year, however, he was forced to resign, for he received still another assignment away from home. This time he became president of the European Mission, replacing the ailing Orson F. Whitney. For two years, from November 1922 to December 1924, he and his family resided in England while he regularly toured the missions of Europe and supervised their activities.

As mission president, Elder McKay made a powerful impression on Saints, missionaries, and non-Mormons alike. He "never wasted time when he was around you," remembered one missionary, and his experience as a teacher gave him some effective methods by which he taught the missionaries important lessons about their own responsibilities. A glass of clear water, for example, became the subject of an object lesson as he held it in front of the elders and commented, "Now you look like that as a young man." Then he placed his fountain pen in the water and, as the ink polluted it, continued the lesson: "When you commit sin you look like that."

During this two-year assignment, Elder McKay's travels

took him also to Armenia, Egypt, and, for the second time in his life, the Holy Land. Clearly he worked hard, and some years later, in 1946, he had every right to give some firm advice to Selvoy J. Boyer as he set him apart as president of the British Mission. "How old are you?" he asked the new president. "I'm forty-nine," came the reply. "Then you're young enough to do something besides sit in London and go to shows," President McKay said. "You visit every missionary every month, oftener if necessary."

One of Elder McKay's most important accomplishments on this mission was a noticeable improvement in the public image of the Church. For years newspapers had been printing all sorts of derogatory articles, based largely on false information about the teachings, practices, and objectives of the Church. Missionaries and other Church members had written refutations, but the papers had refused to publish them. President McKay decided to try a different approach. Instead of simply writing a refutation, he wrote a long letter directly to each of several editors. In his letter to the editor of the *John Bull*, he called attention to the English tradition of sportsmanship and fair play, requesting that the paper tell only the truth about the Latter-day Saints. "A Daniel Come to Judgement," read a large headline in the next edition of the *John Bull*, and beneath it was the complete text of President McKay's letter. At least for the rest of his mission presidency, no more negative articles appeared in that paper, and several other papers followed suit. In Wales, a town council voted to prohibit the Saints from holding public meetings, but a letter from President McKay succeeded in reversing that action also. Few people could resist the strength of his persuasive character.

President McKay set the tone for an increased commitment to missionary work on the part of the members in Europe. As he went about his travels, he urged every Saint to pledge to bring one new member into the Church each year. They should work with relatives, friends, and associates, he told them. "Every member a missionary" became the motto for which he would be credited in later years, but this emphasis really began in 1923 in Europe.

Another important concern was seen in President McKay's persistent plea to the Saints who were eager to immigrate to America. "Stay where you are," he told them, for the time had come when they were to build up the Church in their own lands. This was consistent with a statement issued by the First Presidency in October 1921, urging the missionaries to stop preaching emigration. The Saints could be more useful to the Lord's kingdom by strengthening it in their own lands rather than immigrating to America, where "their hopes will not be realized." Though the gathering had been of great meaning in the history of the Church, the First Presidency said, "we must realize that times and conditions change and that therefore the application of the principles and teachings must change." At the same time, the Saints were promised that temples would one day be erected in their native lands, so that they could enjoy all the blessings of the gospel without worrying about moving to America. As he dedicated the first temples in Europe a little over three decades later, David O. McKay may well have thought of this as a fulfillment of the promises he had made to the Saints in the 1920s.

After Elder McKay returned from Europe, his time was taken up mostly by church service, but also in various civic activities. In 1930, for example, he attended, by invitation from U.S. President Herbert Hoover, a White House Conference on Child Health. The following year Governor George Dern appointed him chairman of Utah's executive committee for child welfare. That same year he was elected president of the Weber College Alumni Association. In 1941 he became a member of the board of trustees of Utah State Agricultural College.

IN 1934, AT AGE SIXTY-ONE, David O. McKay began a new phase of his career in church leadership. At the October conference he was sustained as second counselor to President Heber J. Grant in the First Presidency. First counselor was President J. Reuben Clark, Jr., an international lawyer and American diplomat who had been in the First Presidency since April 1933. Suddenly David O. McKay was thrown into close contact with a powerful man whose personality and administrative style was much different from his own, a man who had had no previous experience in the affairs of church government. It was not long, however, before a great mutual affection and respect built up between the two, and even though they were to differ in approach and attitudes toward some things, they worked very well together in the First Presidency for nearly three decades.

If President Clark's initial appointment surprised some members of the Church, it is clear that Elder McKay's did not. Already, because of his prominence in educational and civic affairs as well as his effective church service, he was known and loved, it seemed, by almost everyone. "President McKay," editorialized the *Deseret News*, "is one of the most beloved of all the authorities of the Church. By his long and successful ministry he has won the complete confidence and hearty esteem of all among whom he has labored."

As David O. McKay entered the First Presidency, he could reflect on much of importance that had taken place since he became a General Authority. The United States had gone through a terrible world war, and, in part, his world tour was a significant symbol of the effort to tie the Church itself together again after the frustrations of that war. The Church was entering a new era of economic prosperity, better public relations, and growth. In addition, there was the beginning of a mild dispersion of the Saints as migration to Utah continued to be discouraged. Various changes had taken place in church administrative programs, including, under the direction of President McKay, the Sunday Schools.

Perhaps the most dramatic problem in this era, however, was the Great Depression, which, beginning in 1929, affected the economic well being of people around the world. The Saints, like many other people, were ill prepared for the economic disaster, but under the direction of the First Presidency a new program was presented in the 1930s. This was the Church Security Plan, later to be more permanently known as the Welfare Program. At the end of the decade, the Second World War broke out, and the leaders of the Church found their work increasingly concerned with all the implications of that tragedy, including the withdrawing of missionaries from most parts of the world, establishing servicemen's programs, and operating church programs under conditions of restricted travel and communications. In his capacity as a member of the First Presidency, President McKay was deeply involved in these and many other serious problems facing the growing church in a rapidly changing society.

At the same time, his busy schedule did not include much relief from civic responsibilities. As early as 1937, Governor Henry H. Blood appointed him chairman of a study committee looking forward to the celebration of Utah's pioneer centennial in 1947. Two years later, on the recommendation of the committee, the state legislature established the 1847 Utah Centennial Commission, and again President McKay was named chairman. Along with a committee of Utah business and professional leaders, the commission planned a statewide celebration that included historical pageants, musicals, educational programs, athletics, sports events, and the erecting of the impressive "This Is the Place" monument at the mouth of Emigration Canyon. All this was heralded as a magnificent celebration, and after it was over President McKay received innumerable tributes for his work.

On January 2, 1951, in his seventy-eighth year, President David O. McKay and his wife, Emma Ray, celebrated their golden wedding anniversary. Most couples at that stage in life look forward to a time of blissful retirement, and certainly the McKays had earned a rest. But neither age nor past achievements are taken into account when it comes to receiving new church responsibilities. In fact, both seem only to add to the likelihood that more assignments will come. Within three months President McKay would take on the heaviest reponsibility of his career, and he would serve in that new capacity for nearly two more decades.

THE QUIET DYNAMICS OF A CHANGE in leadership of the Church were dramatically portrayed in the events surrounding the death of President George Albert Smith and the sustaining of President David O. McKay. Since 1945 Presidents Clark and McKay had served as counselors to President Smith, and since October 5, 1950, President McKay had also served as president of the Council of the Twelve. President Smith, however, had been ill for some months, and as his counselors went to his bedside on April 2, 1951, he did not even remember them. Only then did the full realization of what could happen to himself come to President McKay, even though President Clark had warned him many days before that "the responsibility will be yours." The awesome responsibilities of church leadership were never coveted by David O. McKay, and this new one least of all. On the evening of April 4 President Smith died, and as a result, the First Presidency was dissolved and the responsibility for church leadership fell immediately upon the shoulders of the president of the Council of the Twelve.

The next morning the fourteen apostles, including the two former counselors, sat in a solemn semicircle around the blue altar in the Salt Lake Temple. Demonstrating the order of the priesthood that eliminates personal or political considerations from such matters, the chairs reserved for the First Presidency stood empty. President McKay occupied the first of the remaining seats, and J. Reuben Clark assumed his place in the sixth, according to his seniority as an apostle. As President McKay began to speak, undoubtedly the same profound feeling came to the other apostles that suddenly overwhelmed Elder Spencer W. Kimball. "I saw him as president of the Church," he later wrote. "There was no doubt in my mind. It was a soul-satisfying feeling. It was hardly a light — it was more like a sudden flood of warmth and into my mind came the thought: '*A prophet's mantle.*'"

Arrangements were made for going ahead with the annual general conference and for the funeral on Saturday, April 7. On Sunday afternoon, April 8, the apostles met again in the temple and Elder Joseph Fielding Smith, next to President McKay in seniority, proposed that David O. McKay become president of the Church. The proposal was seconded by the next in seniority, Elder Stephen L Richards, who was also one of President McKay's closest lifelong friends. The sustaining vote was unanimous.

At that point the apostles received a surprise, but one that represented President McKay's personal commitment to the importance of seniority. Everyone expected him to choose President Clark as his first counselor, for that seemed only natural as a result of the two decades he had already served in that capacity. For a moment, then, there was silence when President McKay indicated that he would like to have Stephen L Richards as his first counselor and J. Reuben Clark, Jr., as his second. In his mind it was simply a matter of seniority, and Elder Richards had been an apostle longer. President Clark expressed no dismay at all. After he had been sustained by the quorum, and again the next morning in the general conference, he simply remarked that "one takes the place to which one is duly called, which place one neither seeks nor declines." "A perfect reaction," commented Elder Kimball, and as the new First Presidency took the reigns, the love and mutual respect the three men held for each other became abundantly clear. President Clark became President McKay's first counselor in 1959 when, upon the death of President Richards, Elder Henry D. Moyle was added to the First Presidency.

Tall, robust for his advanced age, distinguished looking, with a full head of wavy white hair and with eyes characterized by one newsman as "fiercely tender," David O. McKay not only acted like but also looked the part of a prophet. He would need all the strength and insight his years of experience — combined with the inspiration he was entitled to — would give him, for the Church itself would see some dramatic changes and face some serious problems during the two decades of his administration.

The Church was not only growing, but was also becoming truly international in nature. There were over 1.1 million members when President McKay took over, and by the time he died in 1970, that number had more than doubled. Some 30 percent of that growth was the result of missionary work, and much of it was taking place in Asia, Latin America, and other countries around the world. One of the challenges of President McKay's administration was to provide the full services of the Church, including the organization of wards and stakes and the building of temples, in these far-flung places.

It was an important symbol of the modern age, then, when David O. McKay, as president of the Church, went to Europe in the summer of 1952 on what may have been the most significant trip of his career. He visited nine countries during June and July and made the long-awaited announcement that a site had been selected for a temple in Berne, Switzerland. This was the inauguration of a new era for the Church, for it represented the beginning of temple building outside the American continent. In order to accomplish the objective of building temples not only there but also in other parts of the world, it was also announced that the temple in Berne would be smaller and less expensive than other temples, and it was clear that this would be the pattern for many temples to come. Three years later President McKay returned to Europe, where he not only dedicated the Swiss Temple on September 11, but also broke ground for a temple near London.

During his years as president, President McKay's dignity, warmth, and charm won friends and new respect not only for him but also for the Church. A simple experience as he visited the queen of the Netherlands in 1952 illustrates the point. She had scheduled a half hour for the visit, and President McKay carefully watched the time. When the half hour was up, he politely thanked the queen and began to leave. "Mr. McKay," she said, "sit down! I have enjoyed this thirty minutes more than I have enjoyed any thirty minutes in a long time. I just wish you would extend your visit a little longer." After more persuasion from her, he sat down again. At that point a coffee table was wheeled in, and the queen poured three cups of tea, pushing one each to President and Mrs. McKay. When neither of the McKays began to stir their tea, the queen asked, "Won't you have a little tea with the queen?" No, President McKay explained, the Latter-day Saints did not believe in drinking stimulants, and they believed tea to be a stimulant. "I am the queen of the Netherlands," she responded. "Do you mean to tell me you won't have a little drink of tea, even with the queen of the Netherlands?" "Would the queen of the Netherlands ask the leader of one million, three hundred thousand people to do something that he teaches his people not to do?" he asked in return. "You are a great man, President McKay," she replied. "I wouldn't ask you to do that." Many such simple stories suggest the quiet grandeur with which this modern prophet conducted himself, gaining the respect of the people of the world.

President McKay's travels took him to many places and for many purposes. A brief chronicle of his activities outside Utah will only suggest his tireless activity and busy schedule. In 1951 he attended the Church's annual pageant at the Hill Cumorah, went to Los Angeles to break ground for a temple, and attended a conference of prominent men in the nation called by President Harry S Truman. In 1952 he met with over a thousand young Latter-day Saints in the Los Angeles area, attended several other meetings there, dedicated a chapel in Nevada, gave an impressive Easter address over the National Broadcasting System, dedicated a monument in Georgia erected in memory of a missionary who had been killed there in 1879, dedicated two more chapels in Nevada, made his far-reaching trip to Europe, returned to Los Angeles in August to consult on the construction of the temple, and spoke at a stake conference in Idaho Falls.

The year 1953 was especially busy. He visited California, Arizona, Texas, and Nebraska, where, on the anniversary of Brigham Young's birth, he dedicated a new steel bridge, the Mormon Bridge, that spanned the Missouri River at the point where the Mormons ferried across it in pioneer days. Clearly, the public relations function of the president of the Church was becoming highly significant. From Nebraska he went on to Washington, D.C., where he attended, by invitation of Secretary of State John Foster Dulles, a conference on American foreign policy. In July he addressed the national council of the Boy Scouts of America in Los Angeles. There he received a special citation honoring him for his many achievements and stating that "[as] an ardent supporter of scouting, one of his outstanding decisions as president of the Church was the recommendation that the Cub Scout program be adopted for the younger boys of the Church." Later he was principal speaker at a pioneer celebration in Snowflake, Arizona. In August, he flew to Europe, where he dedicated temple sites in Switzerland and England. During the same trip he made a nostalgic visit to the birthplace of his father near Thurso, Scotland. In October he made a business trip to Moses Lake and Yakima, Washington, in the interest of the church-owned Utah-Idaho Sugar Company, of which he was president, and in December he laid the cornerstone of the Los Angeles Temple. Finally, on December 20 he delivered a nationally broadcast Christmas message on the Columbia Broadcasting System's "Church of the Air" program. All this was in addition to his regular heavy administrative responsibilities and public activities in Utah, and in the year that he turned eighty.

Early in 1954, the venerable church leader was off again, this time on a 32,000-mile trip that took him to missions in South Africa, South America, and Central America. He was accompanied to South Africa by President A. Hamer Reiser of the British Mission, who reported that "President and Mrs. McKay are the world's most wonderful travelers; always pleasant, relaxed, thoughtful of everyone; everything always in order; forthright and cheerful." While in South Africa he made an important decision regarding the priesthood. Previously, because of the Church's policy that, at the time, kept blacks from holding the priesthood, it was also policy in South Africa not to grant it to anyone who could not trace his ancestry out of that area. On this trip, however, President McKay felt inspired to modify the policy, so that the genealogical test did not apply. While this did not change the general priesthood policy, it clearly softened the excessive rigor with which it was sometimes implemented, and represented the liberal spirit that characterized President McKay. Later in the year he traveled on church and other business to Wisconsin, New York, Ohio, Chicago, and Nevada.

The following year, continuing in his desire to "feel the pulse" and catch the spirit of the Church around the world,

President McKay made a 45,000-mile trip to the missions of the South Seas. The nostalgia of that trip, as he remembered the powerful experiences of his 1921 world tour, was profound, and when he returned to America he announced that a temple would be built in New Zealand. Later in the year his travels took him to Los Angeles, Washington, D.C., and Europe. In August he broke ground for the temple in England, and in September he had the pleasure of dedicating the temple in Berne. Back in America, he rounded out the year's travels by attending church activities in Arizona and California.

Never before had a president of the Church traveled so widely and participated in so many activities that drew such wide public attention. President McKay was clearly determined to promote to the fullest the worldwide nature of the Church. Even in his eighties and nineties he hardly slowed down, and space simply does not permit a continuing chronicle of all he did. Briefly, however, at least a few more highlights must be noted. In 1956 he dedicated the Los Angeles Temple. In 1958 he dedicated the New Zealand Temple, the Church College of New Zealand, the London Temple, and the Church College of Hawaii. These activities came in the midst of a continuing heavy travel schedule, which was interrupted twice so he could enter the hospital to have cataracts removed from each eye. That same year, during his trip to England, he paid a nostalgic visit to his mother's birthplace at Merthyr Tydfil, Wales.

In 1961 President McKay made his ninth trip to Great Britain, this time to dedicate the million-dollar Hyde Park Ward meetinghouse in London. On this trip he visited Merthyr Tydfil again and unveiled a plaque at the home where his mother was born. So touched was he by a children's chorus that sang at the ceremony that he promised to return for the dedication of the Merthyr Tydfil chapel. In 1962 he returned to Scotland, where he organized the first stake in his ancestral homeland. There could be no doubt that this illustrious descendant of Clan McKay was the ideal example of the clan motto: "with a strong hand." The following year he kept his promise to return to Merthyr Tydfil, where he dedicated the new chapel.

In 1964 President McKay was invited by U.S. President Lyndon B. Johnson to visit at the White House, where President Johnson asked for, and received, a pledge of spiritual help and support. Also in 1964 he dedicated a temple in Oakland, California. In 1966, for the first time in his life, he visited important church historic sites in Missouri, approving the purchase of an additional 140 acres of land at Adam-ondi-Ahman. That year he turned ninety-three, and by that time his extensive travel schedule seemed to be slowing down.

ALL OF THESE TRAVELS were only public manifestations of the growth and progress of the Church over which David O. McKay presided. At the same time, he had his regular administrative responsibilities to deal with, and these included some important and far-reaching decisions. The youth program, for example, was dear to President McKay's heart, and it was a significant alteration when he approved changes that allowed young men to be ordained to the offices of teacher and priest at ages fourteen and sixteen, respectively. In 1952 he approved the Church's official adoption of the Cub Scout program, under the direction of the Primary Association. In January 1960, he addressed the first of a series of youth firesides. Some 200,000 young people gathered in 170 different places where, over a closed-circuit radio hook-up, they heard him discuss gospel ideals related to courtship and marriage.

In the field of education, President McKay continued to promote the expansion of seminaries and institutes of religion, as well as church schools in various areas of the world where educational opportunities for young Latter-day Saints were limited. He also strongly supported the expansion of the Church's Indian education program, which included placing young Indian students from reservations, where their opportunities were limited, in the homes of Latter-day Saints in other areas.

At the college level, the dedication of the Church College

of Hawaii in 1958 was of special significance to President McKay, for it fulfilled a promise he had made to the Saints at Laie in 1921. A few years earlier, the First Presidency had made the difficult decision to make Ricks College a two-year institution rather than a four-year school, noting that it would have "greater destiny as an integral and permanent part of the school system by being a first class junior college." Brigham Young University was to become the major institution, and during President McKay's administration that school grew in dramatic proportions, both numerically and in academic excellence, and in 1960 it began to offer doctoral degrees. At the same time, after long and controversial deliberations, President McKay decided not to approve the plan of expanding the Church's junior college program. Ricks College, Church College of Hawaii, and BYU would remain the Church's basic institutions of higher education. Meanwhile, the organization of student wards and stakes on the campuses of these schools, as well as in connection with other schools attended by large numbers of Latter-day Saints, did much for the spiritual growth of the youth.

During these years President McKay found himself at the center of a few political issues that affected the Church. In 1954 the Utah legislature authorized the transfer of three junior colleges, once owned by the Church, back to the Church. Governor J. Bracken Lee urged the move in order to save money for the state, and President McKay made it clear that the Church was willing to operate the schools on a sound financial basis. In a subsequent referendum, however, the people of the state voted against the move. Beyond that, the Church was constantly being accused of attempting to influence the votes of people, and a number of church leaders were not reluctant to speak out on issues of national importance. This was all right, as far as President McKay was concerned, but he was equally concerned that Latter-day Saints not consider the political opinions of individual leaders to be the official stand of the Church. In 1960, commenting on a report that church leaders had decided they would promote the fortunes of one national political party over the other, President McKay declared with all the persuasive power he could muster, "This report is not true, and I take this opportunity here, publicly, to renounce such a report as without foundation in fact." There were Latter-day Saints who favored both political parties, he went on to explain, and the General Authorities would treat both parties impartially. Under President McKay's direction, the Church issued a number of public statements forbidding the use of chapels for any partisan political purpose.

There were other issues, however, on which President McKay was not neutral. As it became clear that the political and economic philosophy of Communism was threatening basic democratic institutions around the world, his denouncement of Communism was uncompromising. He also took a firm stand on a liquor-by-the-drink issue, for he considered this to be a moral issue and well within the realm of the Church's official concerns. Under his direction the First Presidency issued official statements with regard to the tense civil rights struggles of the 1960s. A 1969 statement read, "We believe the Negro, as well as those of other races, should have his full constitutional privileges as a member of society, and we hope that members of the Church everywhere will do their part as citizens to see these rights are held inviolate."

President McKay took an active interest in the civic affairs of Salt Lake City. For most of his presidency, until he became so infirm in 1969 that it was no longer possible, he held weekly breakfast meetings with the head of the Salt Lake area Chamber of Commerce and the publisher of the Salt Lake *Tribune*. These meetings provided important opportunities for church and civic leaders to learn of one another's concerns and reach agreements in many important areas of mutual interest.

Within the Church, a number of administrative changes occurred in the 1960s. Many years earlier President McKay had been concerned with better correlation between the various instructional programs. While he was president, an important coordinating council came into being, under the leadership of Harold B. Lee of the Council of the Twelve, which directed a number of significant refinements in church curriculum. President McKay also inaugurated the position of Regional Representative of the Twelve. The needs of the rapidly growing Church required that the Twelve receive some help in overseeing the affairs of the various stakes and missions, and the Regional Representatives were important in helping to provide that assistance.

President McKay was a dynamic leader in the field of missionary work. In 1961 he conducted the first world seminar for mission presidents. There the presidents were instructed in the new proselyting plan, "A Systematic Program for Teaching the Gospel," as well as many other suggestions for more effectively spreading the gospel. The theme President McKay introduced while he was mission president in Europe nearly four decades earlier was revived, and "Every member a missionary" became a popular slogan churchwide. In addition, the Mormon Pavilion at the New York World's Fair in 1964 and 1965 attracted thousands of visitors and resulted in considerable new interest in the Church.

There were many other important accomplishments during President McKay's administration. Among them, to name only a few, were the beginning of the use of modern technology, as seen in the use of films and recordings to enhance the temple ceremonies and the move to an automated membership record program; the rapid growth of genealogical research opportunities through microfilming; the dedication of the huge record vault in a granite mountain near Salt Lake City; and the organization of the Translation Department at church headquarters, which brought together a variety of important translation services for the Church.

In 1961 President McKay authorized a far-reaching innovation that began to lift some of the heavy burden the Council of the Twelve carried in supervising the rapidly multiplying stakes of the Church. That year it was decided the members of the First Council of the Seventy would be ordained to the office of high priest. This gave them full authority, under the direction of the Twelve, to preside at stake conferences, reorganize stakes, and ordain high priests to head the stakes.

As THE WORK BECAME HEAVIER, President McKay's advancing age began to affect his ability to move as fast and function as effectively as earlier. As a result, in 1961 he called Elder Hugh B. Brown of the Council of the Twelve to be a counselor to the First Presidency. A few months later President Henry D. Moyle died and President Brown became President McKay's second counselor. In 1965, President McKay selected two additional counselors, Joseph Fielding Smith and Thorpe B. Isaacson, to assist him and his regular counselors in the work of the First Presidency. In 1968 Elder Alvin R. Dyer also was named as a counselor to the presidency. Some members were surprised at what seemed to be breaking a tradition when these extra counselors were named, though it was soon pointed out that earlier presidents had done the same thing. It was clear that President McKay was not afraid of whatever innovations were necessary for the progress of the Church.

On December 10, 1962, a fitting tribute was paid to President McKay by business and civic leaders in Salt Lake City. A gala banquet and program was arranged by a committee composed entirely of prominent non-Mormons. Heartfelt tributes were paid to him, honoring him for his outstanding service to the Church, the state, and the nation. U.S. President John F. Kennedy sent a congratulatory telegram that read, in part, "I am happy . . . to commend you for your long and devoted service to God, to your state, and your country. The bond of Christian brotherhood which has marked your religious pronouncements has helped tie our people to those of other nations in a deeper spirit of Christian faith." Seven years later it was reported that in a national public opinion poll conducted by the Gallup organization, 1,501 adults were asked, "What man that you have heard or read about, living today in any part of the world, do you admire the most?" David O. McKay was among the top five religious leaders listed in the responses.

The distinguished awards and honors received by President McKay throughout his life were numerous. They included an Honorary Doctor of Laws from Utah State University (1950), Honorary Doctor of Humanities from Brigham Young University (1951), Honorary Doctor of Letters from the University of Utah (1951), Honorary Doctor of Letters from Temple University (1951), Silver Buffalo and Silver Beaver awards from the Boy Scouts of America (1953 and 1956), the Golden Medal of the Greek Archdiocese of North and South America (1955), the Exemplary Manhood award from BYU Associated Men Students (1968), and the Distinguished American award from the National Football Foundation and Hall of Fame (1968). Well known in religious, business, and civic groups, David O. McKay was not only an inspired and outstanding church leader but also a superb ambassador for the Church throughout the nation and around the world.

As he advanced in years, people spoke with amazement of the dynamic energy with which he still conducted himself. A special article in the *Improvement Era* commemorating his eighty-fifth birthday noted that even at that age, President McKay began his day long before the sun was up, and that usually his automobile was the first one in the church parking lot. He often reached the office by seven o'clock, and his daily schedule included endless meetings, consultations, and appointments as well as paying attention to the hundreds of details involved in carrying out the routine of his position. Evenings, too, were crowded with church work, including public appearances, but he nevertheless continued to find time to study and to be with family members.

Inevitably, of course, the dynamic church leader's advancing age made itself apparent. A series of strokes and heart attacks in the 1960s eventually had the effect of thickening his speech and visibly weakening his body, but his keen mind remained active. He moved into a special apartment in the Hotel Utah, and it was there that his counselors met him and continued to conduct much of the business of the Church. It became increasingly difficult, however, and much more of the responsibility began to fall to the counselors.

In April 1968 President McKay was able to attend two sessions of the general conference, though his messages were read by his son David Lawrence. The following April another son, Robert, read his opening message. Still, his infirmities did not completely debilitate him during this last year of life. On July 9 he attended ceremonies celebrating the opening of the new hospital that bore his name in Ogden, and two weeks later he rode in the Days of '47 parade in Salt Lake City. That October he was unable to attend general conference sessions, but messages from him were read at the meetings. "Spirituality," his closing message read, "is the consciousness of victory over self. It is the realization of community with Deity. No higher attainment can be reached than that."

Three months later, on January 18, 1970, David O. McKay died in Salt Lake City, having served as a General Authority longer than any other person up to that time. "He was loved and respected and revered by millions of people who now mourn his passing," said President N. Eldon Tanner at the funeral. "During his whole life he was a true exemplar of the life of Christ."

SOURCES

Several good books containing sermons and writings of President McKay are readily available in libraries. For more intimate glimpses into his life, the following readings are suggested: Llewelyn R. McKay, *Home Memories of David O. McKay* (Salt Lake City: Deseret Book, 1956); Clare Middlemiss, comp., *Cherished Experiences from the Writings of President David O. McKay* (Salt Lake City: Deseret Book, 1955); Jeanette McKay Morrell, *Highlights in the Life of President David O. McKay* (Salt Lake City: Deseret Book, 1956); David L. McKay, "Remembering Father and Mother, President David O. McKay and Sister Emma Ray Riggs McKay," *Ensign*, August 1984, pp. 34-40. Many more articles, stretching over several decades, may be found in the pages of the *Improvement Era*, the *Ensign*, and other church publications.

JAMES B. ALLEN is professor of history and head of the History Department at Brigham Young University. A native of Logan, Utah, he earned his Ph.D. in history at the University of Southern California. He is author of articles in professional journals and a biography of William Clayton (University of Illinois Press). He is co-author of *The Story of the Latter-day Saints* (Salt Lake City: Deseret Book, 1976); *Manchester Mormons: The Journal of William Clayton* (Santa Barbara, Calif.: Peregrine Smith, 1974); *Mormonism and American Culture* (New York: Harper, 1972); and *Mormons and Gentiles: A History of Salt Lake City* (Boulder, Colo.: Pruett, 1984).

JOSEPH FIELDING SMITH

Joseph Fielding McConkie

It is fitting that the tenth president of The Church of Jesus Christ of Latter-day Saints be a man tithed for the work of the Lord even before his birth. His mother, Julina Lambson Smith, wife of Joseph F. Smith (who would yet become the sixth president of the Church), desired a son to bear his father's name. Like Hannah of old, she went before the Lord and vowed a vow. If the Lord would give her a son, she would consecrate the child's life to the Lord's service. Her pleading was heard, and in the tenth year of their marriage she gave birth to a son. By the quiet whisperings of the Spirit, Julina knew that this son would be called to serve in the Council of the Twelve.

The child was the tenth to be born into this polygamist family. Both of Joseph F. Smith's other wives had given birth to sons, and each had desired to have her firstborn bear his father's name. "Papa would not consent," Edna, the third wife, explained. He said that "the name was to go to Julina's son," since Julina was the first wife. And so the child was given the name Joseph Fielding Smith, Jr., and was raised to sense that there was something sacred in the name he bore. Within the family, he now shared his name with his father; his granduncle the Prophet Joseph Smith; his great-grandfather Joseph Smith, Sr.; and Joseph Fielding, the brother of his grandmother Mary Fielding Smith, wife of Hyrum. The name Joseph was held in such reverence in the family that the use of the nickname "Joe" was not tolerated even in reference to one who was an enemy to the faith.

Thus the voice of the father was to become the voice of the son; jointly their years in the apostleship would span in unbroken chain more than a hundred years. The Church has never known two men more loyal to the testimony of the Prophet Joseph Smith than this father and son. Joseph Fielding, Jr., would yet be told in a patriarchal blessing that his labors would "stand as a wall of defense" against those seeking "to destroy the evidence of the divinity of the mission of the Prophet Joseph" and that in his defense of the Prophet he would "never be confounded."

JOSEPH FIELDING SMITH, JR., was born July 19, 1876. That was the summer that Custer met his fate at the hands of Crazy Horse and Sitting Bull at the battle of the Little Big Horn. Ulysses S. Grant occupied the White House and Brigham Young, the Lion House. Seven years earlier a golden spike driven at Promontory Summit in northern Utah had united railroads from the east and west and officially brought the pioneer era to an end; yet much of the work of colonization was left to be done. Livelihood in the Territory of Utah was for most the family farm, and chores the common lot of children. It was a time of making do or doing without.

Joseph Fielding Smith's birthright was noble, if not pretentious. It was one rich in the opportunity to work and sacrifice. He was born into a home well furnished with love, faith, lots of children, and little of anything else. He was amply blessed with all the things that money cannot buy, though few that it can. His was not a life encumbered with the distractions of ease and comfort. As we have noted, at the time of his birth his father had three wives and nine children. Joseph F. Smith would yet take two more wives; thirty-three children would be added to the family by birth and another five by adoption. Of a certainty, when it was necessary to do without, there were a lot to do it with.

A journal kept by the father between 1870 and 1881 gives

us some sense of the austerity of the times. The entries, which are brief, even terse, may themselves be an evidence of the scarcity of pencil and paper and perhaps even time. For November 7, 1879, we read: "I took my little Joseph F. to the Coop. and changed his boots for a larger pair." That his children would have shoes on their feet during the coming winter months was a blessing worth recording. And we note that the old shoes were not discarded but exchanged for the larger pair, which themselves were probably not new. Of these years the father said, "[We] were tugging away with all our might to keep body and soul together." In later years he recollected a Christmas in which he had not so much as a single cent to buy anything for his children. "I walked up and down Main Street, looking into shop windows—into Amussen's jewelry store, into every store—everywhere—and then slunk out of sight of humanity and sat down and wept like a child, until my poured-out grief relieved my aching heart; and after a while returned home, as empty as when I left."

In the spring of his fourth year, while playing outside, little Joseph F. was bitten by a stray dog. Noting the incident, his father's journal entry reads: "I shot him." History attests that it was the dog, not Joseph, that was shot. In the summer and fall the family would make trips up the canyons east of Salt Lake City to pick berries. Little Joseph, now five years old, was anxious to help. The journal reads: "Joseph F. climbed a tree to pick berries and fell, his leg catching in the forks and hung him up until I took him down." To add injury to insult, an annoyed yellow jacket wasp then stung him. The entry concludes: "We worked hard most of the day picking berries. I picked a peck."

The stringency of the times did not impede the spirit of revelation. Under the date of January 23, 1881, Joseph F. Smith recorded the following, which took place at a stake conference in Ogden: "Pres. W. Woodruff spoke about an hour. He prophesied that I should occupy the position in this church once occupied by the Prophet Jos. Smith. I was greatly surprised. And will here say that this can only be fulfilled if God designs it and I live long enough and continue faithful." The entry that immediately follows noted: "My cow ran away." Though the Smiths were a family with their eyes directed to the heavens, the necessities of life kept their feet firmly on the ground.

Such was the home in which the Lord chose to mold the spirit of one called and ordained to the apostleship even before his birth. And what more fitting place to raise a prophet than in the home of a prophet? His mother, a prophetess in her own right, had been raised in the home of George A. Smith, a cousin and close associate of the Prophet Joseph Smith. George A. Smith was called to the apostleship at the age of twenty-two, the youngest to be called to that position in this dispensation. Each of the wives by whom he had children would play a part in molding the character of Joseph F. Smith's sons and daughters. There was Sarah Ellen Richards, daughter of Willard Richards, apostle and counselor to Brigham Young; Edna Lambson, younger sister to Julina; Alice Ann Kimball, daughter of Heber C. Kimball; and Mary Schwartz, niece of John Taylor. Their lot was not easy; yet they were women of faith who worked together and loved each other's children as their own.

DURING THE IMPRESSIONABLE YEARS of Joseph Fielding's youth, the combined powers of earth and hell were united in an attempt to destroy the kingdom of God on earth. The 1880s witnessed a united effort on the part of Satan's priests, a malicious press, and unprincipled politicians and other pretended do-gooders to pass antipolygamy legislation. Their efforts were successful in driving church leaders into exile, forcing scores of Saints from the boundaries of the United States, disincorporating the Church as a legal entity, escheating church property, and essentially denying the Saints every right for which their forefathers had spilled their blood in the Revolutionary War.

Prosecution quickly turned to persecution, and from the time young Joseph Fielding was baptized by his father until he was fifteen years of age, his father was in exile. President John Taylor had been especially concerned to have Joseph F.

out of the way, because as an officiator and recorder in the Endowment House, he had a detailed knowledge of the plural marriages that had been performed. During this period, Joseph F. Smith filled a mission in Hawaii under the assumed name of J. F. Speight. He also hid right under the noses of those who were looking for him, serving a mission in Washington, D. C., under the alias of Jason Mack (his maternal great-granduncle), where he labored for the admission of the Territory of Utah to statehood.

Several times during this period, the Smith home was raided and searched by marshals looking for Joseph, Sr. When this happened, the children were interrogated and threatened, but they refused to give even their own names. Those were experiences never to be forgotten. These visits also forced some of the wives into seclusion to avoid being subpoenaed. During this period Julina redoubled her efforts to see that her children were taught the gospel. "She used to teach me, and put in my hands, when I was old enough to read, the things that I could understand," President Smith later recalled. "She taught me to pray, . . . to be true to my duties as a deacon and as a teacher . . . and later as a priest. . . . I had a mother who saw to it that I read, and I loved to read. I used to read the books that were prepared for the Primary children and for Sunday School children in those early days. . . . I usually had a book in my hands when I was home." He read the Book of Mormon before he was ordained a deacon. The hayloft or the shade of the poplar tree in front of the old Smith home on Third West often served as his classroom, and the written word his teacher. Though he enjoyed playing ball with his brothers, he loved reading more. His thirst for knowledge was never quenched, and his love of books became a lifelong courtship.

When Joseph Fielding's father returned from exile in Hawaii, it was still necessary for him to remain in seclusion. This created occasions when the family could gather around their father and be instructed in the principles of the gospel. His long absence made the instruction of those occasions even more precious, and the family gave careful attention to the counsel of their patriarch. "It can be said in truth," Joseph

Fielding said, "that the older children who remember these happy scenes in the midst of anxiety have never forgotten what they were taught, and the impressions have remained with them and will likely do so forever."

These were the years in which young Joseph Fielding learned the value of hard work and witnessed in the life of his saintly mother the meaning of service. She took a course in obstetrics and became a licensed obstetrician. In the years that followed, she brought nearly a thousand babies into the world and would say with pride, "I never lost a mother or a baby." This service, which was often given free, included going daily for five or six days to care for the mother and her newborn child. Often it was Joseph's duty to drive her buggy. "I wondered," he said, "why babies were so often born in the middle of the night."

Many of his youthful hours were spent milking cows and working on the family farm in Taylorsville. On one occasion when he and his younger brother George were loading hay, he had a close brush with death. They had stopped by the Jordan River to stack some bales and give their team of horses a drink. Because they had a skittish horse, Joseph told George to stand by the head of the team and hold their bridles until he could climb up on the wagon and take the reins. Instead, George went back and started up the binding rope. As he did so, the horses started with a sudden jerk and Joseph was thrown down between them on the doubletree.

The thought, "Well, here's my finish," flashed through his mind. But something turned the horses and they ran into the canal, while he was thrown clear of their hooves and the wheels of the wagon. Joseph, much shaken, got up, told George what he thought of what he had done, and hurried home. He was met en route by his father, who was coming to the fields, having received a strong impression that one of his sons was in danger.

Were young Joseph called upon to illustrate the inspiration of his father, he could think of no better evidence than the invitation that Joseph F. extended to a daughter of one of his boyhood friends in Nauvoo to live in the Smith home while she attended the University of Utah. She was a tall, stately girl with pretty features and dark hair. Her name was Louie Shurtliff. Louie came to get a teaching certificate and got a marriage certificate to go along with it. It is said that it was love at first sight between her and Joseph Fielding, though it was not until after she had completed her three-year course at the university that she and her knight in a new ZCMI suit graduated into the state of marital bliss. Her wedding gown was the beautiful white dress she wore at graduation, and their first home was with the Smith family as they sought to save the money for one of their own. They were married April 16, 1898.

They had been married a year when Joseph received a call from President Lorenzo Snow to serve as a missionary. He was set apart by his father, who also ordained him a seventy at that time. Undoubtedly some tears were shed as he and his young bride parted. Louie returned to her family's home near Ogden, where she would teach school and wait for those golden years she and Joseph would spend together when her soldier of truth returned from his mission to England.

Among those with whom he traveled to the mission field was his brother Richards, who had received his call at the same time and was assigned to the same mission. Missionary work at this time was largely ineffective, and Joseph Fielding Smith did not baptize a single soul on his mission. It was rare for anyone to treat the missionaries with civility. Most of the people they met refused to speak to them; those who did usually berated them and assured them that they "already knew all about Mormonism." Even the members seemed lackadaisical, and meetings were often canceled because no one but the missionaries showed up. Still one can see the mission field as an important training ground for the young elders. Here they saw all the blessings of gospel living sharply contrasted with the lifestyle of the world. They learned about bitterness and enmity; about threats and mobs; about sin and darkness; and even about dirt and fleas and bad food. They met the devil and saw his works and felt his spirit and came away with an appreciation for the gospel that can be gained in no other way. They studied the gospel and learned to defend it and became very practiced in doing so. Here the steel of testimony was forged.

In seeking to bless others with the gospel, none are more blessed than the missionaries. Such was the blessing that a wise father sought for his sons. "May God bless you, my boys," wrote Joseph F. Smith to Joseph, Jr., and Richards (who had been named after his grandfather Willard Richards), "and keep you safely from all harm, prosper you in your mission, make you instrumental in doing much good, seal indelibly upon your minds the testimony of His truth and knowledge of the divine mission of the Prophet Joseph Smith and of the fidelity of his friend and associate Willard Richards whose blood flows in your (R's) veins. Both your grandfathers, Hyrum and Willard, were true men, men of intelligence, wisdom and inspiration, and either of them thought their own lives worthless in comparison to the faithful performance of their duties and the importance of the restored Gospel, for which they lived, labored and died. Be as true to those holy principles as your fathers have been and your reward will be sure and most glorious." Such have always been the rewards and blessings associated with missionary work, irrespective of the reception the missionaries are given by those to whom they are sent.

JOSEPH FIELDING SMITH returned from his mission in June 1901. It was a time of joyous reunion with Louie, and a time of dreams and plans for the future. His first concern was that of employment—finding a job with the kind of a salary that could make dreams a reality. A tempting offer almost immediately presented itself, but there were strings attached. The job would have taken him into some undesirable situations and surrounded him with company that was less than the best. Joseph struggled with the decision for a few days; then, still feeling quite uncertain, he sought counsel from his father. In their discussion, he explained how the position had become available. The man who previously held it had fallen into temptation because of his surroundings and had been dismissed. An inspired father simply responded, "My son, the best company is none too good." Joseph rejected the offer, and shortly thereafter he obtained more modest employment in the Church Historian's Office, a position that led to his appointment as assistant church historian in 1906.

When Lorenzo Snow passed away in October 1901, Joseph's father, then the senior apostle of God on earth, was called to preside over the Church. During the next seventeen years, Joseph Fielding did all that he could to lighten his father's load. Many an evening was spent helping him catch up on correspondence. The years 1903 through 1911 were especially difficult because of intense anti-Mormon sentiment both locally and nationally. These were the years in which the Salt Lake Ministerial Alliance, with the help of the Salt Lake *Tribune*, waged a vicious war of words against the Church, using Reed Smoot as their whipping post. Elder Smoot, a member of the Quorum of the Twelve, had been elected to the United States Senate. The unseated incumbent, Thomas Kearns, purchased the *Tribune* and hired a bitter apostate, Frank J. Cannon, as his editor. The Church in general and Joseph F. Smith in particular were deluged with calumny. During the course of one week, the paper described President Smith with the following epithets: greedy, lawbreaker, lecher, immoral, ruthless, sordid, viperous, insane, wicked, withered limb, apostate, outcast, traitor, anarchist, rebel, and atheist.

Swept along in the current of his own hatred, Cannon expanded his attacks to include Joseph's older brother Hyrum, who had been called to the Quorum of the Twelve at the time their father became the president of the Church, and to Joseph himself. In 1907, when George Teasdale, a member of the Twelve, passed away, a headline in the *Tribune* read: "SMITH IS SLATED FOR APOSTLESHIP." In bold type came the following: "Death of George Teasdale Paves Way for Elevation of Royal Scion — Joseph F., Jr., To Be Hit By A Revelation — Grim Reaper Brings 'My Son Hyrum' One Step Nearer Regal Succession."

A rather lengthy article then suggested that "while the humbler communicants" of the Church may have thought that Joseph F. Smith would "see the future apostle in a great, flaring vision, . . . 'wise men' knew differently," and that Elder

Teasdale's successor would "be chosen as Joseph F. may will without assistance, divine or otherwise." Under the caption "Joseph F. Jr., the Man," the article continued: "When Joseph F. Smith had three vacancies in the quorum to fill at the April conference in 1906, he refrained by a heroic effort, which almost burst a bloodvessel, from naming a Smith at that time." The article then observed that Joseph F. Smith, Jr., had been made assistant church historian at that conference, succeeding Orson Whitney, who was called to the apostleship. "This minor office," the *Tribune* observed, "furnished his inspired father with an excuse for putting him on the payroll and gave him a chance to 'learn the ropes.' Since then his father has kept him busy. Not being gifted with the ability to write history — the position in which the tithepayers support him — he has been sent around to stake conferences and inflicted upon the long-suffering Saints as a preacher. He is said to be more ignorant, arrogant, overbearing and bigoted than even his half-brother, Hyrum M. Smith the heir-apparent."

The article concluded with the announcement that Joseph F. Smith was trying to outlive all the other apostles so that Hyrum could succeed him as the president of the Church. Unfortunately the article did not tell its readers how one goes about trying to outlive someone else.

During this period Joseph and Louie built and moved into a home and became the proud parents of two daughters. During a third pregnancy in 1908, Louie became very ill. For weeks Joseph devoted himself almost entirely to her care and looking after the children. On March 30, 1908, Louie died of complications associated with her pregnancy. A heartbroken father closed the doors to their dream home and took his little daughters to the Beehive House, then used as the home of the president of the Church, so that they might be cared for by their grandmother and their unmarried aunts.

The months that followed were difficult and lonely. Knowing that it is not good for a man to be alone and that little Josephine and Julina needed a mother, President Joseph F. Smith counseled his son to remarry. Joseph, Jr., was more inclined to seek a companion in prayer than in courtship, but despite this imbalance in faith and works, the Lord responded. On the staff at the Historian's Office was a vivacious young lady by the name of Ethel G. Reynolds. She was the daughter of George and Amelia Schofield Reynolds. Her father is best remembered for his exhaustive concordance to the Book of Mormon, a work he began while imprisoned as a polygamist. His was the famous test case in which the Supreme Court sustained the constitutionality of the antipolygamy legislation. Ethel was both pretty and bright, and the fact that she was the daughter of faithful parents made her even more attractive to Joseph Fielding Smith. Love of the Lord and loyalty to the Church were inherent to her nature. Joseph and Ethel were married November 2, 1908, in the Salt Lake Temple by President Joseph F. Smith.

As JOSEPH FIELDING SMITH WALKED through the gate of the Salt Lake Temple grounds to attend the concluding session of general conference in April 1910, one of the gatekeepers asked him, "Well, who is going to be called to fill the vacancy in the Council of the Twelve?" Joseph Fielding replied, "I don't know, but there is one thing I do know—it won't be me and it won't be you." He continued on into the meeting, taking a seat in the congregation.

Conducting the business of the conference, Heber J. Grant read the names of the General Authorities for a sustaining vote. About thirty seconds before President Grant got to the point where he would read the name of the newly called apostle, Joseph Fielding Smith received a witness of the Spirit that his name would be read. So it was. The following day, April 7, 1910, Joseph F. Smith ordained his son an apostle and set him apart as a member of the Quorum of the Twelve. Joseph Fielding Smith, who was thirty-three years of age at the time, would spend the next sixty years traveling throughout the Church and the world, teaching the gospel and bearing his special witness of the Savior. Then, after six decades of apostolic service, he would be called to preside over the Church as its president.

The following Thursday, when the Twelve met with the

First Presidency in their regular temple meeting, Joseph Fielding was assigned to accompany Elder George F. Richards to the Bear River Stake for a stake conference. As the Church was smaller in those days, two of the brethren would visit a stake together. "We would travel as far as we could by train," President Smith reminisced, "and then the local brethren would meet us with a white top or a wagon. Sometimes we continued on horses or mules or by ox team. Many times we slept out under the stars or in such houses or cabins as were available." Often such assignments would occupy weeks of travel time. How interesting it would have been to this young apostle to know that he would return to many of these same places in a matter of hours by plane and car in future years.

The life and labors of Joseph Fielding Smith were prophetically capsulized in the two patriarchal blessings he received. In a blessing given after his call to the apostleship, Patriarch Joseph D. Smith declared, "You were called and ordained before you came in the flesh, as an Apostle of the Lord Jesus Christ, to represent his work in the earth." Some seventeen years earlier, when Joseph Fielding was nineteen years of age, John Smith, the Patriarch to the Church, had prophesied, "It shall be thy duty to sit in council with thy brethren, and to preside among the people." Now in harmony with that same spirit, and undoubtedly without the knowledge of the earlier blessing, Joseph D. Smith declared, "And you will indeed stand in the midst of this people a prophet and a revelator to them, for the Lord has blessed you and ordained you to this calling and it will come upon you as naturally as night shall follow the day."

These inspired patriarchs did more than just announce President Smith's foreordination as a "mighty man in Israel." They identified the special mission that would be his. Uncle John Smith told his nephew that his life had been "preserved for a wise purpose," that there was much for him "to do upon the earth," and that it would be his "privilege to live to a good old age." He instructed him to hold up his head and lift up his voice "without fear or favor as the Spirit of the Lord shall direct," and promised that the blessings of the Lord would rest upon him. Joseph was promised the spirit of revelation and that he would be given both "word and sentiment" so that he might "confound the wisdom of the wicked and set at nought the counsels of the unjust."

Joseph D. Smith gave utterance to President Smith's mission in these words: "You have been blessed with ability to comprehend, to analyze, and defend the principles of truth above many of your fellows, and the time will come when the accumulative evidence that you have gathered will stand as a wall of defense against those who are seeking and will seek to destroy the evidence of the divinity of the mission of the Prophet Joseph; and in his defense you will never be confounded, and the light of the Spirit will shed its rays upon your heart as gently as the dews that fall from heaven, and it will unfold to your understanding many truths concerning this work that have not yet been revealed."

BRUCE R. MCCONKIE, who edited a three-volume work of President Smith's doctrinal teachings entitled *Doctrines of Salvation*, said of him: "Joseph Fielding Smith is the greatest doctrinal teacher of this generation. Few men in this dispensation have approached him in gospel knowledge or surpassed him in spiritual insight. His is the faith and the knowledge of his father, President Joseph F. Smith, and his grandfather, the Patriarch Hyrum Smith."

"I never did learn to deliver a discourse," said Joseph Fielding Smith, "without referring to the scriptures." When he stood behind the pulpit to teach the Saints, his attitude was one of solemnity. He was not an entertainer or storyteller. He was a modern Isaiah, a Jeremiah, a Nephi, or a Jacob. The best of the world's ethics were to him as skim milk. He preferred the cream of restored truths. If a sermon did not justify the death of Christ at Calvary or the death of his grandfather, Hyrum Smith, and that of his granduncle, the Prophet Joseph, then he did not feel that it was worth giving.

He was unyielding in the defense of truth and impatient with doubt and lack of faith. Having never known doubt, he had a hard time understanding it in others. He honestly could not remember a time when he did not know that Joseph Smith was a prophet and that the Church is true. He was born with a testimony. Though gentle and forgiving with the transgressor, he had little tolerance for the sophistry of men. If it was in the scriptures, he believed it — and he expected others to do the same.

Truth was his standard and scriptures his measuring rod. He taught the principle thus: "It makes no difference what is written or what anyone has said, if what has been said is in conflict with what the Lord has revealed, we can set it aside. My words, and teachings of any other member of the Church, high or low, if they do not square with the revelations, we need not accept them. Let us have this matter clear. We have accepted the four standard works as the measuring yardsticks, or balances, by which we measure every man's doctrine.

"You cannot accept the books written by the authorities of the Church as standards of doctrine, only in so far as they accord with the revealed word in the standard works.

"Every man who writes is responsible, not for the Church, for what he writes. If Joseph Fielding Smith writes something which is out of harmony with the revelations, then every member of the Church is duty bound to reject it. If he writes that which is in perfect harmony with the revealed word of the Lord, then it should be accepted."

His loyalty to principle was such that for years while he was a member of the Quorum of the Twelve, he would decline an annual invitation of a member of the First Presidency to attend a Christmas open house because it was held on the Sabbath. Yet his loyalty to the Brethren was such that when a man came into his home to complain about one of the leaders of the Church and refused his quiet invitation to quit, Joseph Fielding Smith, with one hand on the fellow's neck and the other on the seat of his pants, escorted him out of the house and off his property.

Though President Smith was the most prolific writer the Church had known, he never sought to be such. The twenty-five books that bear his name were printed to supply the demand for copies of his discourses or to respond to a pressing need for sound instruction on particular subjects. Often this was at the urging of the Brethren. When Heber J. Grant was the president of the Church, he wrote to Joseph Fielding Smith saying that he was the "best posted man on the scriptures of the General Authorities" and instructing him to take care of himself because he was so greatly needed.

The more prominent of his written works were *Essentials in Church History*, a succinct history of the Church first published in 1922; *The Way to Perfection* (1931), a discussion of doctrinal principles; *The Life of Joseph F. Smith* (1938), the story of his father; *The Signs of the Times* (1942), a compilation of talks dealing with events of the last days; *Man, His Origin and Destiny* (1954), written to refute the theories of men and to testify that we are indeed the children of our divine Father; *Doctrines of Salvation* (1954-1956), a three-volume work of doctrinal insights; and *Answers to Gospel Questions* (1954-1966), a five-volume work recording answers to a variety of questions sent to him over the years and originally answered in the *Improvement Era*. President Smith also edited two very significant works, *Teachings of the Prophet Joseph Smith* (1938), and *Gospel Doctrine* (1919), the sermons and writings of his father, Joseph F. Smith. He also wrote the words for a number of hymns, including "Does the Journey Seem Long?" and "We Are Watchmen on the Tower of Zion." These hymns have been sung by the Tabernacle Choir on their national broadcast.

THOUGH THE LIFE OF JOSEPH FIELDING SMITH was devoted to the study and teaching of the gospel, nothing was of greater importance to him than his own family. "True greatness," he taught, "is found only in the family." The scriptures say that "where your treasure is, there will your heart be also," and despite the many absences occasioned by his office, his heart was always with his family. His union with Ethel was blessed with nine children, giving him eleven in all—six daughters and five sons. A larger house was built for them on Douglas Street, a house filled with books, good music, and much activity. President Smith delighted in gathering his family around him in the evenings to tell them stories from the scriptures or the history of the Church. These occasions often included the bearing of testimony, which included not only expressions of love for the Lord but also expressions of love for each of his children and their mother. He wanted his children to live properly and knew that he must see that they were taught properly.

Often he would relate stories at the breakfast table, before the children went to school. It was not uncommon for him to lose track of the time, which necessitated leaving the prophets in some kind of a dire predicament and his children in anxious anticipation of the story's conclusion. Before they moved from their home on Second West to Douglas Street, he was able to conclude some of his stories as he walked the children to school on his way to the Church offices.

As to discipline, his heart was too tender to spank his children, so he had to discipline them with love. When one of the family did something that warranted correction, after discussing the matter with the offending party, he would put his hands on the child's shoulders, look him in the eyes, and say softly, "I wish my kiddies would be good." The knowledge of his love did much to encourage obedience.

Obedience, love, and even testimony did not make a family immune to sorrow or heartache. In the summer of 1937, Joseph Fielding's wife, Ethel Reynolds, passed away after a long illness. She was only forty-seven years of age. The cause of death was a cerebral hemorrhage, which came as a relief to other complications that the doctors had not been able to successfully treat. Close on the heels of this sorrow came the nation's involvement in the Second World War. President Smith's four older sons were called into military service. Each served honorably. Lewis Warren, the second son, gave his life in that service. That the lives of both Lewis and his mother were exemplary of faith, devotion, and goodness did much to bring solace to a sorrowing family.

Recognizing that a loving companion is a reservoir of strength even to the strongest of men, and that even an apostle doesn't make much of a mother, Joseph Fielding Smith resolved to marry once again. Courtship for an apostle and the Church's most prolific writer was at best terribly awkward. To family and close friends it must have seemed a little amusing to see this man, so confident behind the pulpit, so tongue-tied and uncertain as he tried to respond to the feelings of his heart. Finally, a letter of proposal was written, and after four days of anguish, it was personally delivered. A long weekend conference assignment intervened, and the hoped-for message of acceptance was received. Then the courtship and the process of getting acquainted could begin. On April 12, 1938, Joseph Fielding Smith was sealed for time and eternity to Jessie Ella Evans. Aunt Jessie, as she was known to the family, was a gifted contralto. She sang the lead for the American Light Opera Company in New York for three years. She was offered a contract with the Metropolitan Opera Company, which she declined to return to Utah. "The Lord told me to do his service in Utah," she explained. Thus President Smith would affirm that she was in the right place at the right time for the right purpose. For the next thirty-three years she traveled with him throughout the world, singing her way into the hearts of the Saints.

SHORTLY AFTER APRIL CONFERENCE IN 1939, Joseph Fielding Smith, by assignment of the First Presidency, commenced a tour of the European missions. His new bride, Jessie, accompanied him on what proved to be a most timely and exciting assignment. In June he presided over a conference for mission presidents in Lucerne, Switzerland. Prominent note was taken in this conference of the unsettled political conditions in Europe.

By August it was apparent that Germany was about to open hostilities against Poland, and word was received from Salt Lake City that all missionaries in Germany should be reassigned to neutral countries. President Smith directed the missionaries in the East German Mission to go to Denmark, and those from the West German Mission were to go to Holland. When Holland refused entrance to the missionaries, they were sent instead to Denmark. At this time President Smith prophesied that because the Danish people had helped the missionaries, they would be blessed. Those who experienced Nazi occupation have testified that the Danes were spared many of the problems experienced by the other occupied countries.

Germany's invasion of Poland and the subsequent declaration of war by England and France put an end, for the time, to missionary work in Europe. Foreigners were expelled, and President Smith assumed the responsibility to direct their return to the United States. This was accomplished on twenty-three ships, most of them freighters that had been improvised to handle passengers. With the aid of divine providence, all of the missionaries safely returned. Those who had not completed their missions were reassigned to stateside missions. It was November before President and Sister Smith returned home having completed that assignment.

TEMPLE AND GENEALOGICAL WORK were among the special loves of President Smith. He served as a counselor in the presidency of the Salt Lake Temple for sixteen years and as its president for another four. He was one of the moving forces behind the Genealogical Society of Utah and was the first editor and business manager of the *Utah Genealogical and Historical Magazine,* which began publication in January 1910. His determination and dedication are illustrated in the publication of the first issue of this magazine. His family had been placed under quarantine because his daughter Julina had contracted scarlet fever. Elder Smith worked on the manuscript at home, treated it with an antiseptic, and then placed it in a box by the front gate. From there it was taken to the printer and the galley proofs prepared. These were then sent to him for approval. He checked them, fumigated them, and once more placed them out by the front gate for collection. He served in leadership positions in the Genealogical Society until it was assimilated into other Church programs in 1940.

Joseph Fielding Smith also had an intense interest in the history of the Church. He felt it to be the most important history in the world, and he labored accordingly to see that it was the most accurate. He began working in the Historian's Office in 1901, was made an assistant Church historian in 1906, and Church Historian in 1921. He served in that position until he released himself when he became president of the Church in 1970. He held the office longer than any other man in the history of the Church. He was proud to have served in the same position once held by such notables as Willard Richards, George A. Smith, Wilford Woodruff, and Franklin D. Richards.

AT THE DEATH OF GEORGE F. RICHARDS in August 1950, Joseph Fielding Smith became acting president of the Council of the Twelve. He was set apart as the president of the quorum in April 1951, when David O. McKay became president of the Church. In October 1965, he assumed the additional responsibility of serving as a counselor to President McKay, who was then ailing in health. He served both as the president of the Council of the Twelve and as a counselor to the First Presidency until he became the president of the Church on January 23, 1970.

At the time he became the president of the Church he had served as an apostle for almost sixty years and was himself ninety-three years of age. With a twinkle in his eye he liked to say that his first assignment in the Church was to go with Brigham Young to dedicate the St. George Temple. He then slyly added, "I was one year old then." His youthful memories included discourses given by Wilford Woodruff and association with many who knew the Prophet Joseph Smith. From the time of his call to the time of his death on July 2, 1972, his life spanned that of forty-two other apostles and four other presidents of the Church.

A renewal of strength attended the call of Joseph Fielding Smith to preside over The Church of Jesus Christ of Latter-day Saints as its prophet, seer, and revelator. Despite his great age, he continued to travel throughout the world to teach and testify of the Savior and the restored gospel. During the first year of his presidency he presided over special meetings in California, Idaho, Arizona, Mexico, and Hawaii. Highlights of the following year included his return to the British Isles, for an area conference, where he had served as a missionary seventy years earlier, and his trip to Independence, Missouri, to dedicate a new visitors' center. His special interest in the youth of the Church is evidenced by talks given to students at Snow College, Ricks College, the College of Southern Utah, University of Utah, Utah State University, Brigham Young University, and the Church College of Hawaii.

Some have wondered why the Lord would call a man at such an advanced age to the demanding task of presiding over the Church. For many it represented the placing of a divine seal of approval upon his life and works. Those feelings found confirmation in the October 1970 general conference. "All my days," President Smith said at that time, "I have studied the scriptures and have sought the guidance of the Spirit of the Lord in coming to an understanding of their true meaning. The Lord has been good to me and I rejoice in the knowledge he has given me and in the privilege that has been and is mine to teach his saving truths. . . . What I have taught and written in the past I would teach and write again under the same circumstances." Thus quietly and with a modesty characteristic of him, President Smith affirmed for the Church that his teachings of a lifetime — whether written or spoken — were countenanced by the special inspiration of his office.

It seems fitting that the announcement that Monday night be reserved as family night be made in the administration of this man whose own feelings were so strongly riveted to his family. President Smith never stopped teaching his own family that salvation was not found in offices but in the family unit and in honoring covenants.

In his discourses as the president of the Church, Joseph Fielding Smith continued to emphasize the necessity of being true and faithful to the testimony of the restoration. Joseph Smith had said that if we were to take away the Book of Mormon and the other revelations of the restoration, we would be no different from any of the other squabbling sects of Christendom. President Smith wanted it clearly understood that though we are in the world, we are not of it. One instance in which he emphasized this theme was at the dedication of the visitors' center in Independence, Missouri. In that historic setting, with descendants of Joseph Smith's family present, he reviewed the promise the Lord had made to Joseph Smith while he was incarcerated in the jail at Liberty, Missouri. "The ends of the earth," the Lord had said, "shall inquire after thy name, and fools shall have thee in derision, and hell shall rage against thee; while the pure in heart, and the wise, and the noble, and the virtuous, shall seek counsel, and authority, and blessings constantly from under thy hand." (D&C 121:1-2.) President Smith declared, "I for one want to be numbered forever among those who seek counsel and authority and blessings as they have come from this great prophet."

In his call to preside over the Church we see the fulfillment of the prophecy of the patriarch, that he would "stand in the midst of this people a prophet and a revelator to them." In that which he taught and wrote over the course of a lifetime, we find the fulfillment of the promise that the Spirit would unfold to his understanding many truths concerning the gospel that had not yet been revealed.

The Lord has never chosen to exempt his prophets from the heartaches of the flesh. On August 3, 1971, after thirty-three years of marriage, Jessie Evans Smith passed away. For the third time Joseph Fielding Smith was bereft of his closest earthly companion. From the time of their marriage, Jessie Evans had been at his side. She had been with him in virtually all his travels, sharing her testimony in song, and showing the Saints the soft and mellow side of her apostle of truth. Always pleased to share her musical talent in these meetings, she often asked President Smith to join her in a duet. With a feigned reluctance he would do so, suggesting that it was more of a "do it" than a "duet."

The firmness with which President Smith taught gospel principles aptly represented his own uncompromising commitment to the Lord. He avoided the very appearance of evil. He did not like the use of such words as *heck* or *darn* even in anger because they were too close to unbecoming speech. *Gosh* and *gee* were also unacceptable in his family because of

335

their closeness to the sacred name of deity. The strongest language that one could evoke from him was, "He makes my tired ache."

Illustrating his respect for authority, one of his daughters tells the following story: "We were driving Dad and Aunt Jessie home from a General Authority party and were about to pass a slow moving car when he noticed that President McKay was in it. Instinctively he responded, 'We don't pass the President!'"

A great leader must first be a great follower, and President Smith proved himself that. On a Sunday evening shortly after he became president of the Church, my wife and I took our little family up to visit him. While he lost himself in conversation with our little girls, we chatted with Aunt Jessie. She mentioned that because of a stake conference schedule, they would fast with their ward twice that month; in addition, President Smith would fast each Thursday, that being the day the First Presidency and Council of the Twelve met in the temple. That meant that he would be fasting six times that month. My first thought was, Why does he fast with the ward? After all, he is the president of the whole Church, and he fasts for them weekly! My second reflection was that it was interesting that such a thought occurred to me but that it had never occurred to him.

Among his habits of a lifetime was that of punctuality. "He never rushes to a meeting," his secretary said. "He always goes early." For instance, if the Council of the Twelve were to meet in the temple at eight-thirty, he would go at eight o'clock to see that everything was in order. It is doubtful that he was ever late for anything. He used to say, "I always allow time for a flat tire." He also wore a watch on each wrist. This was because he traveled so much and was often passing through different time zones. He liked to have one set on the time at home and the other set on the time where he was.

President Smith believed in the doctrine of work. "People die in bed," he cautioned, "and so does ambition." One of his sons recalled, "Somehow it seemed immoral to Dad for us to lie in bed after six o'clock. Of course I only tried it once. Father saw to that." Responding to the question, "How do you get so much done?" President Smith said, "It's in the bag," meaning that he was a brown-bagger, and that by not having to go out for lunch, he saved three hundred hours a year.

He was also doggedly independent and expected to do things for himself. He never quite accepted the machine age. He did almost all the typing for his many books himself on his trusty old manual typewriter. Having never been taught to type, he used what he called "the Bible method — seek and ye shall find."

Though always busy, he was never too busy for his family. He preferred his office door left open and instructed his secretary that if she saw members of his family, children or grandchildren, she was to go get them and bring them in to see him. On one occasion I passed his outer office door without going in. His secretary, Ruby Egbert, came out and got me. She said she would be in trouble if President Smith knew she had let one of the family go by without stopping to see him. I was escorted into his office and was greeted with a kiss as was his custom. After a brief visit I stood to leave, and he arose, came around the desk, and put his arm around my shoulder and walked me to the door. As we reached the door, he pulled me around so that I faced him, and said, "Always remember that you have the blood of prophets in your veins." Such was his way of reminding his family of their heritage and their responsibility to live worthy of it. There was no more dominant or obvious theme in his life than that of being true to his heritage. "In all my life," he said, "whenever I've been tempted, one thought has always come to me: what would my father think of that?"

He was proud of the name Smith and told his family that in the beginning everyone was named Smith. Then when they sinned, they had to change their name. For years, when the General Authorities set missionaries apart, it was his responsibility to assign the missionaries to a particular General Authority. Often in reading their names, when he came to one difficult to pronounce he would just shake his head and say, "Oh, I wish everyone was named Smith."

His was a quiet faith. He did not talk much about spiritual experiences, yet they were common to him. His son Joseph, Jr., shared such an experience. As they were returning home from a conference in Vernal, Utah, their vision obscured by a heavy rain, they took a wrong turn in Duchesne, which led them up Indian Canyon. As the storm increased in volume, the road became slippery in places and was covered with mud in others. Near a very deep chasm in the road, they got stuck. Attempts to push the car free were without avail. Joseph recalls that his father said, "We have done all we can. We will call upon the Lord." He then did so, telling the Lord that they needed his help to right the mistake they had made. He told the Lord of the danger of their situation and reminded him of important appointments that awaited them in Salt Lake City.

As the prayer concluded, the storm abated, the car was freed, and a wind came up and dried off the road sufficiently that they were able to safely wind their way back to the main highway. As soon as they reached low ground, the storm commenced again, stalling traffic in the immediate area for several hours. When they wound down Provo Canyon, they were stopped by a highway patrolman, who asked where they had come from. When informed that they had come through Indian Canyon, the officer said, "That's impossible! It's reported that all the bridges in that area have been washed out." The headlines of the next day's paper reported two hundred cars stranded in the area from which they had escaped.

Jeraldine Bangerter recalls hosting President Smith when he toured her husband's mission in Brazil. After a mission conference, they returned to the mission home for dinner. At the conclusion of the dinner, President Bangerter asked President Smith if he would like to take a short rest before they commenced the remainder of the day's activities. President Smith was well into his eighties at the time. "No," he responded, "I'm not tired. What I would like to do is talk about the scriptures." As Sister Bangerter cleared the dishes off the table, the brethren got their scriptures and began to talk. She recalls that President Smith thumbed through them and spoke of various passages as if they were old personal friends. An hour slipped by and President Smith stood to stretch; as he did so, he raised his hand above his head and said, "If we don't study these scriptures, we will be held accountable."

The thought worked on her. She loved the Lord and wanted to study the scriptures, but with eight children, two still in diapers, and a husband to support, it seemed impossible to find the time. Excusing herself to get them some water, she left the room but continued to wonder about her standing with the Lord. Realizing that someday she would have to face the Lord, she decided that she had better face President Smith now and find out just what her plight would be. She returned to the room and confessed to President Smith that she had not studied the scriptures the way she ought to, but that she worked hard to be a good mother and to protect her husband's time so that he would be free to do so. "What is going to happen to me?" she asked. "Can I ride on Grant's coattail?" Her question was greeted with a stern look, and President Smith's voice was firm in response. "Well, I guess so," he said, and those who knew him would catch the twinkle in his eye, "if you will bake him a pie once in a while!"

President Smith liked pie and he liked children; he liked good books, and he loved to hear Jessie sing. What he did not like were unnecessarily long meetings, gum chewing, especially in church, and tobacco and its stench, any time, any place. When one of the major tobacco companies used the slogan "the thinking man's filter and the smoking man's taste," he wrote to the company and suggested that the slogan ought to be "the stinking man's filter and the filthy man's taste." Shortly after his letter was sent the slogan was dropped, though his suggestion for a new one was not taken.

In setting apart new bishops, President Smith would tell them that if they "made any mistakes in judgment, they were to make them on the side of mercy." Frequently some of the brethren observed that if it were necessary for them to be judged for any reason, they hoped that Joseph Fielding Smith be their judge. His daughter Amelia recalls an occasion when a peddler came to his door and was turned away by one of the children, since the peddler had nothing that the family needed.

When their father learned of it, she said, he sent the children to find the woman, with the instruction that none in need were to ever be turned away.

Though he was gracious to all men, President Smith had little use for those who thought themselves to be intellects and who delighted in traducing the faith of others. A man who had not grown up in an active church family but who, because of the influence of good friends in college, gained a testimony and became active in the Church, recalls an interview with President Smith. "He told me I had done everything backwards. He said, 'You are supposed to go to college to lose your testimony, not gain it.'"

THOUGH JOSEPH FIELDING SMITH SERVED as an apostle for more than sixty-two years, he constantly taught his family that the blessings of the kingdom of heaven were not associated with office or position. His doctrine was that true greatness is found only in the family. In the funeral discourse for a fellow member of the Council of the Twelve, he said that the thing that was the most impressive in the apostle's long life of service was that he had received the ordinances of salvation and lived up to the covenants he had made. Having been true to that standard, Joseph Fielding Smith passed away quietly on July 2, 1972, just a few days before his ninety-sixth birthday. "He was a man without guile," said President N. Eldon Tanner, "and his passing was as near a translation as possible."

Such was the life and testimony of a man who could say, "I have a perfect knowledge that the Father and the Son appeared to Joseph Smith in the spring of 1820 and gave him commandments to usher in the dispensation of the fulness of times." As to the office he held, he said that it is God's work: "He chooses men and calls them to be instruments in his hands to accomplish his purposes, and he guides and directs them in their labors. But men are only instruments in the Lord's hands, and the honor and glory for all that his servants accomplish is and should be ascribed unto him forever."

SOURCES

As a grandson of President Smith, I have drawn much of the material in this chapter from my association with him or that of other family members with whom I have talked. Published sources include Joseph F. McConkie, *True and Faithful: The Life Story of Joseph Fielding Smith* (Salt Lake City: Bookcraft, 1971); Joseph F. McConkie, "Joseph Fielding Smith: A Family View" (Brigham Young University: Sperry Symposium, January 26, 1980); and Joseph Fielding Smith, Jr., and John J Stewart, *The Life of Joseph Fielding Smith* (Salt Lake City: Deseret Book, 1972). Unpublished sources include Joseph Fielding Smith's missionary journal (copy in possession of the author); letters of Joseph Fielding Smith from his father (copies in possession of the author); and journal of Joseph F. Smith (1879-1883), which is in the Library-Archives of the Church.

JOSEPH FIELDING MCCONKIE is associate professor of ancient scripture at Brigham Young University, with degrees also from that institution. A native of Salt Lake City, he directed the LDS Institute of Religion in Seattle and has been a chaplain in the United States Army. He is the author of *True and Faithful: Joseph Fielding Smith* (Salt Lake City: Bookcraft, 1971); *Seeking the Spirit* (Salt Lake City: Deseret Book, 1978); *The Spirit of Revelation* (Salt Lake City: Deseret Book, 1984); and *Gospel Symbolism* (Salt Lake City: Bookcraft, 1985); and co-author of *Sustaining and Defending the Faith* (Salt Lake City: Bookcraft, 1985). He is a grandson of President Joseph F. Smith.

HAROLD B. LEE

Leonard J. Arrington

On the afternoon of April 20, 1935, Harold Bingham Lee walked down the stairs of the Church Administration Building in Salt Lake City and went out to his car. Awed with the weight of a new calling, he drove up the winding road to the head of City Creek Canyon and into a little grove called Rotary Park. Stopping the car, he got out and began to walk. A spring breeze blew through the trees, which were just beginning to show their tiny buds. There in the park, as he later recalled, "I sought my Heavenly Father. I sat down to pore over this matter, wondering about an organization to be perfected to carry on this work. I received a testimony on that beautiful spring afternoon that God had already revealed the greatest organization that ever could be given to mankind. . . . All that was needed now was the organization to be set to work, and the temporal welfare of the Latter-day Saints would be safeguarded."

That unexpected spring drive was the aftermath of a morning that Elder Lee had spent with President Heber J. Grant and his counselors Anthony W. Ivins and J. Reuben Clark, Jr., discussing plans for what was later to become the Church Welfare Program. Elder Lee had been chosen by the First Presidency to act as director in the implementation of a bold, innovative economic relief program that would deliver thousands of Latter-day Saints from the despair of physical want incurred by the Great Depression, during which the United States had suffered the worst financial catastrophe in its history. Even the industrious Beehive State felt the pangs of the national disaster. Utah, which had bustled with prosperity only a few years before, was feeling the pinch of destitution. In Salt Lake City, as in Seattle, Boston, and San Francisco, the breadlines and soup kitchens dramatized the failure of the American dream.

At the time he was called to design the welfare program, Elder Lee was serving as Salt Lake City commissioner, an office to which he had been first appointed and then elected. He knew the problems. Each day, as he supervised the maintenance of city streets, he saw the solemn faces of fathers, once proud and prosperous, now frantically searching for ways to feed their families. He saw the vacant faces of children who could not understand why their parents no longer brought home armloads of groceries.

For half a decade before this call, Brother Lee had served as president of Pioneer Stake, a group of 7,300 Saints of whom 4,800 were unemployed or receiving government relief. He saw the massive problem not in statistical or economic terms, but in human terms. How will Brother Jones buy enough coal to keep his family warm for the winter? How will Widow Campbell buy medicine for her daughter with pneumonia? What can be done to improve the mental, physical, and spiritual well-being of each person in the stake?

As the First Presidency knew, Harold B. Lee was unusually gifted with the ability to administer large-scale programs—to devise means of solving massive problems in a personal way. This spiritual trademark was the result of seeds, sown in his youth, that blossomed first in the welfare program and later in his vigorous leadership of a church that was evolving into an international force for good. Many years later, after he had been sustained as a prophet, seer, and revelator of the Church, he declared: "No longer can this church be thought of as the 'Utah church,' or as an 'American church.' The membership of the Church is now distributed over the earth in seventy-eight countries, teaching the gospel in seventeen different languages. This greatly expanded church population is today our most challenging problem. . . . It poses some great challenges to the leadership of the Church to keep pace with the many problems." This broadened perspective came as the result of a life of administrative responsibility and lifelong experience in developing and executing programs to benefit people.

THE CLASSIC OPENING PHRASE with which Nephi begins the Book of Mormon, "Having been born of goodly parents," might well have been written by Harold B. Lee. He descended from men and women of vision, insight, and courage. His lineage is composed of pioneers who were valiant both spiritually and physically—ancestors who passed on a tradition of faith, love, and insight to the young man who would later become the prophet, seer, and revelator of The Church of Jesus Christ of Latter-day Saints. In many ways he was instrumental in making his forebears' dreams of an industrious Zion a reality for their progeny.

The story of the Lee family in America begins in 1745, when William Lee endured the difficulties of an emigrant ship to begin anew in North and South Carolina—the land of plantations and opportunity. In America he was wounded in the American Revolution and was left for dead after the battle of Guilford County Courthouse in the Carolinas in March 1781. He was found in this abandoned state by a nurse, whom he later married. Out of this union came four sons; the youngest was Samuel.

Only two years after the Church was organized, Samuel's sons, Francis, Alfred, and Eli, and their families accepted the restored gospel and were baptized. They suffered through the vicissitudes, the mobbings and murders of Jackson County, Far West, and Nauvoo, and took part in the great migration to the Great Basin. While making their trek west, the Lee brothers were met by their father, Samuel, at Winter Quarters, and he was baptized after they arrived in Tooele, Utah.

After the arduous crossing of the Great Plains, the Francis Lee family—for Francis had married by then—settled in

Tooele, west of Great Salt Lake City, and then were called by President Brigham Young to colonize St. George. In unquestioning obedience the family journeyed to the vermilion cliffs and greasewood-covered land of southern Utah. Not long afterward they were called again to move, this time to Meadow Valley, Nevada, situated in the southwest part of Utah Territory, which at that time included Nevada. There, in a place later named Panaca, they built a "dugout"—a cozy clay cubicle with a roof of wooden poles. They were the first permanent settlers in Meadow Valley.

On one occasion two Indians entered the small family dugout when only Jane Johnson Lee, wife of Francis, was at home. One of the braves motioned that he wanted the gun in the corner, but Jane refused to give it to him. When he started for the gun, she hit him with a piece of wood, knocking him down. As the Indian recovered, he drew his bow and aimed an arrow at her. Again wielding a piece of wood, she pounced on him. She broke his bow and arrows, and he scrambled for safety, lucky to have escaped with his bones intact. In later events Sister Lee proved to be a close friend and trusted associate of the Indians in the region. Francis, Sr., and Jane remained in Meadow Valley the rest of their lives.

The two sons of this sturdy pioneer couple married sisters. The McMurrin girls, converted from Scotland, had walked with a handcart to Salt Lake City, accompanied by their father, who was a cooper. Samuel Lee married Margaret, and Francis, Jr., married Mary. In the days when childbirth was a risky business—when a sterile delivery room and a doctor were rare—Margaret was pregnant twelve times, and eleven times was without a surviving newborn. Only one child survived, the twelfth, Samuel Lee, named after his father. Then Margaret died. A premature baby, Samuel was so small that a finger ring could be slipped over his hand onto his arm.

Mary McMurrin nursed the motherless child along with her own baby until her health failed. Then she and her husband journeyed to Salt Lake City with the children and left baby Samuel with his grandmother McMurrin, who cared for him until he was sixteen. When his faithful grandmother died,

Samuel, now grown to young manhood, went north to Cache Valley to live with an aunt. There he found his wife. While living in the village of Clifton, Idaho, he met dark-haired, dark-eyed Louisa Bingham.

The marriage of Samuel and Louisa in the Logan Temple in 1895 established a union to which six children were born. Their home was described as "out on the string, three miles north of the store." The store was the only commercial enterprise in the town, and the string was a small road that was either muddy, dusty, or snow-covered, depending on the season. "Aunt Susan" Henderson served as midwife in the area, since the nearest hospital and doctor were many miles away. On a windy day, March 28, 1899, Aunt Susan saw Harold Bingham Lee draw his first breath.

HAROLD CHARACTERIZED HIS CHILDHOOD WELL when he said, "We had everything that money could not buy." Though money was scarce around the turn of the century, the Lee children never knew they were poor because of the many entertainments available to them. There was Dudley's Pond, where barefoot boys went to swim. At another pool, on Bybee's farm, the future prophet was baptized a member of the Church at the age of eight.

The country life was not without its risks, nor Harold's childhood without its misadventure. When he was very young, he swallowed a chunk of lye, thinking it was candy. According to a story in the *Deseret News* in 1934, "Except that his grandmother, his mother, and a quantity of olive oil were handy this story would not be written."

When he was five, Harold visited the neighborhood schoolhouse, where the teacher was delighted and surprised that he could write the alphabet—and his name as well. Impressed with his precociousness, the teacher directed that the overall-clad boy begin school a year earlier than most children his age. The Lee children rode two miles to school in a two-wheeled cart pulled by a small sorrel pony driven by their mother. According to Harold's brother, Perry, they bounced into the small school every day dressed in knee pants with white starched cuffs folded back over the coat sleeves and white sailor-collars draped down over the shoulders. "And then there were the ringlets," Perry added. "Carefully combed and painstakingly curled, they dangled down our backs for all the world to see — and pull — and scoff. Harold was sent to school at the age of five, still with his mass of beautiful hair. It may be that then was the first time he went into training for the hard knocks of life to come. Suffice to record that those curls caused more skinned knuckles and black eyes than either politics or religion. Finally he had had enough, and I remember how our mother wept when he purloined a pair of scissors and literally 'sawed' off one of the frontal danglers, spoiling the whole effect, which made it necessary to delete the remainder — a welcome relief. He was at last a boy — a fat, chubby one and a pet of all the teachers."

Harold's grandfather Bingham worked as a deputy warden in an Idaho penitentiary. Because the prison was nearby, a pack of bloodhounds was kept at the family homestead to search for escaped convicts. When the hounds howled in the night in search of a missing prisoner, Harold's spunky grandmother would usher him and his brothers and sisters into a small room and lock the door. She did not believe that children should receive "unfavorable impressions."

The Lee farm brought in little money, since its abundant harvests of wheat and potatoes sold at a very low price. To augment the family income, Samuel contracted for grain cutting, drilling wells, and building irrigation canals.

In recalling his childhood in an address to young people, President Lee said, "We began to 'do chores' shortly after daybreak so we could 'start' with the day's work by sun-up. When the day's work was finished, we had yet to do our evening 'chores,' usually by aid of a lantern. . . . Sleep requirements did not admit of too frequent frivolities. Returns from our labors were small and usually came on a once-a-year basis at harvest time. Homes of that day went through the summer with but very little ready money, but from our cows we were provided milk, butter, and cheese; in our granaries there was usually sufficient wheat to be taken to the mill for flour and cereals. We had our own chickens and garden and fruits in season."

The Sabbath was always a day of rest on the Lee farm. Church matters were of primary import, since Harold's father served for many years in the bishopric and his mother in the Young Women's Mutual Improvement Association. Dudley's Pond was off-limits for swimming on Sunday; instead the Lee family gathered around to study, sing, and enjoy the family spirit while resting from their daily work.

While Harold enjoyed few of the "store-bought" joys that were the result of increasing industrial development in the United States, he had many worthy compensations. He always had enough to eat, enough to wear, clean air to keep his mind alert, and a family bonded together by covenant and love. He could ride on one of the family horses to the top of the nearby Rocky Mountain range and look across the golden waves of wheat at harvest time and feel the quiet, powerful comfort of being in harmony with nature. By the side of the clear, cold mountain brook, he could lie in his bedroll and gaze up at the millions of tiny candles in the sky and ponder questions to which he would later find answers. He knew the satisfaction of sitting around a family table to a hearty meal—piles of whipped potatoes, home-grown corn on the cob, and finger-thick steaks—after a day of hearty toil. In the fall he ate delicacies like "head cheese" when the pig was butchered to provide home-cured hams and bacon to last out the cold Cache Valley winters.

The family piano was the household gem. On that fine old instrument, sometimes with a Scottish lady by his side, Harold learned to play the lively marches he especially liked. These lessons started a diversified interest in music that he later found useful when he served as chairman of the Church Music Committee.

New sounds were always brightening the Lee home. Sometimes it was grandma humming a hymn as she churned the butter, or mother calming a colicky baby with a soft lullaby, or Harold practicing his scales on the piano. Perhaps the grandest sound contribution, at least in decibels, was introduced on the day when brothers Harold and Perry were in bed spotted with measles. They heard the family horses coming through the yard; soon their smiling father entered with two shining instruments — a cornet in one hand and a baritone horn in the other. Thereafter the bubbling, brassy sound of the Lee brothers' horns resounded through the house. As they quickly became proficient, they joined the Silver Cornet Band of Clifton, which furnished entertainment for parades and festive occasions such as the 24th of July. When they attended high school, Harold practiced on the slide trombone; he later joined the Preston Military Band and a group that furnished silvery music for the fox trots and waltzes of church and school dances.

When the Lee boys had completed all of the grades at the local school, they were sent to the Oneida Stake Academy in Preston, Idaho, to complete their high school education. Every day they rode horses fifteen miles to the Church-operated secondary school, where, when he was only thirteen, Harold met a classmate by the name of Ezra Taft Benson, with whom he was later associated in the Council of the Twelve.

At Oneida, in addition to his musical abilities, Harold demonstrated his ability as a debater and public speaker. When he and his partner, Sparrel Huff, took the negative on the question of abandoning the Monroe Doctrine and defeated the hitherto unbeaten rivals from the Fielding Academy at Paris, Idaho, Harold and his fellow debaters were feted by their peers as conquering heroes.

Harold's interest in sports, particularly in basketball, won for him election as athletics manager. This was the "plum" of all the student offices, since the manager was permitted to travel, expenses paid, with the teams wherever they went. This gave him a chance to see the surrounding areas and prepare for the active, gregarious life ahead of him.

Student rivalries spiced the student life at Oneida. During his final year there, Harold and the other graduating seniors posted their class flag at the top of the flagpole only to find the next morning that the juniors had removed it. Adding insult to injury, the underclassmen had shredded the flag as well. A brief explanation of the situation states matter-of-factly that "fisticuffs followed."

After high school, Harold decided to train as a teacher at the Albion State Normal School in southwestern Idaho. During the summer of 1916, when he was just barely seventeen years of age, he prepared himself to pass the certification examination in fifteen subjects. During this time he lost more than a pound of weight for every subject, but was rewarded when he learned that he had scored an average of 89 percent on the tests.

The Silver Star School near Weston, Idaho, is where Harold B. Lee started his teaching career in a little one-room schoolhouse at age seventeen. In bartering for his salary, the young schoolmaster drew lots with the school board to determine whether he would receive sixty-five or sixty dollars — and lost! However, the kindhearted board did approve a living expense of fifteen dollars for board and room. Harold was principal of the school, the only teacher, the custodian, the groundskeeper, and everything else.

When Harold was hired as the principal of the Oxford School a year later, he received a boost in pay to ninety dollars a month and an additional challenge, since many of the pupils were older than he. In spite of the fact that many of the students had reputations as being rough and tough, the new principal solved the situation and earned their respect by playing basketball with them during the lunch period. From that administrative position he gained valuable experience as well as friendships that were long-lasting and rewarding. During his employment in Oxford, he traveled by horseback from the Clifton farm. He spent his spare time in community activities, in perfecting his musical talents, and in improving his teaching skills.

During Harold's years as Oxford School principal, his father was the bishop of his home ward at Clifton. Many evenings when he returned home, Harold and his brothers helped their father load a sack of grain or a bundle of clothes into the back of the pony cart. The load disappeared into the sunset as their father cared for the sick and needy in dignified silence, protecting the pride and confidence of the families he helped. This simple, Christian program suggests the successful welfare program Bishop Lee's son would design in 1935.

AFTER HAROLD HAD TAUGHT SCHOOL for nearly four years, his bishop-father recommended that he serve a mission. His call to the Western States Mission came from President Heber J. Grant. For the first time Harold was called Elder Lee, a title by which he would be known as an apostle and prophet for nearly half his life. For two or three years prior to his mission call, he had been the organist in the Clifton Ward as well as the trainer and organizer of a girls chorus. When he prepared to leave on his mission, the young ladies whom he had coached and taught brought him a gold ring as a symbol of their respect and friendship.

In the locked annals of mission records is a simple, graphic report prepared by President John M. Knight concerning the service of young Harold B. Lee from November 11, 1920, to December 18, 1922. The character sketch fits the man: "Qualifications—As a speaker, 'Very Good.' As a presiding officer, 'Very Good.' Has he a good knowledge of the Gospel? 'Very Good.' Has he been energetic? 'Very.' Is he discreet and does he carry a good influence? 'Yes.' Remarks: 'Elder Lee presided over the Denver Conference with marked distinction from August 8, 1921, to December 18, 1922. An exceptional missionary.'"

While he was a missionary, Elder Lee had a tracting companion by the name of Willis J. Woodbury, who used to carry a stack of black-covered scriptures in one hand and a cello case in the other. When invited into a home, the two would open the case and begin. Elder Woodbury would stroke the bow across the cello while Elder Lee acompanied on the piano. Their music prepared listeners to be more receptive to the gospel message. Elder Lee was a natural leader among missionaries and members and was influential in bringing more than forty persons to the waters of baptism.

After he was released from his mission, Elder Lee spent a

short time in Clifton, then went to Salt Lake City to court a young lady by the name of Fern Lucinda Tanner, whom he had met in the mission field and had admired from a distance. Bright, talented, and beautiful, Fern was a scripturalist of unusual ability. After a short courtship they were married in 1923 in the Salt Lake Temple just two months after he had been established as a principal in the Granite School District in Salt Lake County. This marriage was blessed with two daughters, Maurine and Helen.

During the years after marriage, the Lees established a home on the west side of Salt Lake City, a home that became a gathering place for young people. Fern became a favorite neighbor through her gentle, gracious manner and her wise counsel. Harold worked at his brother-in-law's grocery store as well as at a gasoline station, while attending night school at the University of Utah. He also took a number of correspondence courses. He served as principal of the Whittier School and later the Woodrow Wilson School in the Granite District. During the summers he augmented his school salary with employment that included selling meat for Swift and Company, checking out Salt Lake City street department equipment, and serving as watchman and tram checker at the yards of the Union Pacific Railroad Company. He also worked as a salesman for the Foundation Press, a company that sold a "master library," including beautiful illustrated Bible story books. In 1928 he was appointed intermountain manager for the firm.

During this period Harold was also active in the Church. Soon after he moved to Salt Lake City, he was called as the M-Men instructor in the Poplar Grove Ward, and the next year he served in the Sunday School superintendency. In 1926 he became the superintendent of the religion class in Pioneer Stake—a program that later merged into the seminary program of the Church. In the same year that "Lucky" Charles Lindbergh took off from Roosevelt Field in New York, Harold B. Lee was called to serve on the stake high council. A year later he was appointed stake superintendent of the Sunday

School. When he was only thirty-one years old, he was set apart to preside over the Pioneer Stake in Salt Lake City—the youngest stake president in the Church at the time.

What was it like to grow up in the Lee family in the 1920s? Helen Lee Goates says that her earliest recollections relate to the nightly ritual in which the family of four (father Harold, mother Fern, Maurine, and Helen) knelt in family prayer. They lived on Eighth South in a little home Brother Lee had bought from his father-in-law. A sleeping porch had been added to the back of the house and was equipped with space heaters designed to keep out the frost. Maurine and Helen, just fifteen months apart in age, slept on the porch. Since it was very cold in the winter, they had their prayers in the living room; then their father would take one of them in each arm, carry them out to the sleeping room, and tuck them in. When they were a little older and were too big for him to carry in that way, the gentle father would put one of them on his back and carry the other in his arms—and out they'd go to bed each night. As he tucked them in, according to Helen, he always had some endearing words to say to them. "Daddy knew how important it was in the lives of his little girls to feel that he loved them. This little nightly ritual demonstrated that he loved us, was concerned for us."

Helen recalls her earliest memory of her father's teachings about Heavenly Father. "One time when we were still very small, we went in company with another family or two on a hike up to Timpanogos Cave [near Provo, Utah]. We had our lunch and the plan was to hike up after lunch. Mother had some limitations on her health, so she wisely decided against making the climb with us. Maurine and I started out with our father, each of us holding to one of his hands. Mother was full of admonitions and advice: 'Now stay close to Daddy, don't let go of his hand, don't get too close to the edge of the trail,' and so on." Helen remembers moving a little closer to her father, gripping his hand a little tighter, and saying, "Oh, Mommy, you don't have to worry about us. As long as Daddy's here, we'll be just fine. We'll be safe."

As they started out, she says, her father's mind was on

this remark she had made, and it apparently started him thinking. Helen continues: "As we walked along the trail that day, Daddy talked to us about the fact that as long as he was there, he would indeed do everything he could to keep us safe from harm. But there was a greater lesson that might be learned. He went on to say that there would be dangers other than physical dangers that we would encounter. There would come a time in our lives, he said, when we would realize that we needed someone else besides just a Daddy to keep us safe. So we talked about our Heavenly Father, that he loved us every bit as much as our earthly father did, and that he would be with us wherever we were, wherever we went. Whatever the circumstances, whatever the dangers, we could always call on this unseen Heavenly Father to guide us and help us."

As the children grew older, the family moved into a larger home at 1208 South Eighth West in Salt Lake City. President Lee worked hard to improve the home and its surroundings, proving his competency as a do-it-yourself man. Up early in the morning to work in the yard, and working late every evening he was free, he developed a lovely backyard that was used by his family and their many friends. He did all of the landscaping himself, installing a beautiful board fence, fish pond, pagoda, benches at strategic spots, and a brick fireplace for barbecues. His daughter Helen recalls:

"Daddy learned in his early years that if he was going to accomplish anything, he was going to have to move fast. And I mean that literally. His movements were always very quick, and I suppose that as he got busier and as his life became more complicated, he just had to move at top speed to get everything done—especially with a big yard to take care of. He'd come in from work, greet all of us, then upstairs he would go and change his clothes, wasting not a minute. In his old clothes, he'd start to cut the lawn before supper, while mother was still getting things on the table. It might be that he'd get a call—somebody wanted him to come and administer to him or somebody needed counsel or help. He would race back in, put on his suit again, take care of the administration or other business, come back, change his clothes again, work for a while, and then go off to an evening meeting. He wouldn't have had time to do all that if he moved at a normal pace."

In 1932 an elected Salt Lake City commissioner, Joseph H. Lake, died, thereby vacating the office to which he had been elected thirteen months earlier. Shortly thereafter the remaining city officers prevailed upon Harold B. Lee to accept an appointment to the position. He was then thirty-three years of age. After careful consideration, he resigned his post with the Foundation Press and was unanimously approved in the new post. A year later, in a regular election with a field of twenty-five candidates, he was chosen by a sizeable margin to continue as city commissioner.

One of the most beneficial projects sponsored by Commissioner Lee was the replacement of the seven old-style garbage wagons with three new, automatically controlled, enclosed garbage trucks, the initial cost of which was paid for in the first year through reduced operating costs.

IN THE MEANTIME, the good times of the 1920s were brought to an end by the stock-market crash of 1929. The Great Depression settled like a dark cloud over the nation. Factories closed down, the number of unemployed workers rose sharply, farm prices declined, and millions of families found themselves without the income to buy food and clothing.

Even as the cloud descended, Harold B. Lee and his counselors in the stake presidency, Charles S. Hyde and Paul Child, initiated a creative alternative to demeaning charity programs. "Job relief without charity" became a meaningful slogan in Pioneer Stake. The carefully calculated program, executed and designed after much prayer, instituted on a grand scale what the young stake president had seen his father develop in Clifton—a bishop's storehouse to provide for the needy. A warehouse was obtained at 333 Pierpont Avenue in Salt Lake City, and unemployed workmen put it in shape for storage and work projects. Through drives for contributions, fruit bottles, clothing, and furniture were obtained to supply goods for processing and dispensing. Sewing and reconditioning operations were also carried on. Workmen were sent out to help farmers with the harvest, their pay consisting of a portion of the crop.

Soon the storehouse was transformed into a nerve center of enterprises that provided hundreds of Saints with work, food, and goods to sustain them. Pioneer Stake also fostered forty acres of subsistence gardens and, at a cost of only five thousand dollars, built a gymnasium and recreation center from the shambles of an abandoned warehouse. This edifice was the culminating effort in a stakewide budget system, which was later transformed into a recreation program in which all members could participate, regardless of their circumstances. The new building allowed all stake activities to be centralized and coordinated. While serving as stake president, Harold also developed a specialized program of leadership development and teacher training—programs that were later adopted worldwide by the Church and continue to function in the present Church organization.

At no time was the impact of economic despair more intensely felt than at Christmas. President Lee's practical empathy is illustrated by two incidents he related in a talk to the Deseret Industries workers during their annual Christmas dinner in 1973:

Our little girl went across the street with her Christmas doll to show the neighbor, and soon came back crying. She was crying because Donna Mae, the neighbor girl, didn't have any gifts for Christmas. Santa Claus had not come to her house.

Then, too late, we remembered that the father of the family had been out of work. Although he was not a member of the Church, we tried to share our Christmas with the children. For me it was a very difficult Christmas. I did not enjoy the dinner that I sat down to that day, because I, as stake president, had not become acquainted with the people in my stake.

The next Christmas we made preparations. We made a survey, and we found that we had more than a thousand people who needed help during those difficult times. So we made ready by gathering toys and taking them to the old storehouse. Then the fathers and mothers came and helped fix the toys, putting them together, dressing dolls, and sewing things.

We had oranges and apples. There was roast beef and all the trimmings for Christmas dinner. The bishops arranged to have it delivered to all the needy families, and then called me to let me know that all had been visited.

357

One morning after a heavy snow had blanketed the streets of Salt Lake City, President Lee went out to supervise the removal of snow.

I saw a little boy. He didn't have a warm coat, or gloves, or overshoes. It was bitter cold so I stopped and brought him into the car. The heater was going, and as he got warm I inquired if he was ready for Christmas.

"Mister, we aren't going to have any Christmas. Daddy died six months ago. Now there is only Mom and me and two younger children. We don't have much."

Probing deeper, I asked where he was going and he replied that there was a free movie uptown that morning and he wanted to go to that. That was all the Christmas he was going to have. I got his name and address and I told him that I would see to it that he did have a Christmas at his home.

President Lee had told his family about the little boy who was to have no Christmas. They too were concerned. He called the bishop to be assured that the family had been provided for. He concluded, "That year when I sat down to my Christmas dinner I felt that I could enjoy it, because, as far as I knew, every family in my stake was having a good Christmas."

On April 20, 1935, came the culminating event to all the spiritual, mental, and physical preparation that Harold B. Lee had experienced up until then: "The call of the First Presidency for me to come to their office [came] on a day that I shall never forget—April 20, 1935. I was city commissioner in Salt Lake City. I was a stake president. We had been wrestling with this question of welfare. There were few government work programs; the finances of the Church were low; we were told that there wasn't much that could be done so far as the finances of the Church were concerned. And here we were with 4,800 of our 7,300 people who were wholly or partially dependent. We had only one place to go, and that was to apply the Lord's program as set forth in the revelations."

President Lee continued: "It was from our humble efforts that the First Presidency, knowing that we had had some experience, called me one morning asking if I would come to their office. It was Saturday morning; there were no calls on their calendar, and for hours in that forenoon they talked with me and told me that they wanted me to resign from the city commission, and they would release me from being stake president; that they wished me now to head up the welfare movement to turn the tide from government relief, direct relief, and help to put the Church in a position where it could take care of its own needy."

After receiving the call, President Lee reacted and performed with the insight and innovation that had always been his custom. However, being modest and dependent on the Lord to guide his firm hand, he recorded the following reaction to his new responsibility: "There I was, just a young man in my thirties. My experience had been limited. I was born in a little country town in Idaho. I had hardly been outside the boundaries of the states of Utah and Idaho. And now to put me in a position where I was to reach out to the entire membership of the Church, worldwide, was one of the most staggering contemplations that I could imagine. How could I do it with my limited understanding?"

It was then that he took that solitary walk in Rotary Park. "As I kneeled down, my petition was, 'What kind of an organization should be set up in order to accomplish what the Presidency has assigned?' And there came to me on that glorious morning one of the most heavenly realizations of the power of the priesthood of God. It was as though something were saying to me, 'There is no new organization necessary to take care of the needs of this people. All that is necessary is to put the priesthood of God to work. There is nothing else that you need as a substitute.' "

With this spiritual assurance and a life that was prepared for service to the Lord, Harold B. Lee delivered his letter of resignation to the city and became the originator, under the direction of President Heber J. Grant, of a series of projects and programs first called the Church Security Program, and later the Church Welfare Program.

THE CHURCH WELFARE PROGRAM presented President Lee with monumental problems during the days when national economic devastation was most severe. Manpower, materials, finance, and organization were all independent challenges that required coordination and insight to manage. Besides the tremendous logistical problem, there was the awesome task of administering the new program in the face of criticism from those who felt that subsidy should be kept within the province of secular government. Constantly seeking divine inspiration, President Lee used the existing Church organization for execution of the plan. Stakes, wards, and branches were organized into regions, each of which carried out planned assignments under local priesthood direction.

While traveling through Zion's stakes to explain Church welfare, President Lee often quoted from the 115th section of the Doctrine and Covenants: "Arise and shine forth, that thy light may be a standard for the nations; and that the gathering together upon the land of Zion, and upon her stakes, may be for a defense, and for a refuge from the storm, and from wrath when it shall be poured out without mixture upon the whole earth." Applying the meaning of that declaration, he rephrased the scripture to convey an immediate message: "I have caused you to be organized into stakes of Zion that you might provide a defense, a refuge, and a protection for my people."

President Grant issued an official statement concerning the new plan. The Church Welfare Program was established by prophets "to set up a system where the evils of the dole will be abolished and where independence, thrift, industry, and self-respect can again be established among our people." From that declaration, Brother Lee, along with committee members Mark Austin, Campbell M. Brown, Stringham A. Stevens, Henry D. Moyle, and William E. Ryberg, established a program built upon three foundations:

1. The program was not new, but was merely the incorporation of traditional Church philosophy into a workable program of cooperation to meet the demands of Latter-day Saints with financial problems.

2. The program was instituted through the existing Church organization.

3. All activities and projects were designed to help the

people to help themselves rather than to provide a simple subsidy. Those receiving food and commodities were expected to work for them, if at all possible. In Brother Lee's own words, "Every member of the Church gives what he is able to give and receives in return whatever he needs for the sustenance of himself and his family."

In outlining the operating rules, he prescribed the following steps to make the program successful: "There must be no idleness in the Church; we must learn the lesson of self sacrifice; we must master the art of living and working together; we must practice a greater brotherhood in our priesthood quorums."

From these simple steps developed a plan that one world-famous economist praised for these reasons: "First—The Church has a magnificent organization. Second—It provides strong central authority centered in the General Authorities and in the priesthood. Third—The people have the will to sacrifice."

President Lee explained: "The bishops' storehouses in our day, as in other days, stand throughout the land as symbols of great faith translated into action. . . . Through the workings of this program of Church-directed welfare activities, every needy Church family may be aided by the Church in its efforts to become independent members, to do all possible with the aid of near relatives to help themselves. . . . Until those in need can be placed on jobs in private industry at a salary or wage sufficient to supply their needs, or have been rehabilitated on an independent basis, those who are able bodied are expected to work on Church-owned and -operated projects in production, processing, storing or distributing food, clothing, fuel, or household commodities that there may in our day 'be meat in the [Lord's] storehouses' both for themselves and their unfortunate neighbors."

By the time the program had been in effect for nearly a year, many had recovered confidence in overcoming the desperation they had felt only months before. Thousands of Saints had risen from the valley of despair to the mountaintops of hope. Through thought, prayer, and experience, President Lee had instigated a program that would convert dreams into reality. Much of his empathy and zeal to help the poor came from his own experience. In speaking of those who had known want, he said: "I have loved you. I have come to know you intimately. Your problems, thank the Lord, have been my problems, because I know, as you know, what it means to walk when you have not the money to ride. I know what it means to go without meals to buy a book to go to the university. I thank God now for these experiences. I have loved you because of your devotion and faith. God bless you that you won't fail."

AT AGE FORTY-TWO, this man of faith and experience, this confident yet humble servant of the Lord and of the people, was called as an apostle of The Church of Jesus Christ of Latter-day Saints. On April 6, 1941, thousands of arms rose to the square as Saints from around the world provided their sustaining vote for the humble young man who filled the place that had been made vacant by the death of Elder Reed Smoot. On that occasion John A. Widtsoe wrote the following prophetic tribute to Elder Lee: "He is full of faith in the Lord; abundant in his love of his fellow men; loyal to the Church and State; self-forgetful in his devotion to the gospel; endowed with intelligence, energy, and initiative; and gifted with eloquent power to teach the word and will of God. The Lord to whom he goes for help will make him a mighty instrument in carrying forward the eternal plan of human salvation. . . . He will be given strength beyond any yet known to him, as the prayers of the people ascend to the Lord in his behalf."

When he responded at conference to his call, Elder Lee attested to his humility and trust in the Lord when he said, "Since nine o'clock last night I have lived an entire lifetime in retrospect and in prospect. . . . Throughout the night, as I thought of this most appalling and soul-stirring assignment, there kept coming to me the words of the Apostle Paul, 'Let us therefore come boldly unto the throne of grace, that we may obtain mercy, and find grace to help in time of need.'. . . Therefore I shall take the word of Apostle Paul. I shall come boldly unto the throne of grace and ask for mercy and his grace to help me in my time of need. With that help I cannot fail. Without it I cannot succeed."

As a member of the Twelve Elder Lee shouldered many responsibilities, including the chairmanship of the music, general priesthood, and servicemen's committees. In addition, he continued to serve as the managing director of the General Church Welfare Committee; as adviser to the general board of the Primary Association; and as a member of the publications, garment, and expenditures committees.

He continued to enjoy music and often, when visiting wards and stakes, would surprise the members by offering to render his services on the piano or to act as organist. While he played "Midnight Fire Alarm" at home, his daughters pranced around the room. He played hymns and "family music" to the delight of his immediate family and their friends. He played the organ or piano for the Council of the Twelve at their weekly meetings in the temple. Both of his daughters became accomplished musicians—Maurine on the piano and Helen on the violin. He then transported them about the Salt Lake Valley as they performed for various church and school groups.

During World War II, when many young members of the Church were off to war, Elder Lee was asked to give a series of Sunday evening radio talks under the title "Youth and the Church." These lasted for several months. His daughter Helen explained how he brought his family into the project: "My sister and I were then in our late teens, so Father was very much interested in our reactions. He was very much aware of the kind of problems we were facing at that particular time in the history of the world, and we regularly discussed the things that he was going to talk about. He always had three talks that he was working on. He was putting the finishing touches on the one that he was to give the coming Sunday, then one for the following week that would be in a rough draft form, and then a third one that he had just begun outlining. He would bring the scripts home that he was working on, read them to us, and we would discuss them at the dinner table in a free exchange of ideas. We'd say, 'Oh no, Dad, you can't say that. It just isn't like that,' or else 'You'll have to say that differently.' Then we would all go with him each Sunday evening to the Tabernacle where he gave these talks. Such experiences drew us closely together." These talks were published under the title *Youth and the Church*, and later expanded as *Decisions for Successful Living*.

As he traveled to all corners of the Lord's kingdom, Elder Lee always bore an assured testimony of the gospel of Jesus Christ. He inspired missionaries, members, and leaders, and spent many hours counseling with young people. He lifted his voice in eloquence to comfort the forlorn and bereaved, as when he traveled to the troubled land of Korea in 1955. Dressed in fatigues, he comforted, reassured, and calmed those who had suffered physically and spiritually in that war-torn land. Those servicemen who felt his firm, kind hand and were soothed by his compassionate words will never forget the comfort he brought to them. As chairman of the Church's servicemen's committee during World War II, Korea, and Vietnam, he worked hard to establish programs that would offer servicemen the full blessings and opportunities of the gospel.

Though often in peril because of his health, President Lee maintained a rigorous schedule working to build the kingdom of God. Perhaps it was through his own battle for health that he was able to sharpen his understanding of and empathy for others.

In 1962 while he was visiting a stake conference in Henderson, Nevada, Elder Lee received word that his beloved companion was ill and hovering near death. He rushed home to the bedside of the woman who had been his wife for nearly forty years and found her slipping away. Following her death, his soul-searing grief took him through many dark days, wrestling with his spirit and emotions. Eventually, in the same courageous manner with which he faced such challenges all his life, Elder Lee recognized the gospel as a beacon guide through any storm.

While Elder Lee was in Hawaii on Church assignment in 1966, his daughter Maurine (Mrs. Ernest J. Wilkins) passed away. He felt again the pangs of grief. Elder Gordon B. Hinckley of the Council of the Twelve, who had been Elder

Lee's close friend for many years, said, "These searing experiences, difficult to bear, served to increase his sensitivity to the burdens of others. Those who have sustained similar losses have found in him an understanding friend and one whose own tested faith has become a source of strength to them."

In a speech given at a memorial service honoring Latter-day Saints who had lost their lives in the Vietnam conflict, Elder Lee said these comforting words: "Having gone through some similar experiences in losing loved ones in death, I speak from personal experience when I say to you who mourn, do not try to live too many days ahead. The all-important thing is not that tragedies and sorrows come into our lives, but what we do with them. Death of a loved one is the most severe test that you will ever face, and if you can rise above your griefs and if you will trust in God, then you will be able to surmount any other difficulty with which you may be faced. . . . So to you who have lost loved ones, . . . we say to you that faith can lift you beyond the sordid trials of the day and point you to the glorious tomorrow that can be yours."

In 1963 Elder Lee married Freda Joan Jensen, an accomplished woman in her own right, having excelled as an educator and administrator and as a member of the general boards of the YWMIA and the Primary Association. Together they established a happy home warmed with love and gracious hospitality, a home supportive of Elder Lee's heavy Church responsibilities.

WHEN DAVID O. MCKAY was president of the Church, the Church Correlation Committee was established to coordinate the teaching and organizational functions with the governing body of the priesthood. Elder Lee was called to employ his proven skills to tighten up the kingdom's structure and undertake an extensive research program into the materials, methods, and curricula of all the Church programs and auxiliaries. As a result of this effort, there was a general refinement in teaching programs and organizational structure.

Paralleling Elder Lee's service in Church programs came opportunities to serve and excel in civic capacities. In 1957 he was named to the board of directors of Union Pacific Railroad Company — many years after he had spent the summers as a tram checker in the railroad yards. The next year he was asked to serve as a member of the board of the Equitable Life Assurance Society. Later he was made president of the Salt Lake Oratorio Society; he also served on the directing committee of the National Red Cross and became chairman of the board of Zions First National Bank. He was honored with honorary doctorates from Utah State University, Brigham Young University, and the University of Utah, and received numerous service awards, including the Silver Buffalo Award presented by the Boy Scouts of America.

When David O. McKay died in January 1970, the reins of Church leadership came into the worthy, capable hands of President Joseph Fielding Smith, who chose Harold B. Lee as his first counselor and N. Eldon Tanner as his second. This succession of leadership not only made Elder Lee president of the Council of the Twelve, but also necessitated his release from the committees on which he had been working so he could devote his full time to the business of the First Presidency. While serving in this capacity, he refined his skills as an administrator and continued to work on improving the efficiency of church programs. Under his leadership, teacher and bishop training programs were strengthened, and the size and scope of the worldwide missionary program was expanded.

On July 2, 1972, President Joseph Fielding Smith sat peacefully in an armchair as the finger of God touched him, and he slept. With his passing, the mantle of prophet fell upon Harold Bingham Lee. Of President Smith's death, President Lee said: "He seemed in that brief moment to be passing to me, as it were, a sceptre of righteousness as though to say to me, 'Go thou and do likewise.'"

As his consciousness of his calling as the earthly shepherd of Christ's flock descended upon him, President Lee's spiritual courage ascended to meet the challenge. He spent many hours in prayer and meditation. "The morning after my call came," he said, "as I knelt with my dear companion in prayer, my heart and soul seemed to reach out to the total membership of the Church with a special kind of fellowship and love which was like the opening of the windows of heaven, to give me a brief feeling of belonging to the more than three million members of the Church in all parts of the world."

On Friday morning, July 7, 1972, the Council of the Twelve met in a special room of the Salt Lake Temple to set apart the new prophet. President Gordon B. Hinckley, a member of the Twelve at the time, wrote of that occasion: "There was no doubt in the minds of the members of the Council of the Twelve who should succeed him [President Smith] as President of the Church. . . . In that quiet, holy place, with subdued hearts, they sought the whisperings of the Spirit. All hearts were as one in response to those whisperings. Harold Bingham Lee, chosen of the Lord, schooled from childhood in principles of the restored gospel, refined and polished through thirty-one years of service in the apostleship, was named president of The Church of Jesus Christ of Latter-day Saints and Prophet, Seer, and Revelator. The hands of all present were laid upon his head, and he was ordained as the anointed of the Lord to this high and incomparable calling."

The next month President Lee flew to Mexico City to preside over the greatest assembly of Saints ever held in Latin America. More than 16,000 members from Central America and Mexico met to receive inspired instruction from the General Authorities. One young Latter-day Saint from Tampico said, "To be able to sit and listen to his words and to know and feel in your heart that you are listening to a prophet of God is one of the most beautiful experiences in my life, especially to know that these men have the authority from our Lord to lead and organize us."

Later President Lee journeyed to the Middle East, where, with his wife, he traveled the dusty roads of the Holy Land and walked the roads that Jesus walked. He read the scriptures on the shore of the Sea of Galilee and passed through acres of olive groves in the thick heat of Israel. While there he also organized the first branch of the Church in Jerusalem.

In October 1972, he was formally sustained at a Solemn Assembly in the Salt Lake Tabernacle. President N. Eldon

Tanner conducted the official reorganization of the First Presidency and sustaining of the General Authorities and officers of the Church. After each motion, an audible wave of approval traveled through the historic Tabernacle as the voting procedures went quorum by quorum, obtaining the approval of each group.

When the sustaining ordinance had been completed, the new prophet arose to speak: "I find myself without words to express my deep and innermost feelings. . . . On that sacred occasion three months ago when I began to sense the magnitude of the overwhelming responsibility I now assume, I went to the holy temple. There, in prayerful meditation, I looked upon the paintings of those men of God—true, pure men, God's noblemen—who had preceded me in a similar calling." He went on to recount the special appointments and talents of the ten men who had served as prophet before him. Recalling Joseph Smith's self-characterization, he said, "At times it seemed as though I too was like a rough stone rolling down from a high mountainside, being buffeted and polished, I suppose, by experiences, that I too might overcome and become a polished shaft in the quiver of the Almighty."

FROM THAT DAY FORWARD, the Church continued to grow and prosper under his modest but firm leadership. Those who worked with him through the years say that there was a new air about him, more holy, more powerful, more compassionate and long-suffering. And so, with a new spiritual dimension added to his long years of experience, President Lee coupled his training with a divine calling to prepare for the Second Coming of the Lord and Savior Jesus Christ.

President Lee's training in the Church Correlation Committee gave him insight into the international tone of the Church. Through his direction, Saints around the world now received materials specifically designed for their culture. New youth programs brought a closer coordination between the Mutual Improvement Associations and the priesthood, and missionary lessons were revised.

The Latter-day Saints had a particular admiration and appreciation for President Lee because of his outgoing personality and love of mingling with the Saints. Commenting on this trait, Elder Paul Dunn of the First Council of Seventy said, "This great prophet somehow makes time to get out among the people. He's at this conference and that conference; and he's gone extra miles to meet the members. The president can't shake hands with every soul in the Church, but he tries. In his brief term as president he has been to area conferences in England, Mexico, and Germany. There have been several tours and scores of youth conferences. He has utilized every opportunity to be with them. The members he has met will never forget him. He has given them renewed devotion and dedication." "There is a communication when spirits respond to one another," President Lee declared. "To understand people, you must feel their spirit. You must mingle among them."

A story that illustrates President Lee's life and character was related in his closing talk at general conference in April 1973:

"I was suffering from an ulcer condition that was becoming worse and worse. We had been touring a mission; my wife, Joan, and I were impressed the next morning that we should get home as quickly as possible, although we had planned to stay for some other meetings.

"On the way across the country, we were sitting in the forward section of the airplane. Some of our Church members were in the next section. As we approached a certain point en route, someone laid his hand upon my head. I looked up; I could see no one. That happened again before we arrived home, again with the same experience. What it was, by what means or medium I may never know, except I knew that I was receiving a blessing that I came a few hours later to know I needed most desperately.

"As soon as we arrived home, my wife very anxiously called the doctor. It was now about 11 o'clock at night. He called me to come to the telephone, and he asked me how I was; and I said, 'Well, I am very tired. I think I will be all right.' But shortly thereafter, there came massive hemorrhages which, had they occurred while we were in flight, I wouldn't be here today talking about it.

"I know that there are powers divine that reach out when all other help is not available. . . . Yes, I know that there are such powers."

In many ways the story is a parable to President Lee's life of service to the Saints. As he traveled for nearly forty years in the interest of the Church, he always had a firm, invisible hand above him to protect and bless him. From his rich early childhood in Clifton, Idaho, doing chores in his overalls, to the carpeted offices of the Church Administration Building, he was firm in following the word of the Lord. His compassion, his warmth, and his love increased as the spiritual veil became increasingly thin between the earthly architect of the world Church and his Almighty Creator.

President Lee was stricken unexpectedly with cardiac and lung complications and died only a few hours later on December 26, 1973, at the age of seventy-four. Funeral services were held in the Salt Lake Tabernacle on Saturday, December 29, followed by interment in the Salt Lake Cemetery. The youngest head of the Church in forty years, he had served as president for only a year and a half. When he was sustained as prophet of the Church at the Solemn Assembly in October 1972, he capsulized well his administration: "The true record of my service in my new calling will be the record that I have written in the hearts and lives of those with whom I have served and labored within and without the Church."

SOURCES

I am particularly grateful to my son Carl Arrington and to Helen and Brent Goates for help in the preparation of this essay. Much of the essay, in a different format, was published in my article on President Lee in Preston Nibley, *The Presidents of the Church* (Salt Lake City: Deseret Book, 1974), pp. 427-57. In preparing this essay, I have relied upon oral histories in the Church Archives; talks, books, and articles by and about President Lee; and personal interviews with President Lee and his brother, S. Perry Lee.

LEONARD J. ARRINGTON is Lemuel Redd Professor of Western History and director of the Joseph Fielding Smith Institute for Church History at Brigham Young University. A former Idahoan, he was awarded the Ph.D. at the University of North Carolina. He is author of *Great Basin Kingdom: An Economic History of the Latter-day Saints*

(Cambridge, Massachusetts: Harvard University Press, 1958); *Brigham Young: American Moses* (New York: Alfred A. Knopf, 1985); and co-author with Davis Bitton of *The Mormon Experience: A History of the Latter-day Saints* (New York: Alfred A. Knopf, 1979); and *Saints without Halos: The Human Side of Mormon History* (Salt Lake City: Signature Books, 1982).

SPENCER W. KIMBALL
Edward L. Kimball

On March 28, 1895, Andrew Kimball sat as a delegate in the constitutional convention that had been convened in Salt Lake City in anticipation of statehood for Utah. At thirty-six, he was one of the youngest of Heber C. Kimball's fifty-two sons. When he got home at five o'clock, he found Olive, his wife, in labor with their sixth child, a nine-pound boy. Andrew recorded, "I took the children in to see him. Clare [age ten] had made up her mind for a girl, was badly disappointed, had a crying spell."

Andrew proposed naming the baby Roberts, because of his admiration for church leader and orator B. H. Roberts, though ironically, on the most controversial issue in the convention — whether women should vote — Andrew was in favor and B. H. Roberts led the opposition. Consequently Olive objected to the name and the baby was named Spencer Woolley Kimball — Woolley after her family.

At that time Andrew served as president of the Indian Territory Mission, principally in Oklahoma, overseeing missionary work from Utah by correspondence and by periodic visits. Between times he earned a living for his growing family as a traveling dry-goods salesman through Utah and southern Idaho. Nearly three years later, as he was selling in central

Utah, he received a call from the Church to replace the ailing president of the St. Joseph Stake, in southeastern Arizona.

Neither Andrew nor Olive had any desire to move to frontier Arizona. Both had lived in Salt Lake City all their lives. They assumed that Arizona would be a forbidding place, hot and desolate, a land of cactus, snakes, and Indian attacks. The little Mormon towns on the Gila River had only recently been settled, whereas Salt Lake City was already fifty years old. These were city folk being asked to become pioneers. Without enthusiasm, but committed to accepting the call, they set out.

SPENCER WAS THREE when the family of eight left Salt Lake City in a rainstorm. The trip to Thatcher, in the Gila Valley, took four wearying days by train through mountains and desert. They found the valley itself a green strip two miles wide along the river. A crowd of well-wishers greeted them. The wind was blowing so hard that scheduled singing was postponed, but the Saints showered them with rose petals.

With help, the Kimballs grubbed out mesquite stumps to make a ten-acre farm, and with Olive's inheritance, they had enough to build a brick house. They were cash-poor, but they got by.

As the stake president, Andrew was the leader of the several thousand Mormons and thus the most important and respected person in southeastern Arizona. Spencer adored his father and tried to emulate him.

Spencer grew up in a Mormon environment, and dependence on the Lord came naturally. After little Leo Cluff, a rancher's son, had been gored by a cow and the doctor gave him up for dead, Andrew blessed him by the power of the priesthood. And he was healed. Another day Spencer's one-year-old sister, Fanny, wandered away. After a frantic search, Clare, sixteen, said they should pray. After family prayer, Gordon, the oldest boy, walked right to where Fanny was sleeping in a large box behind the chicken coop.

As a child Spencer rarely missed a church meeting, often sleeping with his head on his mother's lap. And while he pumped water or milked the cows, he occupied his mind by memorizing things like the Articles of Faith or the Ten Commandments or words of the hymns. Spencer and his mother walked together down the dirt road to the bishop's house, taking tithing eggs. And when they cut hay, Andrew told his boys to get the tenth wagon load, which went to the tithing barn, from the best part of the field.

One hot day, hearing the bell calling children to Primary, Spencer told his brothers, "I've got to go to Primary." His brothers, who were pitching hay up onto the wagon for Spencer to tromp, said, "You're not going to Primary today." He responded, "If Pa were here, he'd let me go." "Well, Pa is not here and you're not going." They kept throwing hay up, but Spencer was already halfway across the field on his way to Primary. He said later, "I've always gotten lots of credit from people for being a very good Primary boy." In truth, the cool chapel was a lot more pleasant than tromping hay in the sun.

Health problems loomed large in most families. Spencer suffered from typhoid fever and facial paralysis, and nearly drowned as a small child. Four of his sisters died in infancy or childhood. His mother died when he was eleven. Seriously ill in her twelfth pregnancy, she went to Salt Lake City for treatment, her strength dwindling. A month later the Kimball children were called out of school and told by the bishop as gently as he could, "Your Ma is dead." Spencer ran out of the house, sobbing uncontrollably. His world had revolved around his small, gentle mother, who had never spoken ill of anyone. On arriving home from school, he said, "I would hang my cap on the hook by the door over the wash dish and holler, 'Ma! Ma! Ma!' But when I found her in the house and she asked what I wanted, I just said, 'Nothing.'" He only wanted to know that she was there. Now she was gone.

Ruth, then thirteen, dropped out of school for a while to mother the family, but after a few months their father felt they needed a mother, and he got their permission to marry again. In the summer he married Josie Cluff, a strong, capable woman who had reared two children of her own. None of them found it easy, not Andrew, not Josie, not the children; but they held on and made it work.

Spencer grew up physically strong and active, good at wrestling and a hard worker. He served his father as business secretary, learning to type and handle correspondence. Andrew expected precision from his sons. He said, "People won't ask how *long* it took to make a cupboard, but how *well* it is made."

Much to his surprise, when Spencer was fourteen the Sunday School superintendent asked him to teach a class; at fifteen he was stake chorister. About this time he heard Susa Young Gates speak at stake conference. When she asked who in the congregation had read the whole Bible, only a few hands went up. Spencer took the challenge and that night began to read by kerosene lamp. In his unfinished attic room he plowed through the Bible, page after page. A year later he finished with a sense of satisfaction.

In the small high school, his classmates elected him president each year. He was the one who, with a friend, caused school to be dismissed when they made rotten egg gas in chemistry laboratory. He was the ringleader when nearly all the boys in school skipped classes on April Fool's Day and were expelled until Spencer, as their spokesman, apologized. He played pranks, but he was not mean. Other boys stole or did senseless damage, such as slashing all the melons in a neighbor's patch. Spencer had no use for such conduct.

Sports occupied him. He starred on the basketball team. The high point of the year came in the high school's challenge game against the University of Arizona, whose team came and played them in a makeshift gymnasium in the basement of the chapel. The high school team won, and Spencer's teammates paraded him on their shoulders. Next night, on a neutral court, they lost, but nothing could take away the thrill of the first victory. When his school participated in a track meet with a makeshift team, the coach recruited him to run the mile. Spencer wrote of the great race, "Away I went and I did fairly well until my wind began to be lost. . . . My loyalty would have taken me to my death, I think, if the mile hadn't finally terminated. I'd rather die than quit. . . . Finally all seemed a blur and on the home stretch all I could see was a large crowd . . . shouting. I fell across the line. My good friends patted me on the back. . . . 'Well, Spencer, you came in third anyway.' Of course, I knew that there were only three of us running."

The twenty-one who graduated in his high school class gave as their class gift a stone pillar on which they generously mounted an engraved tablet listing their names, with Spencer's name at the top. At the graduation ceremonies Andrew Kimball, president of the board, announced that Spencer would not be in college in the fall, but on a mission. Spencer had no indication this was coming, but after he recovered from the shock, he was willing to go. He worked for the summer at a dairy, doing very hard work to earn two dollars a day. At the end of the summer his cigar-smoking non-Mormon boss presented him with a gold watch and held a farewell party for the boy, who had won his respect.

BEFORE LEAVING FOR HIS MISSION, Spencer attended a dance in Thatcher and met a new girl in the valley, Camilla Eyring, but the dance ended before he got around to dancing with her. He went to the Central States Mission where he did country tracting, without purse or scrip, asking for a place to stay among the homes he and his companion called on. One night a backwoods family gave them shelter in their one-room shack. The mother and children disappeared into the attic, while the father and one son shared a cot, leaving the missionaries the only bed. Spencer recognized that as a magnificent gesture.

The work was discouraging. His father wrote, "I am pleased with your game spirit. . . . You are small in stature—so was your sweet mother—but big natured and whole souled. Your hard experiences will enable you to know just a little of what it costs to be a Latter-day Saint and something of what your father and grandfather waded through. . . . It will all come out well and you will have something to tell your posterity."

Not long afterward, his sister Ruth, closest to him in age and his mother-substitute in many ways, died. Grief swept over Spencer, and it took a while for his sense of responsibility to overcome his emotions. But after a year in the mission field, President Samuel O. Bennion assigned him to St. Louis and

soon made him conference president over twenty-five missionaries, all older than he. Spencer worried that he was not
adequate to the assignment. Though he baptized only a handful
of people during his mission, his testimony had solidified. He
received no flash of insight, only a gradual strengthening of
commitment to serving the Lord.

In January 1917 Spencer returned home and soon registered
at the University of Arizona, where he worked hard for his
good grades and earned a little money helping an invalid
woman. He started missing some of his church meetings until
he said to himself, "What are you doing, Spencer Kimball?
You know that is the way out of the Church." He made a new
resolution to be faithful, which he kept.

Working that summer in Los Angeles freight yards, he
walked long miles to his sister's home to save a nickel in
carfare, reading a book as he went. He worked fourteen-hour
days, wheeling loads of up to a thousand pounds. When the
crudeness of conversation about him became more than he
could take, he decided to quit. His boss, reluctant to see him
go, hired him for another job as a freight checker, with easier
work and better pay.

Late in the summer, back in Arizona, he was working on
a ranch, digging a well, when he read in the newspaper about
Camilla Eyring's coming to teach school in the community.
He remembers thinking, "There's my wife. I am going to marry
her." Not bashful, he soon learned that she regularly took a
bus from the school in Thatcher to her parents' home in Pima,
a few miles away. He caught the same bus, introduced himself,
and they spent the trip trying to impress one another. He asked
if he might call on her. She said yes.

The next evening, as Camilla got ready for a dance, Spencer
arrived unannounced. She thought he might stay just a while,
so they sat on the porch. As the time for her date to arrive got
closer, she improvised. She and friends were going to a dance,
and did he want to go along? He said yes. When her date drove
up, she went out and asked whether this friend, who had just
dropped in, could go to the dance with them. Her date could
hardly refuse, but he drove "like the devil was after him," and

at the dance he refused to dance with Camilla, so she danced with Spencer.

Within a very short time Spencer left for Brigham Young University, and they exchanged affectionate letters. Because of the war, BYU had very few students: in public speaking he was the only student, in mathematics there were two, in history four, in theology six. Within only a few days Spencer, too, received a notice to report for a preinduction physical examination, and he returned to Arizona to wait the assembling of the next military contingent from his community.

His parents were away on an extended trip, so he had free use of their car. Since he had no work and no school, he courted Camilla all evening and slept all morning. She had to work all day and sometimes nodded in the classroom. Her students tittered when they saw Spencer waiting for her.

The couple swung on the Eyring gate and walked the railroad grade in the moonlight. Within a month they decided on marriage. They expected Spencer to leave any day. Camilla's family were pleased, but Spencer's parents did not even know of the decision because they were still away. Camilla could not get leave from her teaching position to go to the temple, so they scheduled the marriage for Friday, November 16, in the Eyring home, so they would have at least the weekend. Camilla had decorated the room with tree branches placed to cover holes in the wallpaper.

Spencer's induction kept being put off—indeed, it never took place—and Spencer worked at odd jobs. Camilla began a difficult pregnancy soon after the wedding, and Spencer finally got work in a bank. They rented a tiny house for six dollars a month and set up housekeeping with scant furniture. By summer they had saved enough money to travel to the Salt Lake Temple. The long trip proved difficult for the pregnant woman, but they had the satisfaction of knowing their marriage was sealed. In August Camilla delivered their first child, Spencer LeVan. Complications of childbirth left her in ill health for years.

Spencer knew nearly everyone in the valley and they knew him. He worked in the bank, kept books for a store, played piano in a dance band at nights, and served as stake clerk (which was then a paid employment). The stake had twenty-one units, making supervision of their record keeping a major undertaking. The long hours strained his eyes and made him irritable at home. Then he gave up the dance band and things went better.

In 1921 the bank moved Spencer to Safford, two miles away, and for $2,400 the Kimballs bought their first home, a small white frame house. Pecan and fruit trees and grapevines grew in the yard, and Spencer built a corral for their milk cow. He planted two small palm trees in the front yard to grow up with his family. The following year Camilla bore a girl with blue eyes and a reddish tint to her blond hair. They named her Olive Beth after her grandmother.

The depression of business between 1920 and 1922 hurt the bank where Spencer worked, and he took cuts in pay, happy to have a job at all. But in 1923 the bank still failed. Spencer had invested in the bank as a stockholder, and he lost the $3,000 he and Camilla had scrimped and invested over their six years of marriage.

Fortunately his good reputation produced three job offers. He took the position as chief teller at the Bank of Safford at the same $150 salary he had been receiving. The job gave him more responsibility and allowed him to learn new aspects of banking. He found the other tellers had an "over and short" petty cash box, which they used to adjust their balance at the end of the day. "Why don't you balance exactly?" he asked. They laughed that no one could handle as many transactions each day as they had to without making mistakes. He accepted the challenge, on condition they never take change from his window without his checking it. He balanced to the penny every day.

He had typed some for his father; now he taught himself to type with all his fingers by coming early to work and practicing from a typing book. He found the skill of immense benefit all his life.

In 1924 Andrew Kimball lay dying in Salt Lake City.

Spencer took leave from his bank to be with his father. He wrote home: "Poor father. . . . He throws his hands and pounds the bed and wrings his hands and runs his hands thru' his hair and straightens out and draws up his left leg, the only one he can move and moans and yells with all his strength. All night long every 10 or 15 seconds and repeats it. He cries O! My! over and over and sometimes O My God! How long! for hundreds of times then O! My! Father let me die. It is the most pitiful thing I ever saw. And still he lives on and his heart beats in spite of everything." The stressful time ended two days later.

President Heber J. Grant, a lifelong friend of Andrew's, accompanied the body to Arizona. At the cemetery Spencer broke down, sobbing uncontrollably. He had lost his mother at eleven and now his father at twenty-nine.

President Grant stayed to reorganize the stake over which Andrew Kimball had been president for twenty-six years. He called Harry L. Payne as president and young Spencer Kimball as one of the counselors. Spencer's two older brothers went to President Grant and urged that it was a mistake to put that responsibility on so young a man. President Grant closed the discussion by saying, "Spencer has been called to this work, and he can do as he pleases about it." Spencer and Camilla had talked of his going back to college to become an accountant or teacher, but the calling took precedence.

In 1925 Spencer and Bishop Joseph Greenhalgh began a sideline business of buying installment contracts. Two years later the bishop persuaded Spencer that they could make a go of an insurance and realty agency. After hesitation about leaving a job that paid enough to provide security for his growing family—now five, with the addition of a third child, Andrew Eyring—Spencer decided that the success of his own business would be largely determined by his wit and energy. Though he sometimes thought nostalgically of the secure paycheck, his income rarely dipped lower than his bank salary. The family survived the bad times by living thriftily, and they were even able to save and invest.

IN 1928, WITH BUSINESS PROSPECTS ROSY, Kimball-Greenhalgh bought twenty acres of prime land for $20,000 for development of eighty-two lots. They put in sidewalks and curbs, planted trees, and had begun to sell lots when the stock market crash of 1929 brought the national economy tumbling down. Almost overnight the lots stopped selling. They advertised an auction, hoping to sell some lots on an easy-payment plan. They hired a band and put up decorations and offered prizes. When the time came, the usually blue Arizona skies let loose a downpour, and no one came. Not a single lot sold.

In 1930 Camilla bore a little red-haired boy. They named him Edward Lawrence, after his grandfather Edward Eyring, making four children to care for. During this difficult depression time, barter became standard practice. When Camilla needed shoes for the children, she would ask, "Who owes us money that I can get shoes from?" She longed for the days when she could buy with cash and shop where she wished.

Spencer banked at the Bank of Safford, where he had worked. There were rumors of problems, but partly out of loyalty he left his money where it was. In 1932 the bank failed. The failure swept away not only his personal savings but also the accounts of organizations for which he was secretary or clerk—the canal companies, the Rotary Club, the St. Joseph Stake, estates of which he was executor—about $9000 in all. Kimball-Greenhalgh had $1400 on deposit in another bank, with which they were able to make their outstanding checks good, and that kept their reputation as a credit-worthy business solid. It hurt especially to learn that the failure resulted partly from embezzlement of $23,000 by one of their friends at the bank.

For years the agency did not sell a single lot or house. A little cash insurance business, some brokering of trades, and some miscellaneous income allowed the business to limp painfully along. Spencer wrote, "It is hard to keep optimistic. After a good night's rest I rush down to work all pepped up and ready for anything. In the first couple of hours about six or eight policies are returned (can't pay for them) and down drop my feathers. And by night time you feel like everything is gone to the bad."

The year 1933 brought both the depth of the depression and personal disaster. Shortly before Eddie's third birthday, he came in from play and complained of a sore throat. Vomiting, fever, and muscle weakness followed. The doctor finally made a diagnosis of the dreaded poliomyelitis. Fearfully Spencer and Camilla bundled the baby into their car and raced for Los Angeles, where a specialist put a frightened Eddie in an isolation room. Spencer and Camilla tearfully told him stories through the crack of the door as he screamed. Spencer had to return to the other three children, while Camilla stayed for several months. Daily letters exchanged concerns and advice:

My beloved Husband,
The day you receive this note will mark the sixteenth anniversary of our wedding. . . . Every year increases my love and respect. This separation is bitterly hard but it has made me realize more than ever before how much I have to be thankful for. . . . Never once in the time of our acquaintance have I found cause to doubt or mistrust. The attraction of sex and other things of course combine to make the perfect union but without confidence there can be nothing lasting.

My darling wife,
. . . Sixteen years is a long time for a girl to put up with one man and especially such a poor excuse as I am. . . . We have had our ups and downs, our disappointments and our surprises, our joys and our sorrows, and it has been a wonderful period. I want you to know that I love and appreciate you. You are the finest wife in the world.

Camilla bore the brunt of Eddie's care in succeeding years, often splinting his legs at night and massaging and exercising them daily. Nearly every summer he had another operation. Over the next eight years Spencer and Camilla made fifteen trips to Los Angeles, sometimes taking the other children along as part of a family vacation. Though Eddie had trouble walking, they treated him as they did the other children and expected him to work and do chores. It hurt them to hear him pray, "Bless me so that I can run and play and climb trees like the other children and fight!" But they let him learn, sometimes the hard way, that he could succeed at other things.

In 1934 Franklin D. Roosevelt took office, promising a New Deal. He declared a banking moratorium and issued sweeping banking regulations. Spencer said that these steps would surely mean loss of public confidence in banks and ruin to the country by deepening the Depression, but events proved him wrong. Roosevelt's ability to restore confidence caused money to flow back into the banks. Unemployment continued high, but gradual recovery was under way. Building lots began to sell. Kimball-Greenhalgh moved from a little office in the bank building to a Main Street location.

In the new office Spencer put his desk right out front, so he could see and greet people as they passed. People liked to do business with him, and Kimball-Greenhalgh hired two full-time people to help him. Spencer worked long hours and expected them to work hard too. The business stayed open six days a week, and when overtime came along, none of them expected extra pay. Having full-time help gave him added flexibility, so that he could attend to church responsibilities, such as going to the hospital or speaking at a funeral or traveling to general conference. He said that before he would work again as an employee, he would set up a peanut stand.

When Spencer visited the Eden Ward representing the stake presidency, he saw five boys on the front row acting in unison, crossing their legs, rubbing their chin, shifting in their seat. Finally he realized they were mimicking his movements; he took it as an object lesson.

Spencer contributed to the musical life of the valley. When he was young, he had taught himself to play the piano after only a few formal lessons and he had earned money with friends in a dance band. He led choirs and sang solos in a clear baritone voice. He and three friends formed a quartet, the Conquistadores, which sang frequently at clubs, entertainments, and funerals.

Even though Spencer was gregarious, when someone began to tell a dirty story in his presence he disassociated himself from it. He might interrupt to say, "I've already heard that story." Or if it were at a meal, he would put a big bite in his mouth as the punch line came, to show that he did not share in the joke.

He and Camilla had a circle of good friends who got together often. Spencer was the life of the party, loving to dance and tease and play good-natured pranks. He enjoyed sports — basketball, volleyball, handball, snowshoeing. But when they were hunting, he chose to tend camp and left the shooting to others.

Spencer and Camilla expected their children to work and save, be involved in church activities, take music lessons, do well in school, and go on missions — to be successful in whatever they did. The parents offered consistent support; when the children performed, they could expect to see one or both of their parents in the audience. Frequent physical expression of affection, light discipline, and individual responsibility were their methods, and the children usually responded as their parents hoped.

Spencer LeVan, the first child, was particularly precocious, but all the children excelled as students. Camilla had taught school and Spencer had wished to be a teacher. It pleased them that all their children pursued college education and that three became teachers, but Spencer taught them that educational success was praiseworthy only in the context of a rounded character.

The Kimballs were active in the community. In 1935 Spencer helped establish the first radio station in the area. "I have never seen anything happen in Safford to create such a sensation," he said. "Nearly every store or business place on Main Street has a radio and you can go down the street and hardly miss a word or note." Nearly every charitable drive involved Spencer. Camilla started the local PTA, worked as an election official, served as volunteer librarian, and presented book reviews.

Spencer joined the Rotary Club in 1923 and played the piano for meetings. He enjoyed the fellowship and saw it as furthering many goals in common with the Church. The local club raised money for youth camp and for free lunches for school children. After a term as the Safford club president, Spencer was persuaded by friends to run for district governor. Others perceived Mormons as a self-righteous lot, but Spencer managed to transcend the stereotype. After a year's vigorous campaigning, Spencer arrived at the 1935 convention only to learn that the campaign manager for Harold Smith, his prime opponent, had just dropped dead on the golf course. With the concurrence of his backers, when the convention began Spencer stood and withdrew his candidacy and nominated Harold Smith. After the dramatic moment, people swarmed about, congratulating him on the generous gesture. As a result of his conceding the election in 1935, no one even ran against him the next year.

At the international convention, the international president told the assembled district governors: "You naturally feel good when you visit a club and they stand and applaud you. But it is not *you* they are applauding; it is your position." Spencer remembered that when he received special treatment as a church leader.

As the year of leadership in Rotary ended, Camilla wrote in her journal, "It was a very pleasant experience but I really do not crave publicity. . . . I have a real ambition to learn to be quietly at ease under any circumstances and in any company, to take my place in a dignified yet simple manner. . . . I never expect to come as near the center of the stage again."

As a reward for his unusually productive service, his Rotary district voted to pay his travel expenses to the next international convention, to be held in France. The couple took Camilla's fare from savings and eagerly set off for Europe.

Because Spencer was forty-two and a small-town businessman, they perceived this to be the adventure of a lifetime, probably their only chance to see such faraway places. They sailed from Montreal, where LeVan was serving on his mission. They rushed to the rail to see whales and icebergs on their exciting first voyage. After the convention, they toured Europe for two months, seeing France, Italy, Hungary, Austria, Switzerland, Germany, the Netherlands, Belgium, France, and England. In London Camilla wrote, at the end of the long trip,

"I am so downright homesick tonight I just had to cry a bit. I have seen so much I have reached the saturation point."

SPENCER HAD BEEN STAKE CLERK before his call as a counselor in 1924 and at President Payne's request he continued "temporarily" for three years. When two successive clerks were released after relatively short service, Spencer again resumed double service as counselor and clerk. In 1935 the other counselor suggested that they needed him worse as a clerk than as counselor. When Elder Melvin J. Ballard visited the stake, he called Spencer as stake clerk again. Since the stake clerk received a modest salary, one of Spencer's friends wrote him, "Spencer, I'm disappointed in you. To think that you'd accept the money calling instead of the spiritual calling." She predicted that within six months Spencer would apostatize.

In 1938 Elder Ballard divided the St. Joseph Stake, creating the Mount Graham Stake and calling Spencer as president of the new stake, which ran from Safford, Arizona, to El Paso, Texas. Spencer felt inadequate. When he told Elder Ballard that there were people who would oppose him, the apostle lightly responded, "You can take care of that." Immediately after Elder Ballard set him apart, Spencer and Camilla went to visit some neighbors with whom there had been disagreements about water rights. Each party felt he had been wronged, but each swallowed his feelings and agreed to put the problem behind him.

Travel to each ward in the stake added up to 1,750 miles. Spencer and his counselors visited the wards repeatedly. Stake work involved many things. Spencer started a stake newsletter; he stood by while the doctor amputated a man's leg on a kitchen table; he performed weddings; he counseled the troubled; he administered to the sick; he spoke at funerals.

All through stake conference in September 1941, rain poured down. The Gila River, usually a shallow stream, rose high enough by Monday to flood Duncan, forty miles upriver from Safford. Water swirled down Main Street. Adobe houses melted and frame houses shifted. Spencer provided food and bedding from the interstake welfare storehouse to the homeless families in Duncan, a quarter of them Church members. Property loss was tremendous; whole farms washed away. Spencer correlated the generous relief efforts, including thousands of hours of work by machines in trying to restore the land. In all, it was a triumph for the Church Welfare Program, showing its power to deal with a local emergency.

On Camilla's birthday, December 7, 1941, the news buzzed over the radio that the Japanese had attacked Pearl Harbor. Young men went off to war. At one time 250 from the Mount Graham Stake were serving in the military. The two older Kimball sons and Olive Beth's husband enlisted in the Navy. Spencer served as chairman of a United War Fund campaign and as chairman of the local United Service Organization, and helped with the sale of war bonds and the collection of scrap metal. This typified his dozens of community involvements. He had served on the city council, helped with the Red Cross and the Boy Scouts, raised money for the local college and served on its board. He had worked against repeal of Prohibition and lobbied for requiring schools to teach about the dangers of alcohol. He served as director of the state organization of insurance agents and was named to a governor's commission on education. It is no wonder that he felt pressure, confiding in his journal, "My head whirls. I am bewildered in the impossibility of doing all I must do." On top of that, for ten years he suffered from boils, as many as twenty-four at one time.

In 1940 Spencer and Camilla were able to move into a new, larger, Pueblo-style home built to their own specifications for $5,000. It had six rooms and a bath and a half. By 1942 business was prospering and they had challenging work and church responsibilities. Their twenty-fifth wedding anniversary found them in a mood to celebrate. They sent out six hundred invitations to friends to come to their home, staggering the times so that the crowd would not all come at once, but their friends came and stayed, packing the home till people could not move; they had a grand time. Of this period Camilla said, "We loved the feeling of permanence and security our new home gave us. In fact, we felt we had established an estate where we would end our days."

WHEN SPENCER ATTENDED GENERAL CONFERENCE in April 1943, he was asked to open the conference with prayer and he received dinner invitations from four different General Authorities. He was gratified with what he took to be an expression of the Brethren's satisfaction with his handling of the Duncan flood.

On Thursday, July 8, 1943, Spencer arrived home for lunch just as Eddie said into the telephone, "Here he comes now. Daddy, Salt Lake City is calling!" Though he had often had such calls, in that instant he had an overpowering feeling that he was to be called to a high position, but he thrust it aside as a presumptuous thought. J. Reuben Clark, Jr., counselor in the First Presidency, said, "Spencer, do you have a chair handy? The Brethren have just chosen you to fill one of the vacancies in the Quorum." Spencer had difficulty assimilating what he had heard. "You don't mean me? There must be some mistake. I am so weak." He thought of all the petty things he had done and imagined the people he had offended saying to him, "How could *you* be an apostle of the Lord? You are not worthy. You are *insignificant*. You *can't* do it." Spencer asked if he could come to Salt Lake City to discuss the call and that was arranged. He exchanged pleasantries absent-mindedly and then hung up.

Spencer faced his wife and two children. "They have called me to be an apostle," he said unsteadily. After a silent lunch he lay on the floor to rest, but his mind raced. He reviewed the sacrifices it would require of him and his family, his own limitations, and the commitments he had made to obey the Lord's direction. Tears came, then convulsive sobbing. Camilla stroked his hair, trying to comfort him. "You *can* do it," she reassured him. "You can do anything the Lord asks of you." When he finally returned to his office, with his face flushed, his helper assumed he had been playing handball on his lunch hour.

That night no sleep came, and for six nights, despite near exhaustion, sleep came only fitfully. Camilla knew, but no one else. Day and night he prayed for forgiveness, strength, and assurance. "Please tell me, Lord, that all is well and that

I am acceptable to you." On Tuesday they arrived in Boulder, Colorado, where LeVan and his family lived. Wednesday morning early Spencer slipped out of the house and hiked to the hills, without destination. He nearly stepped on a coiled rattlesnake and wondered if that were a symbol. He wept openly as he climbed, wondering whether he was being called by revelation or because of his efficiency as stake president or because President Clark was his cousin. He desperately wanted confirmation from the Lord. He stumbled up the rough mountainside, without a path, thinking of his parents and grandparents and wondering what they thought of him and his life. Finally he reached a high cliff, where he found a cross of tree limbs. He thought how easily his anguish could be blotted out by falling from that high place. And he thought of Christ's temptation. Then a wave of shame swept over him for even comparing himself with the Master. He lay on the earth and for a long time he prayed, he suffered, he wept.

Finally he received the special assurance he had struggled for. He felt a calm like the dying wind, the quieting wave after the storm is over. His tears stopped; his soul felt peace. Though he had taken a steep, rocky way up, he found an easy path down. This time he knew where he was going.

In Salt Lake City David O. McKay, first counselor to President Grant, reassured him of his call. Because they wanted him to be able to sell his business and home and move his family to Church headquarters in Salt Lake City, they announced his call to the newspapers and radio immediately.

When he returned to Arizona, he had a hard time tending to business because so many people wanted to extend congratulations. "It was inevitable," said some. "I knew it was coming," said others. Then Evans Coleman, who had known Spencer from his boyhood, said, "It's clear the Lord must have called you, Spencer, because no one else would have thought of you."

Farewell parties, stake responsibilities, business affairs, family arrangements all crowded his time. LeVan was married and in the Navy; Olive Beth worked in an office in San Francisco; Andrew and Edward were in high school. By the end of

August, Spencer had moved Camilla and the two younger sons to Salt Lake City to stay with a relative until housing became available.

Then he returned to Arizona, racing to conclude his responsibilities there. He attended three wards of his stake the same day. "All the meetings started out as regular testimony meetings and ended in testimonials for me. I told the boys as we went late to the last two meetings that I was the first corpse I had ever seen that had three funerals in one day and was late for two of them."

Just as school began in Salt Lake City, a polio scare closed down all public gatherings, including schools, churches, movies, dances. Camilla lay ill and homesick; the two boys felt miserable at being uprooted. Andrew, sixteen, acted like a caged lion. He was losing his last year in the high school, where he would have been class president and a star athlete. Spencer wrote a long epistle to his children, expressing love, acknowledging their sacrifices, and calling for their commitment. He expressed his personal feelings of inadequacy, "but I have accepted the work. I am relying on you to help me." The crisis blew over.

It seemed to Spencer that everyone in Arizona wanted to have a party for him or invite him to dinner, but on the train he wrote to Camilla, "There was not a soul came to say good-bye. . . . I have been so much honored I am ashamed to mention it, but you, knowing my weakness for demonstration of appreciation, will understand me. Now I have forgotten that. And now I am on my way to the great adventure of my life."

October conference began. Seven thousand hands raised to sustain Spencer as an apostle of Christ. Afterward he knelt before the invalid president, Heber J. Grant, and received his ordination to the apostleship. He accepted the admonition "to make this cause and this labor first and foremost in all your thoughts."

BEING AN APOSTLE brought many new experiences—stake conferences, mission tours, temple sealings, setting apart missionaries, meetings with General Authorities. The Church in 1943 had 146 stakes and 38 missions, with about 900,000 members, a large share of them within one hundred miles of Salt Lake City. A major part of his work entailed dealing with people, their joys and especially their problems. Through his door streamed a prospective missionary wanting to bear his testimony, a young man who had been unable to admit to his bishop serious sins, a woman unreconciled to the death of her son in the war, a deserted wife, an engaged couple asking him to perform their temple marriage, a bickering married couple, a young woman asking whether she should marry a young man who seemed to be losing his testimony, a man who demanded excommunication to express his anger at his bishop. Other times he went to them—a mentally ill patient at the Veterans' Hospital, a neighbor suffering from cancer, an alcoholic who called him for help, a youth in trouble with the police, a blind man who needed someone to accompany him through the temple.

His first mission tour was of the Western States Mission. He and the mission president pushed hard, holding more than forty meetings and traveling 4500 miles by car in seventeen days through Colorado, New Mexico, Nebraska, South Dakota, and Wyoming. In Wyoming a public official advised them not to try to get to Rawlings through snowdrifts, but Spencer knew that a congregation would be waiting. They carried an ax, firewood, extra blankets, and finally reached their destination by way of a long detour.

No apostle brought greater concern for details to his stake conference assignments. He did his homework and analyzed statistical reports. After he returned home he wrote with specific suggestions and asked for follow-up reports.

He had a marvelous memory for people. After a stake conference, a young woman shook his hand and said, "I thought you might remember me because I am Blanch's sister." He replied, "No, I remember you because you're Julia."

Spencer did not spare himself in traveling, working, counseling, and administering to the needs of the people. He gave many blessings and sometimes had a clear sense that he was inspired. Other times he could not tell. Usually he asked the Lord for a blessing, "if it be thy will," but sometimes he promised recovery and trembled afterward with the responsibility.

Visiting in the homes of stake leaders nearly every week, he would play the piano for the children and sing with them. "They'll forget my sermons, but they'll never forget my songs." And he was quick to help with the milking. In one such place he was followed at the next conference by Bishop Marvin O. Ashton, who reported jokingly that as he drove up to the stake president's farm, there on the gate hung overalls and a milk bucket for him.

President Grant died in May 1945 at eighty-eight, after twenty-six years as president. This man had been an apostle for thirteen years before Spencer's birth. Spencer rushed home from visiting the Eastern States Mission to participate in the funeral and in the naming of the new president.

During President Grant's last several years, J. Reuben Clark, Jr., and David O. McKay, his counselors, had handled most Church affairs. George Albert Smith at seventy-five was the senior apostle. Some urged that if succession inevitably followed seniority, the president would almost always be an old man, but discussion in the Quorum resulted in unanimous agreement that George Albert Smith should succeed to the presidency.

Spencer worked in the Heber C. Kimball family organization as president, starting a newsletter, reprinting his grandfather's biography, and gathering genealogy records. His position as a General Authority stirred new interest and pride in the family.

His first involvement with really poverty-stricken Church members occurred during a three-week mission tour in Mexico. The people's faithfulness in the face of great difficulty impressed him deeply. One of the dancers in a program wore a suit belonging to a missionary, who went to bed because he had no other clothes.

In 1947 Spencer was assigned to try to reconcile factions in a rural ward torn by dissension. They met at seven in the evening. He listened for hours as people denounced one another bitterly. In his turn, he proposed that if the people could not forgive one another, it might be necessary to dissolve the ward. Some still resisted, and he quoted scriptural incidents and admonitions about forgiving. There was still hardness. Finally he preached with power, from the scriptures, that those who refuse to forgive others commit the greater sin. And at two in the morning the meeting finally ended in tears of forgiveness. He admonished them that they must never again raise the dead issues, and he later wrote each family individually to reinforce his admonition.

He enjoyed telling stories about himself: A Primary class came in with their teacher, who obviously had primed them with pictures of the apostles. She said to the children, "Now, who can tell me who this man is?" For a long while no one spoke, until a boy, scratching his head, answered, "I know I've seen that mug somewhere." Another time a person came up after stake conference and said, "I'm glad you came, Brother Richards. I always used to get you mixed up with Elder Lee."

Spencer became deeply involved in missionary work to the Indians in 1946 when President Smith called him into his office and said, "I want you to look after the Indians in all the world." In a patriarchal blessing, Samuel Claridge had said to Spencer, "You will preach the gospel to many people, but more especially to the Lamanites." He had long wondered how it would come about.

Soon afterward he woke in the night with a strange foreboding. He felt something horrible in the room and sensed an enemy, unseen but very real, trying to destroy him. He sweat and fought until he remembered from the temple ceremony that he could use the power of the priesthood to rebuke the evil spirit. He did so. Afterward he wondered whether the work he had just begun offered some special threat to Lucifer.

Spencer began to travel on the reservations, meeting with members, teaching the gospel, blessing the sick, assessing attitudes and problems, trying to deal with the hostility of ministers of other churches who opposed letting missionaries live on the reservations or chapels be built. Progress was slow.

In 1947 a harsh early winter left many Navajos close to

starvation, and Spencer stirred up interest in helping them by writing articles for newspapers and magazines, giving talks, contacting service clubs, and petitioning Congress. A caravan of food and clothing made its way to relieve the immediate suffering. But he concluded, as he became better acquainted with the chronic problems, that education and improved roads were the keys to long-term improvement of Indian conditions.

During that same winter, a seventeen-year-old Indian girl, Helen John, who worked in the sugar-beet fields in Utah, begged her employers to let her stay in a tent on their farm all winter so she could go to school. When they asked Golden Buchanan of the stake presidency for advice, the idea opened up in his mind to place Indian children in Latter-day Saint homes during the school year. He immediately wrote to Elder Kimball, and a few days later the apostle showed up on his doorstep. He asked the Buchanans whether they would themselves take Helen into their home as if she were their daughter. After a prayerful night, they agreed. Homes were found for other children, and the program grew until by 1954, under Elder Kimball's encouragement, it became an official Church program, with sixty-eight children. It grew to nearly five thousand children before improved conditions on the reservations caused the number to decline.

To the Indians, Spencer preached responsibility for their own progress; to the whites, he preached the need to accept and to help. "The only difference between us and the Indian is opportunity. Racial prejudice is of the devil and of ignorance."

THOUGH HIS WORK caused a heavy drain on his energies, Spencer did not stop for anything. While he was touring the Indian mission in 1948, the car stuck in the desert sand. He and Golden Buchanan pushed their utmost again and again to get it free. That night agonizing pain struck. It passed and Spencer determined to finish his tour. After a week more, he had pushed himself to exhaustion. When the results of an electrocardiogram were in, his doctor insisted that Spencer quit Church work for a month. That seemed impossible, so he decided that he would just be careful. That night pain struck again, and a few days later more severe pains. He lay awake through the night discussing funeral plans and family finances with Camilla, thinking he was about to die.

As he recovered from this heart attack, he felt deep depression about failing his responsibility. After seven weeks of house confinement, he was driven by Golden Buchanan to the Navajo Reservation, where they pitched a tent near the hogan of Howela Polacca. Spencer read and rested and walked a little and carved a crude self-portrait in sandstone for two peaceful weeks. He returned to work, feeling good, but just a week later the pain returned, and the First Presidency sent him to California to be away from calls and callers. To occupy himself, he worked out a twenty-five-foot time line on a roll of shelf paper, showing in parallel columns the secular and religious history of the world.

After six weeks by the sea, he returned to Salt Lake City and reported for duty. President Smith urged him to be careful, said that he and the church loved him, and kissed him on the forehead. Such gestures Spencer recorded and treasured.

For several years, when Spencer became fatigued or under stress from dealing with people's problems, the pains in his heart would return, but he did not tell his Brethren. A year after the heart attack, he found himself back in Arizona. He invited a friend who seemed to be drifting spiritually to go camping with him. The friend offered to buy the food, but Spencer said they would not need any food, because he hoped they would fast. They camped out from Saturday to Monday at a meadow in the high mountains, read the scriptures, prayed, and talked out the friend's erroneous concepts. When they prepared to leave, the car would not start. They worked at length with no results. Then they prayed for help, and after a moment's further tinkering, the car started. Gradually the friend grew back to full faith.

In 1950 Spencer began to worry about persistent hoarseness. A cancer specialist found a suspicious spot on one of his vocal cords and took a biopsy under anaesthetic. As an orderly wheeled Spencer back to his room, the young man uttered a profanity. Spencer, half-conscious, pleaded, "Please don't say that. I love Him more than anything in this world. Please."

The doctor concluded there was no cancer but that the cord needed to be cauterized. Spencer put that off and received a priesthood administration instead. His voice returned with strength, and the doctor decided cauterization would not be needed.

GEORGE ALBERT SMITH DIED at the time of general conference in April 1951, on his eighty-first birthday. Spencer wrote of the temple meeting to name a successor that when David O. McKay, president of the Quorum, stood to speak, "I saw him as the President of the Church. . . . There was no doubt in my mind. It was . . . like a sudden flood of warmth and into my mind came the thought: 'A prophet's mantle.'" Spencer considered this manifestation an indication of divine favor.

President McKay was seventy-seven, but vigorous and even youthful in comparison with his predecessors. He brought dynamism to the missionary effort and traveled more widely than any president ever had.

Spencer received the assignment to deal with cases involving sexual immorality and homosexuality, and he counseled hundreds of troubled people. Themes related to these problems began to surface more often in his sermons. He preached on modesty, calling for "a style of our own," and he talked about the difference between love and lust. Each such talk brought him more counseling to do. He said once during a mission tour, "When they fail to take care of their marriage, they'll come to the point of divorce and sit in my office and say they don't love one another, that they never did." He went on heatedly, "That's a damned lie!"

On the other side he received great satisfaction in meeting with competent, faithful stake leaders each weekend.

Assigned to visit the stake in which he lived, he thought about testimony meetings when few stood, and sacrament meetings with secular music instead of hymns, and decided, after earnest prayer, to simply confront his neighbors with their worldliness and lack of spirit. In his talk he asked them to stop addressing one another as doctor, colonel, judge; in the Church everyone is brother or sister. He told them to support one another and to enter into the spirit of the Lord's work more. While the statistics looked good, the people lacked something important. After the scolding he expected resentment, so he was surprised at the numerous expressions of appreciation for his directness and practicality.

After he toured a mission, he usually wrote individual letters to the families of the missionaries he met. He carried a staggering load of correspondence, doing much of the typing himself. He wrote long letters of encouragement to all manner of people. One Christmas a group of fifty Indian children each sent him a letter. He responded with fifty long, individual letters of thanks and admonition.

Camilla once received a bouquet of roses with an anonymous note, saying that Spencer had gone out of his way to help someone on crutches manage a package. "Since he is the type of man who would appreciate a gift to you more than to himself, it pleases me to send you these roses."

In February 1955, President McKay announced that rather than maintain a General Authority in Europe to preside over the ten missions there, he would periodically assign a General Authority to tour the missions. Spencer received the first such assignment. Delighted, he mailed instructions to the missions and asked for a proposed schedule of meetings. When the schedules came, he returned them with the request to "double the number of meetings."

In Europe a devastating war had reduced many major cities to rubble. Despite this, he urged the Saints in the thirteen countries he visited to stay where they were and build up Zion there. A new temple, accessible to them, would soon be dedicated in Switzerland.

In the Netherlands he went for an early morning walk on the beach and returned to the mission home with a young man in tow. The youth spoke only a little English and Spencer had brought him back to receive a pamphlet on Joseph Smith.

By the time the Kimballs arrived in Switzerland for the

temple dedication, Spencer had spoken to half of the 36,000 Latter-day Saints in Europe and had met with a thousand full-time missionaries. Despite the stress, his body held out until the assignment ended. Then he came down immediately with a bad cold.

Spencer returned to the United States and the routine of stake conference visits, counseling, and shoring up the some-times-sagging work among Indians. He and Elder Mark E. Petersen drove to the Navajo reservation to get signatures of four tribal councilmen on a petition to allow Church buildings on the reservation. In one day they traveled over four hundred miles of nearly impassable roads, getting stuck in deep sand repeatedly, before they could get one signature. Another day produced a second. With that kind of commitment on his part, he was bothered when a member of the Twelve, after having visited the mission, reported that not much progress was being made. He saw the other apostle as not realizing how difficult the work would be and how much progress had been made since the beginning, just ten years before.

In December 1956, en route to a stake conference in Arizona, Spencer had a strong feeling he should go the long way around, by way of Las Vegas, but he shrugged it off because the roads seemed good and the snow light. Coming down the mountain through the Kaibab forest, Spencer and Camilla suddenly confronted a truck stuck in the road and they skidded off, heading straight downhill. In the bottom of the ravine Spencer found he was only shaken up, and he said, "Well, Mama, I guess we are all right," but Camilla groaned in pain, "No, I am dying." With help he managed to bend the fender away from the tire and get the car out along a wood road back to the highway. The car struggled back thirty-five miles to Kanab, where Camilla went into the hospital with broken ribs, punctured lung, and cuts and bruises.

Spencer went on to his appointed conference in Arizona by bus. Just a few days before Christmas, after twelve days in the hospital, Camilla returned home, and on Christmas day she prepared turkey dinner for twenty-three family members.

The hoarseness that had disappeared after a blessing in 1950 came back. When Spencer visited the New York Stake in February 1957, he arranged to see a throat specialist. He approached the occasion fearfully, thinking of his sister's terrible suffering with cancer, but then calm came over him as he considered that he had lived long enough to see his children well settled and had given thirteen years of service as an apostle. Dr. Martin concluded from a biopsy that Spencer had "borderline malignancy" and that eventual removal of the larynx was indicated. Spencer saw only a bleak future. Even if he should survive, how could he do his work without a voice? He put the decision off.

While his throat recovered from the biopsy, he had to be silent, writing rather than speaking. A man in the Church offices consulted with him, speaking while Spencer typed his half of the discussion. Finally he said, "You know, Brother Kimball, I've dealt before with people who were deaf and dumb, but you're the first person I've known who was just plain dumb." Most people assumed that because he could not speak he was also deaf, so they tended to shout. On the other hand, a little grandson assumed things must be secret and whispered in his ear. A friend at a dinner club remarked, "Well, at least you can eat."

Gradually he began to whisper. Four months after the biopsy, his throat was not healing; so at President McKay's direction, Spencer, Camilla, and Harold B. Lee went back to New York. This time Dr. Martin prescribed immediate removal of the larynx. The apostles explained the unique importance of Spencer's voice and obtained a commitment that the surgeon would take as little tissue as possible; that meant one vocal cord entirely and part of the other.

The operation would mean the end of a normal voice, and over the weekend Spencer talked freely, almost frantically. Intellectually he accepted the decision, but he struggled in spirit until Elder Lee administered to him. When he awoke he had a four-inch incision down his neck and a tube in his windpipe. For weeks that seemed interminable, he suffered. The infected wound healed slowly. He wrote hundreds of letters on his typewriter. Finally he tried out his voice and found there still was a weak, rough rasp—not much, but it was something, and he determined to make the most of it.

When he received his first assignment following the operation, to help two other apostles dividing a stake, he participated in nine hours of meetings with constant intense pain from a giant carbuncle on his stomach, but he said nothing because he was so glad to be back in the work.

Six months after the operation, he attended stake conference in the Gila Valley. Elder Delbert L. Stapley, the appointed visitor, invited him to speak. Spencer feared public speaking, but he decided that he would never find a more sympathetic audience for his gruff voice. He started by telling his friends that he had gone to New York and fallen among cutthroats. They laughed, and he knew he could still handle public speaking.

IN 1959 SPENCER VISITED THE MISSIONS in Argentina, Chile, Uruguay, Paraguay, Brazil, and Peru. Among other problems, he had to advise on a policy for couples who wanted to be baptized but were living together while legally married to others. The former marriage had dissolved in fact, but the law had no provision for divorce. By custom the government authorities simply ignored the technical crime. Spencer recommended that if the people had done what they could to regularize their relationship and were faithful to one another, they should not be denied baptism. He also saw a number of members of the Church who were black or of mixed blood and felt great sympathy for them in their inability to receive the priesthood.

People were always his first concern. As he visited one stake, a bishop asked if he could bless a dying man in the hospital. Between meetings they raced to the hospital and ran up the stairs and down the hall. As they entered the room, the bishop recalled, "there was an amazing change. Elder Kimball seemed to have all the time in the world." They visited unhurriedly, administered to the man, and took their leave. Once out the door, they ran to the car and sped back to the conference, arriving just after the afternoon session had begun.

Still concerned with work among the Indians, Spencer and Elder Petersen got permission to show a motion picture about the Indian student placement program to the Navajo tribal council. When the time came to show the film, only a handful of people showed up; a wrestling match at the fairgrounds proved too much competition. They felt heartsick, because they believed the film would influence the council's attitude toward the Church. After they prayed for help, they received permission to show the film the next day. Just before they were to show the film, the power failed; they suspected sabotage. It appeared that the meeting would go on and their chance would be lost. But the vice-chairman, whom they expected to be hostile, invited them to say something while they waited for an extension cord. Finally the film started, but sunlight washed out the picture; then clouds moved in to darken the room. Elder Kimball thanked the Lord as he watched doubtful looks change to attention and interest. The council took a standing vote of appreciation for the Church's interest in Indian education.

In October 1960 the Church sent Spencer to organize four new stakes in Australia and New Zealand. While there, he had the grievous responsibility of participating in the excommunication of several missionaries who had become involved in sexual immorality. He mourned the fact that any of twenty missionaries might have been able to prevent the tragedy if they had just reported the situation to the mission president before problems became acute.

Spencer and Camilla came home by completing the circuit of the globe. In India they met with Mangal Dan Dipty, a young preacher who had become converted after reading Church literature and receiving a spiritual manifestation that what he read was from God. They explained the gospel to him and discussed the likely consequences of his baptism, that he would lose friends and family and his position, and that he would be alone, perhaps the only Latter-day Saint in a vast area. But he persisted, and after three days together Spencer decided he could not refuse this brave young man. He performed the baptism in a muddy river.

They continued on through the Near East and Egypt to Jerusalem. After a lifetime of studying the scriptures, they thrilled at being in the places they had read about. Shrines erected over most places made it hard to recapture the past, except at the Garden Tomb. There especially they prayed together in gratitude for their knowledge of Christ. Later that same year they returned to experience Christmas in Bethlehem, but they were sorely disappointed at the crowds and hubbub. Only in the silence of the hillside where the angels announced Christ's birth to the shepherds did they capture the sense of what it might have been like.

Travel is a major part of an apostle's life. Airplane travel greatly expanded Spencer's range. Once when airplane trouble caused his trip across the Great Plains to take twelve hours, he wryly noted that he had new sympathy for the pioneers. He made missionary contacts on planes. He helped strangers. In a Chicago airport, stranded by bad weather, a pregnant young mother stood in line trying to get a plane to Michigan. She had a hungry, wet two-year-old on the floor, whom she was pushing along with her foot because she was threatened with miscarriage. A man offered her help and got people to let her move up in the line. Then he held her child while she arranged a flight. Later, from a picture, she recognized the stranger as Spencer Kimball.

As an apostle he often felt spiritual guidance, as when he interviewed potential stake leaders and felt a kind of recognition when the right man came in. But he spent much of his time in detail work. He helped write a new handbook for stake and ward leaders, chaired the church budget committee, worked on a new hymnbook and continued to be responsible for the Indian work.

Twelve thousand Indians now belonged to the Church. Spencer promoted their cause tirelessly. When a young white woman's parents came to him, objecting to her plan to marry an Indian man, he told them that while there might be adjustment problems for two people with such different backgrounds, there was no wrong in it. He performed the wedding, though the bride's parents refused to attend.

In 1963 he became a member of the missionary committee. Often at conferences he called to the stand boys who were twelve and asked, "What will you be doing when you are nineteen?" If they did not know, he reminded them that they would be serving a mission; then he would give them each a dollar for their missionary fund. He sometimes called up girls, too, and gave them a dollar toward the expense of traveling to the temple for their marriage. A friend gave him a box of silver dollars labeled "Seeds for the Spencer W. Kimball Missionary Garden."

In 1964 Elder Kimball visited the seven missions in South America. When he had visited there five years earlier, there were 9,000 members on the continent. Now a thousand missionaries were baptizing a thousand members a month. Poverty and runaway inflation made it impossible for members to come to temples in the United States. "One day we must have a temple in South America," he thought.

The next year he was assigned, with Elder Franklin D. Richards, to supervise those same missions. When they were about to offer a prayer on a hilltop in Quito, dedicating Ecuador for the teaching of the gospel, some tourists happened along. Spencer invited them to participate in the brief service. At a hotel Elder Kimball asked their waiter whether he would like his children to receive "food" that would benefit them forever. He arranged for the missionaries to visit the man's family. He also struck up acquaintance with a likely looking shoeshine boy in the park and corresponded with him for some years, hoping that he might accept the gospel.

At seventy-two the hard travel of several trips a year to South America wearied Spencer, but he felt strength coming from purpose and specific divine blessing. Once in Chile the Kimballs slept three nights in the mission car while being driven long distances from one conference to another. When the tour ended, a mechanic looked the car over and concluded it was impossible for the car to be running because the generator brushes were completely worn off.

While the Kimballs and a mission president and his wife waited through the night in the cold airport lounge at Bogota, the president's wife refused to take Spencer's coat, so he waited until she was asleep, then covered her with his coat. He and the mission president, too cold to sleep, walked about the lounge all night, discussing missionary work.

Spencer obtained permission from President McKay to begin proselyting among the millions of Indians in the Andean Altiplano, many of whom spoke only their Indian dialect. He spoke to these Indians personally for the first time at a street meeting at a junction of paths in the Indian town of Peguchi. More than a hundred gathered to hear the mission president tell them that the Book of Mormon was a record of their people. Elder Kimball then told of the visit of Jesus Christ to their ancestors and endorsed the four missionaries as bearers of truth. As he described Christ's descent out of heaven, all eyes looked to the skies. He had never felt more stimulated by a meeting, and he saw in the responsiveness of the Indians a precursor of great things.

Even though Spencer was basically apolitical, he saw some political trends in the United States that disturbed him, especially increasing government taxation and regulation and increasing military involvement by the United States in Vietnam, with its effect on availability of young men to serve missions. Widespread disrespect for authority and the destructive riots in American cities also bothered him. In the name of civil rights, BYU and the Church were made targets because the Church did not confer the priesthood on blacks. Missionary deferments from military draft also came under legal attack.

After four years with the South American missions, Elder Kimball was reassigned to supervise the Church in Great Britain. One hundred thirty years before, his grandfather had helped reap a mighty harvest of converts in England. Spencer felt the spirit in Britain somewhat lax now. Despite the Saints' difficult conditions, he thought they could do more to send missionaries, support missionary work, and build sacrament meeting attendance and home teaching up from very low levels. Part of the problem was discouragement stemming from "baseball baptisms." Under his urging, a strong effort was made to find and reclaim those young people who had been summarily baptized, but when that failed, their names were dropped, to allow concentration of effort on real converts. Camilla traveled with him, helping the mission presidents' wives with meetings for the women and looking after Spencer.

He wrote in his mid-seventies, "It seems to me that friends of my own age are very old and are getting feeble. . . . I still feel so vigorous." But he still had occasional chest pains and a bad back, and some renewed problems with his throat. Of a typical day he wrote, "I started out very miserable and found myself wondering if I could get through the day, but . . . I seemed to become intoxicated with my work and forgot myself and it was a good day."

THE WORLD AND THE CHURCH have always had moral problems, but Spencer perceived them as growing more widespread and more virulent. For years he had preached repentance. In 1969 he published a book, *The Miracle of Forgiveness*, on which he had been working for ten years in spare time, usually the few weeks in the summer when he had no stake conference appointments. He had often said that there were already books enough, but he finally put into writing his feelings about how people could and should become reconciled to the Lord after making mistakes. The book grew out of long experience and deep personal concern and knowing that even active Latter-day Saints needed his message. Once as he was setting apart a bishop's counselor, he put his hands on the man's head and quickly said, "Did I interview you for this position?" The man said, "No." The apostle then took each of the bishopric aside for an interview, and the counselor who had given him pause proved to have been guilty of repeated acts of adultery.

A woman came to him in the temple and asked, "Do you remember me?" Embarrassed, he admitted he did not. Relief lighted her face. "You worked and prayed with my husband

and me until three o'clock in the morning. If after these nineteen years of repentance you do not remember me or my sins, perhaps the Lord will also remember them no more. Thank you."

The book obviously met a need, going into half a million homes in the next fifteen years. Hardly a mail went by without letters of appreciation.

In January 1970 President McKay died, after nineteen years as president of the Church. Two-thirds of the members had known no other president. The number of stakes had grown from 180 to 500. The Council of the Twelve named Joseph Fielding Smith president of the Church, despite his ninety-three years. President Smith called Harold B. Lee, the next in seniority, as a counselor in the First Presidency and set Spencer apart as acting president of the Twelve.

When biopsy showed a recurrence of cancer in Spencer's throat, he considered treatment options. Then a bombshell burst. A diagnostic probe showed his growing fatigue resulted from impending heart failure, but there seemed no point in a heart operation unless the throat cancer could be checked. Twenty-four cobalt treatments succeeded in destroying the cancer, and then the heart operation could proceed. He had perhaps a seventy-five percent chance of survival and the hope of five or six more good years, but he wondered whether it made sense to "fight so hard to extend my life when perhaps my time had come." President Lee urged him to submit to the operation, saying that he still had work to do.

Dr. Russell Nelson performed the operation, bypassing a clogged artery and putting in place a steel and plastic ball-and-cage heart valve. The doctor later said he felt divine guidance in the operation; it had gone perfectly in every detail. He sensed that the man whose heart he held in his hands would preside over the Church.

During Spencer's recovery, in July 1972, President Smith died suddenly and quietly just before his ninety-sixth birthday. Harold B. Lee succeeded him, making Spencer Kimball president of the Twelve and second in seniority. Spencer and Camilla prayed earnestly for President Lee's welfare, not only for the usual reasons, but because the awesome responsibility of presidency might fall upon Spencer if the younger and more vigorous President Lee should happen to die first.

December 26, 1973, evening. Spencer received a call from Arthur Haycock, President Lee's personal secretary, that the president lay suddenly very ill. Spencer rushed to the hospital. He asked President Marion G. Romney for instructions, and President Romney said there was nothing to do but wait. By nine o'clock President Lee had passed away. President Romney then turned to Elder Kimball, now the senior apostle, and asked him, "What would like you me to do?"

ON SUNDAY, DECEMBER 30, 1973, the Council of the Twelve named Spencer Woolley Kimball the twelfth president of the Church. He had been an apostle for thirty years. At seventy-eight and with his health history, most people thought his administration would be a rather short, "caretaker" period. One little boy, brought into his office to shake his hand, said frankly, "I wanted to see you before you died."

At President Lee's funeral, Spencer said, "A giant redwood has fallen and left a great space in the forest." He had to fill that space, yet he was not alone. One night he felt President Lee's spirit near, reassuring him. Another night, half sleeping, he saw his father. He felt the Lord's guidance in many of his decisions: business decisions, spiritual decisions, public relations decisions. The demands on his time were incredible, but he tried to see visitors whenever he could; he did not want to be isolated from the people.

He had assumed he knew what it might be like to be president of the Church, but he had had no idea of the extra stress in bearing ultimate earthly responsibility for the welfare of 3.3 million people. Everything he said and did carried an unaccustomed weight.

At a seminar for Regional Representatives just before general conference in April, he talked about missionary work, and the unused capacity in the Church, a talk similar to talks he had given before. He urged that the Lord would open doors only when the Saints were prepared to walk through them, and he asked, "Are we prepared to lengthen our stride?" Now that he spoke as the prophet, people responded. The number of missionaries, which had already been growing, climbed even more rapidly.

After the conference where Spencer was first sustained as president, Spencer and Camilla opened their home to friends and relatives to enjoy a buffet meal Camilla had prepared. Because of threats, the city had posted a police patrol car outside. During the evening Spencer left his guests, filled a plate with food, and slipped out to take it to the officer on duty.

For many years the president had not needed security, but with demonstrations against the Church by nonmembers and threats from dissidents, the Church had for several years been providing full-time security, with consequent loss of privacy. But the security was designed to protect him from harm, not to cut off contact. On New Year's Day when the family had gathered for dinner, four teenage boys rang the bell and asked to meet President Kimball. He invited them in and visited, then posed with them for pictures. When he learned they had not eaten, he had Camilla prepare food for them. A family member later asked whether all of that was necessary. He replied, "I belong to all the people, not just to my family."

He tried to reduce secular responsibilities in 1975 by resigning nearly all corporate directorships to which he had fallen heir. And he sought to reach more of the people. He began announcing new and smaller temples to be built all over the world, first in São Paulo, then Tokyo, then dozens more over a period of years. He held a series of thirty-eight solemn assemblies for instructing Church leaders, and he increased area conferences from one a year to several each year.

In 1975 Adney Y. Komatsu became an assistant to the Twelve, the first non-Caucasian General Authority. Then in October President Kimball activated the First Quorum of the Seventy. Among those called to that quorum were Charles Didier of Belgium and George P. Lee, a Navajo, and soon thereafter General Authorities were called from half a dozen other nations.

Later President Kimball introduced other important administrative changes, an emeritus status for aged or ailing General Authorities, and the status of temporary General Authority.

In the winter of 1976 President Kimball arrived in Samoa for the first of nine area conferences in the Pacific. He and Camilla both fell suddenly ill, with high temperatures and nausea, later diagnosed as viral pneumonia. Though miserable, they did not consider turning back. When they arrived in New Zealand, the fever had broken, and Spencer managed a television interview and luncheon with the prime minister. Then, after a two-hour remission, his fever returned and he went to bed.

In New Zealand also, Spencer asked President N. Eldon Tanner to represent him at the Saturday evening cultural program. During the evening he woke with a start; his fever had broken again. He asked Dr. Nelson, who watched over him, "What time was that program to begin this evening?" "At seven o'clock, President Kimball." "What time is it now?" "Almost seven." "Tell Sister Kimball we're going." As they drove into the stadium, just after the opening prayer, the crowd erupted in a deafening outburst. The young man who had just offered the invocation had prayed, "We three thousand New Zealand youth have gathered here prepared to sing and to dance for thy prophet. Wilt thou heal him and deliver him here."

Later in the year, after an area conference in Denmark, the president and several apostles went to visit the chapel where the Thorvaldsen statues of Christ and his apostles stand. Though the chapel was closed for renovation, the custodian showed them around. When President Kimball declared to the custodian that he stood in the presence of living apostles, the man wept.

The year 1977 was designated International Women's Year, to focus on women's concerns, and in the United States feminist organizations used the occasion to push for ratification of the Equal Rights Amendment. In 1974 Barbara Smith, general president of the Relief Society, and the *Church News* had expressed opposition to the ERA, and in December 1976 the First Presidency had issued a statement to the same effect. Spencer favored equal treatment for women, but he felt that the ERA was not the proper way.

The Church received heavy criticism for its opposition to the ERA, and publicity came to a peak with the excommunication of Sonia Johnson for her verbal attacks on the Church. More publicity attended the effort of the National Organization of Women to disqualify Mormon federal judge Marion Callister in a case involving Idaho's effort to rescind its ratification of the ERA.

President Kimball wanted to express his regard for the women of the Church, and he felt pleased the next year to be asked to dedicate the Relief Society Monument to Women in Nauvoo, Illinois. He also convened the first general women's meeting in the Church, sent by closed circuit communication to 1,400 locations.

The first of eight area conferences in Latin America in 1977 brought 25,000 Saints together in Mexico City from as far away as fifteen hundred miles. At its conclusion the congregation burst into spontaneous singing and waved white handkerchiefs. He waved back with his handkerchief. The Saints crowded near the president at every opportunity. Sometimes the crush seemed frightening. Camilla also spoke at each conference, reading her talk in Spanish.

In Bogotá an Indian district president from Ecuador, in white linen trousers and sandals and with braided hair hanging down his back, offered one of the prayers. It seemed fitting that President Kimball spoke on the Savior's disapproval of class distinctions.

In the high altitude of La Paz, Bolivia, visitors gasped for breath. Though urged to save his strength, President Kimball insisted on shaking hands with everyone at the conference. He explained, "They came long distances to see the prophet. I will not disappoint them."

Five heads of state received him on this trip, responding warmly to his explanation of what the Church stands for, particularly in terms of honesty, industry, and commitment to family.

While traveling, Spencer and Camilla primarily attended to church business, but they took opportunities for some sightseeing—Disney World, the water show at Cypress Gardens, an art show, a Shakespeare play, a professional baseball game, an ice show. They rode in the 24th of July parade in Salt Lake City, he wearing a big Stetson and she a pioneer-style dress.

In August 1977, President Kimball went to Europe to install a new temple presidency in Switzerland and to visit Poland. He had requested that while he waited a few days to go into Poland, meetings be arranged in the Italian missions. When he asked why the time was not fully scheduled, Arthur Haycock, his secretary, explained that they were just trying to save his strength. President Kimball responded, "I know you're trying to save me, but I don't want to be saved, I want to be exalted!" Extra meetings were arranged.

After long negotiations, special ambassador-at-large for the Church David Kennedy had succeeded in obtaining legal recognition of the Church from the communist government in Poland. Legal status did not open the door to proselyting, but it did allow for freer communication, for holding church meetings for the handful of members there, and for teaching those who expressed interest.

The communist Minister of Religion received the Kimball party respectfully, refraining from smoking or drinking in their presence. The ministry arranged a tour of places of historic interest, and late in the evening, after a private choral concert in the cathedral, the archbishop of Warsaw invited them to his adjacent residence. Camilla first thought it was just another building to look at, and when she saw the long flight of stairs, she asked if she could just sit down to wait for the others and rest her painful arthritic knees. In a few moments four priests appeared with a chair and proposed to carry her upstairs in it. Alarmed at that prospect, she rushed up the stairs, sore knees and all, to find that the archbishop had a table of refreshments waiting for them.

Early the next morning the small party met with a few others in a downtown park for a dedicatory prayer under an overcast sky. As President Kimball concluded, the sun came out.

BACK IN SALT LAKE CITY, during a meeting President Kimball suddenly had great difficulty breathing, and he was rushed to the hospital. Dr. Nelson, who had performed his heart surgery, came to his room and found him looking deathly ill. At the president's request, Dr. Nelson gave him a blessing in which he felt inspired to promise speedy recovery, even before the doctors could diagnose his condition, so that he could return to his work without missing any significant appointment. The diagnostic tests were inconclusive, and by the next day President Kimball was feeling better. That evening he left the hospital, and the next day he flew to Canada to help install a new temple presidency, having missed no significant appointment.

President Kimball stressed the keeping of personal journals and the writing of family history as part of the Saints' obligation to strengthen family ties and do genealogical research. For years he had been an assiduous journal keeper, and in 1977 his journals provided the primary resource for a biography on his life.

During general conference in April 1978, the Kimballs had to move temporarily to an apartment in the Hotel Utah for security. The concern stemmed from the ongoing trial of followers of Ervil LeBaron for the murder of Dr. Rulon Allred, leader of a polygamous group. Camilla said, "The apartment is beautiful, but I still feel that I am in prison."

On June 8, Camilla was working in her garden when the telephone rang. Her daughter, Olive Beth, asked excitedly, "Have you heard the news?" "What news?" "About the revelation that all worthy men can receive the priesthood!" Camilla wept in joy and relief. For some time she had known that something weighed heavily on her husband's mind, but she did not know what it was. She had thought it might be a serious problem with one of the General Authorities, but now she understood that he must have been concerned about whether the revelation would cause dissension in the Church, as Wilford Woodruff's 1890 Manifesto had done.

Nothing so dramatic as this revelation had happened in several generations. The electrifying news that every race could receive the blessings of priesthood and temple caused nearly universal rejoicing, not only because of the extension of blessings but because it demonstrated the principle of continuing revelation. The General Authorities did not elaborate, but let the announcement of the revelation speak for itself.

Within a few days Joseph Freeman, Jr., received the Melchizedek Priesthood, and he and his wife and two sons could go to the temple to be sealed as a family. Marcus Martins, the first black missionary called after the revelation, began serving in his home country of Brazil in August, and his father was called to serve in a stake presidency soon after.

With his deep concern about people, President Kimball felt humbly grateful to have been God's instrument to open these doors. But after the burst of great excitement, he turned back to the business of building the kingdom little by little.

In the summer of 1979 Spencer had a frightening dizzy spell that the doctor diagnosed as a tiny stroke. When Spencer complained, "I have no balance," Dr. Nelson reassured him, "That will pass." Spencer responded, wryly, "What won't?" A second such incident got him thinking about dying. "We have our bags packed," he explained. His eyesight also faded, so that in an area conference in Toronto, for the first time he turned his talk over to Arthur Haycock to read.

He needed help walking. It appeared that he was sliding rapidly downwards. When he went to BYU to speak to 20,000 students, he had to ask President Dallin Oaks to finish reading his talk. But his sense of humor had not left him; at the lunch BYU provided for the Kimball family, he expressed thanks for "the delightful repast. We're so glad to be able to eat with our family without having to provide the food."

The next day his weakness was so pronounced that he was hospitalized for tests. His condition was diagnosed as a subdural hematoma (blood and fluid inside the skull pressing on the brain), requiring emergency surgery. Providentially his anticoagulant medicine had been stopped in preparation for a scheduled cataract operation; the brain operation could proceed without fear of uncontrolled bleeding. Dr. Sorensen drilled a burr hole through the skull, and the fluid, under pressure, spurted out. The doctor predicted that perhaps President Kimball would be able to attend general conference in October, but he would surely not be able to participate. In fact, however, Spencer spoke five times. And after conference he traveled to Jerusalem.

Members of the Church had raised $1,000,000 by private subscription to establish a garden for the city of Jerusalem on the Mount of Olives to commemorate the dedicatory prayer of Orson Hyde. On his way to Israel, President Kimball went to Arab Egypt, where he was greeted by government officials, and in his remarks and dedicatory prayer at the Orson Hyde Garden, he specified his concern for all the children of Abraham, Arab and Jew alike.

About Thanksgiving time, pressure built up again inside his skull, requiring a second operation similar to the first. This time the operation required his missing area conferences in New Zealand and Australia. As he was recovering from the anaesthetic, he showed his great need for affection. He fancied that he had attended a dinner for a thousand people and, to his distress, no one had set a place for him. No one said even, "We're glad to have you here, president." In reality, on his eighty-fifth birthday a program in the Salt Lake Tabernacle and a banquet for 2,000 people in the Hotel Utah suggested how many friends honored him.

Area conferences resumed, and he participated again. His talks were typed with letters four times normal size so that he could read them. In general conference in April 1981, President Kimball reported that since October he had traveled 50,000 miles, holding area conferences in the Orient and in the Pacific Islands, and flying to South America and Puerto Rico and the Dominican Republic.

But numbers could never tell the whole story. After the

meeting in Santo Domingo, he had already gone to bed when a busload of people arrived hours late because their bus had broken down. They had come far and would have to turn right around to return for work the next day, so Arthur Haycock asked President Kimball if he would be willing to greet them. More than that, the president delivered to this small group the same message that he had presented in the earlier meeting.

He was clearly slowing down, but he had set things in motion that came to fruition. New editions of the standard works became available, a project he had been encouraging for a number of years. Later the Book of Mormon received a new subtitle: Another Testament of Jesus Christ.

In May 1981 the First Presidency issued a statement critical of arms buildup in the United States and specifically opposing the basing of MX missiles in the Utah-Nevada desert. Partly in response to this, President Reagan referred the proposal back to the military for further study.

Spencer's heartbeat slowed to a dangerous level, so after performing the marriage of a granddaughter in the Salt Lake Temple, he went to the hospital for the installation of a pacemaker.

The University of Utah conferred on both Spencer and Camilla Kimball honorary degrees. The citation for him emphasized his role in helping to make the Church international and universal, with indirect reference to the revelation on priesthood. Camilla's citation stressed her exemplary life, particularly her promotion of education and personal growth for women.

IN JULY 1981, with all three members of the First Presidency ailing, President Kimball felt impressed to call Gordon B. Hinckley to be a third counselor in the First Presidency. Shortly afterward the president showed a sharp decline in his strength, and a brain scan showed a third subdural hematoma in the same area as before. More than a burr hole was needed; Dr. Sorensen removed a five-square-inch oval of bone from Spencer's forehead and afterward wired it back in place.

Recovery this time progressed very slowly. Rumors made

their appointed rounds — that he had suffered a stroke, that he had two heart attacks, that he was totally incapacitated, that he lay in a coma. Occasionally the sense of humor that helped him be a survivor still surfaced. One nurse asked teasingly, "President Kimball, can you tell me when the Second Coming will be?" He said, "Why? Are you ready?"

He was determined to get well. When he suffered a stress ulcer and nearly bled to death, a nurse came in to give an infusion of blood. She tried for a half hour to find a vein that would receive the large needle. She said, placatingly, "I guess you don't want this, do you." He roused enough to say, almost fiercely, "I *do* want it."

He recovered enough to carry on some of his responsibilities, but he was in fragile health. He suffered a painful partial collapse of a vertebra; he had an abdominal hernia; he once lapsed into a coma for four hours; his eyesight faded to nothing; he had glaucoma; he slept poorly at night and might then fall asleep even in the middle of a meal; fluid retention required a salt-free diet; skin cancers had to be removed; one fall resulted in a cut forehead and black eye, while another required seven stitches; he suffered a minor stroke; a toothache required a root canal job; and he suffered for a time with gouty arthritis. It was a time that required great patience. One day as a nurse tried to shave him with an electric shaver, she worked for several minutes with no results. Spencer said puckishly, "Perhaps it would work better if you took the cap off."

Despite his problems, it seemed that every time general conference approached, he received a new surge of energy and was able to attend most sessions, but he had to rely on others to carry the work forward. He spoke for the last time in public in April 1982, but even that brief talk represented a struggle.

His influence continued to be felt, despite his relative inactivity. The programs he had helped initiate had their own momentum. After the death of President Tanner, President Hinckley assumed major responsibility for conducting the affairs of the First Presidency, but he was always careful to acknowledge that he conferred with and acted with the approval of the president. Serious weakness and short-term problems alternated with periods of relative strength for the president, but he dressed each day and was usually able to attend the weekly meetings in the temple with his counselors and the Twelve. He had little to say, but he was there, enduring to the end, despite a tired, worn body.

Near the end of President Kimball's life, in one of the temple meetings, the apostles came in turn to offer greeting. Elder Marvin J. Ashton, knowing that the aged prophet was practically blind, said to him, "President Kimball, I am Marvin Ashton." Spencer took his hand, paused, and then finally said simply, softly, "Marv Ashton, I love you." That was all he said. That was all he needed to say.

On November 5, 1985, Spencer Kimball, ninety, passed quietly away. His funeral not only filled the Tabernacle, but also reached by satellite a multitude of Saints who knew he loved them, too.

SOURCES

The major published sources for this chapter are Edward L. Kimball and Andrew E. Kimball, Jr., *Spencer W. Kimball* (Salt Lake City: Bookcraft, 1977) Caroline E. Miner and Edward L. Kimball, *Camilla* (Salt Lake City: Deseret Book, 1980); Edward L. Kimball and Andrew E. Kimball, Jr., *The Story of Spencer W. Kimball: A Short Man, A Long Stride* (Salt Lake City: Bookcraft, 1985).

EDWARD L. KIMBALL is Ernest L. Wilkinson Professor of Law at Brigham Young University. He holds a B.S. degree in history and LL.B., LL.M., and S.J.D. degrees in law from the Universities of Utah and Pennsylvania. A son of President Spencer W. Kimball, he is co-author of *Spencer W. Kimball* (Salt Lake City: Bookcraft, 1977); *The Story of Spencer W. Kimball: A Short Man, a Long Stride* (Salt Lake City: Bookcraft, 1985); and *Camilla* (Salt Lake City: Deseret Book, 1980), as well as books and articles on law.

EZRA TAFT BENSON
William G. Hartley

Laying the eleven-pound, nearly dead newborn boy aside, the doctor frantically labored to save the life of the mother, Sarah Dunkley Benson. Meanwhile her husband, George T. Benson, Jr., a man of great faith, anointed and blessed the baby, and then the child's two grandmothers grabbed him and dipped him back and forth between basins of warm and cold water.

Priesthood blessing and desperate dunkings triggered a loud cry and robust life in the child. God wanted this baby to live to fill a long and righteous mission so he could one day lead the Church. Sarah also survived and in time bore ten more children.

During the firstborn's long lifetime, he seemed to be guided by two special "character genes." Perhaps he inherited a patriotic gene from his ancestors John Perry Benson, who fought in the American Revolution, and Benoni Benson, one of the Massachusetts Minutemen. Perhaps he received an energized "spiritual gene" from the great-grandfather for whom he was named, Ezra Taft Benson, an apostle and one of the original 1847 Mormon pioneers.

THE NAMESAKE, EZRA TAFT BENSON, was born on August 4, 1899, in the Mormon village of Whitney, Idaho. The community's fifty families, about three hundred people, were all Latter-day Saints—after the sole nonmember converted.

The child, who was called "T" as a youth, was the oldest son in a frugal farm family. They lived in a two-room stucco house on a forty-acre farm, where they produced livestock, sugar beets, potatoes, and wheat. They had a small dairy, and work horses were their "tractor." The parents taught their children honesty, industry, and "doing your job."

At age four, Ezra drove a team of horses on a harrow. He rode horses to herd cattle, was responsible for milking several of the family's seventeen Holsteins, thinned sugar beets, dug potatoes, shocked wheat, and forked hay. The Bensons had eight head of work horses, and Ezra shoveled out the barn, harnessed the horses, curried them, and worked them on the dry farm.

Ezra's father and his grandfathers were farmers who enjoyed their vocation, and his father encouraged the Benson sons to try out new methods of farming and to practice what they learned. Farm life taught Ezra the importance of working hard and instilled in him a love for agriculture, traits that one day would help him become the most important farm leader in the United States.

The farm home had no electricity, and one of Ezra's chores was to clean the chimneys of the oil lamps. Water for baths and washing came from a well George Benson had dug, and Ezra's arms often grew tired from pumping water for the family's needs. A joyous occasion was the day his mother turned a tap in the kitchen and water came out. When he was in his teens, he and his father went to a nearby forest, cut down and hauled trees for telephone poles, and installed a phone system in the farmhouse, with the help of a technician. Ezra helped dig post holes and string wire for the telephone and the electricity. When the family switched on their first electric light, one bulb in each room, they were thrilled. Ezra also helped dig by hand trenches for the community's water system, which tapped a spring two miles east of the farm.

But all was not work on the Benson farm. The children enjoyed swimming in the creek, picking wildflowers, ice skating and sleigh riding in the winter, riding horses, and playing with newborn puppies and calves. Some Saturday afternoons their father played basketball with his sons or took the family to town for recreation. Occasionally he took them on short vacations and on outings to Bear Lake. He and the boys camped, fished, and went boating together. Ezra often recalled with fondness the closeness of the family. They "sang together, played together, prayed together, and stayed together." One of his vivid memories was the aroma of homemade bread (his mother baked twelve loaves at a time). "We would persuade Mother to let us take the top off a loaf, put butter on it, and eat it in our hands," he remembered.

George and Sarah believed in the gospel of Jesus Christ, and they taught its principles to their children. One day when Ezra came in from the fields, he saw his mother bent over the ironing board, with newspapers spread on the floor. As she ironed, beads of perspiration gathered on her forehead. The boy asked her what she was ironing. "These are temple robes, my son," she told him. "Your father and I are going to the temple at Logan." Then she put her flat-iron on the stove, sat down by her son, and told him about the importance of temple ordinances. These were "sweet memories about the spirit of temple work" that blessed his family, he later said.

Ezra was baptized and confirmed on August 4, 1907, on his eighth birthday. Some five years later, he was shocked to see his parents crying as they drove up to the house in their one-horse buggy. His father had received a letter from "Box B"—a mission call from Church headquarters. To finance the mission, the Bensons sold their dry-farm land and rented out the part of their farm that had cash crops. They retained their pastureland and dairy herd.

While George was serving his two-year mission in the Midwest, the family made sacrifices. But the spirit of missionary work, which they shared through his letters, so filled the home that all seven sons served missions as young men, and all of the daughters served in their later years. When George returned, he was called to the bishopric; he served later as a bishop, high councilor, and member of a stake presidency.

When Ezra was about fifteen, his parents read in the *Deseret News* that Latter-day Saints should have family home evenings. "Father said that the message was the word of the Lord to us," he said, "and we were going to start right then." From that time forth, they often spent home evenings regularly, reading the scriptures and singing together.

In an article published in *Reader's Digest* in November 1954, Ezra Taft Benson shared with America "The Best Advice I Ever Had." He told how his father once said to him, "Remember that whatever you do or wherever you are, you are never alone. Our Heavenly Father is always near. You can reach out and receive his aid through prayer." This lesson stayed with the youth throughout his life.

Ezra began elementary school at age eight, and then attended high school at Oneida Stake Academy in Preston, Idaho, three miles away by horseback, buggy, or sleigh. One of his classmates at Oneida Academy was Harold B. Lee, who preceded him into the Council of the Twelve in 1941 and later became eleventh president of the Church.

Ezra enjoyed school and, being tall, eagerly played on the basketball team. During the spring planting and the fall harvest seasons, he often missed school to help on the farm. To earn spending money, he set muskrat traps on his way to school, checked them on the way home, skinned any muskrats he caught, dried the pelts, and sold them to a fur house in Chicago. When he was about seventeen, he was hired by a neighbor to thin an acre of sugar beets, a full day's work for a seasoned adult. Laboring with a short hoe from sunrise to sundown, he completed the acre in one day. The surprised farmer paid him in two five-dollar gold pieces and two silver dollars. "I've never felt so well-to-do since," Ezra later recalled.

Ezra loved to read whenever possible, usually in the evening, on Sundays, and on stormy days. Often his father would have him or one of his brothers or sisters read to the family an article in the *Improvement Era* or the *Deseret News*. Among the youth's favorite books were the scriptures, *Life of Benjamin Franklin*, Bunyan's *Pilgrim's Progress*, and Leo Tolstoy's *Where Love Is, There God Is Also*.

At the Oneida Stake Academy, Ezra learned two valuable lessons. During a test, when he turned to borrow a knife to sharpen his pencil, the teacher falsely accused him of cheating. Ezra received a tongue-lashing and at first was barred from playing in the upcoming basketball game. He felt deep pain from being branded a cheat and liar. Later he said, "Looking back, I know that lesson was God-sent. Character is shaped in just such crucibles." It taught him that he must always avoid even the appearance of evil. It taught him that he must be fair with people by not judging them simply by appearances.

About age nineteen, Ezra became a scoutmaster in the first troop Whitney had. His twenty-four scouts competed in a boys chorus competition and won, forcing him to keep his promise that a win earned them a thirty-five-mile hike over the mountains to Bear Lake Valley. The boys decided to clip all their hair off so they would not need combs and brushes. The barber sheared them all, including the two scoutmasters, and then said he would not charge for the haircuts if he could shave the scoutmasters' heads. Sheared boys and bald scoutmasters spent three weeks camping and hiking together.

EZRA GRADUATED FROM ONEIDA ACADEMY in 1918, near the end of World War I. He entered the military just before the deadly influenza epidemic of 1918 swept his camp. That fall, due to acute labor shortages for the sugar-beet harvest, servicemen were given furloughs to help. Ezra felt prompted to request leave to go home a day earlier than his buddies and was stricken with the flu shortly after reaching home. His family nursed him and he fully recovered, but two of his close military companions died of the disease.

By late 1919 Ezra enrolled at Utah State Agricultural College (now Utah State University) at Logan, Utah. He could only afford to attend winter term, so he took correspondence courses during spring, summer, and fall. In college he was called "Taft" instead of "T."

One fall day in 1920, while he and a cousin stood on a curb near the college, a girl drove by and waved. "Who is that?" Ezra asked. "Flora Amussen," the cousin replied. She drove by again and waved. "If I come down here this winter," Ezra announced, "I'm going to step her." "Heck you will," the cousin said. "She's too popular for a farm boy."

City life had been her background. Flora, the daughter of a Danish-immigrant jeweler and watchmaker, lived with her widowed mother in a large home. The Amussens were people of culture and refinement. On campus Flora was one of the most popular girls, a tennis champion, Shakespearean actress, girls' athletic club president, and studentbody vice-president. She drove her own car.

Nevertheless, Ezra asked her for a date that winter, and she accepted. Soon the two saw in each other traits they liked. Their courtship extended seven years, long enough for both to fill Church missions.

Ezra was ordained an elder on July 13, 1921, just before he left on his mission. On August 1 he and eighteen other missionaries arrived in Liverpool, England, aboard the steamer *S. S. Victorian*. After meeting mission president Orson F. Whitney, for whom Ezra's hometown was named, Ezra and Elder Russell Hodgson went to Carlisle, in the Newcastle District of England's lake region.

According to mission records, Elder Benson participated in a baptism held two months later at the public baths in Carlisle. With twenty-five Saints and investigators present, Elder Ralph Gray spoke on baptism and Elder Benson discussed the Holy Ghost. Three persons were baptized and confirmed. On his mission, Elder Benson proselytized, worked with members, and spoke at branch conferences. In August 1922 he helped confirm nine newly baptized converts. A month later, at the South Shields Branch conference, he and Elder James Palmer delivered gospel discourses to about eighty listeners.

In February 1923 Elder Benson became president of the Newcastle Conference. A month later at the South Shields Branch conference, he complimented branch officers on their "splendid" reports and the "good spirit manifested" by each. He encouraged them to continue to keep in mind the mission's motto for 1923: "Every Member a Missionary." On April 26 he baptized six persons at Sunderland, and during the rest of his mission he participated in several more baptisms. Occasionally he sang a solo at church meetings. In July 1923, at a special conference in London, he sang as part of a double quartet.

Elder Benson liked to recall memorable experiences from his missionary days. One occurred at Newcastle, where he learned a lesson about obeying priesthood counsel with exactness. Anti-Mormon feelings had become so strong that the mission president ordered no more tracting or street meetings. But Elder Benson and his companion had already scheduled and publicized a street meeting, so they decided to go through with it. While they preached, nearby pubs closed and soon a crowd of rowdies gathered and threatened to trample them or throw them in the river. The elders became separated in the crowd. Suddenly a large man stepped to Elder Benson's side and declared that he believed the missionary, and the crowd backed off. A policeman rescued Ezra and helped him return to his apartment. His companion arrived home soon after that. Elder Benson blamed the near-mobbing on his ignoring his president's instructions.

Late in his mission Elder Benson had another memorable experience. Despite strong anti-Mormon feelings locally, he and his companion were invited to travel to South Shields Branch to speak. "Many of the people over here do not believe the falsehoods printed about us," they were told. "If you'll come, we're sure that we'll have a great meeting." The elders fasted and prayed and decided to go. Elder Benson studied hard to speak on the apostasy.

"There was a wonderful spirit in the meeting," he said. After his companion spoke, he then talked "with a freedom I had never experienced before in my life. When I sat down, I then realized that I had not mentioned the apostasy. I had talked on the Prophet Joseph Smith and borne my witness of his divine mission and to the truthfulness of the Book of Mormon." After the meeting, several people came up, and some nonmembers told him, "Tonight we received a witness that the gospel is true as you elders teach it. We are now ready for baptism." This was, he felt, an answer to his prayers.

On November 8, 1923, the Saints held a farewell social in Elder Benson's honor, before his return home. According to a report of the occasion, he received "many valuable gifts from the Saints and elders. He thanked them for their support and exhorted them to live the gospel they had embraced and then enjoy the blessings promised by the Lord. The hall was filled with Saints and friends." He had served under two mission presidents, both of them apostles: Orson F. Whitney and David O. McKay.

FOLLOWING HIS MISSION, Ezra enrolled at Brigham Young University. While he finished his bachelor's degree, with a double major in animal husbandry and marketing, Flora filled a mission to Hawaii. He graduated with honors in 1926, earning a scholarship to Iowa State College in Ames.

Ezra and Flora were married on September 10, 1926, in the Salt Lake Temple. His former mission president, Elder Whitney, performed the sealing. That same day they left for Iowa in a Model-T Ford truck, camping out along the way in a leaky tent. Ezra's scholarship provided them $70.00 a month to live on. For a year they lived on this salary in a $22.50 one-room apartment at the Lincoln Apartments, sharing with three other couples a cement shower down the hall.

Ezra earned his master's degree in agricultural economics. (He is the first president of the Church to have completed an advanced college degree.) He praised Flora for sacrificing for him. In 1952, for example, he told BYU students that she came "from a family of some means" and had to "turn her back on a lot of that and was willing to sacrifice to become a farmer's wife, to go out on the experiment farm at Iowa State College, and glean squash from the field and pick nuts in order to cut down the food bill." He also said, "She married a man who was heavily in debt. She knows what it is to live on $70 a month and maintain a home."

After graduation, Ezra and Flora returned to the family

farm in Whitney, which Ezra and his brother Orval had bought in 1923. They farmed efficiently, keeping up with advances in technology. They bottled and sold milk, kept a flock of 250 chickens, traded eggs for groceries, slaughtered a hog each winter for food, and produced good field crops. But they struggled to pay off the purchase debt with deflated dollars. Flora recalled, "There were times when we would just get a cow paid for, and then we'd have to sell her to pay the doctor because one of our precious babies had arrived."

Tapping Ezra's practical and college training, Franklin County drafted him to be an agricultural agent. He taught farmers how to rotate their crops, improve their marketing, arrange for loans, use better grains, eradicate noxious weeds, control rodents, and employ better bookkeeping systems. He promoted cooperative marketing of livestock and grain.

In 1929, just before the Great Depression began, the University of Idaho hired Ezra to head a newly created Department of Agricultural Economics and Marketing at the state capital, Boise. There he spent nine years as extension economist and marketing specialist. He traveled throughout Idaho pushing, among other programs, the idea of farm cooperatives. In an effort to market Idaho products nationally, he helped make the Idaho potato famous across America. He disliked New Deal farm measures, so while he explained them to Idaho farmers, he did not promote them. Taking a year's leave, he worked on a doctorate at the University of California at Berkeley.

He served several years in the Boise stake presidency and then became stake president in 1938. As president, he emphasized youth activities and scouting. Since the stake was composed mostly of farm people, there were few who were unemployed. When the Church's welfare program was introduced, he directed members to bottle at home two truckloads of cherries, and 25,000 quarts were sent to Salt Lake City.

IN 1939 EZRA MOVED TO WASHINGTON, D.C., to become executive-secretary of the National Council of Farmer Cooperatives, an organization representing more than 5,000 cooperatives and 2.5 million farmers nationwide. He took the job only after he was assured he would not need to wine and dine government officials. In this position, he represented the co-ops before Congress and various government agencies and traveled widely to discuss management and organization problems.

A year later, he was called to serve as president of the newly formed Washington, D. C., Stake, with Samuel R. Carpenter and Ernest Wilkinson as counselors.

When World War II broke out, President Franklin Delano Roosevelt named Ezra to a special four-man agricultural advisory committee. In 1942 he joined the executive committee of the board of trustees of the American Institute of Cooperation, an organization of farm cooperatives and land grant colleges.

One day a Chicago corporation head visited him. He needed a young man with integrity who lived a clean, moral life. Someone had told the man to hire a returned Mormon missionary, so he asked at his Washington hotel: "Are there any Mormons in Washington?" He was told to contact Ezra Benson. So he did. "Can you give me the names of three or four young men?" he asked. The stake president gave him several names. In the years since then, Elder Benson often told that story in order to teach that "it pays for young men, and young women too, to maintain the standards of the Church and be true to the faith."

EARLY IN 1943 Ezra received two job offers, both offering high salaries. One of them seemed particularly enticing but would require that he move from Washington. He stopped in Salt Lake City to discuss the matter with Elder David O. McKay. While there, President Heber J. Grant sent for him. "President Grant took my right hand in both of his," Ezra recalled, "and looked into the depths of my very soul and said: 'Brother Benson, with all my heart I congratulate you and pray God's blessings to attend you. You have been chosen as the youngest apostle of the Church.'" Elder Benson said, "The whole world seemed to sink. I could hardly believe it was true." He had had no premonition of the call, but his wife did.

The call came on July 26, 1943, and he was sustained at general conference in October. He was ordained and set apart just a few minutes after another new apostle, Spencer W. Kimball. President Grant was very feeble at the time. "He sat in a chair," Elder Benson said, "and we knelt down, and President Grant as a prophet of God put his hands on our heads."

When Elder Benson joined the Council of the Twelve, the Church had 837,000 members and 146 stakes, with no stakes abroad. Missionary work abroad had, for the most part, been suspended due to the war. General Authorities usually traveled in pairs to conferences or to missions, traveling by train or boat and seldom by plane.

On February 4, 1946, several months after World War II ended, Elder Benson arrived in London to assume presidency of the European Mission. His main purposes were to reopen missions and alleviate suffering among the Saints in Europe.

After establishing a new mission headquarters in London, he and his secretary, Frederick Babbel, systematically visited the countries of Europe. As they hammered out working relationships with various government and army officials and with the International Red Cross, persistence and prayer opened doors and changed decisions that at first blocked them.

Elder Benson contacted local LDS leaders and inspected remaining Church-owned buildings. He was eagerly greeted by the European Saints, many of whom had lost contact with the Church during the war.

At Karlsruhe, Germany, the Saints extended their meeting two hours, waiting for him to arrive. When he reached the partly bombed-out building, almost the entire congregation was in tears, for they had not seen a representative from Church headquarters for six years or more. Eager to hear him, they extended their meeting and then insisted on shaking his hand before he left.

Elder Benson found the Saints in great need of food, clothing, and, in some cases, fuel. The local leaders needed automobiles. Mission literature was unavailable, and many branches needed new meetinghouses or repairs on existing ones.

Destruction in the war zones shocked Elder Benson and taught him firsthand what atrocities unrighteous leaders could perpetrate. He was particularly heartbroken to stand on rubble that once was the Jewish ghetto in Warsaw, and under which perhaps 200,000 bodies were still buried. This scene helped him in future years to raise a warning voice that freedoms can easily be lost.

Seeing the ravages of war firsthand, he rejoiced when welfare goods finally reached the needy Saints. "I shall never forget as long as I live the arrival of our first welfare supplies, particularly those that entered Berlin," he said. He and Richard Ranglack, a German Saint, went to a battered old warehouse that was under the control of the International Red Cross, with armed guards standing at attention to prevent stealing by hungry people. In the warehouse, boxes were piled almost to the ceiling. They took down several. The first one contained cracked wheat. Brother Ranglack ran his hands through the wheat, then broke down and cried like a child. "Brother Benson," he said, "it is difficult for me to believe that people who have never seen us could do so much for us."

Elder Benson tackled the urgent problems of relocating LDS refugees from Poland. The mission home in Berlin overflowed with ragged, hungry, and sick refugees. He authorized the establishment of refugee camps, one south of Berlin and one near Frankfurt, to which food and other welfare supplies were shipped from the States and from other European countries.

In less than a year, President Benson traveled more than 60,000 miles. He bore his testimony in thirteen countries. He was instrumental in supplying clothing, bedding, and food for thousands of war-weary Saints. On August 10, 1946, he rededicated the land of Finland for missionary work. He authorized the printing of 5,000 copies of the Book of Mormon, Doctrine and Covenants, and Pearl of Great Price in German. He organized branches, purchased properties, and rejuvenated missionary work in Europe.

In his farewell address to the European Saints in September 1946, he asked them to "be not cast down" and to have unwavering faith that "God still rules. He is at the helm." He called for them to live Church standards and be loyal to Church officers. Then, as an apostle, he issued a solemn warning to rulers and peoples "to repent of their evil ways" in order to avoid future war in Europe.

RETURNING TO THE UNITED STATES, Elder Benson resumed his normal labors as a member of the Twelve. He enjoyed his Church associations, as he told the Saints at general conference in October 1948: "I do not know exactly what heaven is going to be like, but I could ask nothing finer over there than to have the pleasure and joy of associating with the type of men and women I meet in the leadership of the stakes and wards of Zion and the missions of the earth."

In the April 1950 conference, he discussed "a rather miraculous drama that is taking place today before our very eyes," largely unnoticed. He referred to the steady gathering then taking place of Jews to the Holy Land.

Before speaking at general conferences, he sought the Lord's help. In October 1950, for example, he told the Saints how his son had come to him after the morning session and said, "Dad, I've observed you've been fasting and praying a good deal during this conference. I just wanted to come in and tell you that I have been doing the same. The Lord bless you." His wife said that the younger children had suggested they kneel in family prayer with him even though they had had family prayer earlier without him. "I am grateful," he noted, "for the support of our families."

His family now included four daughters and two sons: Reed, Mark, Barbara, Beverly, Bonnie, and Beth. He and Flora had wanted to have twelve children but could not. She joked that "if we'd only had twins each time, we would have reached our goal."

In late 1952, Elder Benson learned that he was being considered for a cabinet post as Secretary of Agriculture in the administration of President-elect Dwight D. Eisenhower. He sought direction from President David O. McKay and was told, "If the opportunity comes in the proper spirit, I think you should accept." Having fasted and prayed with his wife about the matter, Elder Benson met with President Eisenhower, who told him that the country needed a spiritual tone in government. Besides, he argued, "You can't refuse to serve America." And so, after he and his wife fasted and prayed, Elder Benson agreed to join the cabinet for at least two years. Until then, no clergyman had served in a cabinet post for some one hundred years. Elder Benson was the first Latter-day Saint to hold a cabinet position.

Before he was sworn into office, Elder Benson visited Washington, D. C., and strolled from the Capitol down past the Washington and Lincoln monuments. "As I walked, I reviewed in my own mind the history of this, the greatest nation under heaven," he said. He read the inscriptions on the walls of the Lincoln Memorial, pondering the messages. "I presume that never in my life has there come to my heart such a feeling of gratitude and thanksgiving for my citizenship in this land, choice above all others."

He brought to his new job several strongly held beliefs about government and politics. Politically, he called himself a "conservative conservative" who wanted government control reduced. In *Farmers at the Crossroads*, he wrote: "I love this nation. It is my firm belief that the God of Heaven raised up the founding fathers and inspired them to establish the Constitution of this land." America, he added, "is not just another nation. It is a great and glorious society with a divine mission to perform for liberty-loving people everywhere." "I'd rather be dead than lose my liberty," he repeatedly told those trying to regulate the farmers.

He wished more Americans understood that people had to pay for government spending. "The Federal Government has no funds which it does not, in some manner, take from the people. And a dollar cannot make the round trip from Oklahoma, Iowa, California, or even Maryland, to Washington and back, without shrinking in the process."

Religion, he felt, should be a vital force in government.

"My faith is the dominant force in my life," he declared, "and I would not want to hide it. If one's faith does not rule his life, then either his faith is not giving him enough or he is not giving his faith enough." He often said that "in the long run, what is right is the best politics."

He proposed a simple yardstick for measuring good and bad laws: "The supreme test of any government policy, agricultural or other, should be 'How will it affect the character, morale, and well-being of our people?'"

This former Idaho farmer who admitted he "disliked Big Government" inherited a huge department, with 78,000 employees scattered in 10,000 locations. He became responsible for the food needs of 160,000,000 Americans, for the grading and classifying of commodities, and for protecting the nation from insects, bad meat, and crop failures. He became director of the nation's largest money-lending agency, the Commodity Credit Corporation. He became "the biggest butter, cheese, and dried milk man in the country" and the largest dealer in grain, cotton, and other commodities. And he assumed leadership of the most extensive electrification project and soil, water, and timber conservation operations yet tried in history.

In January 1953 Flora Benson helped her husband decorate and stock his Washington apartment, where he would live alone for five months until she could move the children from Utah. After she left, he said, "for the first time, it was suddenly more than I could bear. The job ahead seemed too big, the load too heavy, loneliness too sharp a pain. I broke down and wept aloud."

The Bensons bought a house in the Crestwood subdivision, fifteen minutes from his office. In this home the younger children spent most of their growing-up years, and their father found a retreat and sanctuary from his heavy responsibilities. In *Cross Fire*, he tells how he looked forward to weekends, family nights, and evenings at home: "What a difference a home makes. What a difference there is in knowing that at the day's end, you will return to those you love, to your own house and yard, to a place of peace that is truly your own."

In 1953, the old World War II price supports were still in

place, causing U. S. farmers to produce more in order to receive the guaranteed prices. A mammoth surplus of commodities resulted, forcing farm prices to fall. It was "a grade A mess," Secretary Benson said. Once in office, he began the most extensive review of farm problems ever conducted, and reorganized the department to make it more efficient and reduce its giant budgets.

"Cross fire" is the apt phrase to describe his problem-filled years with Eisenhower. Those years, he said, were a "steady round of decisions and emergencies." He persuaded President Eisenhower that farmers needed flexible, lower price supports, not the existing rigid, high ones. In Congress, however, flexible supports faced strong opposition. Secretary Benson lobbied hard with Senate and House of Representatives agriculture committees for his programs, causing controversy and creating political enemies. He helped shape three major agriculture laws passed by Congress in 1954, 1956, and 1958, which laws he felt were "limited steps in the right direction" of sound farm policy. He also faced several major crises, ranging from a beef glut to an outbreak of hoof-and-mouth disease in Mexico and to Dust Bowls in the drought-stricken Southwest.

As an apostle in government, he found many occasions to demonstrate or explain the gospel and had several government-related spiritual experiences. A staff member described him as being "not a ministerial man in appearance or manner. He would be taken for a well-groomed businessman, over six feet tall and weighing 200 pounds. He greets you with a pleasant smile and has an easy laugh." He was known and accepted as both a nondrinker and a nonsmoker. "When he goes to gatherings where there is drinking, as is necessitated by his official position, he doesn't hold a glass of ginger ale to give the appearance of having a highball. Although he adheres to his standards, he does not impose them on others. It is perfectly all right to drink or smoke in his presence, but somehow very few people do."

President Eisenhower, at Secretary Benson's suggestion, saw that each Friday morning cabinet meeting was opened with silent or verbal prayer. Secretary Benson insisted that his own Department of Agriculture staff meetings on Thursdays be opened with verbal prayer.

Soon after his swearing-in, he announced that he would not take part in any secular activities on Sunday, except for extreme emergencies. The President, the Department of Agriculture, and the press, radio, and television respected his wish.

He was attacked politically as soon as he started, possibly because he was given to making such public statements as one made in St. Paul, Minnesota, in February 1953: "We need, as we need no other thing, a nationwide repentance of our sins. In our rush for the material things we have, indeed, forgotten to serve the God of this land. We must look beyond the dollar sign. Our greatness has been built on spiritual values and if we are not surviving, we must find again what we once had and now have lost—the inner strength that comes from obedience to divine law. Without such blessings, the future of the nation is insecure."

In March 1953 Flora Benson and their daughter Barbara were in an automobile accident in Utah. Sister Benson was unconscious. By phone, Elder Benson arranged for his son Reed to go to Utah from Texas to help and to give her a blessing. The next day, despite a full round of work, Elder Benson fasted and prayed until dinner. Finally, at 9:30 P.M., he learned that his wife was conscious and would be all right. "It was the longest night and day I spent in Washington," he recalled.

In jest and in earnest, the Secretary gained a reputation for having a pipeline with God. In October 1955, for example, one member of his staff, Earl Butz, told him, "Remember always that many of your friends feel that a great source of your personal strength is that you walk beside God, whereas most of the rest of us only report to Him."

By 1953 drought had plagued Texas for four consecutive years. Secretary Benson inspected the area, conferred with Governor Allan Shivers, and suggested that the Governor proclaim a day of fasting and prayers for rain. When two inches of rain fell on San Antonio soon after he left, a Texas newspaper reported, "Benson really has contacts that are out of this world."

Cabinet wives occasionally hosted luncheons for one another. In May 1954 Sister Benson hosted Mamie Eisenhower, several cabinet wives, and U.S. Treasurer Oveta Culp Hobby. For weeks she and her daughters planned for the event. "I want to show that it's possible to uphold the standards of the Church and have a wonderful time, too," she said. She informed her guests, in a gentle way, that the Benson family did not serve cocktails, play cards, smoke, or drink tea or coffee, "but we'll try to make it up to you in our own way, and we hope you enjoy our home." Their luncheon included performances by the Benson children and by the Madrigal Singers from Brigham Young University. The guests seemed pleased and complimented the family for a fine social, and Mrs. Eisenhower invited the Madrigals to the White House for a special tour.

On September 24, 1954, American TV viewers who tuned in to Edward R. Murrow's weekly program "Person to Person" saw an unusual interview. Viewers went into the Benson home and saw a typical Mormon family home evening. The press reported that this show brought more fan mail than any other show Murrow hosted.

In late December 1954 the Bensons were guests of their fellow Latter-day Saint and friend, businessman J. Willard Marriott, at the Marriott ranch in Virginia. The guests included President and Mamie Eisenhower, who expressed a wish to see a family home evening. So, by a roaring fireplace on a cold winter night, the Benson family performed, with musical numbers by the four Benson daughters, comic skits, readings, and group singing that included the Eisenhowers.

In the Washington area, Elder and Sister Benson participated in normal community affairs. Sister Benson once was in charge of PTA memberships at Beth's school. One evening after PTA meeting, parents and teachers were surprised to find Secretary Benson sitting with his wife at the tables, accepting PTA dues and memberships. In 1955 she was selected "Homemaker of the Year" by the National Home Fashion League.

The Secretary made an eighteen-day government trip to Latin America in 1955, visiting Cuba, Puerto Rico, Venezuela,

Colombia, Panama, Nicaragua, and Mexico. This trip had special interest for him because it took him into Book of Mormon lands.

In the summer of 1955, the Bensons flew to Europe on a government assignment. While there, they participated in the Swiss Temple dedication. Elder Benson's paternal grandmother was Swiss, and his Ballif kin had taken part centuries before in the Counter Reformation. Publicity about the temple dedication gave him opportunities to discuss the gospel at official state dinners and meetings with heads of nations, members of the cabinet, and prominent citizens.

Farm policy became a sizzling political issue during President Eisenhower's two terms, and critics of Secretary Benson's policies became strident. Calls for and rumors of his resignation peppered reports in the news media. During the 1954 elections, President Eisenhower, responding to charges that Secretary Benson was a political liability, said, "Ezra is the shining star in the firmament of my administration." The administration lost control of Congress that year, but the farm vote proved to be a major source of Republican strength.

Late in 1955 President Eisenhower suffered a heart attack and was hospitalized in Colorado. Elder Benson visited him and told him he was remembered in the prayers of President McKay, seven sessions of LDS general conferences, the Benson family, and the Agriculture Department staff in its Thursday meetings. "In fact," he said, "I guess no man living or dead within my memory has had so many prayers ascended to heaven as you, Mr. President."

Early in 1956 Elder Benson talked with President McKay about whether to drop his government work and return to Church service. He was told to continue as long as President Eisenhower wanted and needed him.

In May 1956, Congress passed an agricultural act that, although not what Secretary Benson hoped for and needed, was in his opinion more good than bad. It created a soil bank, which he had advocated, that promoted acreage reduction and conservation.

Secretary Benson felt that the 1956-1957 period was a critical "time of decision" when the line must be held to avoid a return to "the ruinous high rigid price supports." He declared: "The issue is clear. Is agriculture to manage its own affairs? Or is it to be managed from Washington? Which better serves the farmers' interests—and the nation's interests? Shall government subsidize agriculture in such a manner that it also takes control? Or shall government be kept in the role of servant—or partner—but never the master?"

In 1956 voters reelected Eisenhower, and the Republican Party did remarkably well in the Farm Belt.

During the election campaign, in October 1956, Hungarian freedom fighters revolted against their Communist government, and the rebellion spread from Budapest to the countryside, but it was short-lived. When Russian troops and tanks suppressed the revolt, Secretary Benson declared that he was "ashamed of the apathy" shown by the United States' silence and then by its weak protests: "We had encouraged the captive nations to believe that we would spring to their defense if and when they made a real surge for freedom. Now when the Hungarians had seemed almost on the verge of successful revolt, we had simply stood aghast while the Communist juggernaut rolled over the Freedom Fighters. I was sick at heart."

He decided that if the government would not act, it could at least speak. Early in December he urged President Eisenhower to protest the Russians' brutality through a statement on Human Rights Day, December 10. The President's message, written by Secretary Benson with minor changes by the administration, criticized "the recent orgy of brutality in Hungary" and expressed sorrow and sympathy for "the courageous, liberty-loving people of Hungary." The "Hungarian Massacre," it said, "repudiates and negates almost every article in the Declaration of Human Rights." Regarding this statement, Secretary Benson said that "no project that I helped initiate outside agriculture gave me more satisfaction."

Late in 1957 President McKay visited President Eisenhower in Washington, D. C. He wanted to learn how badly Eisenhower needed Elder Benson. Later President McKay told Elder

Benson, "Mr. Eisenhower indicated to me that you and he had been very close. In fact, the President told me, 'Ezra and I have been just like this' — and he interlocked the fingers of his hands. Then he said, 'I just don't know where I could turn to get someone to succeed him.'"

In October 1957 Secretary Benson took a three-week world tour to promote trade development, visiting Japan, Hong Kong, India, Pakistan, Jordan, Israel, Turkey, Greece, Italy, Spain, Portugal, France, and England. In Hong Kong he met with Saints and missionaries.

In Israel he discussed with Prime Minister David Ben-Gurion several Old Testament prophecies and how in 1841 Elder Orson Hyde, a member of the Quorum of the Twelve, dedicated Palestine for the gathering of the Jews.

During the heart of the hectic congressional campaign in 1958, the Mormon Tabernacle Choir presented a special concert for a black-tie affair in the White House Gold Room. The Eisenhowers listened, enthralled, and requested fifteen minutes of encores. The President then spent an hour mingling with the choir over refreshments in the State Dining Room.

Early in 1959 Secretary Benson visited his friend and fellow cabinet member, Secretary of State John Foster Dulles, who was dying of cancer. In Walter Reed hospital, the two men spoke of their faith in the after-life and of basic religious beliefs. Elder Benson told Mr. Dulles that the Church's General Authorities were praying for him as were prayer circles in the temples. "Ezra, you know that I regard prayer as a priceless help," the dying man said.

While preparing to give an Easter sermon at the Hollywood Bowl on March 29, 1959, Elder Benson thought deeply about Mr. Dulles's impending death. At the sunrise service he explained to 20,000 listeners his testimony of the resurrection. Despite world crises in Korea, Indochina, Lebanon, Quemoy, and Berlin, he said, "the greater crisis by far is that we might forget the Lord."

In midsummer of 1959, Soviet Premier Nikita S. Krushchev visited in Washington, preliminary to President Eisenhower's visit to Moscow planned for the next year. Secretary Benson took the Russian on a special tour through the Department of Agriculture's experiment station at Beltsville, Maryland, preaching when possible the virtues of free enterprise. Afterwards his son Reed, riding in one of the host cars, discussed Christianity and Mormonism for forty-five minutes with Mrs. Krushchev, Mrs. Andrei Gromyko, and others in their party.

That fall Secretary and Mrs. Benson, their two daughters, and three USDA officials toured Yugoslavia, West Germany, Poland, the USSR, Finland, Sweden, and Norway. For the Bensons, the highlight of the trip was the Soviet Union. There, after inspecting several agricultural exhibits and model farms, Secretary Benson asked to visit a church. On their last night in Russia, his guide drove the Americans to the Central Baptist Church, an old stucco building on a dark, narrow cobblestone street close to Red Square.

Services had already started when the Americans entered. Perhaps fifteen hundred persons filled the church to overflowing. When Elder Benson was asked to speak, he told them that he brought greetings from "millions of church people" in the free world. "Be not afraid," he counseled. "Keep God's commandments. Love the Lord. Love one another. Love all mankind. Truth will triumph." Then he bore witness that God lives and that prayer works.

When the Americans walked toward the door to leave, anxious hands reached out to them, waving handkerchiefs, bade them good-bye, and the congregation sang "God Be With You Till We Meet Again." Elder Benson often remembered that pocket of Christians in Moscow: "Seldom, if ever, have I felt the oneness of mankind and the unquenchable yearning of the human heart for freedom so keenly as at that moment."

At general conference in April 1960, during Elder Benson's last year in the cabinet, President McKay complimented him, saying his work would "stand for all time as a credit to the Church and to the nation."

At the close of Eisenhower's second term, members of his administration prepared to leave office. Of the original cabinet in 1953, only Secretary Benson and Postmaster-General Arthur

E. Summerfield served the full eight years. After farewell socials and ceremonies, the Bensons moved back to Salt Lake.

As Secretary of Agriculture, Elder Benson had traveled 600,000 miles, visited 43 countries, held 78 news conferences in Washington, and delivered thousands of speeches across America and on radio and television. Despite controversy about his policies, no one doubted his integrity and courage.

One assessment of his work, offered after his first term but applicable to both, came from Harry J. Reed, dean of Purdue University's College of Agriculture: "He has been quick to offer government aid in times of emergency, of drought, of flood. He has pressed vigorously for more farm research, for more liberal farm credit, for expanded markets—for all of those things which government can and should do to help farmers get their fair share of the national income. But he has been just as quick and firm in resisting unsound measures that might be politically unpopular—measures that would really hurt farmers in the long run instead of helping them. He believes, and I think most farmers will agree with him, that the best politics is to do what's right."

In a 1960 *Report to the American People*, Secretary Benson summed up what he felt were accomplishments and failings of the Eisenhower farm programs. Accomplishments included expanded foreign markets, conservation programs, particularly in the Dust Bowl region, reduction of the growth of food surpluses, a successful school milk program, a Food for Peace program, and progress in research and improvements with the agriculture credit system.

On the negative side, he lamented that surpluses, especially of wheat, had not been reduced and that farmers were caught in a terrible cost-price squeeze. He warned that, although the farm problem had become a serious national problem, increased government controls were not the solution. "Never must this choice nation be permitted to fall prey to a mammoth, centralized, paternalistic government on the pretext that such a government can by decree create and dispense health, wealth, and happiness to a subservient," he declared.

WHEN ELDER BENSON RETURNED to full-time activity in the Council of the Twelve in 1961, he became a Church work-horse. With other General Authorities, he traveled to create new stakes and conduct stake conferences. He visited missions and interviewed missionaries, spoke at general conferences and area conferences, dedicated chapels, and participated in temple dedications. He became a member of the BYU Board of Trustees and served on the Church Board of Education.

From January 1964 to September 1965 Elder Benson presided over the European Mission, which then included eleven missions, 1,500 missionaries, four stakes, and 45,000 Saints in 420 congregations. Mission headquarters were at Frankfurt, Germany. President Benson helped move the European Mission forward on several fronts. To centralize agencies, a Church-owned office building in Frankfurt pulled under its roof the European Information Service, audiovisual department, Presiding Bishop's office, Genealogical Society, building department, legal counsel, translation services, real estate office, and publishing offices for the Church's German language magazine *Der Stern*. Nineteen chapels were built and twenty-five were under construction by local church-service builders and priesthood bearers.

In 1964 the missions baptized 2,000 converts. To aid fellowshipping, missionaries started giving a lesson based on the tract "Baptism, and Then What?" Seven new fellowship lessons were created for post-baptism use. At special meetings, the "Every Member a Missionary" program was stressed among missionaries and members, and the new tract "Building the Kingdom" introduced.

Elder Benson directed the opening of missionary work in Italy in February 1965, after a lapse of more than a century, and soon two dozen missionaries there had good success. He also sent missionaries into Lebanon. Seeing great need for local Saints to fill leadership positions, he directed that leadership seminars be held in each stake and mission.

The Church's newly created European Information Service produced three of every five favorable stories that appeared in newspapers in the missions. The EIS also placed Church literature in libraries and hotels, erected display cases in front of LDS properties, promoted quartets, basketball teams, and concerts, and publicized Church events.

President Benson gave priority to publishing. In the Frankfurt offices, translators worked in eight languages. During 1964 the mission published 128 books and manuals in German. That March the Frankfurt headquarters published the Book of Mormon in Italian. A new program to distribute literature and Church materials to LDS servicemen in Europe was also started.

Missionary and local unit use of audiovisual materials accelerated rapidly. In 1964 the Frankfurt headquarters printed a new tract, "Mormon Pavilion," filled with pictures and text about the New York World's Fair. The film *Man's Search for Happiness* was introduced and shown to some 30,000 persons. In 1965, to replace the World's Fair pamphlet, the office published a brochure entitled "A Church for All the World," as well as several new filmstrips.

President Benson promoted youth conferences. In July 1965, fifteen hundred youths and leaders met at Frankfurt for an all-Germanic youth conference. President Benson's mission report says that "for the first time since the war, our youth enjoyed an MIA sports program, speech festival competition, and MIA music and dance festival program, and MIA roadshow competition."

He returned home from his mission feeling that the Church in Europe was moving in the right direction but was "short on manpower, know-how, and seasoning."

From 1968 to 1971 Elder Benson supervised Church work in Asia, while war raged in Vietnam. In 1969 he dedicated Singapore and Indonesia for the preaching of the gospel. He represented the Church at the 2,500 anniversary observance of the founding of the Persian Empire in 1971. The Church of Jesus Christ of Latter-day Saints was one of twenty-eight world religions represented.

AT PRESIDENT HAROLD B. LEE'S DEATH, Spencer W. Kimball became president of the Church and Ezra Taft Benson, by seniority, was set apart as president of the Council of the Twelve on December 30, 1973. According to fellow apostle Mark E. Petersen, "His call brought to this point in the leadership of the Lord's latter-day kingdom another man of unusual talents and attainments, of unblemished integrity, self-effacing humility, and deep devotion to the Master." Elder Benson was the nineteenth man to preside over the quorum.

As quorum president, Elder Benson directed the committee and work assignments and travels of quorum members. Elder Petersen said of his leadership: "He has led the quorum with great efficiency, constant inspiration, and a never-ceasing flow of love for his Brethren. Their well-being has been a constant concern. Always he has kept their best interests in mind, together with 'what is best for the Kingdom' as he has assigned them to their responsibilities in various parts of the world."

President Benson loved his quorum members. The *Church News* reported that "a spirit of unity, harmony and love among the Brethren characterized his tenure." In 1984 he declared, "I think there is no group of men in this world who are closer to each other than the Council of the Twelve. We just have the most wonderful spirit in our council; we're grateful for it. I don't believe there is a man in that council who would not lay down his life for any of the others. I love them with all my heart."

President Benson's leadership of the quorum bore his imprint as a skilled administrator and facilitator. He was an executive who knew how to assign and delegate to get tasks done. He expected good performances from those to whom he gave assignments. Associates said he always kept a clean desk. In 1973, President Benson and the Twelve received a new group of assistants to help them minister to a burgeoning Church—the newly organized First Quorum of the Seventy.

Early in 1978 he toured Japan, Taiwan, and the Philippines. During that busy week he met with mission presidents and missionaries, dedicated an office building in Tokyo to serve the Asian administration headquarters, and organized Japan's sixth stake.

At the inauguration of U.S. President Ronald Reagan in

March 1981, Elder Benson represented the Church, as did the Tabernacle Choir. He and Sister Benson attended the swearing-in ceremony on Capitol Hill, met privately with President Reagan the same day, and spoke to workers in the Washington Temple and to several Church gatherings.

Through sermons, programs, and plans for the Church, the senior apostle emphasized several concerns, particularly re-activation, temple work, missionary work, and family pre-paredness. Regarding the latter he often said, "The revelation to store food may be as essential to our temporal salvation today as boarding the ark was to the people in the days of Noah."

"Strengthen Your Families" was a theme he often stressed during the 1980s. He urged parents to spend more time at home, to hold family devotionals daily, to instruct children about life's purposes, and to have their family participate in recreation and cultural activities together. He wanted members to enjoy a rich home life similar to what he and his family had experienced. "Complete family love, loyalty, and unity by living the gospel have made our home a bit of heaven on earth," he stated. "Following the program of the Church in the family home evening, the family council, family prayer, and devoted scripture reading has developed faith and testimony in each member of the family. One of our richest blessings has been complete harmony in righteous living in our home."

At times critics and anti-Mormons attacked the Church. President Benson's usual response was to remind leaders and members of the promise found in 3 Nephi 22:17: "No weapon that is formed against thee shall prosper."

In 1978 a horse knocked President Benson to the ground, and he fractured his hip. When doctors put in an artificial hip joint, Sister Benson joked that the joint "is the only thing artificial about him." The accident ended his horse riding days, a recreation he had so much enjoyed since boyhood.

FIVE DAYS AFTER THE DEATH of President Spencer W. Kimball, President Benson called the Quorum of the Twelve into special

447

council to fast and pray in order to pick a new First Presidency. Receiving divine ratification, the quorum ordained and set apart Ezra Taft Benson as the thirteenth president of the Church, on November 10, 1985.

As an apostle for forty-two years, President Benson had served under six presidents: Heber J. Grant, George Albert Smith, David O. McKay, Joseph Fielding Smith, Harold B. Lee, and Spencer W. Kimball. At age eighty-six, he was the second oldest man to become president (Joseph Fielding Smith was ninety-four when he was sustained as president). Unlike his predecessors, President Benson assumed the presidency already well known worldwide.

President Benson chose as his first counselor Gordon B. Hinckley. President Hinckley had served more than four years as second counselor to President Kimball, often directing the day-to-day administration of the affairs of the Church due to President Kimball's failing health.

As second counselor in the First Presidency, President Benson selected Elder Thomas S. Monson, who, in his late fifties, had been a General Authority for twenty-two years. Elder Marion G. Romney became president of the Twelve, but due to his failing health, Elder Howard W. Hunter, next in seniority, was installed as acting president of the Twelve.

On Monday, November 11, 1985, the new First Presidency called a press conference to announce its formation. "This is a day I have not anticipated," President Benson said. "My wife, Flora, and I have prayed continually that President Kimball's days would be prolonged." He told reporters that his heart was filled with overwhelming love and compassion for the Saints and for all people. "I love all our Father's children of every color, creed, and political persuasion. My only desire is to serve as the Lord would have me do."

He went on to reemphasize the threefold mission of the Church: to preach the gospel, perfect the Saints, and redeem the dead. "We shall continue every effort to carry out this mission," he pledged.

During his long life of service, President Benson earned

numerous awards and honors. The Freedom Foundation at Valley Forge bestowed on him four George Washington Honor Medals. In 1957, while serving as Secretary of Agriculture, he received the High Cross of the Order of Merit, the highest decoration the Italian government can bestow, for helping Italy solve food shortages with U.S. surpluses. In 1960 he was named to the Hall of Fame of the Saddle and Sirloin Club of Chicago, and in 1965 he was named to the American Patriots Hall of Fame. The American Farm Bureau Federation awarded him its Distinguished and Meritorious Service award in 1978. He received eleven honorary degrees from such universities as Iowa State, Michigan State, Rutgers, University of Maine, University of Hawaii, University of Utah, Brigham Young University, and Utah State University. In 1975 Brigham Young University established the Ezra Taft Benson Agriculture and Food Institute to improve the quality of life in developing countries.

All his life Elder Benson promoted scouting. He served for many years on the national advisory board and then the executive board of the Boy Scouts of America. Scouting bestowed upon him its highest awards: the Silver Antelope, Silver Buffalo, and Silver Beaver.

In October 1984 President Benson related in general conference an accounting of the boys for whom he once was scoutmaster. He had revisited his Whitney Ward, he said, and found several in ward and stake leadership jobs. He accounted for all but two of his twenty-four boys. Later, at a conference in Arizona, he met one of those boys and found that he had married out of the Church. The two men corresponded until, some time later, Elder Benson sealed the couple and their children in the temple. Later, at a Farm Bureau meeting in Idaho, he encountered the final scout, a man who also had married outside the temple. Before long Elder Benson performed temple sealings for the man, his wife, and their children. The scoutmaster had finished his job.

It is clear that the principle "what is best for the kingdom" has been the guiding principle in the life of Ezra Taft Benson, thirteenth president of the Church.

SOURCES

Books by President Benson include *Farmers at the Crossroads* (New York: Devin-Adair, 1956); *Cross Fire: The Eight Years with Eisenhower* (New York: Doubleday, 1962); *So Shall Ye Reap: Selected Addresses of Ezra Taft Benson* (Salt Lake City: Deseret Book, 1960); and *God, Family, Country: Our Three Great Loyalties* (Salt Lake City: Deseret Book, 1974). Books and articles about President Benson include Frederick Babbel, *On Wings of Faith* (Salt Lake City: Bookcraft, 1972); Gene A. Sessions, *Latter-day Patriots: Nine Mormon Families and Their Revolutionary War Heritage* (Salt Lake City: Deseret Book, 1975), pp. 64-83; Merlo J. Pusey, "Ezra Taft Benson: A Living Witness for Christ," *Improvement Era* 59 (April 1956): 234-38, 266-71, 282-87; Mark E. Petersen, "Ezra Taft Benson: A Habit of Integrity," *Ensign* 4 (October 1974): 15-29; Leonard J. Arrington, "Idaho's Benson Family," and "Ezra Taft Benson: Oral History," in *Idaho Heritage* 9 (July 1977): 14-19. Additional information about President Benson's life and thought can be found in *Conference Reports*, issues of the *Church News*, and *Ensign*, and the Manuscript History of the European Mission, Church Archives, Salt Lake City.

WILLIAM G. HARTLEY earned B.A. and M.A. degrees at Brigham Young University and completed his Ph.D. course work at Washington State University. The former director of the Church's oral history program, he is now assistant professor of history, research historian with the Joseph Fielding Smith Institute for Church History, and director of Family History Services at BYU. His publications include *Kindred Saints: The Mormon Immigrant Heritage of Alvin and Kathryne Christenson* (Salt Lake City, 1982), pamphlets on personal and family history, and articles in *Ensign*, *New Era*, *BYU Studies*, *Utah Historical Quarterly*, and other periodicals and journals.

INDEX

Aaronic Priesthood, 15, 19
Accidents, Wilford Woodruff's life
spared in, 129-30
Agriculture: Wilford Woodruff's
involvement with, 132-33; Ezra
Taft Benson's involvement with,
429-30, 433-43
Animals: Brigham Young's views on,
65; David O. McKay's love of, 292
Anthon, Professor Charles, 13
Apostates, defense of Joseph Smith
against, 50-51, 80
Apostles, 19; calling of Twelve, 29
Ashton, Marvin J., 418
Atwood, Millen, 223
Avard, Sampson, 80

Babbel, Frederick, 431
Ballard, Melvin J., 387
Bancroft, Hubert Howe, 100
Bangerter, Jeraldine, 338-39
Baptism: ordinance of, restored, 15-16;
accompanying organization of
Church, 18-19; Wilford Woodruff's
views on, 123-24
Ben-Gurion, David Ben, 441
Bennion, Samuel O., 377
Benson, Ezra T., 421
Benson, Ezra Taft: birth of, 421;
childhood of, 422-23; school
experiences of, 424-25; becomes
scoutmaster, 425; military
experience of, 425; courts Flora
Amussen, 425-26; missionary
labors of, 426-28, 431-33, 444-45;
graduates from college, 428; marries
Flora, 428; early agricultural
positions of, 429-30; becomes stake
president, 429, 430; becomes an
apostle, 430-31; becomes European
Mission president, 431-33, 444-45;
oversees postwar relief efforts, 432;

family of, 433, 438; work of, as
Secretary of Agriculture, 433-43;
political philosophies of, 434-35,
437, 440-43; lobbies for agricultural
programs, 436; suggests praying for
rain, 437; world tour of, 441; visits
Christians in Soviet Union, 442;
summary of political career of, 443;
becomes president of Twelve,
445-46, urges strengthening of
families, 447; becomes president of
Church, 447-48; awards and honors
of, 449
Benson, Flora Amussen, 425-26,
428-29, 435, 437-38, 442
Benson, George T., Jr., 421, 423
Benson, Sarah Dunkley, 421, 423
Bible: Joseph Smith's revision of, 24;
Wilford Woodruff's love for, 120;
Spencer W. Kimball reads, as youth,
376
Boggs, Lilburn W., 32
Book of Mormon: translation of,
12-17; witnesses to, 17; publishing
of, 17; Brigham Young's experience
with, 47-48; translation of, into
European languages, 99, 161; Heber
J. Grant reads, 223-24; new subtitle
for, 416
Books: given away by Heber J. Grant,
247; David O. McKay's love for,
292-93; Joseph Fielding Smith's
love for, 319; written by Joseph
Fielding Smith, 329
Boyer, Selvoy, 297
Boynton, John F., 149
Brown, Hugh B., 239
Buchanan, Golden, 395-96
Burgess, Margarette McIntire, 35-36
Burton, Rachel Fielding, 188
Bushman, Richard L., 11, 24
Butz, Earl, 436

451